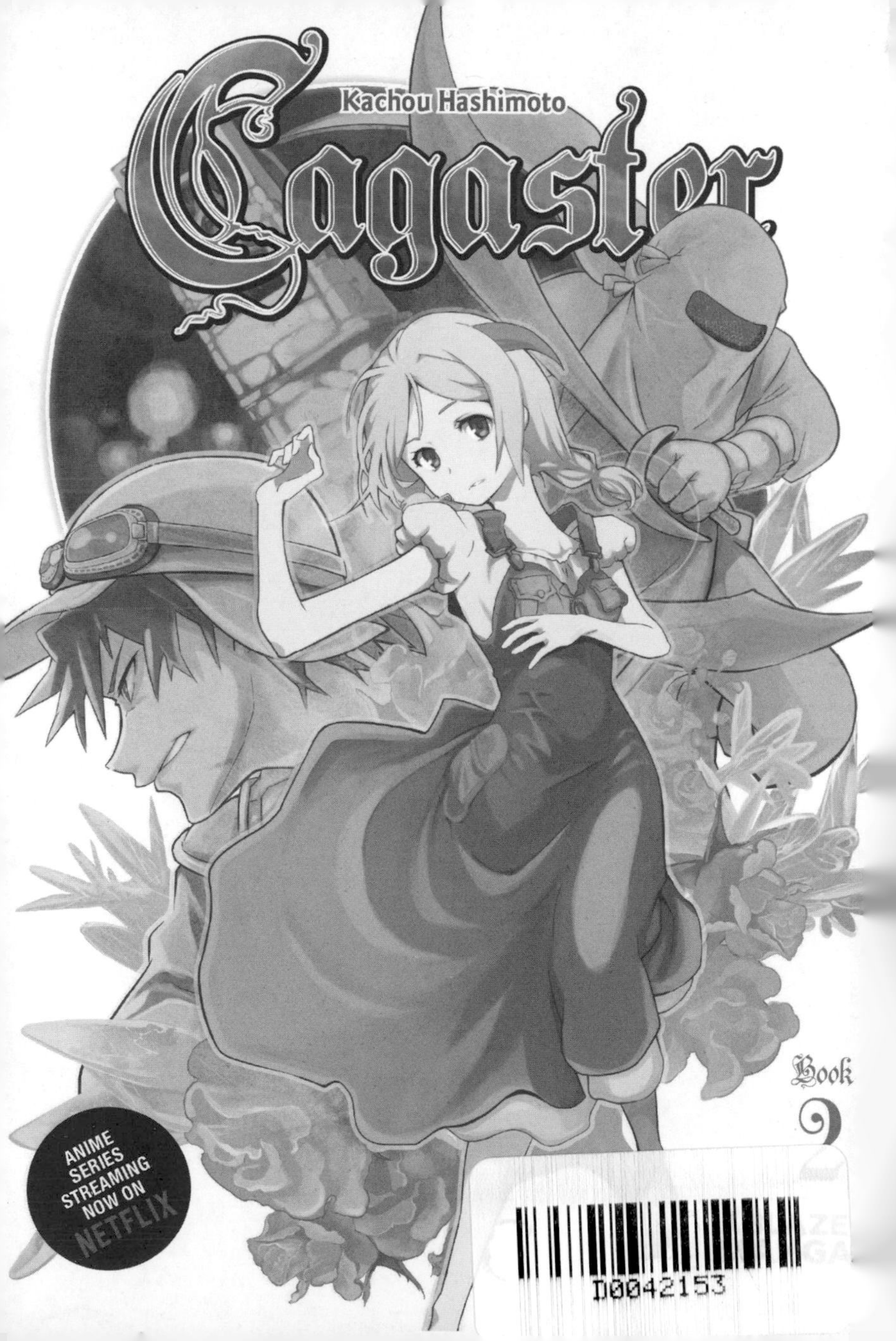
Kachou Hashimoto
Cagaster
Book
2
ANIME SERIES STREAMING NOW ON NETFLIX

Kachou Hashimoto

Cagaster

Book 2

ABLAZE MANGA

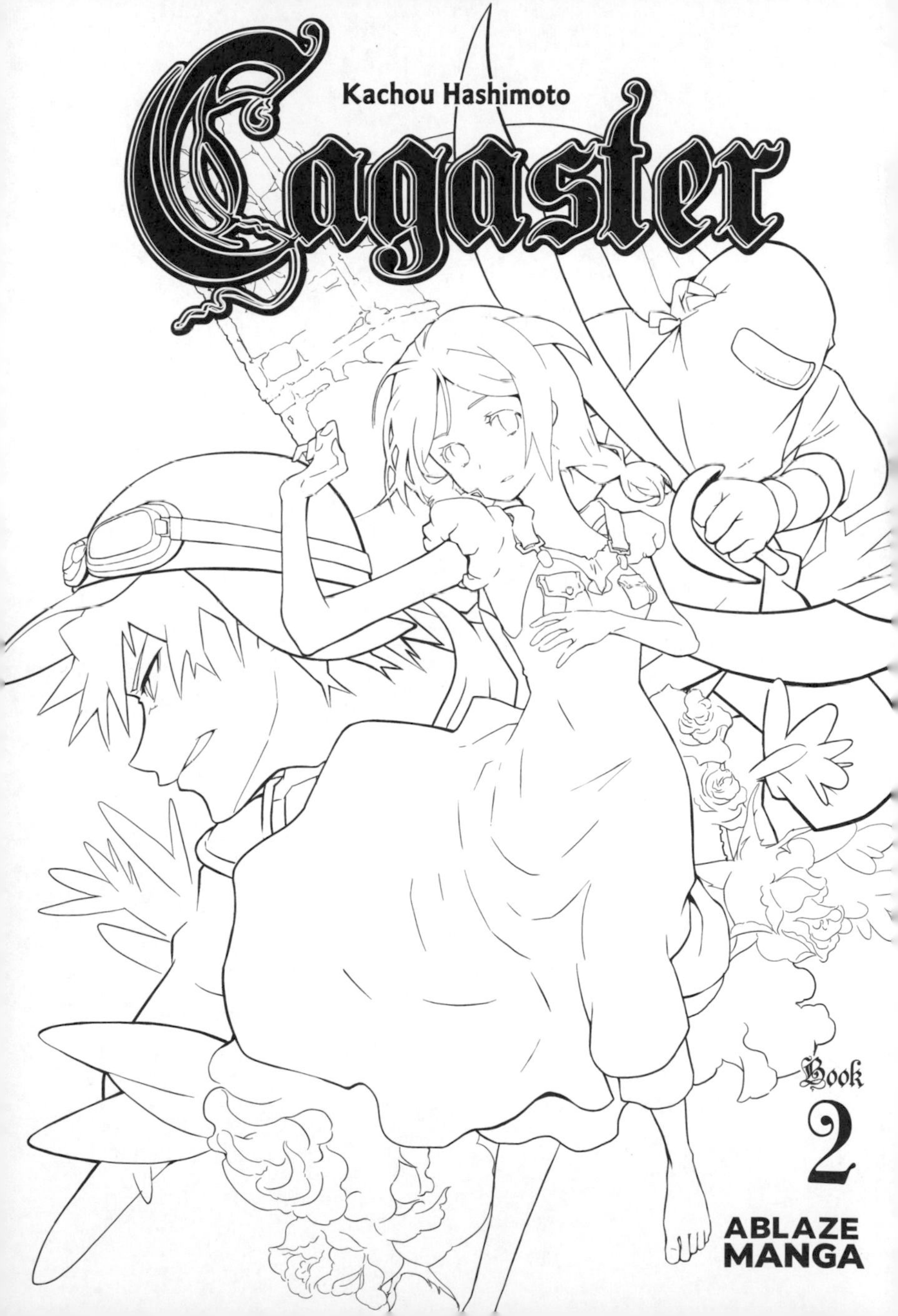

[CHAPTER 6]

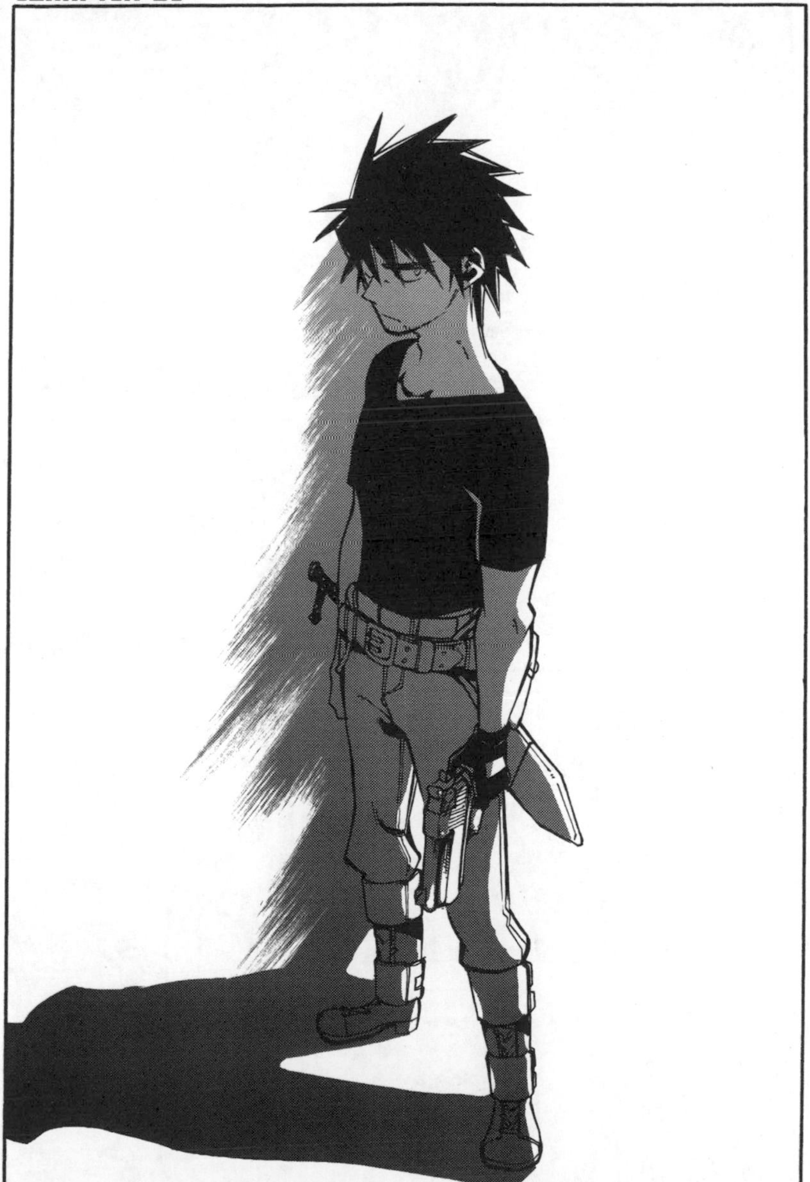

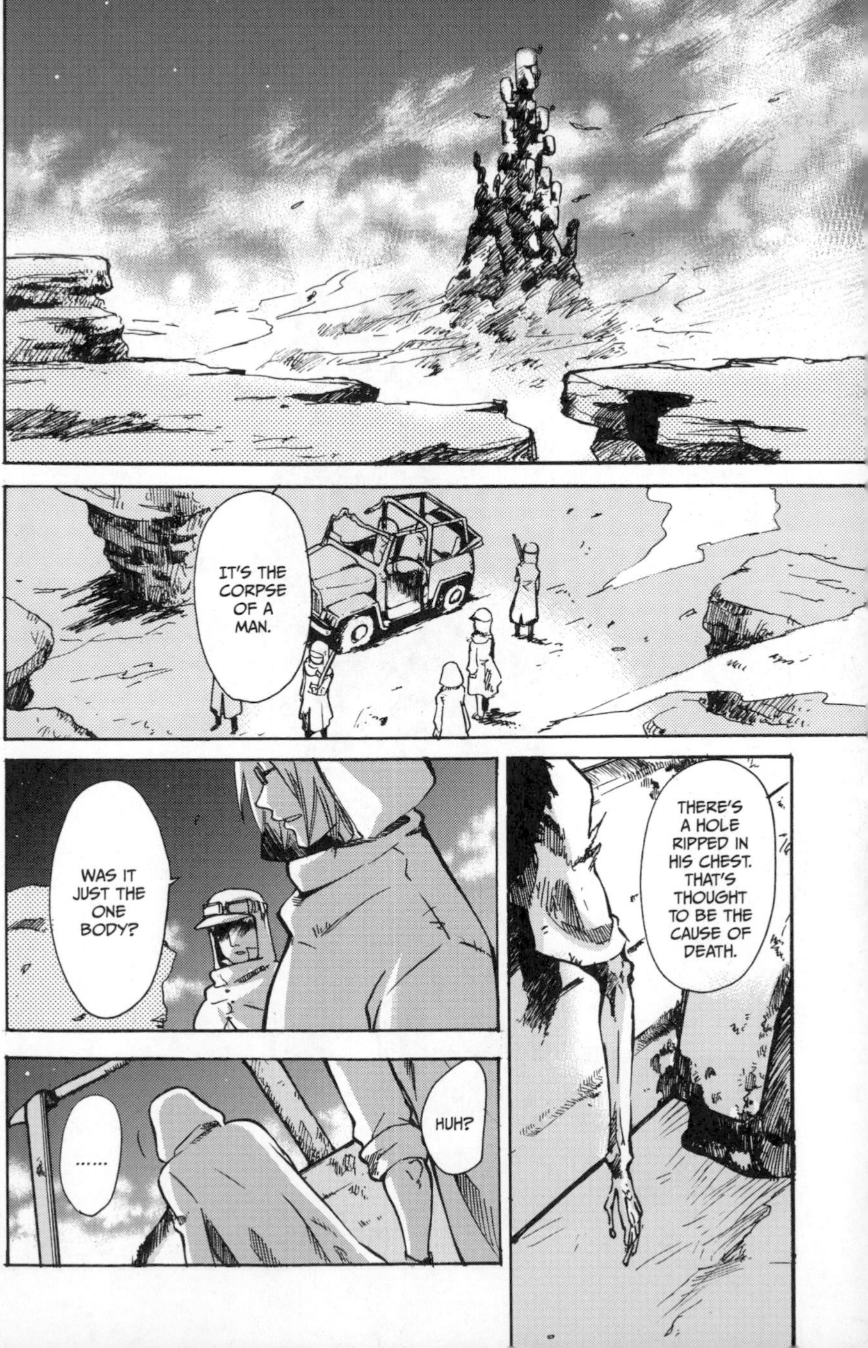
IT'S THE CORPSE OF A MAN.
THERE'S A HOLE RIPPED IN HIS CHEST. THAT'S THOUGHT TO BE THE CAUSE OF DEATH.
WAS IT JUST THE ONE BODY?
HUH?
......

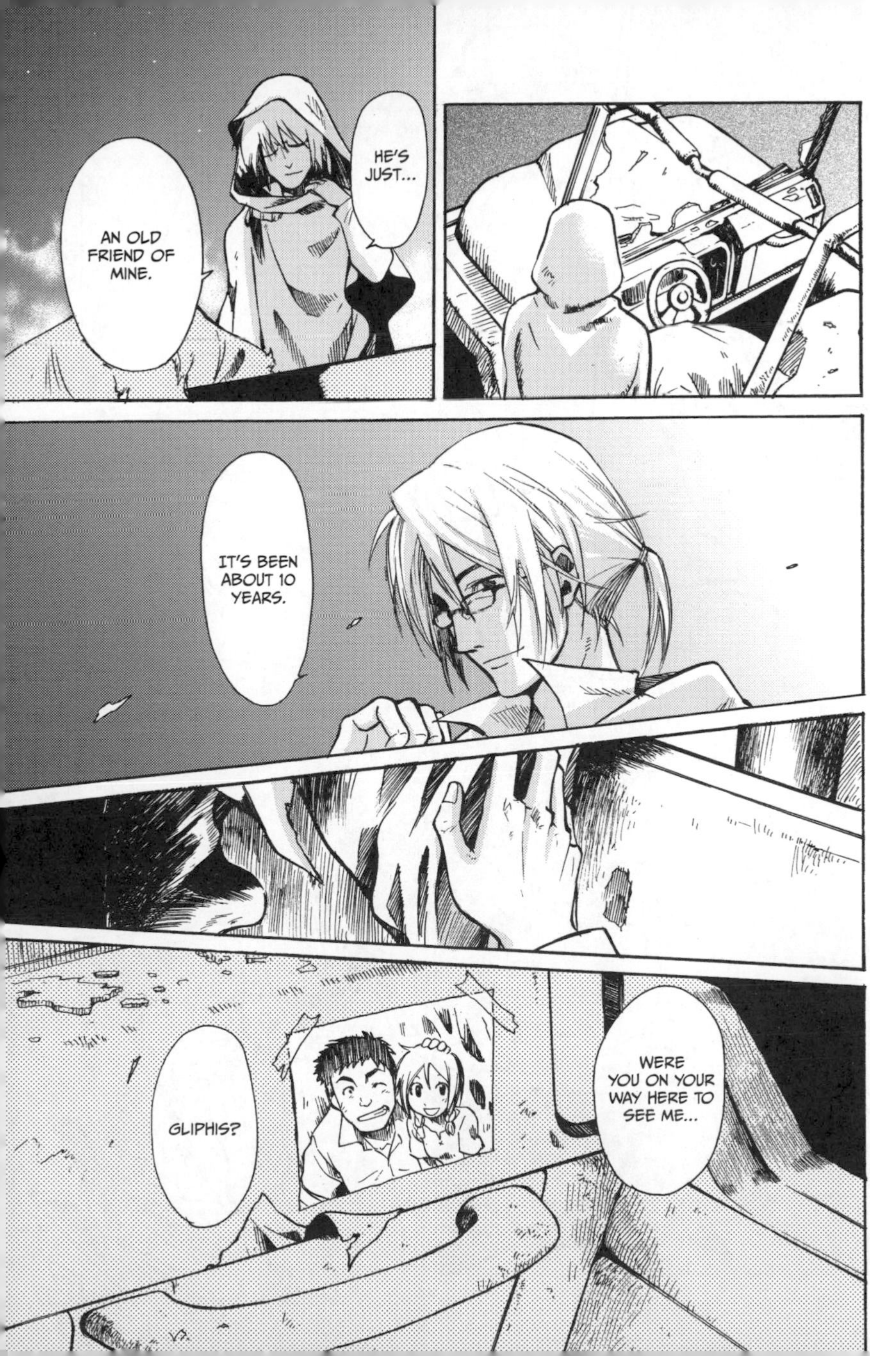
HE'S JUST...
AN OLD FRIEND OF MINE.
IT'S BEEN ABOUT 10 YEARS.
WERE YOU ON YOUR WAY HERE TO SEE ME...
GLIPHIS?

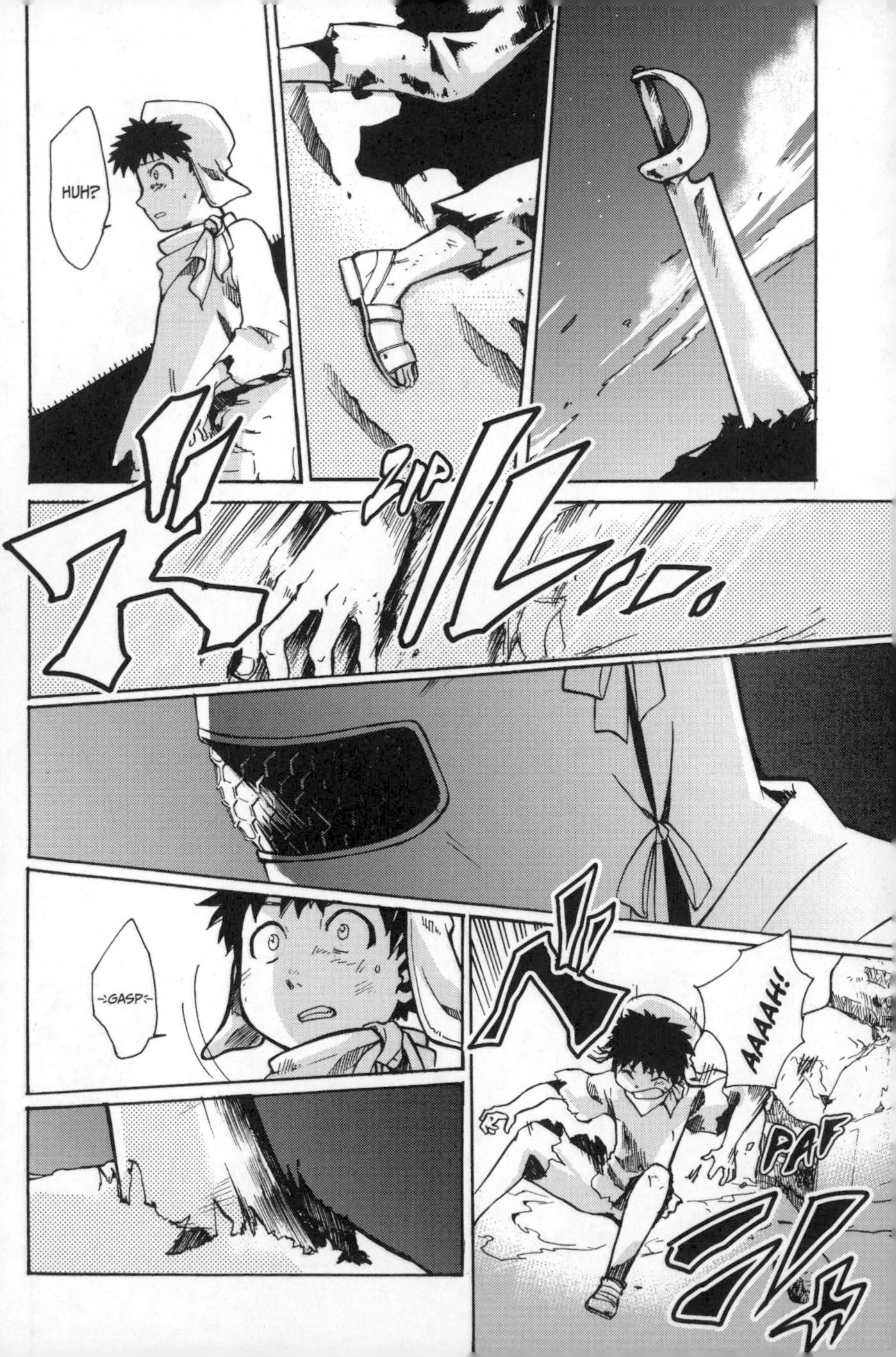
HUH?
ZIP
AAAAH!
PAF
GASP

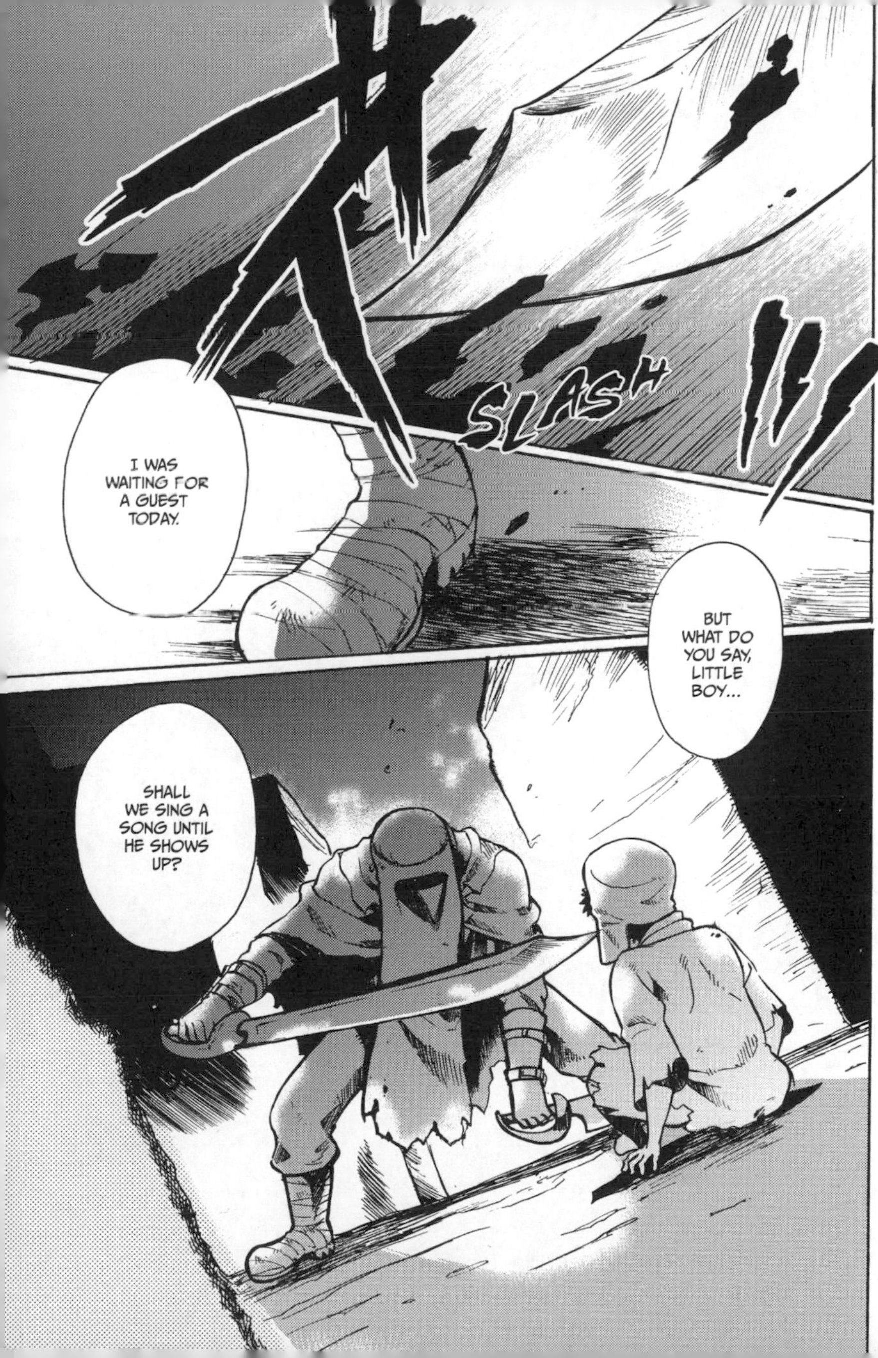
SLASH
I WAS WAITING FOR A GUEST TODAY.
BUT WHAT DO YOU SAY, LITTLE BOY...
SHALL WE SING A SONG UNTIL HE SHOWS UP?

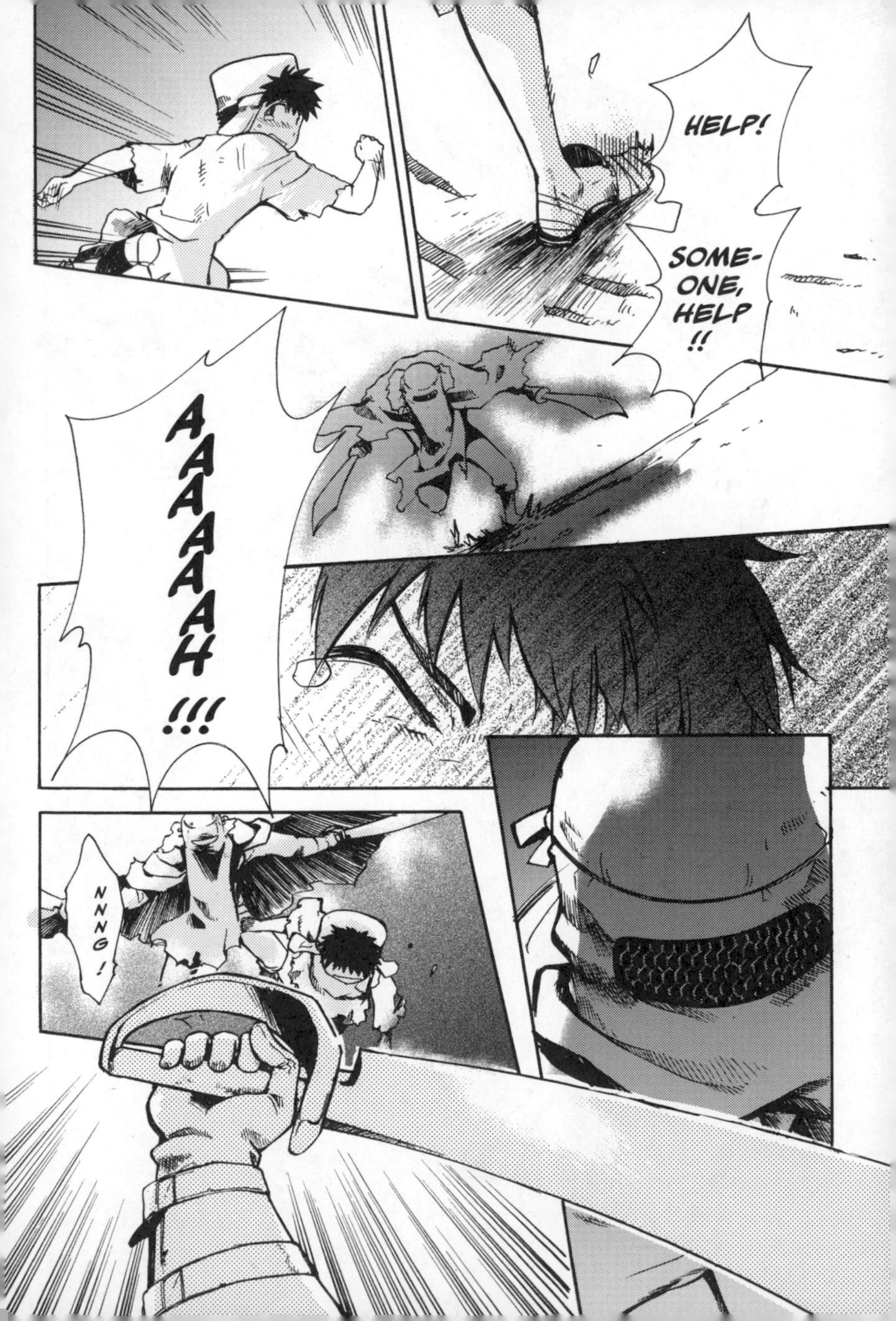
HELP!
SOME-ONE, HELP !!
AAAAAAH !!!
NNNG !

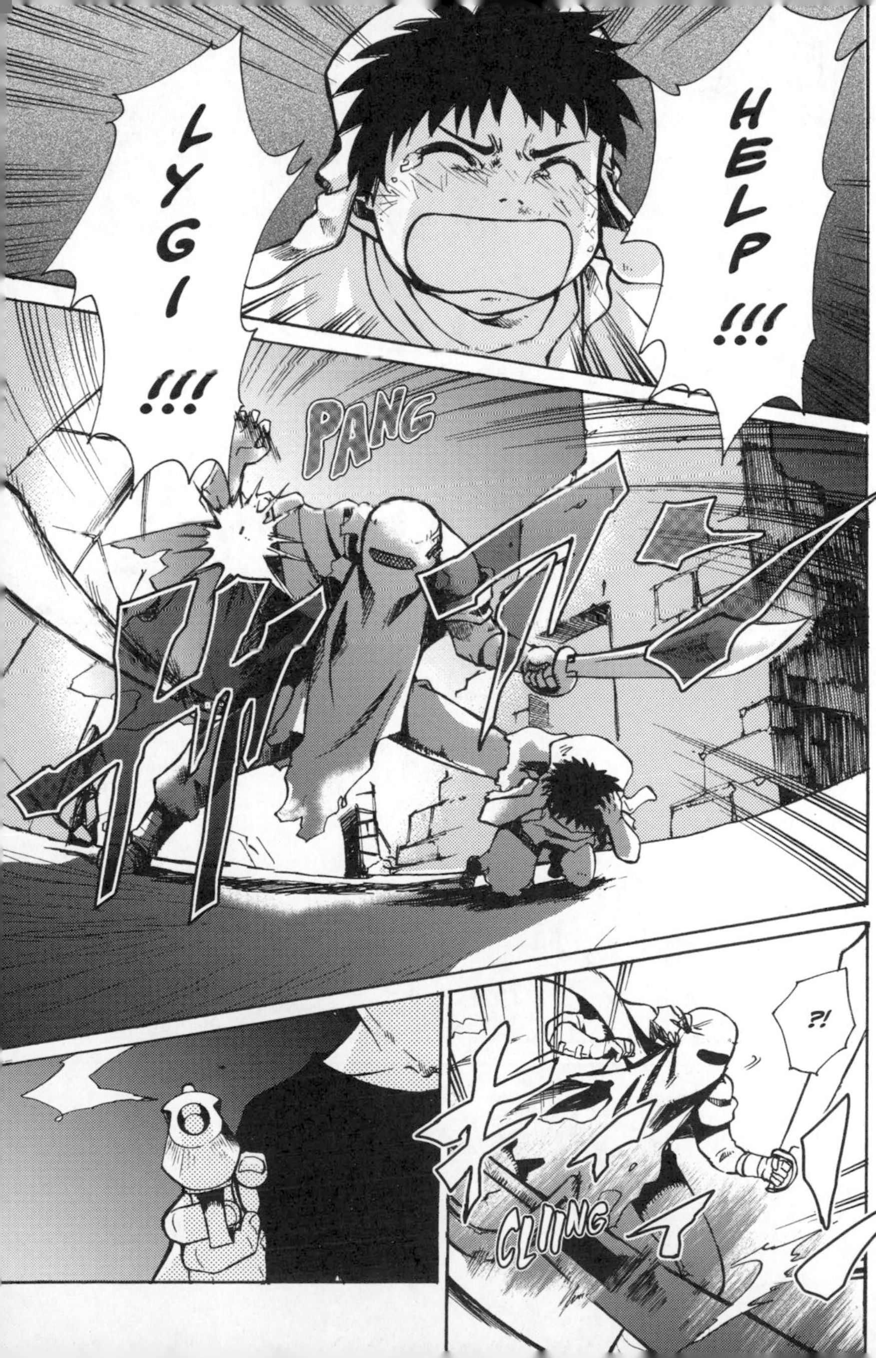
HELP!!!
LYGI!!!
PANG
?!
CLIIING

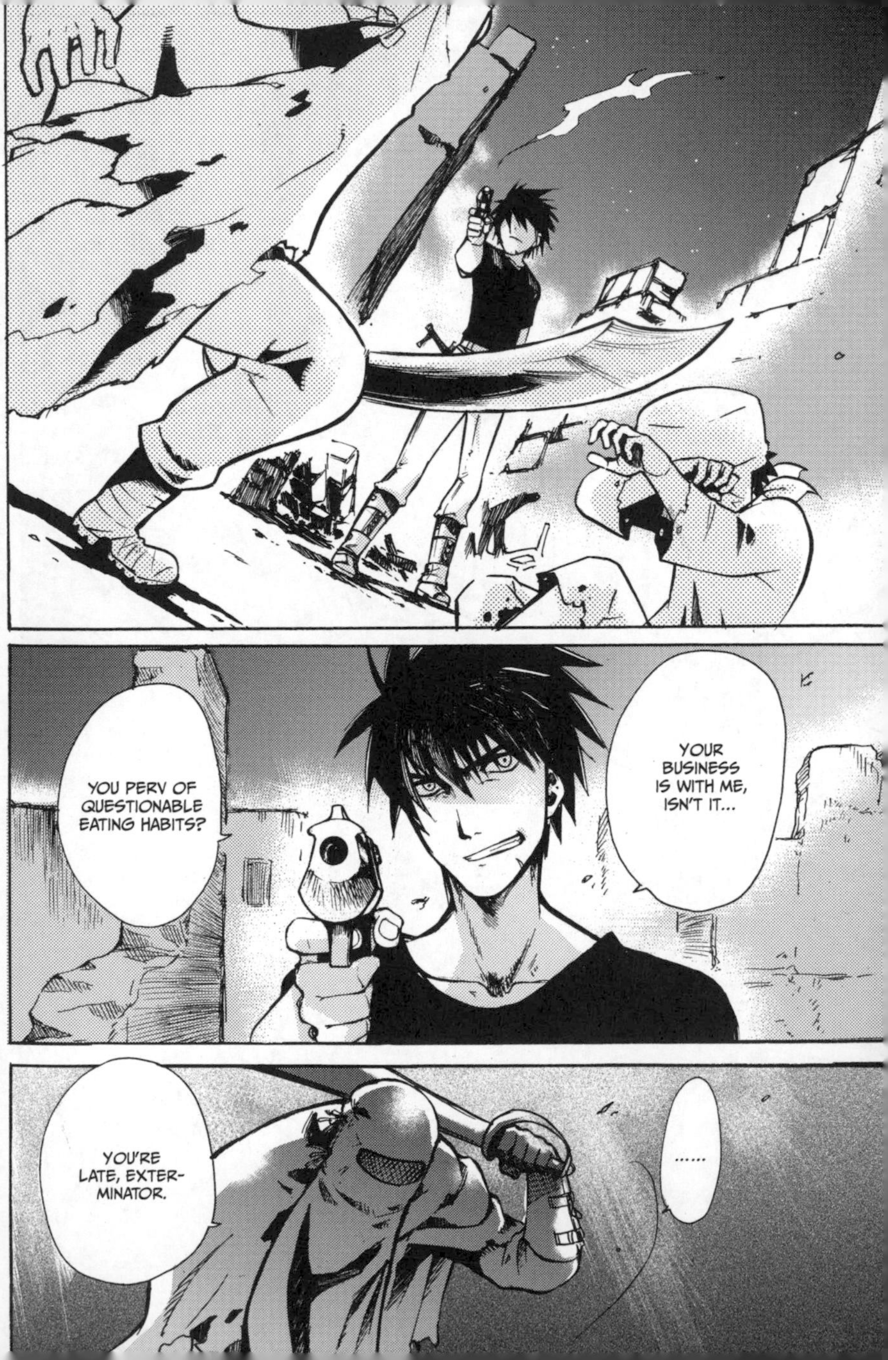
YOUR BUSINESS IS WITH ME, ISN'T IT...
YOU PERV OF QUESTIONABLE EATING HABITS?
......
YOU'RE LATE, EXTER-MINATOR.

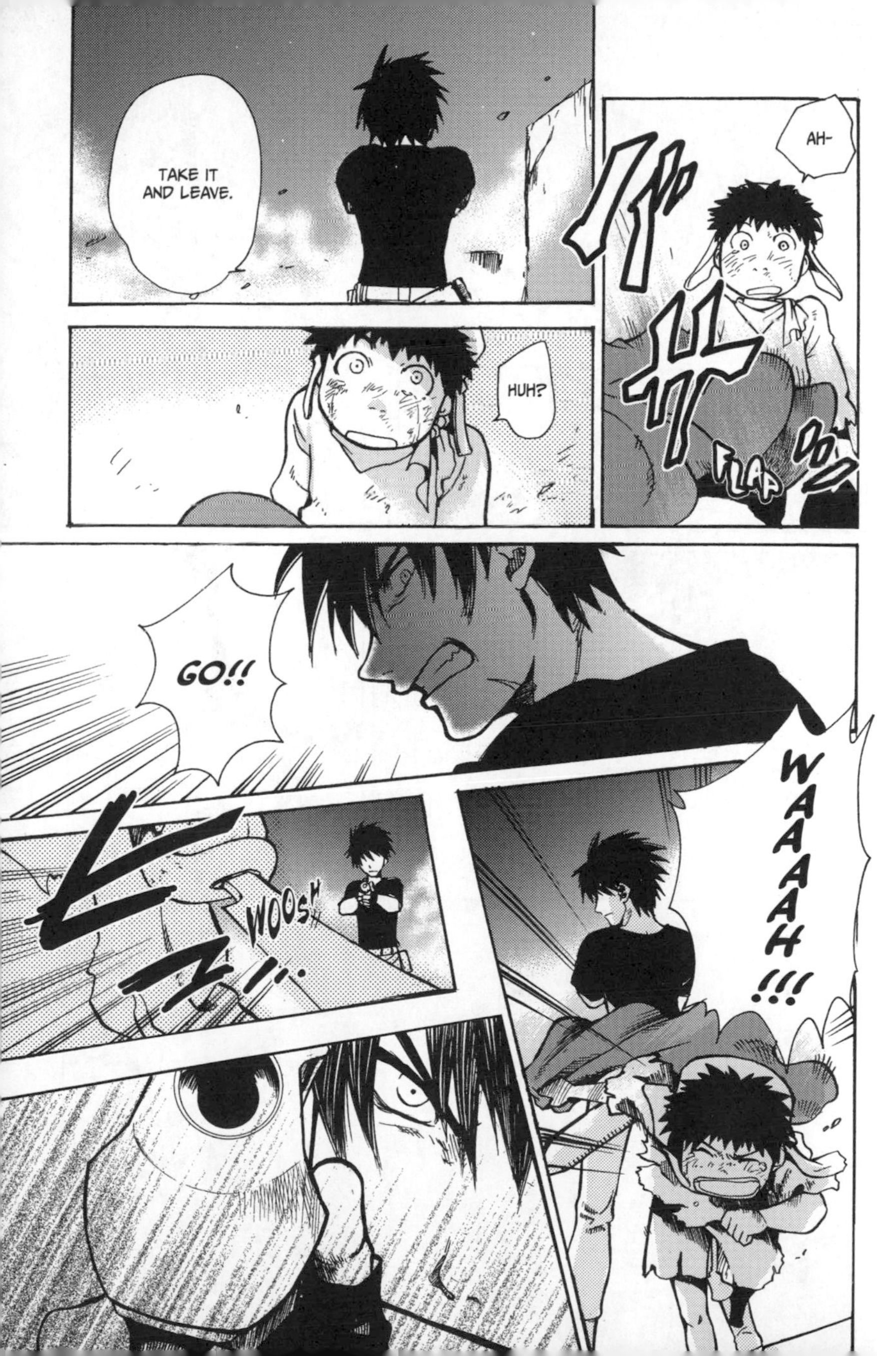
AH-
FLAP
TAKE IT AND LEAVE.
HUH?
GO!!
WAAAAAH!!!
WOOSH

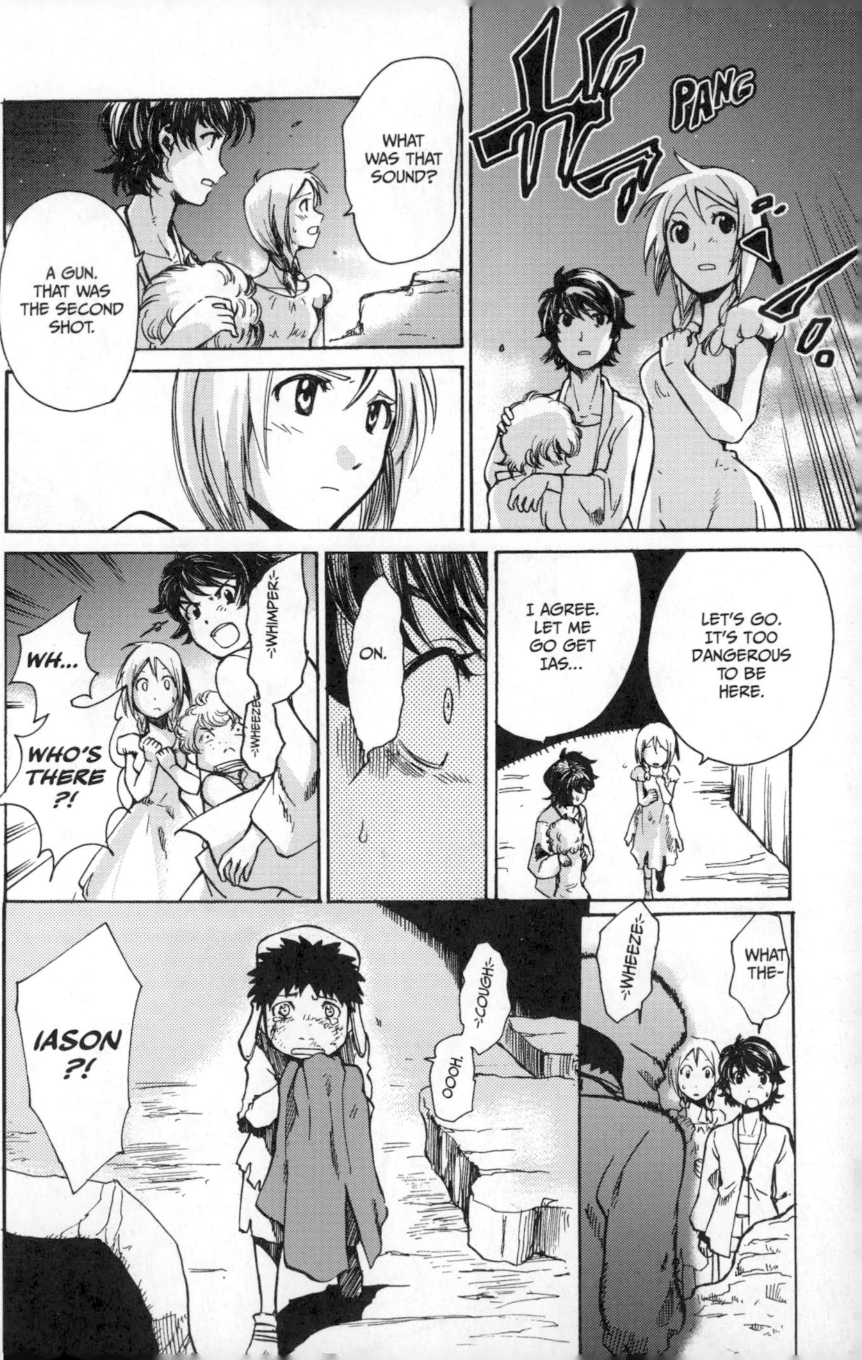
PANG
WHAT WAS THAT SOUND?
A GUN. THAT WAS THE SECOND SHOT.
LET'S GO. IT'S TOO DANGEROUS TO BE HERE.
I AGREE. LET ME GO GET IAS...
ON.
-WHIMPER-
-WHEEZE-
WH...
WHO'S THERE ?!
WHAT THE-
-WHEEZE-
-COUGH-
OOOH.
IASON ?!

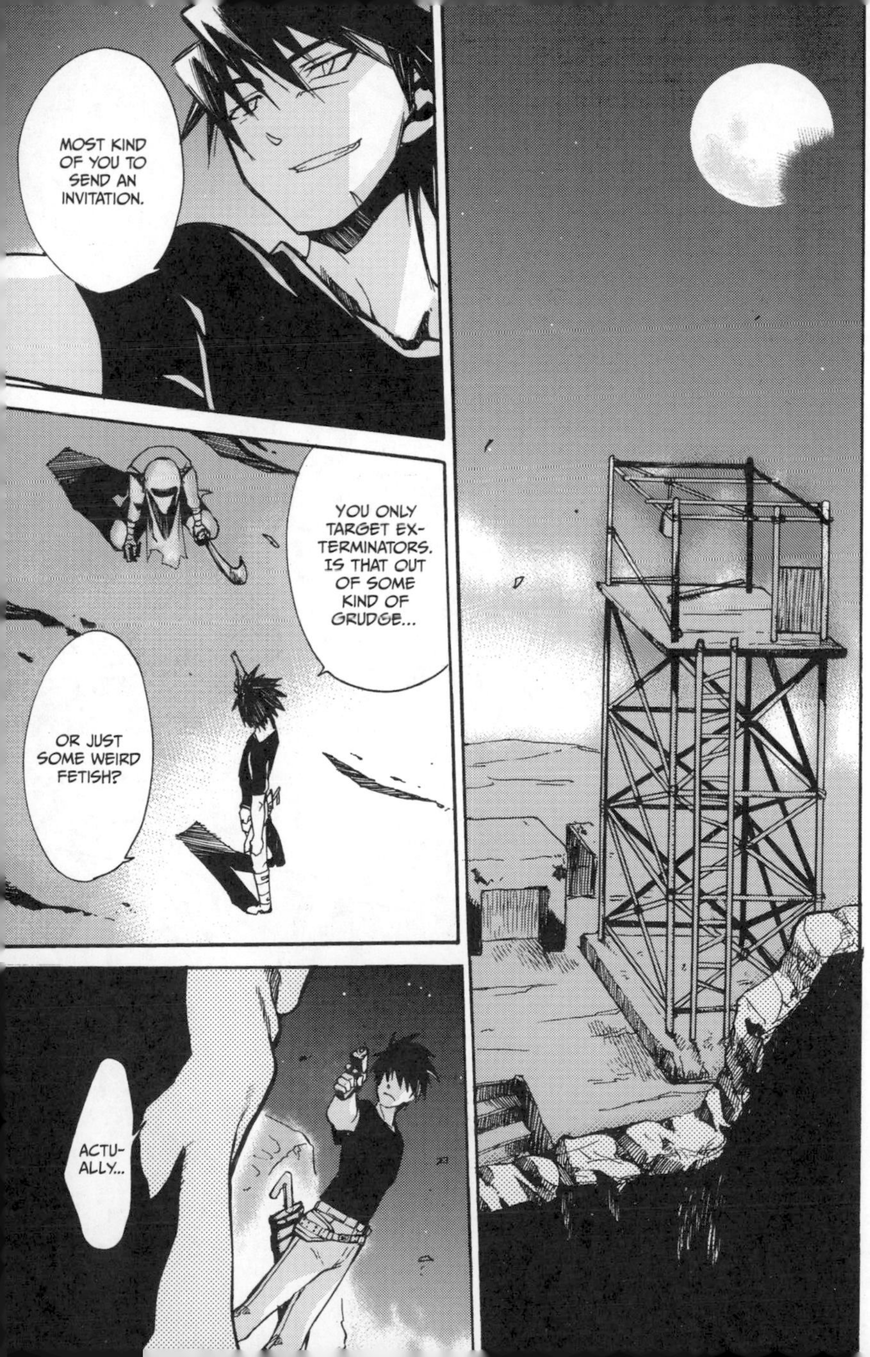
MOST KIND OF YOU TO SEND AN INVITATION.
YOU ONLY TARGET EX-TERMINATORS. IS THAT OUT OF SOME KIND OF GRUDGE...
OR JUST SOME WEIRD FETISH?
ACTU-ALLY...

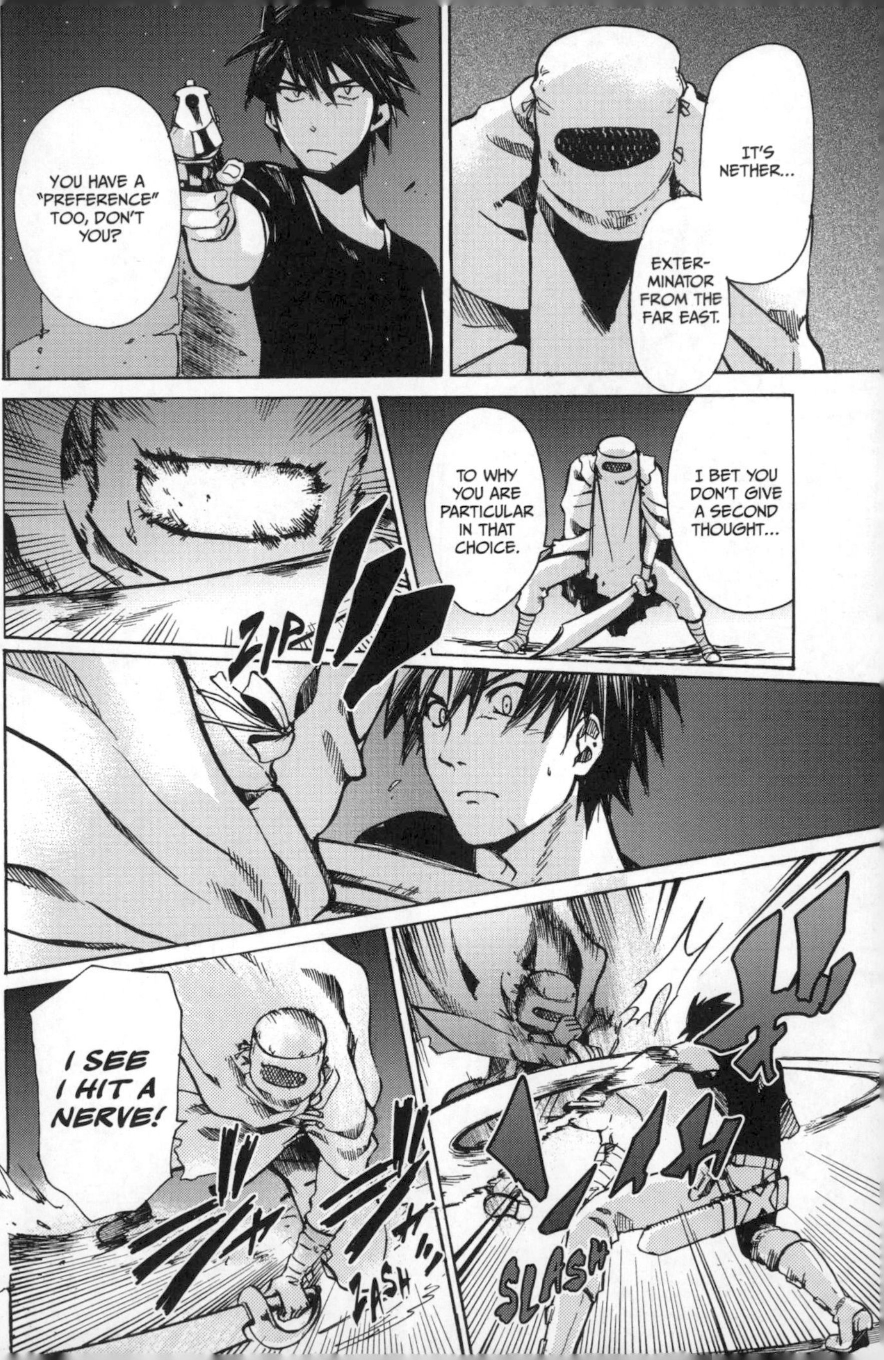

IT'S NETHER...
EXTER-MINATOR FROM THE FAR EAST.
YOU HAVE A "PREFERENCE" TOO, DON'T YOU?
I BET YOU DON'T GIVE A SECOND THOUGHT...
TO WHY YOU ARE PARTICULAR IN THAT CHOICE.
ZIP
SLASH
I SEE I HIT A NERVE!
ZASH

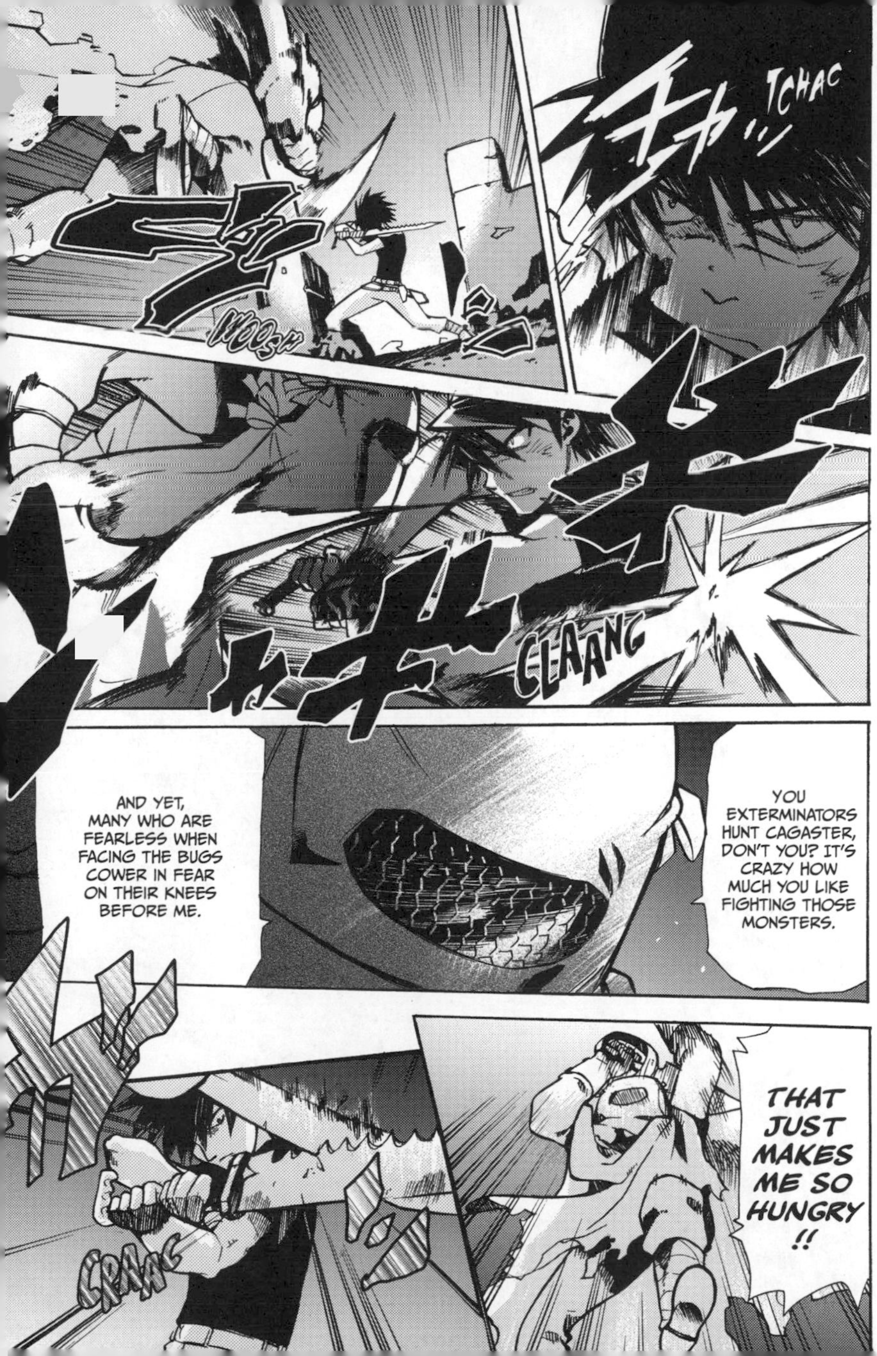
TCHAC
WOOSH
CLAANG
YOU EXTERMINATORS HUNT CAGASTER, DON'T YOU? IT'S CRAZY HOW MUCH YOU LIKE FIGHTING THOSE MONSTERS.
AND YET, MANY WHO ARE FEARLESS WHEN FACING THE BUGS COWER IN FEAR ON THEIR KNEES BEFORE ME.
THAT JUST MAKES ME SO HUNGRY!!
CRAAC

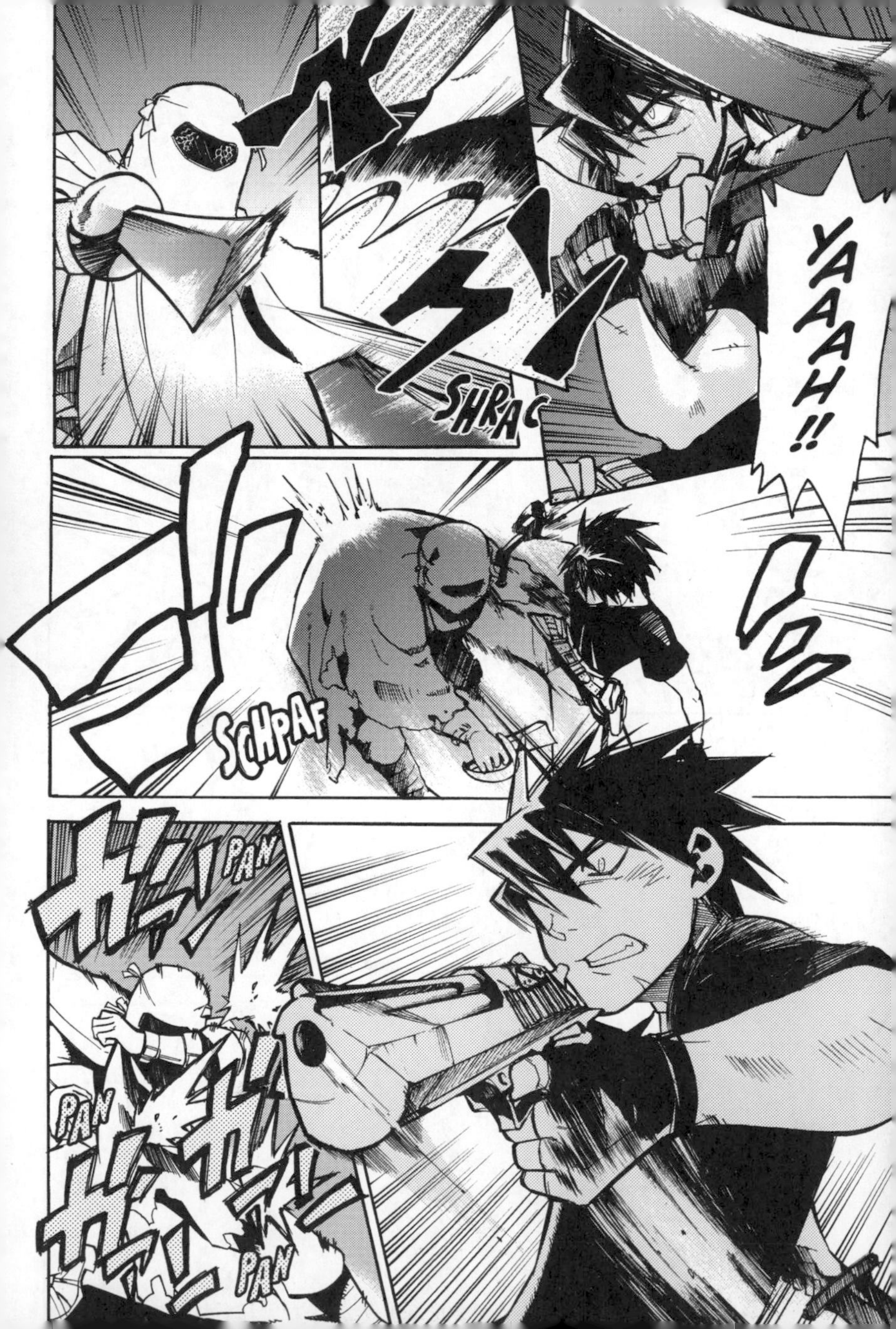
YAAAAH!!
SHRAC
SCHPAF
PAN
PAN
PAN

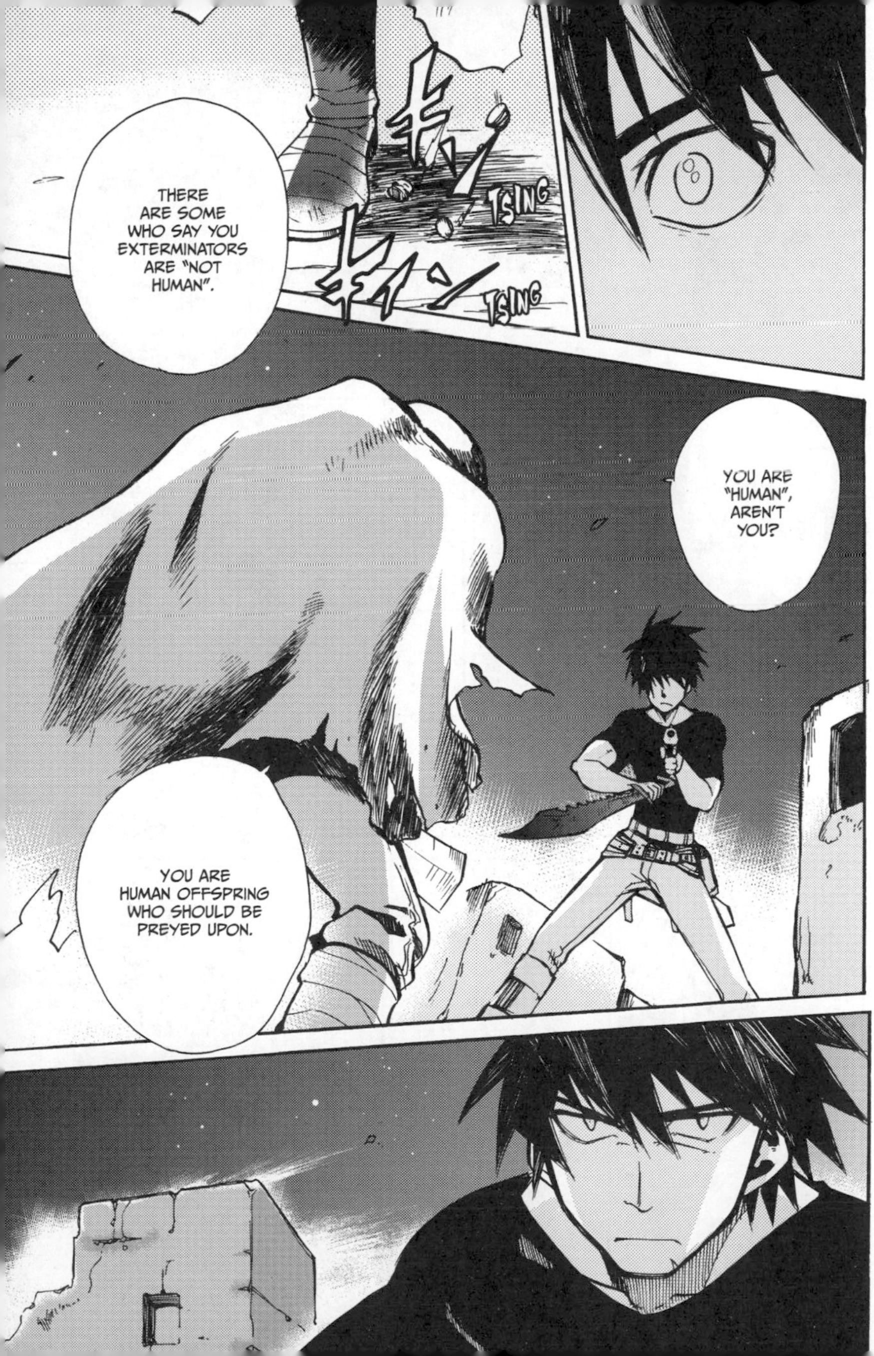
TSING
TSING
THERE ARE SOME WHO SAY YOU EXTERMINATORS ARE "NOT HUMAN".
YOU ARE "HUMAN", AREN'T YOU?
YOU ARE HUMAN OFFSPRING WHO SHOULD BE PREYED UPON.

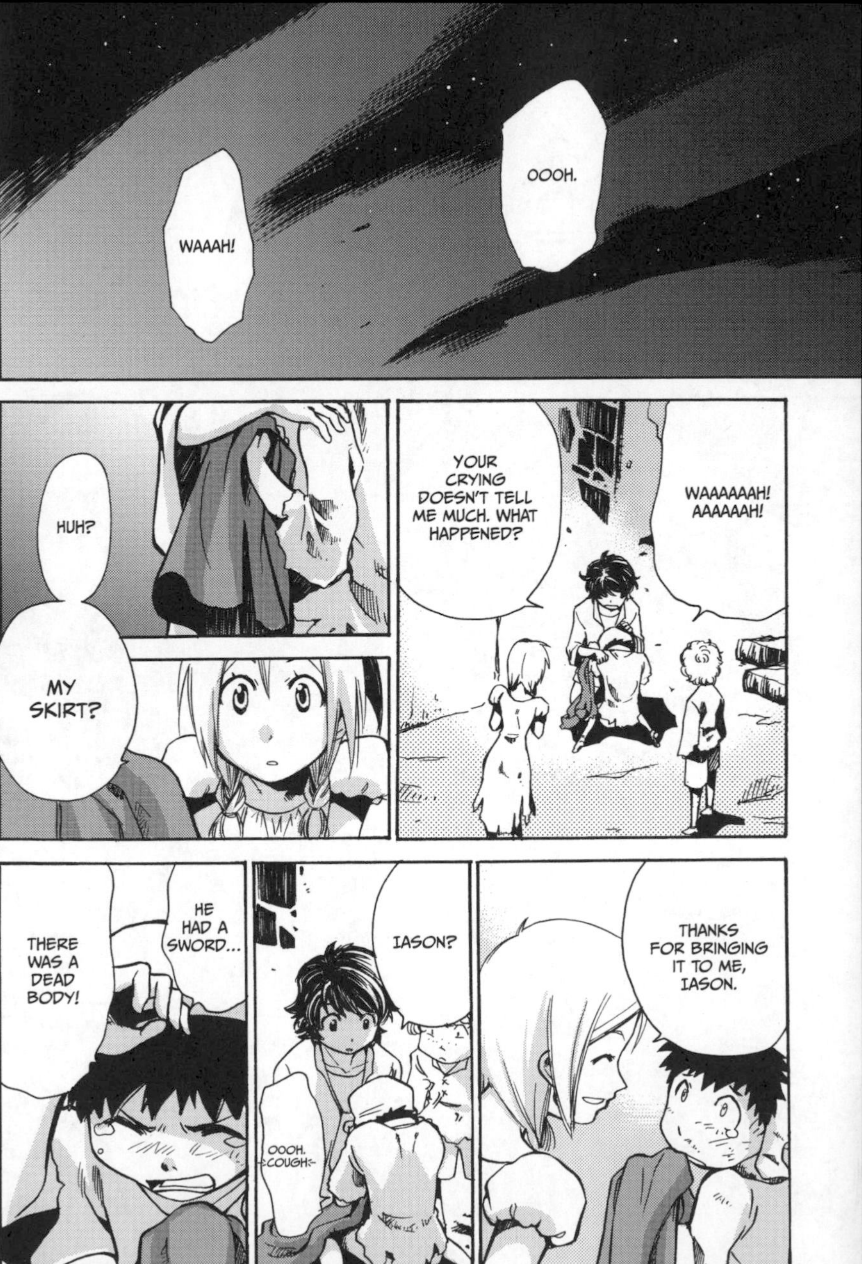
OOOH.
WAAAH!
WAAAAAAH! AAAAAAH!
YOUR CRYING DOESN'T TELL ME MUCH. WHAT HAPPENED?
HUH?
MY SKIRT?
THANKS FOR BRINGING IT TO ME, IASON.
IASON?
OOOH. *COUGH*
HE HAD A SWORD...
THERE WAS A DEAD BODY!

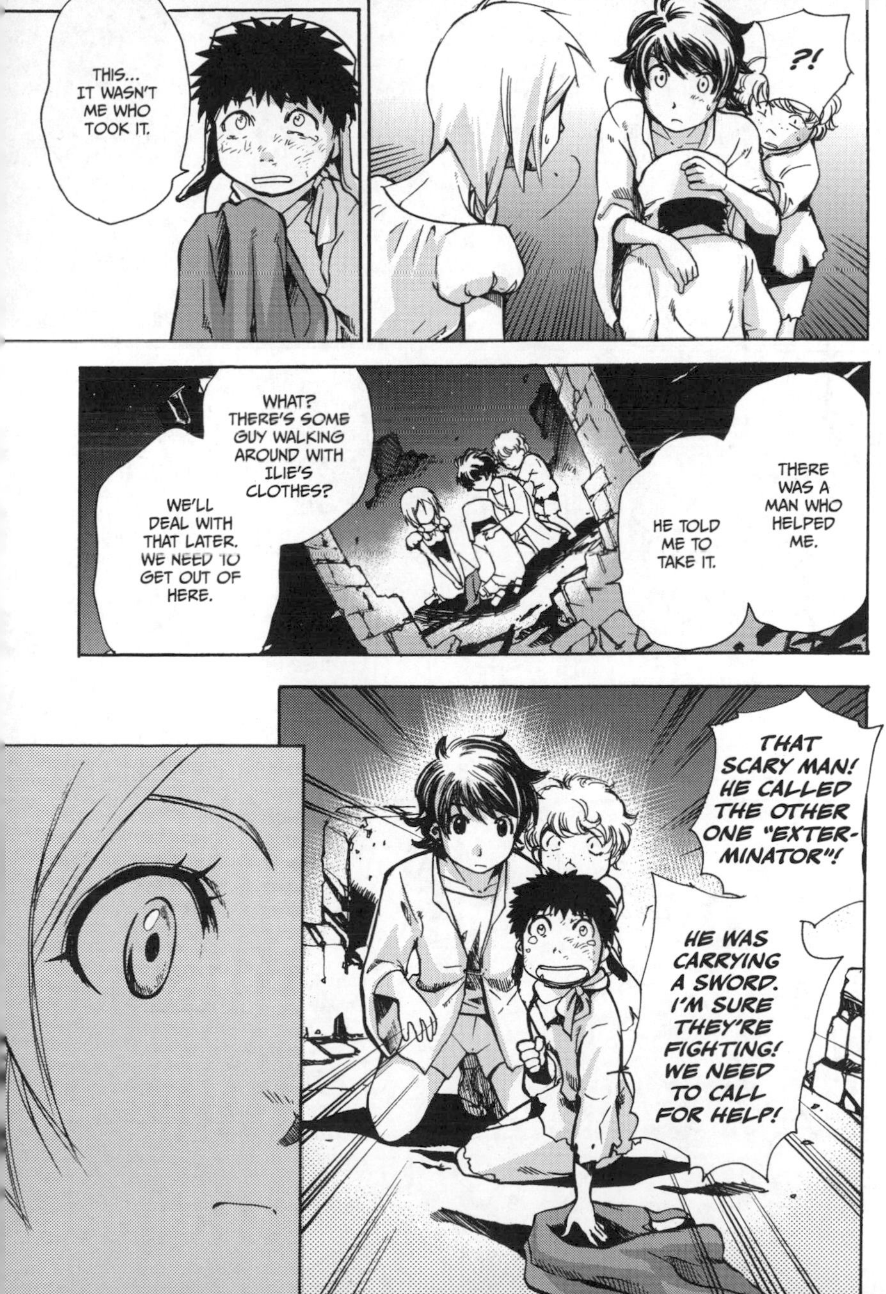
?!
THIS... IT WASN'T ME WHO TOOK IT.
THERE WAS A MAN WHO HELPED ME.
HE TOLD ME TO TAKE IT.
WHAT? THERE'S SOME GUY WALKING AROUND WITH ILIE'S CLOTHES?
WE'LL DEAL WITH THAT LATER. WE NEED TO GET OUT OF HERE.
THAT SCARY MAN! HE CALLED THE OTHER ONE "EXTERMINATOR"!
HE WAS CARRYING A SWORD. I'M SURE THEY'RE FIGHTING! WE NEED TO CALL FOR HELP!

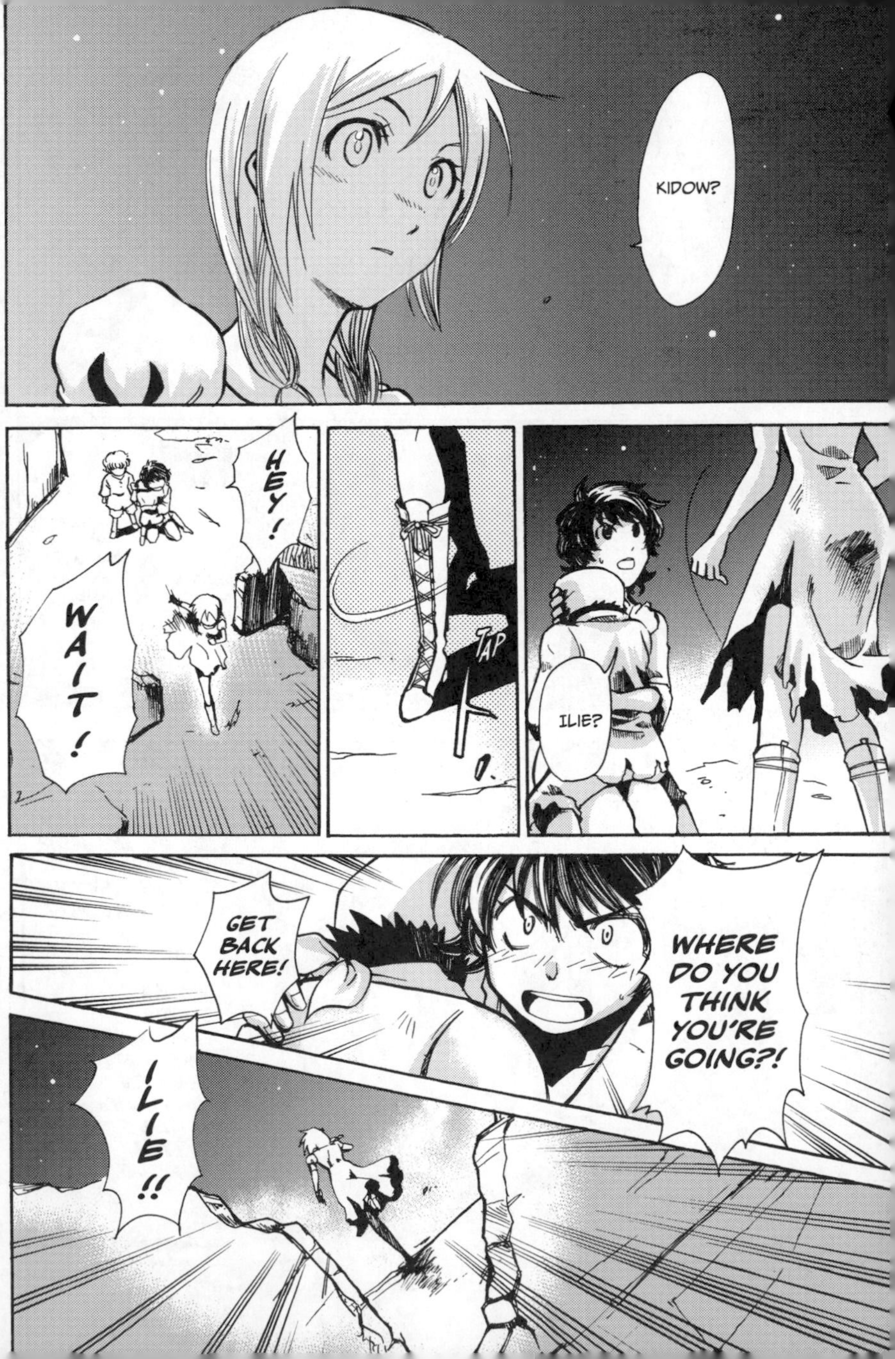
KIDOW?
ILIE?
TAP
HEY!
WAIT!
WHERE DO YOU THINK YOU'RE GOING?!
GET BACK HERE!
ILIE!!

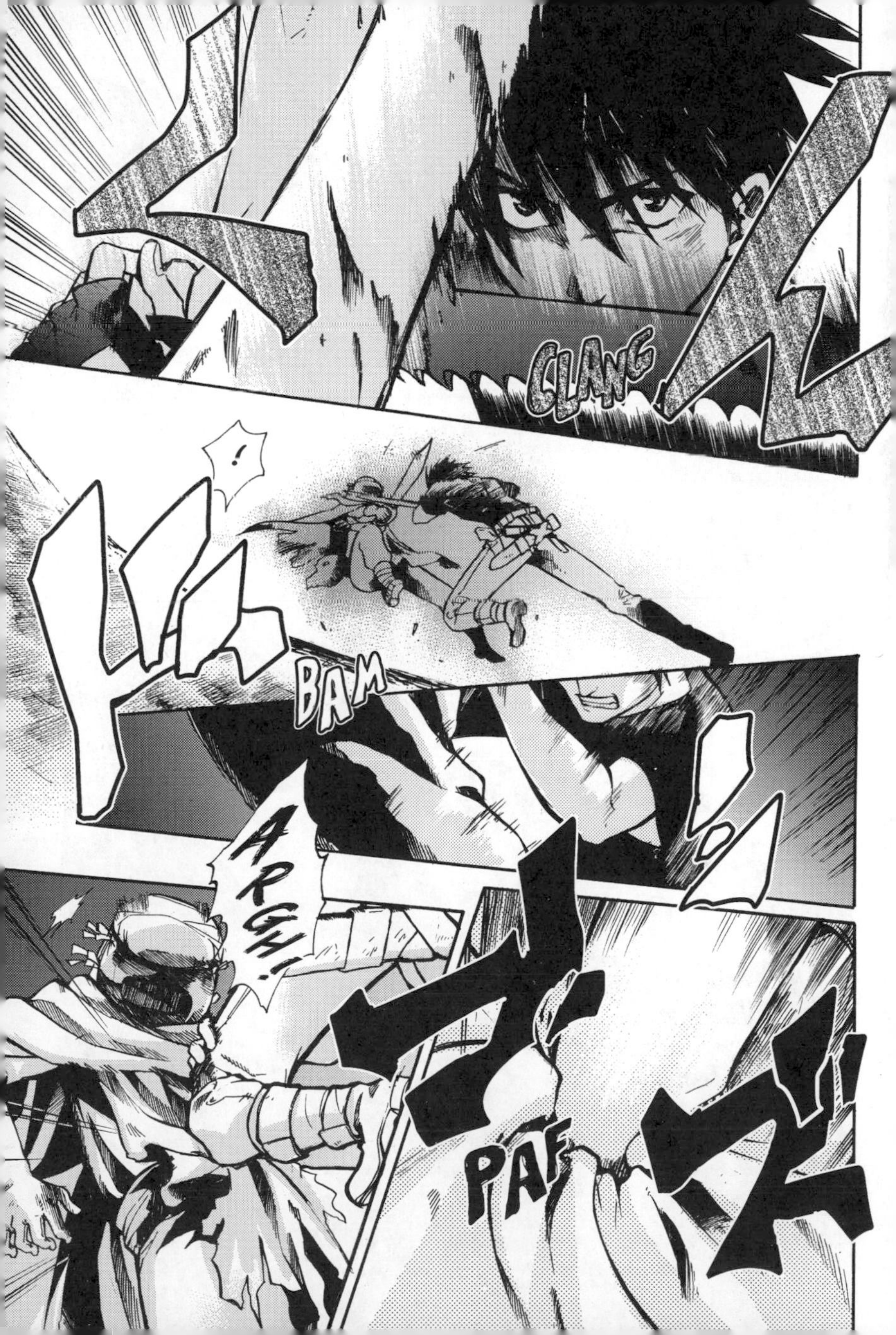
CLANG
!
BAM
ARGH!
PAF

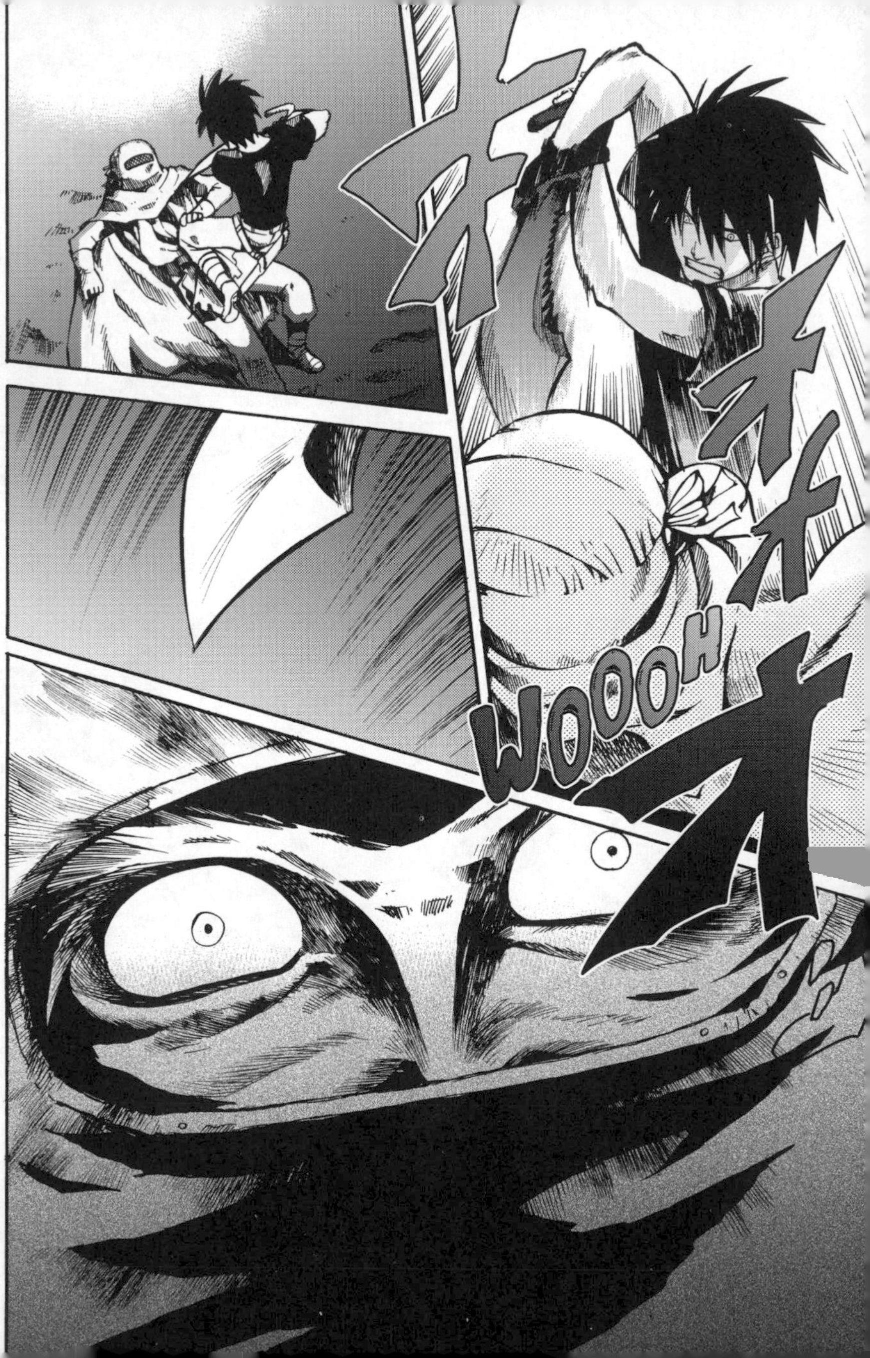
オオオオ
WOOOH

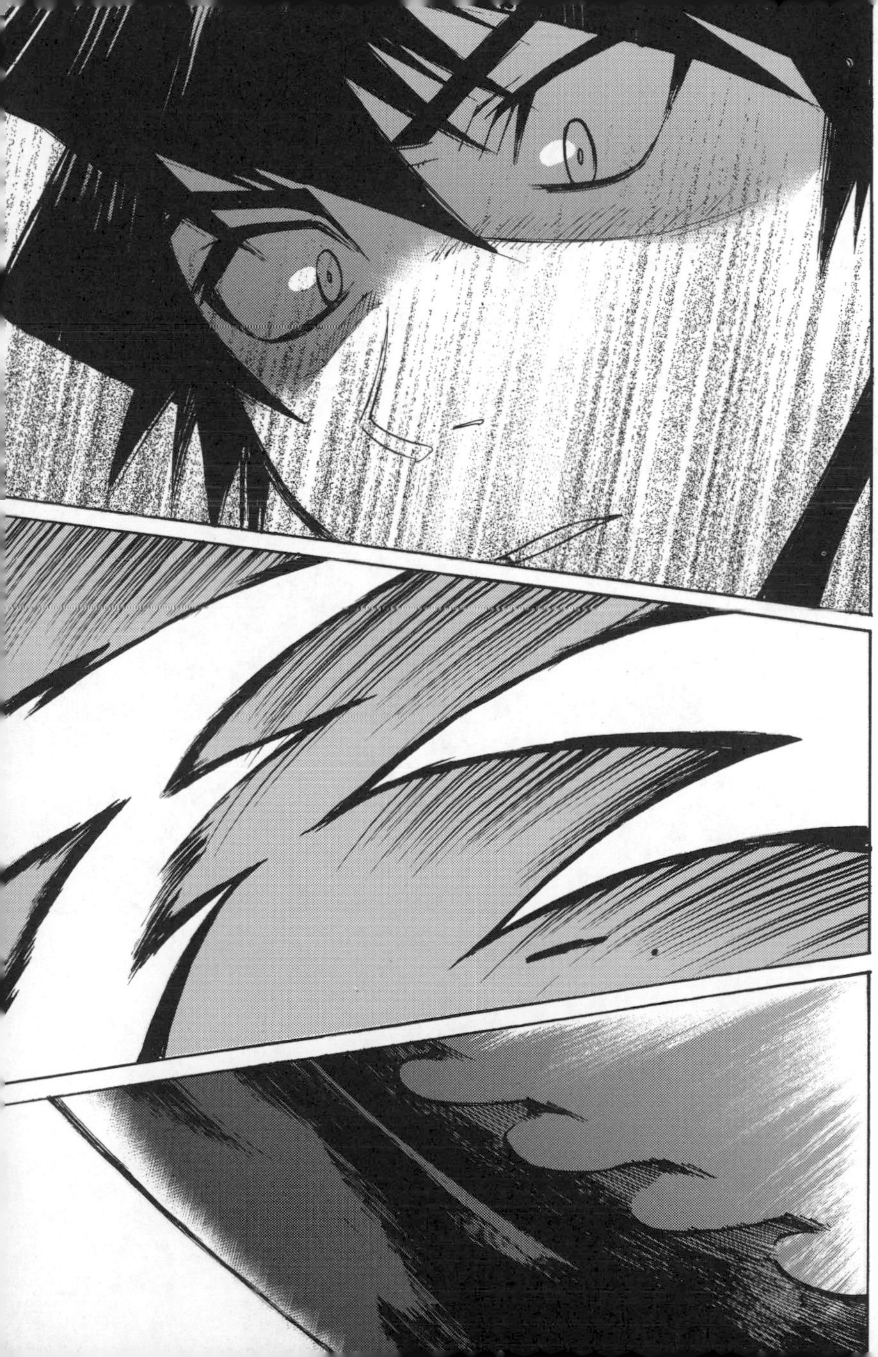

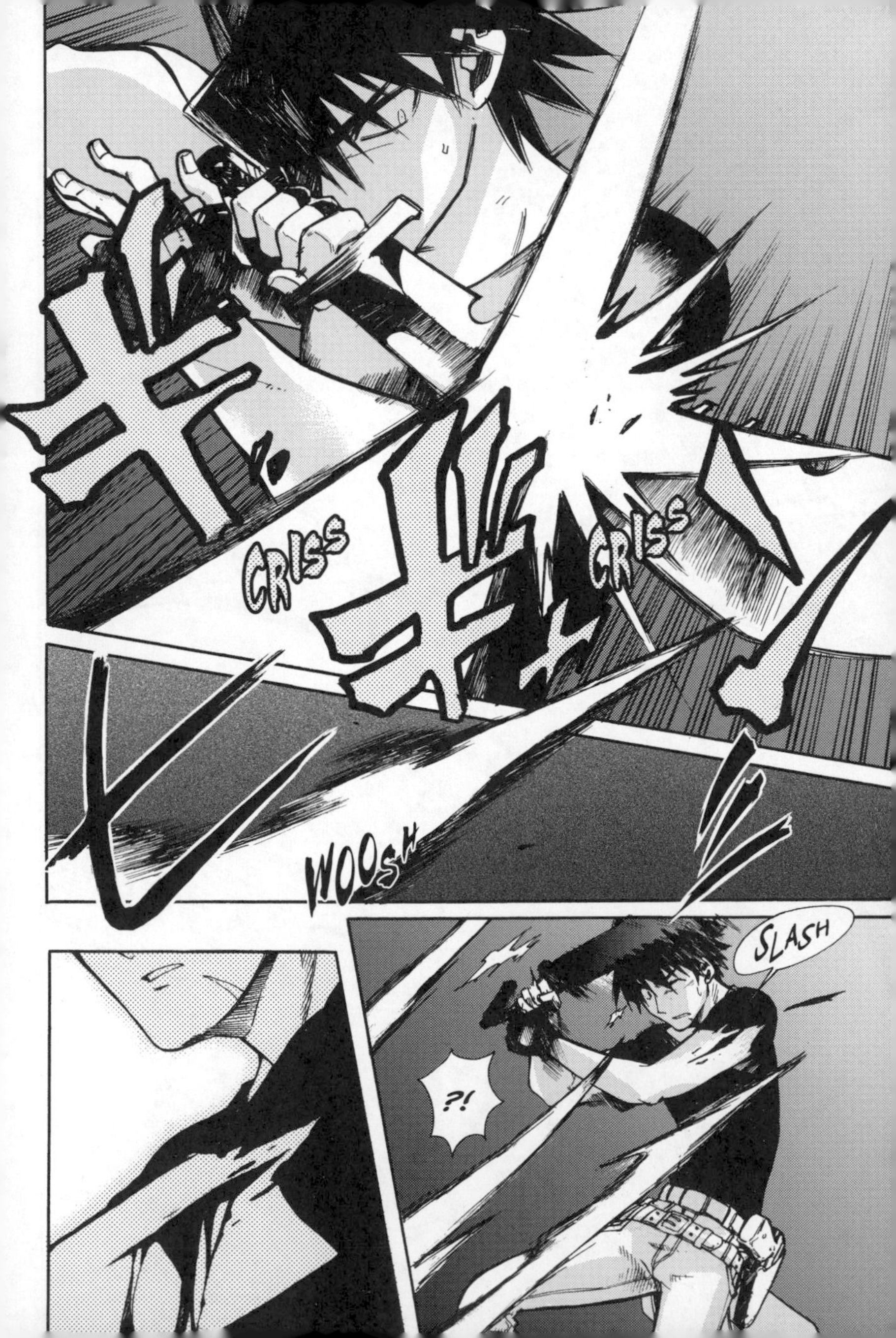
CRISS
CRISS
WOOSH
SLASH
?!

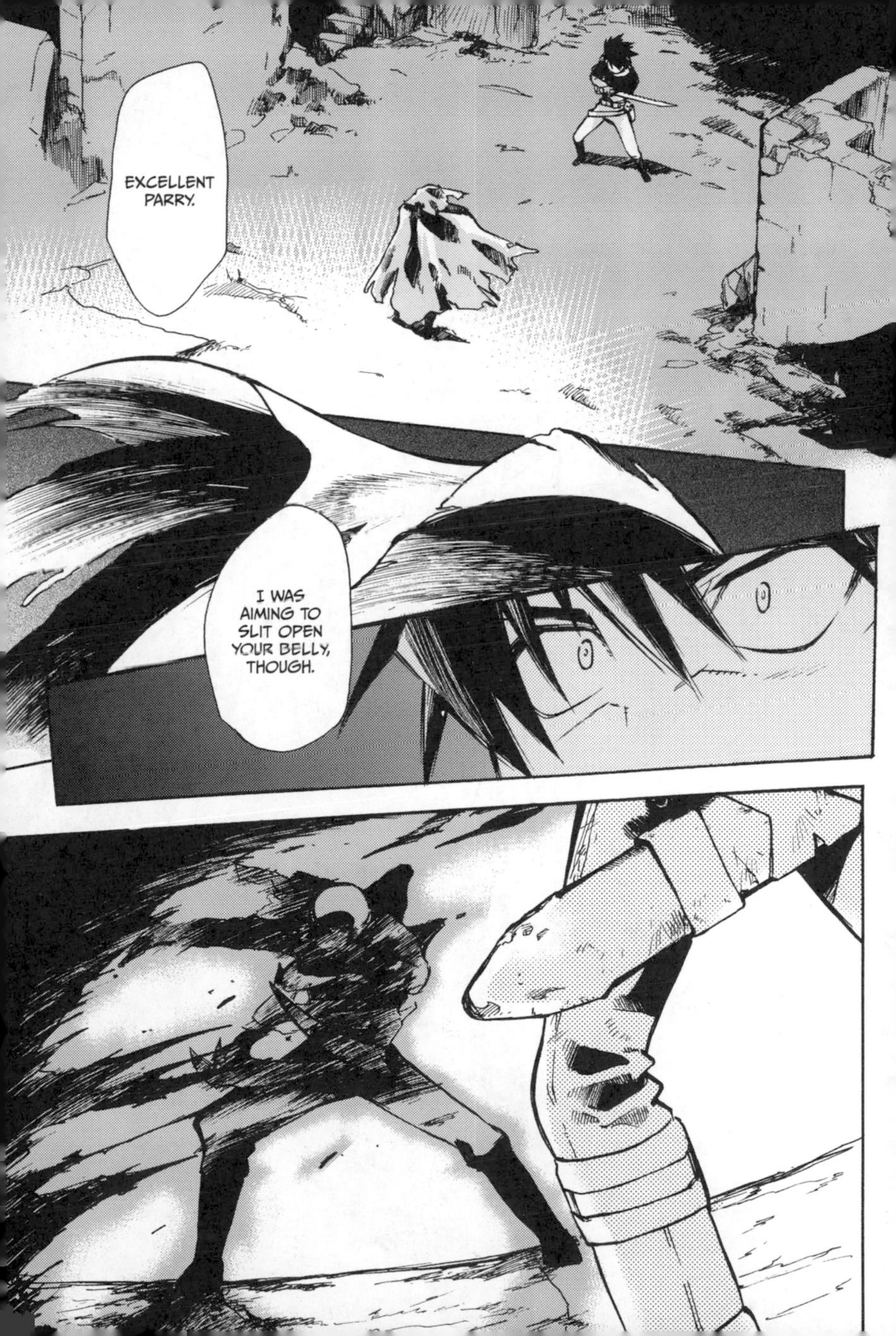
EXCELLENT PARRY.
I WAS AIMING TO SLIT OPEN YOUR BELLY, THOUGH.

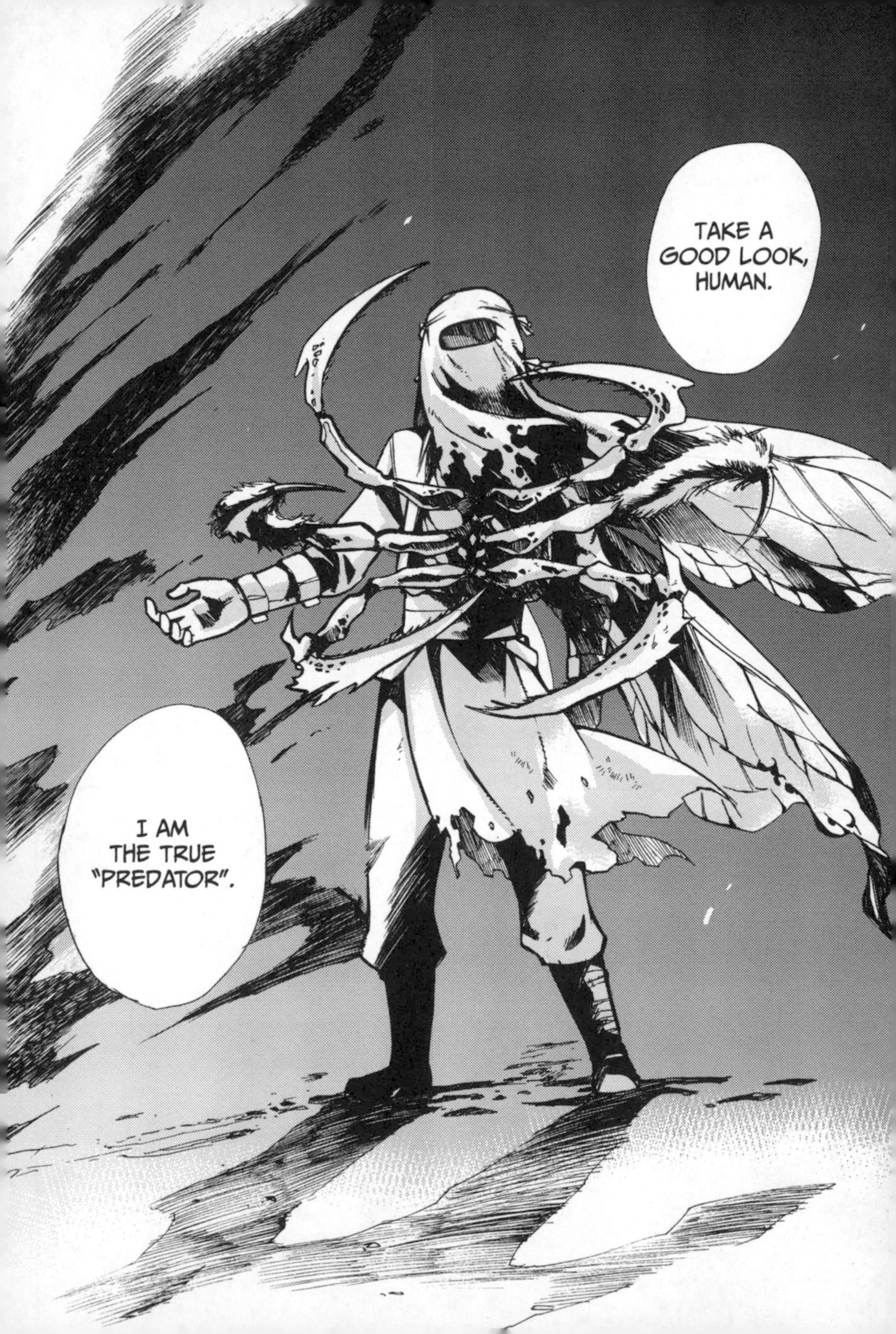
TAKE A GOOD LOOK, HUMAN.
I AM THE TRUE "PREDATOR".

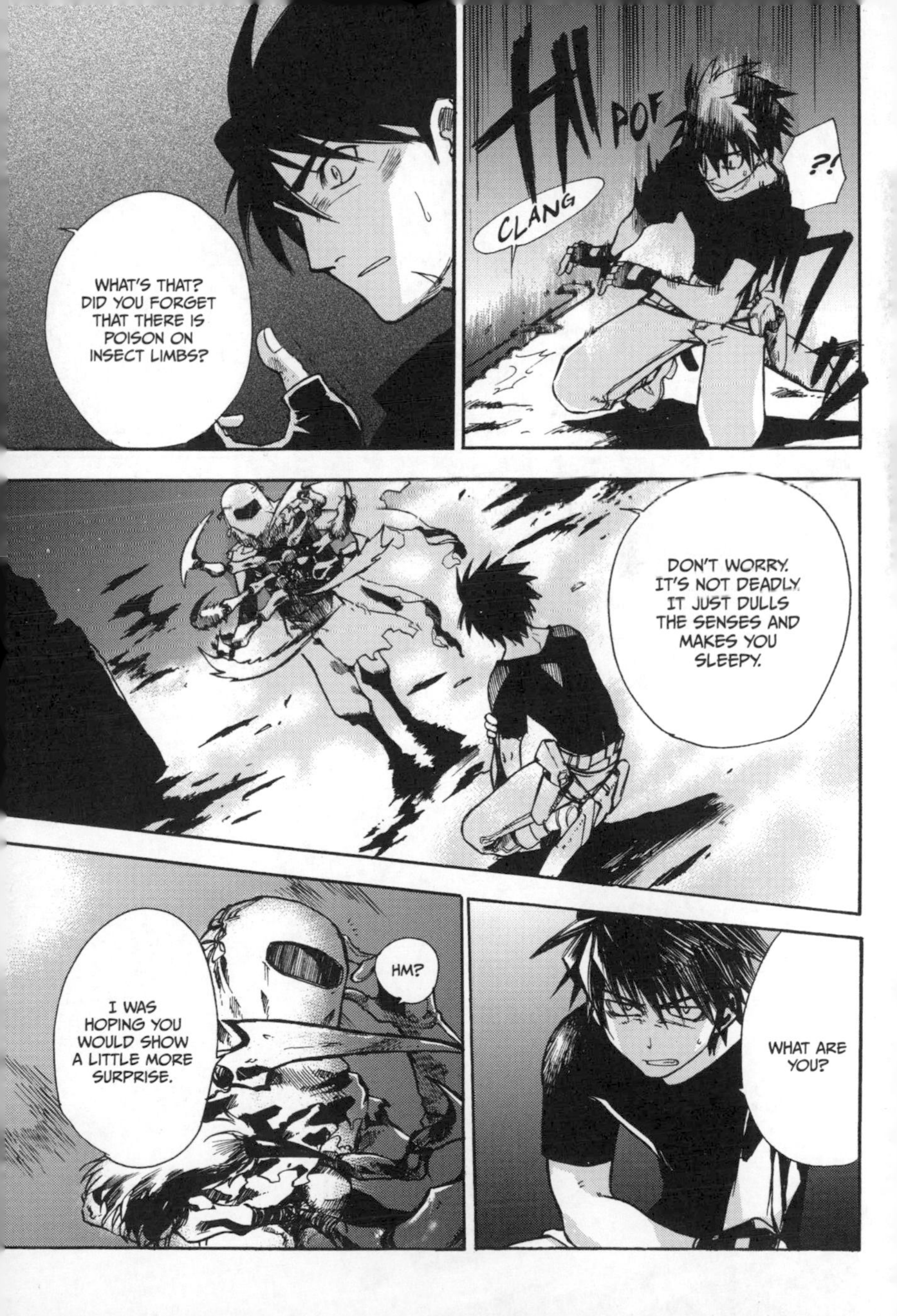
POF
?!
CLANG
WHAT'S THAT? DID YOU FORGET THAT THERE IS POISON ON INSECT LIMBS?
DON'T WORRY. IT'S NOT DEADLY. IT JUST DULLS THE SENSES AND MAKES YOU SLEEPY.
WHAT ARE YOU?
HM?
I WAS HOPING YOU WOULD SHOW A LITTLE MORE SURPRISE.

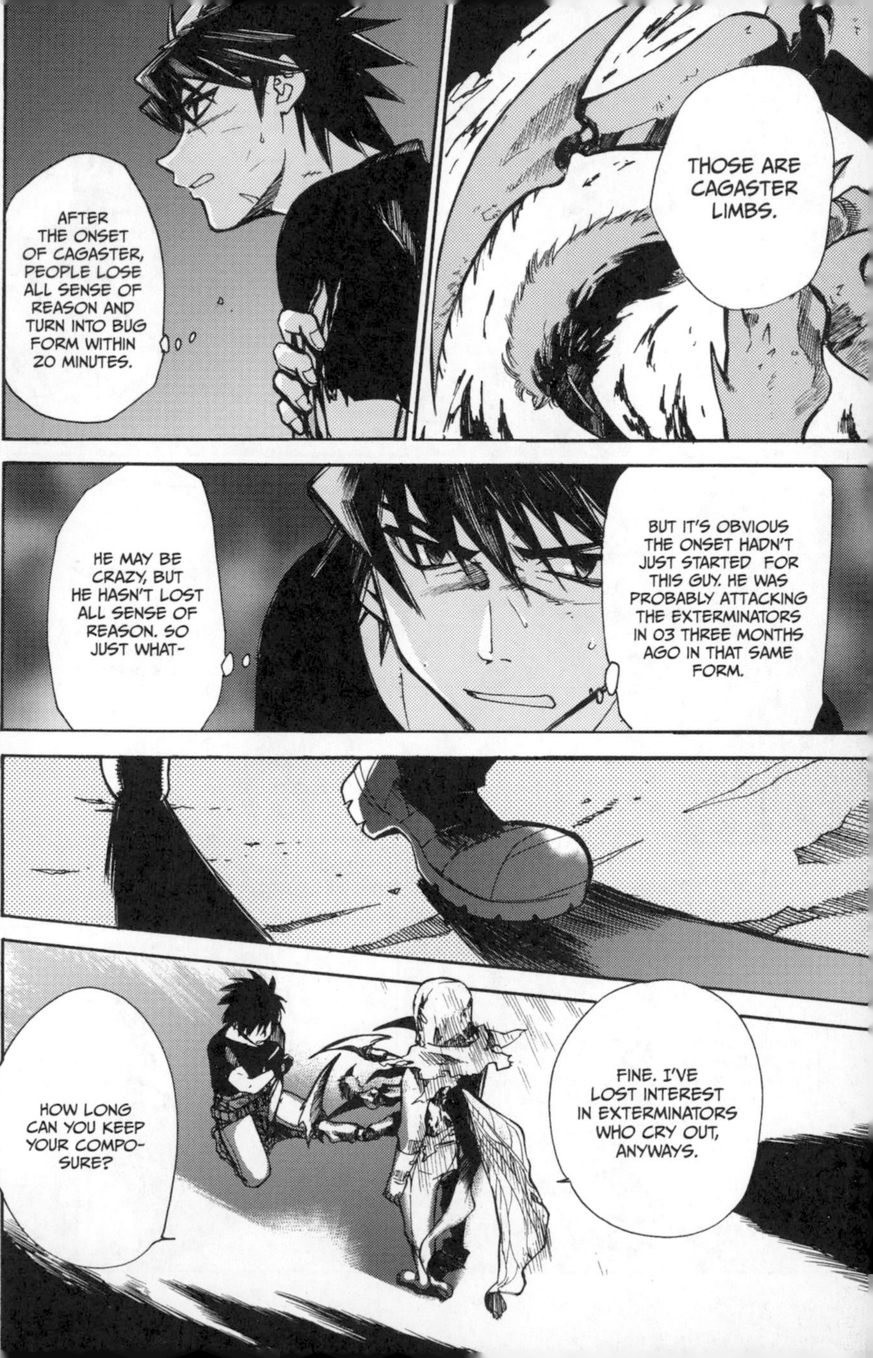
THOSE ARE CAGASTER LIMBS.
AFTER THE ONSET OF CAGASTER, PEOPLE LOSE ALL SENSE OF REASON AND TURN INTO BUG FORM WITHIN 20 MINUTES.
BUT IT'S OBVIOUS THE ONSET HADN'T JUST STARTED FOR THIS GUY. HE WAS PROBABLY ATTACKING THE EXTERMINATORS IN 03 THREE MONTHS AGO IN THAT SAME FORM.
HE MAY BE CRAZY, BUT HE HASN'T LOST ALL SENSE OF REASON. SO JUST WHAT-
FINE. I'VE LOST INTEREST IN EXTERMINATORS WHO CRY OUT, ANYWAYS.
HOW LONG CAN YOU KEEP YOUR COMPO-SURE?

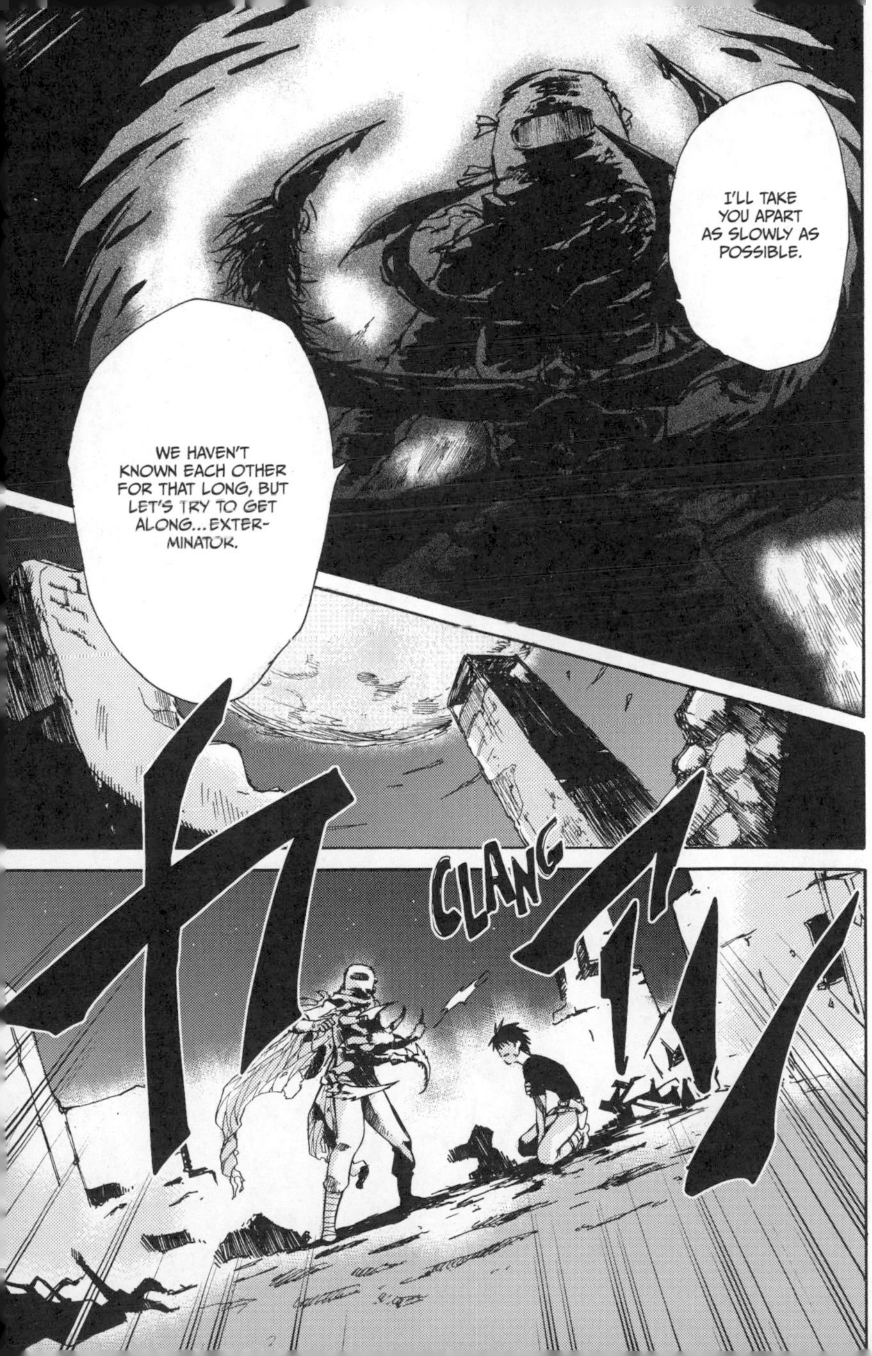
I'LL TAKE YOU APART AS SLOWLY AS POSSIBLE.
WE HAVEN'T KNOWN EACH OTHER FOR THAT LONG, BUT LET'S TRY TO GET ALONG...EXTER-MINATOR.
CLANG

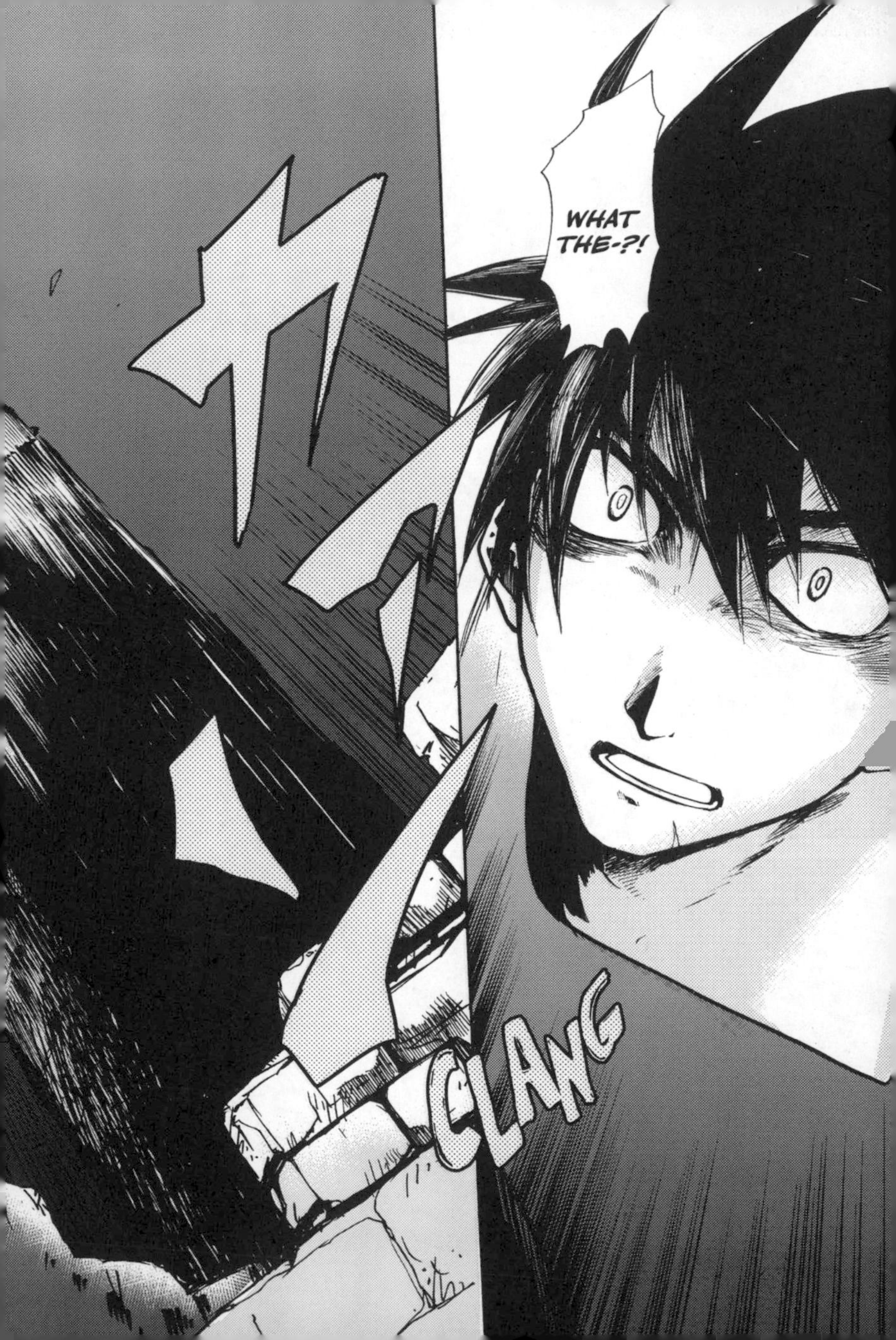
WHAT THE-?!
CLANG

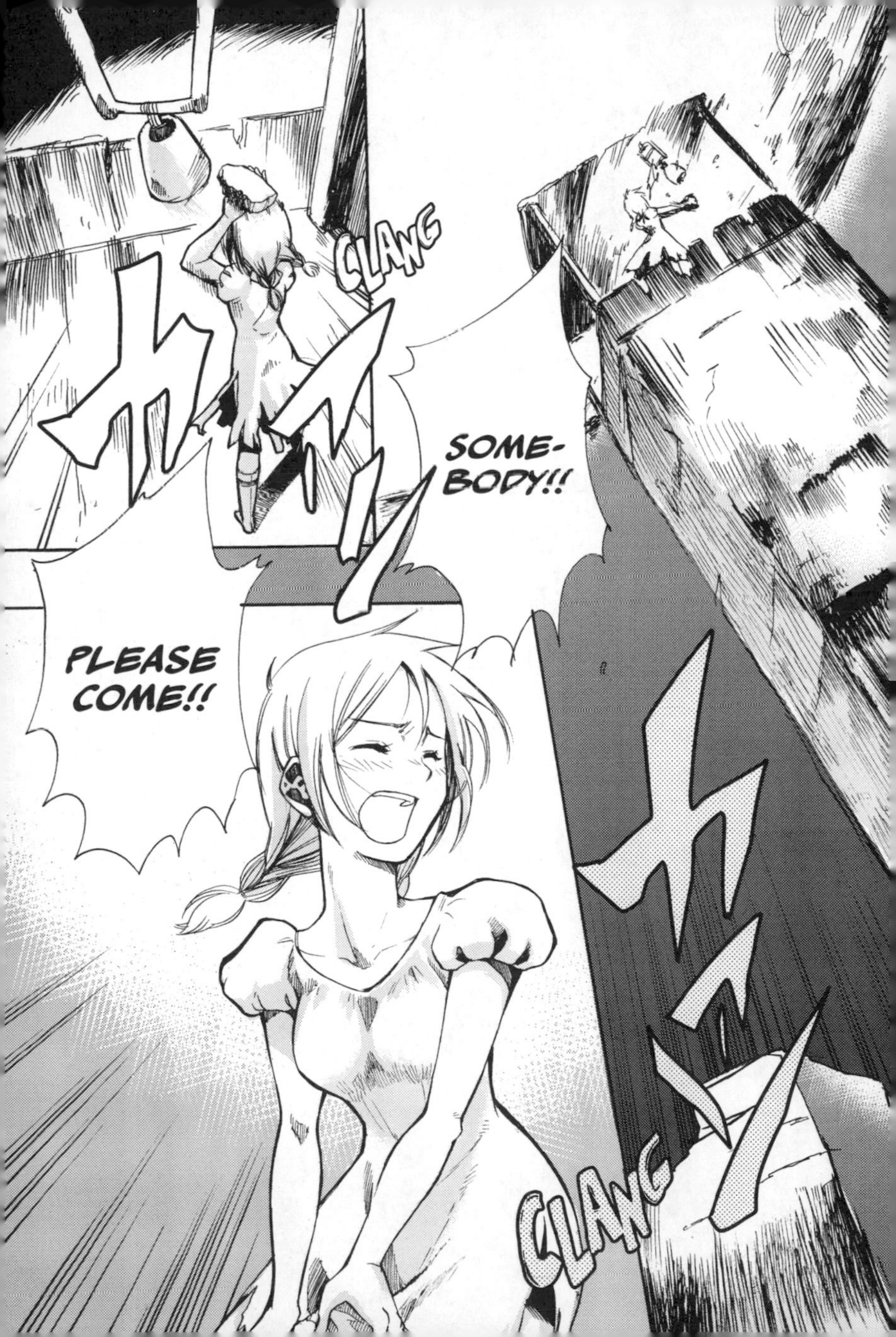
SOME-BODY!!
CLANG
PLEASE COME!!
CLANG

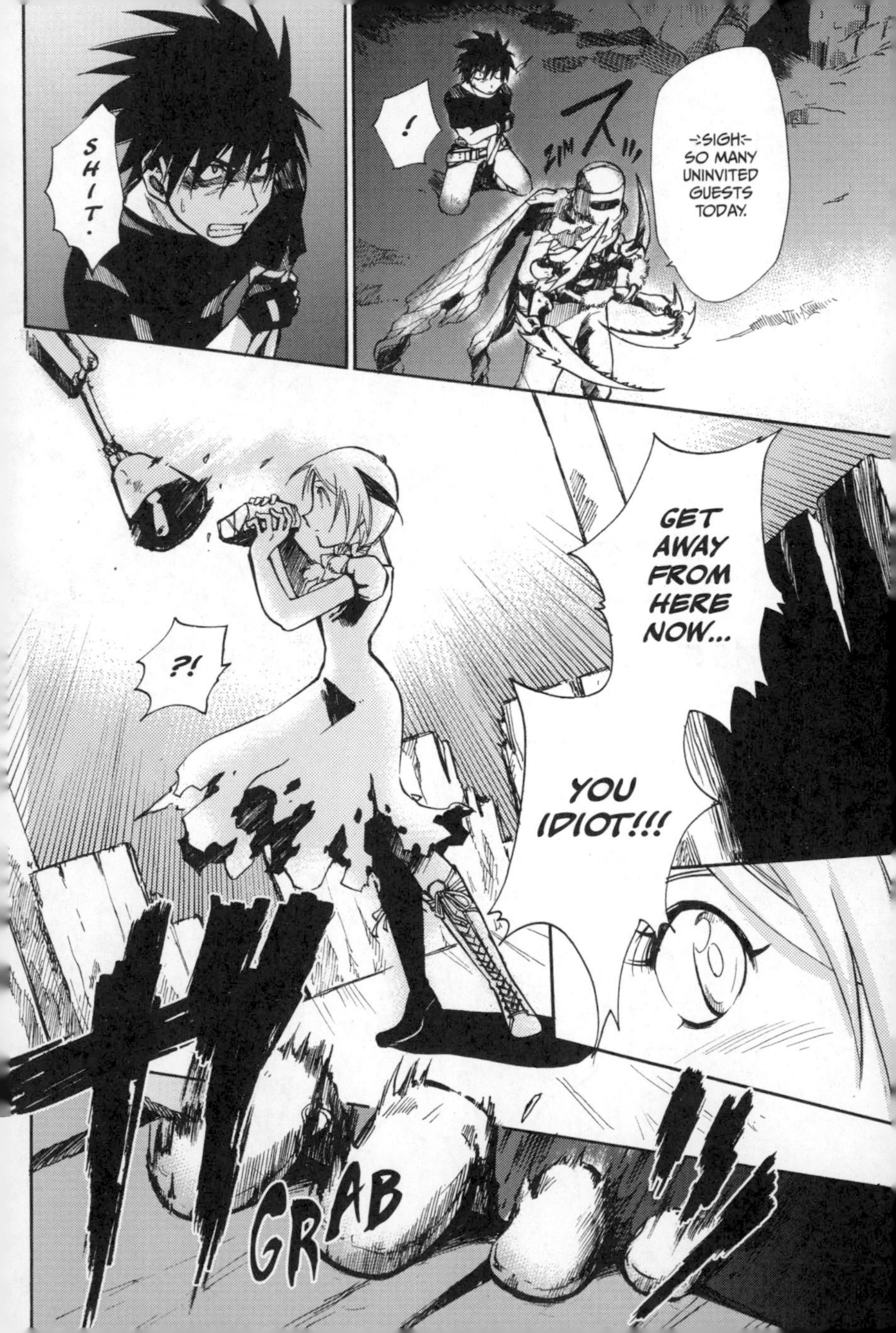
-SIGH- SO MANY UNINVITED GUESTS TODAY.
ZIN
!
SHIT.
GET AWAY FROM HERE NOW...
YOU IDIOT!!!
?!
GRAB

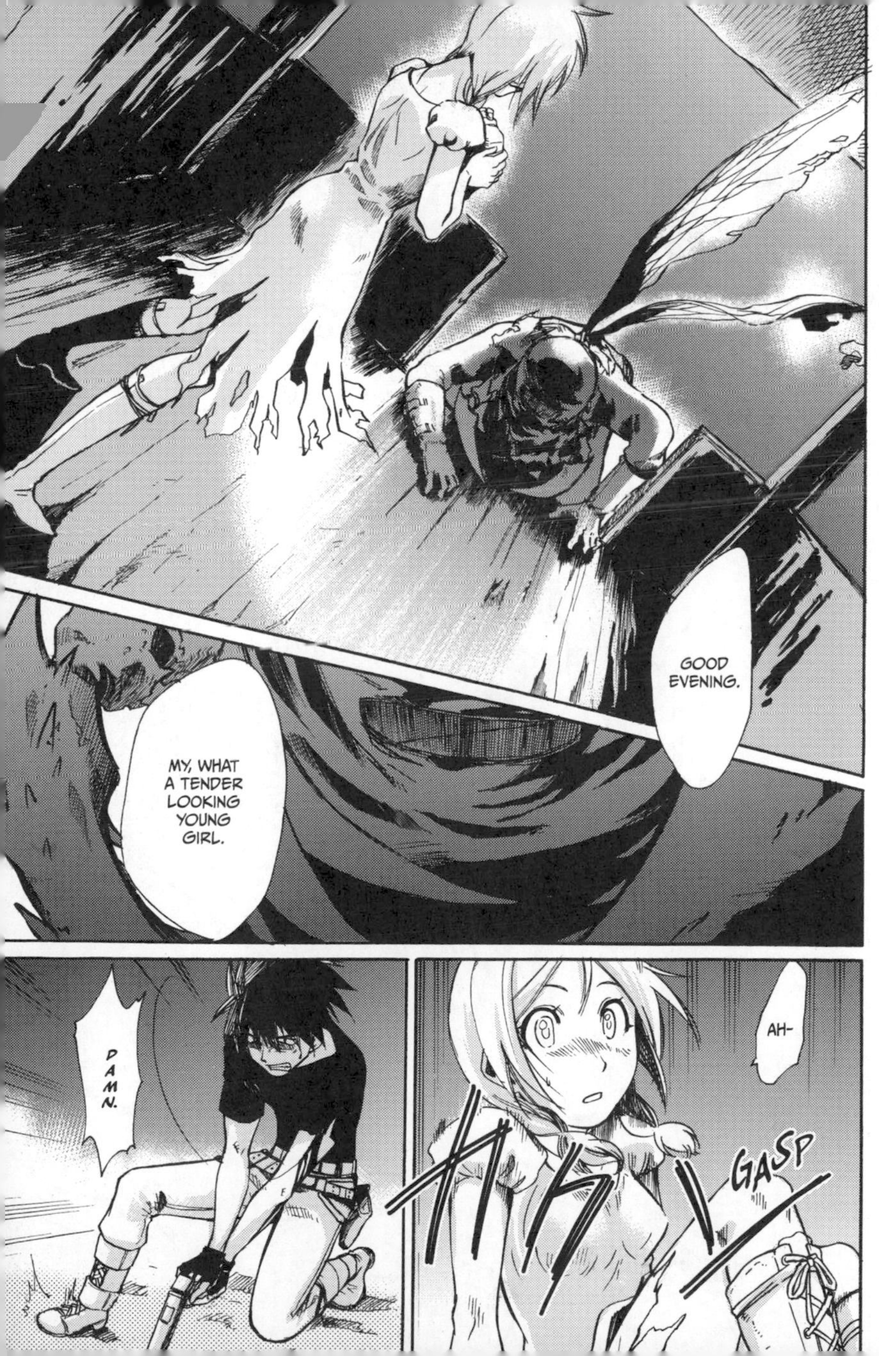
GOOD EVENING.
MY, WHAT A TENDER LOOKING YOUNG GIRL.
AH-
GASP
DAMN.

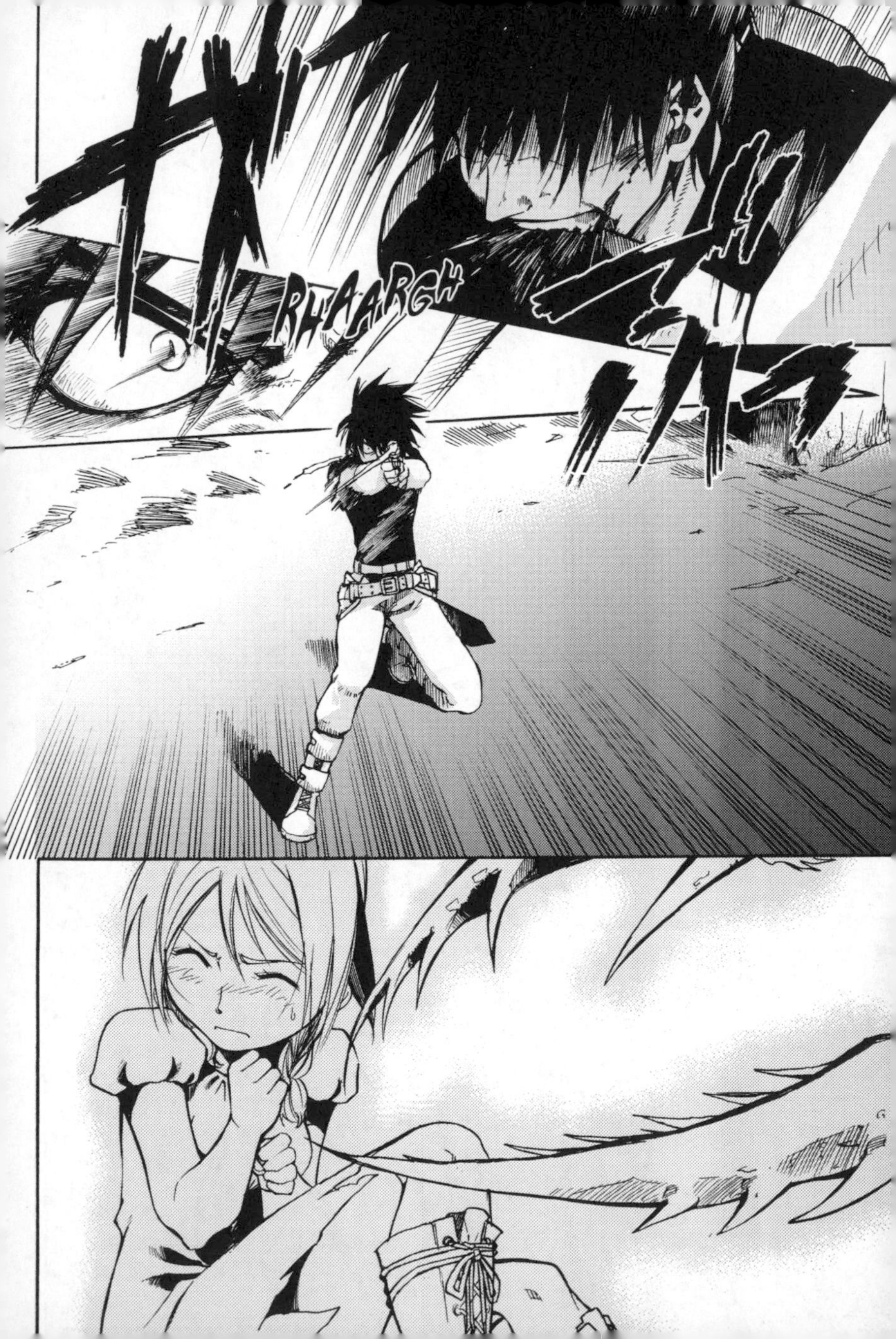
RHAARCH

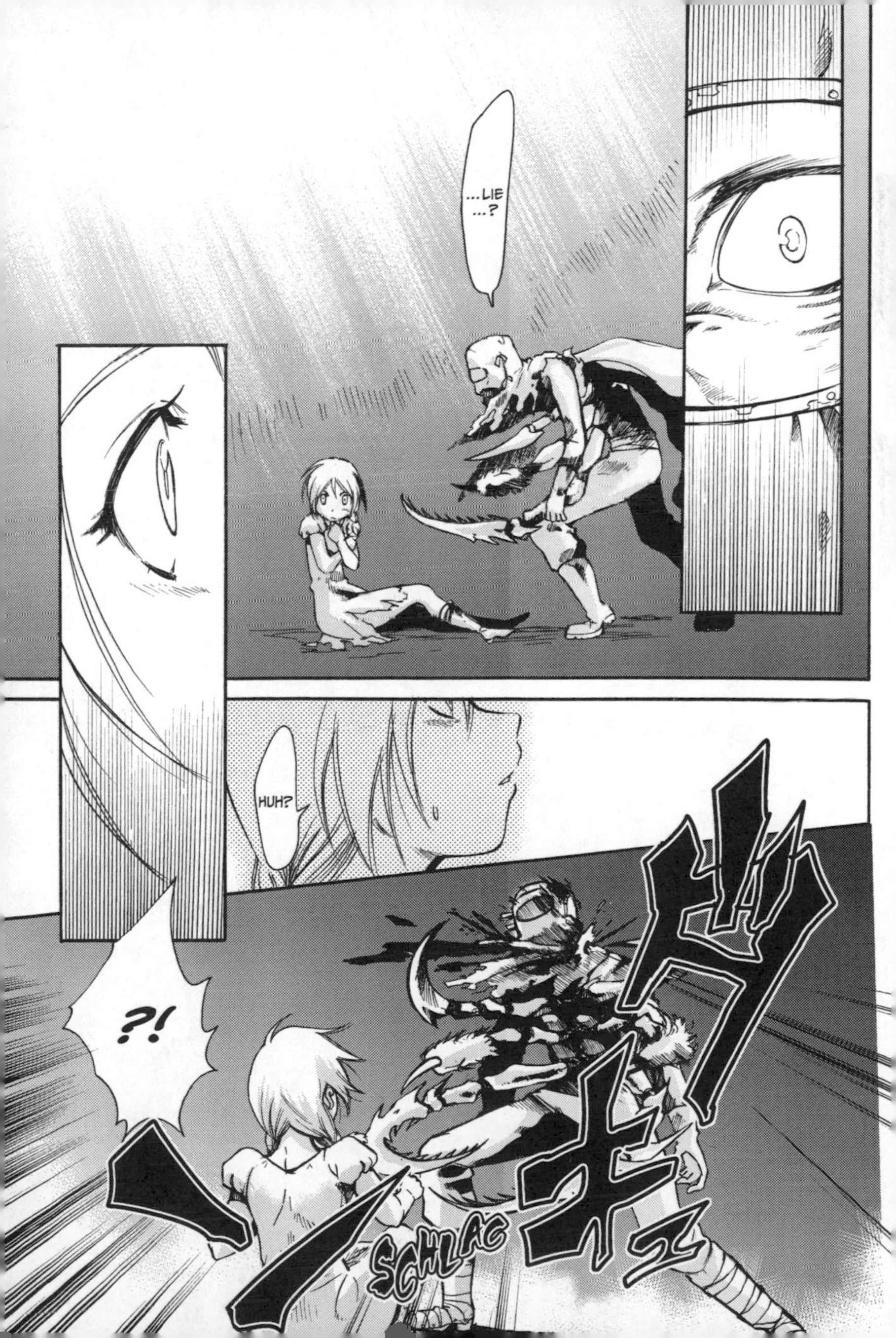
...LIE ...?
HUH?
?!
SCHLAC

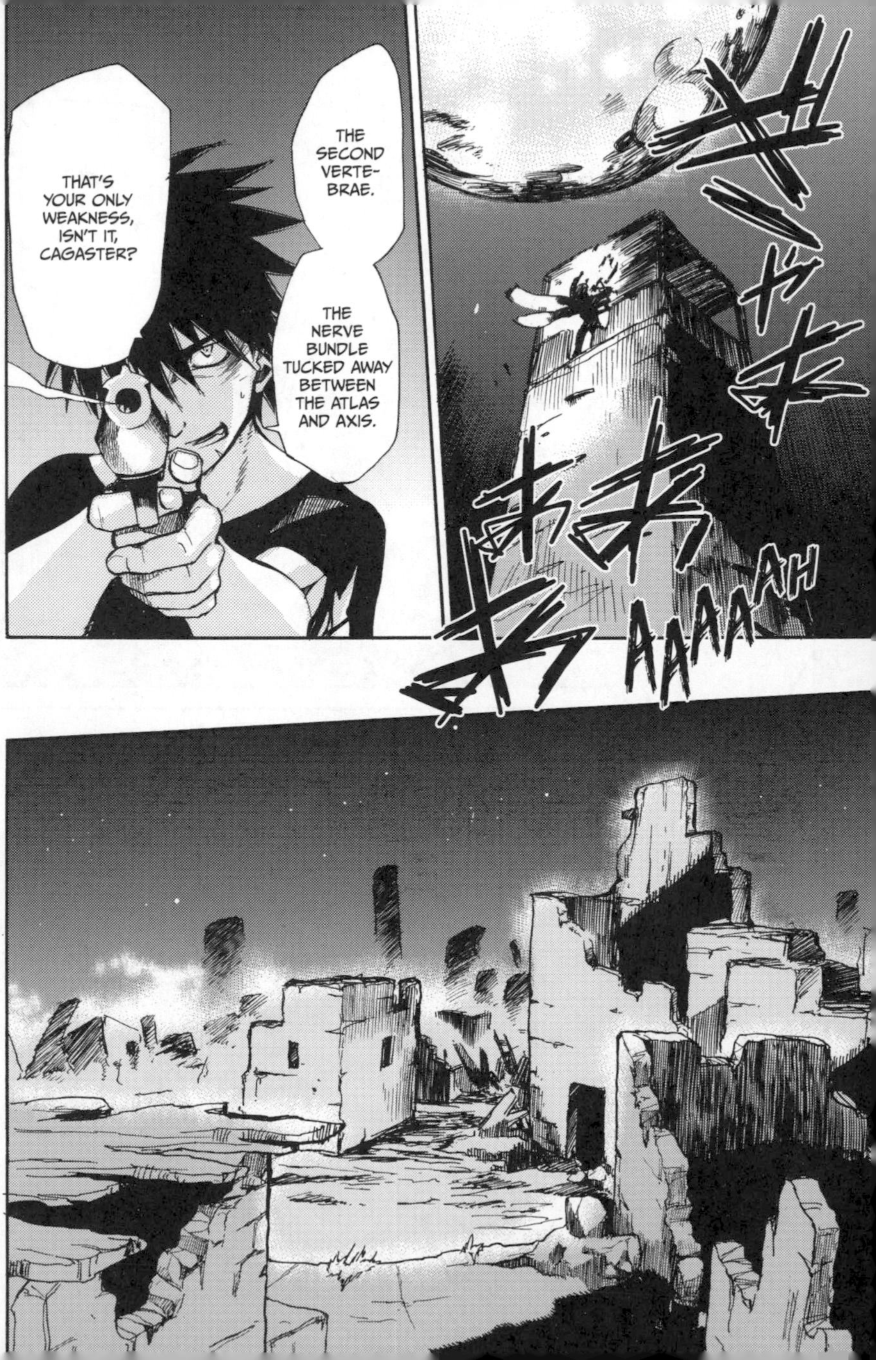
あああ
AAAAAAH
THE SECOND VERTE-BRAE.
THE NERVE BUNDLE TUCKED AWAY BETWEEN THE ATLAS AND AXIS.
THAT'S YOUR ONLY WEAKNESS, ISN'T IT, CAGASTER?

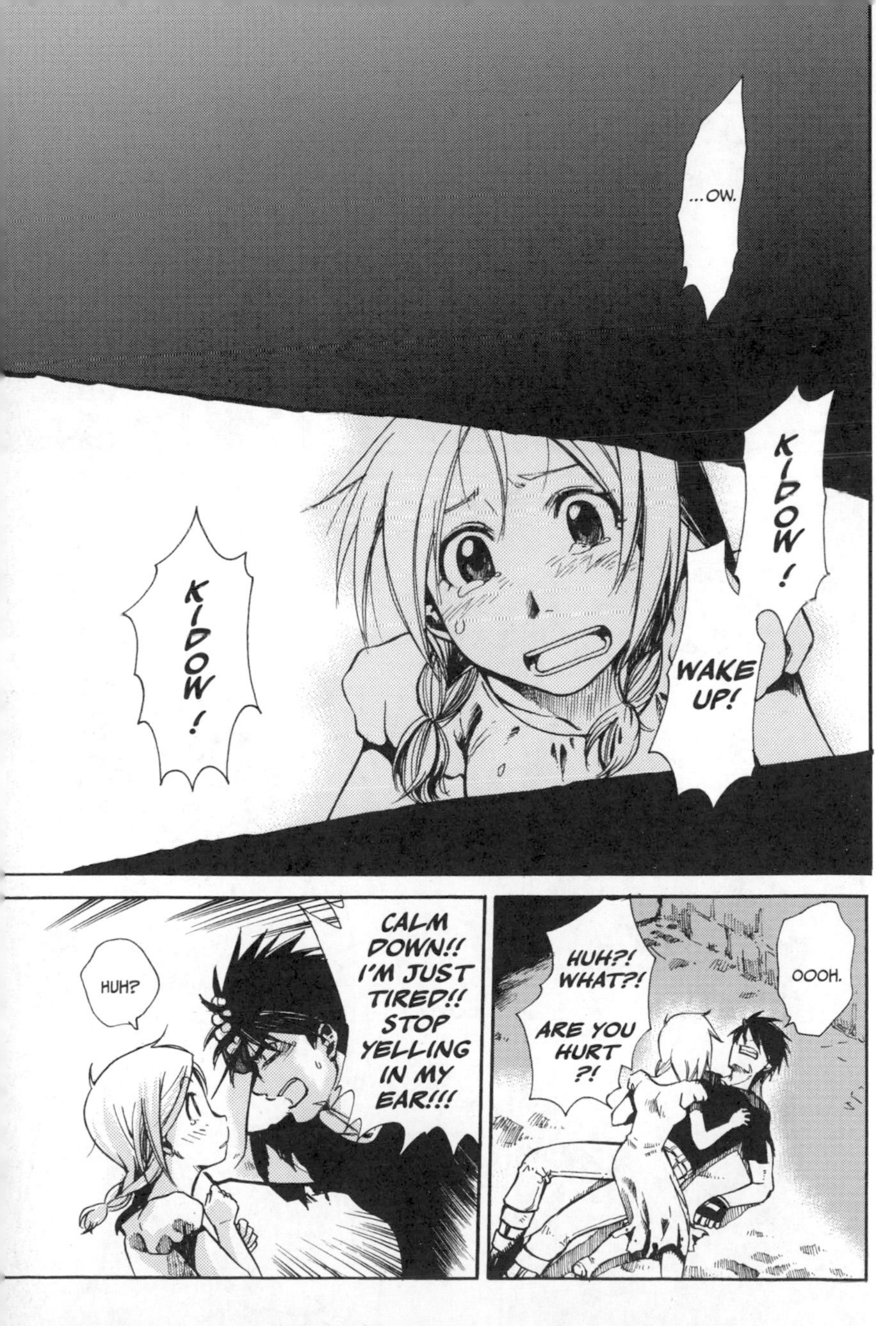
...OW.
KIDOW!
WAKE UP!
KIDOW!
OOOH.
HUH?! WHAT?!
ARE YOU HURT ?!
CALM DOWN!! I'M JUST TIRED!! STOP YELLING IN MY EAR!!!
HUH?

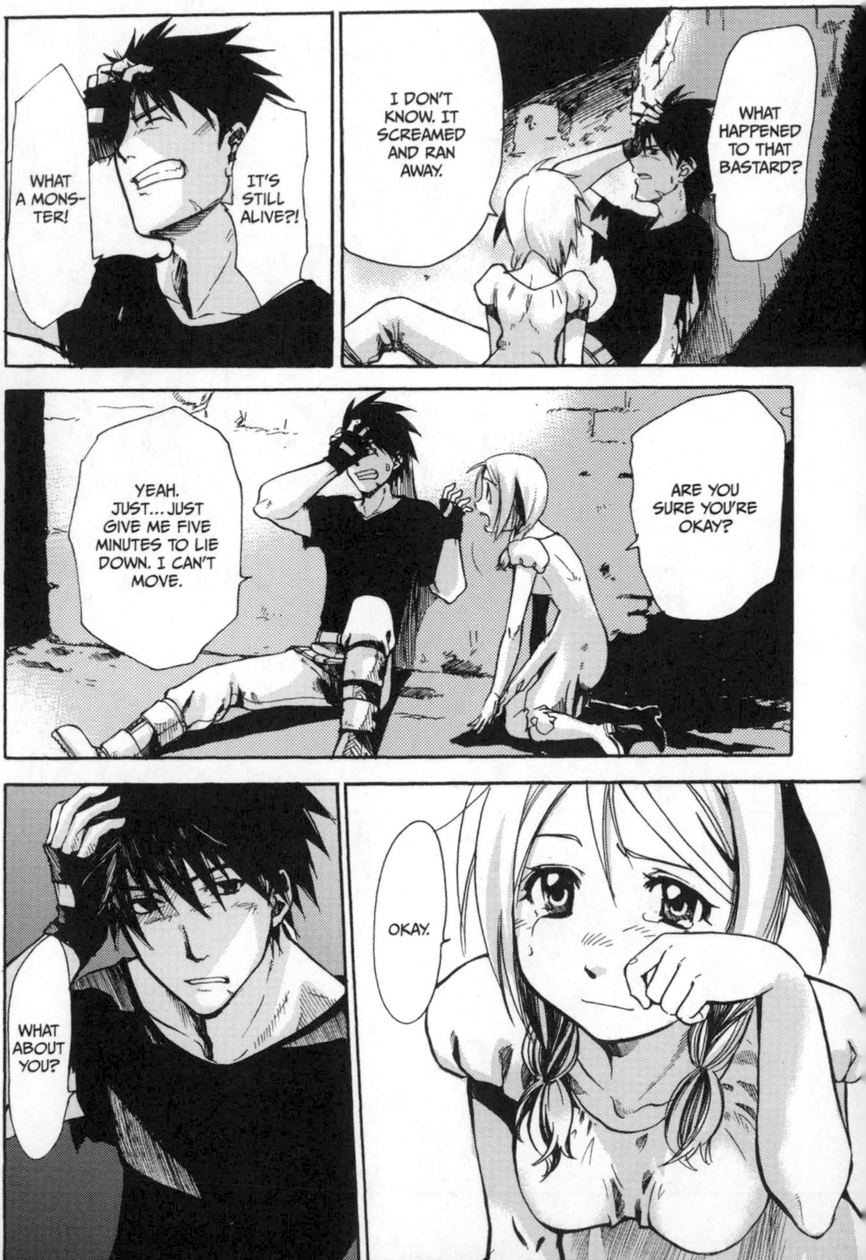
WHAT HAPPENED TO THAT BASTARD?
I DON'T KNOW. IT SCREAMED AND RAN AWAY.
IT'S STILL ALIVE?!
WHAT A MONSTER!
ARE YOU SURE YOU'RE OKAY?
YEAH. JUST... JUST GIVE ME FIVE MINUTES TO LIE DOWN. I CAN'T MOVE.
OKAY.
WHAT ABOUT YOU?

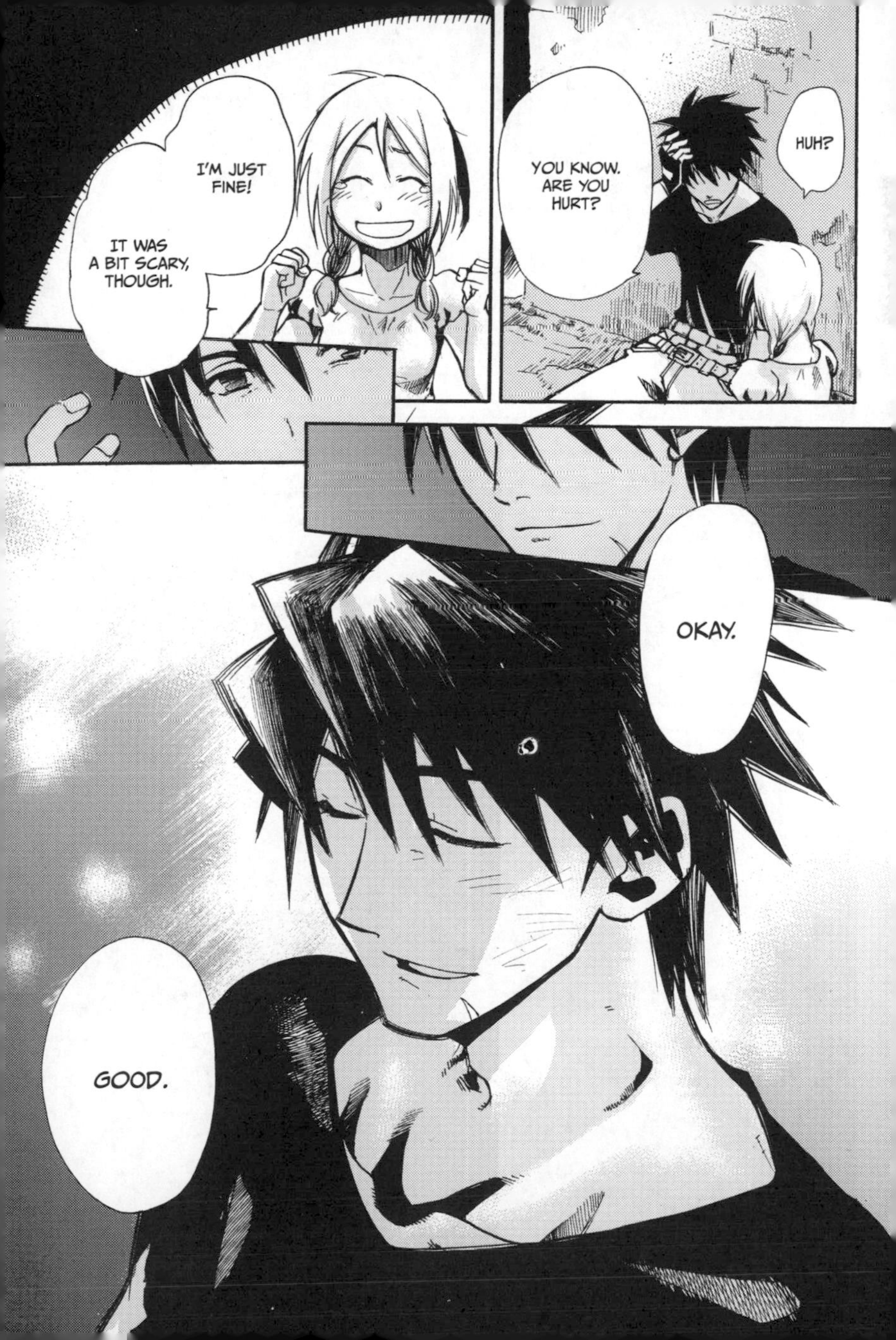
HUH?
YOU KNOW. ARE YOU HURT?
I'M JUST FINE!
IT WAS A BIT SCARY, THOUGH.
OKAY.
GOOD.

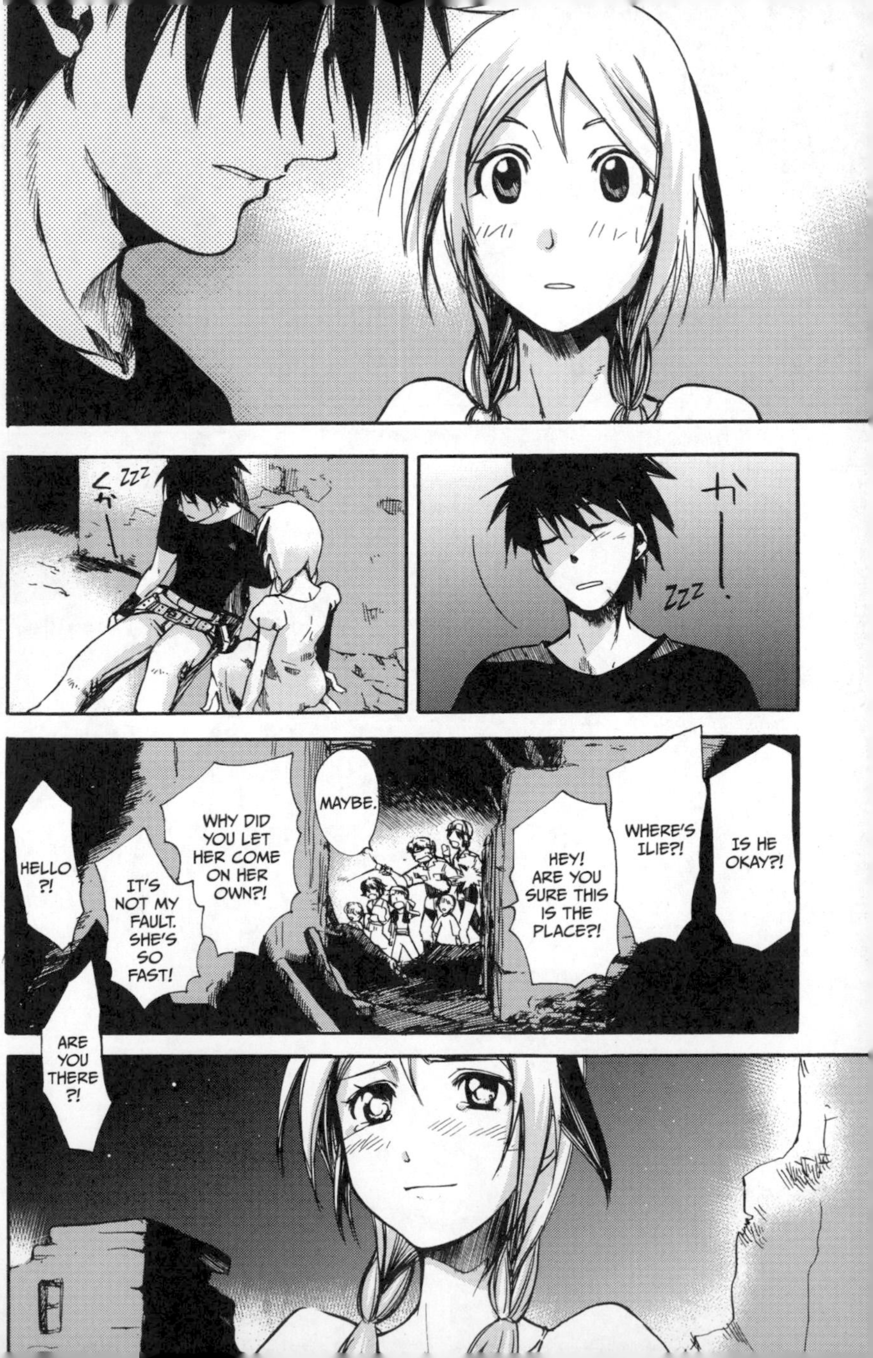
かー！
Zzz
くか
Zzz
IS HE OKAY?!
WHERE'S ILIE?!
HEY! ARE YOU SURE THIS IS THE PLACE?!
MAYBE.
WHY DID YOU LET HER COME ON HER OWN?!
IT'S NOT MY FAULT. SHE'S SO FAST!
HELLO?!
ARE YOU THERE?!

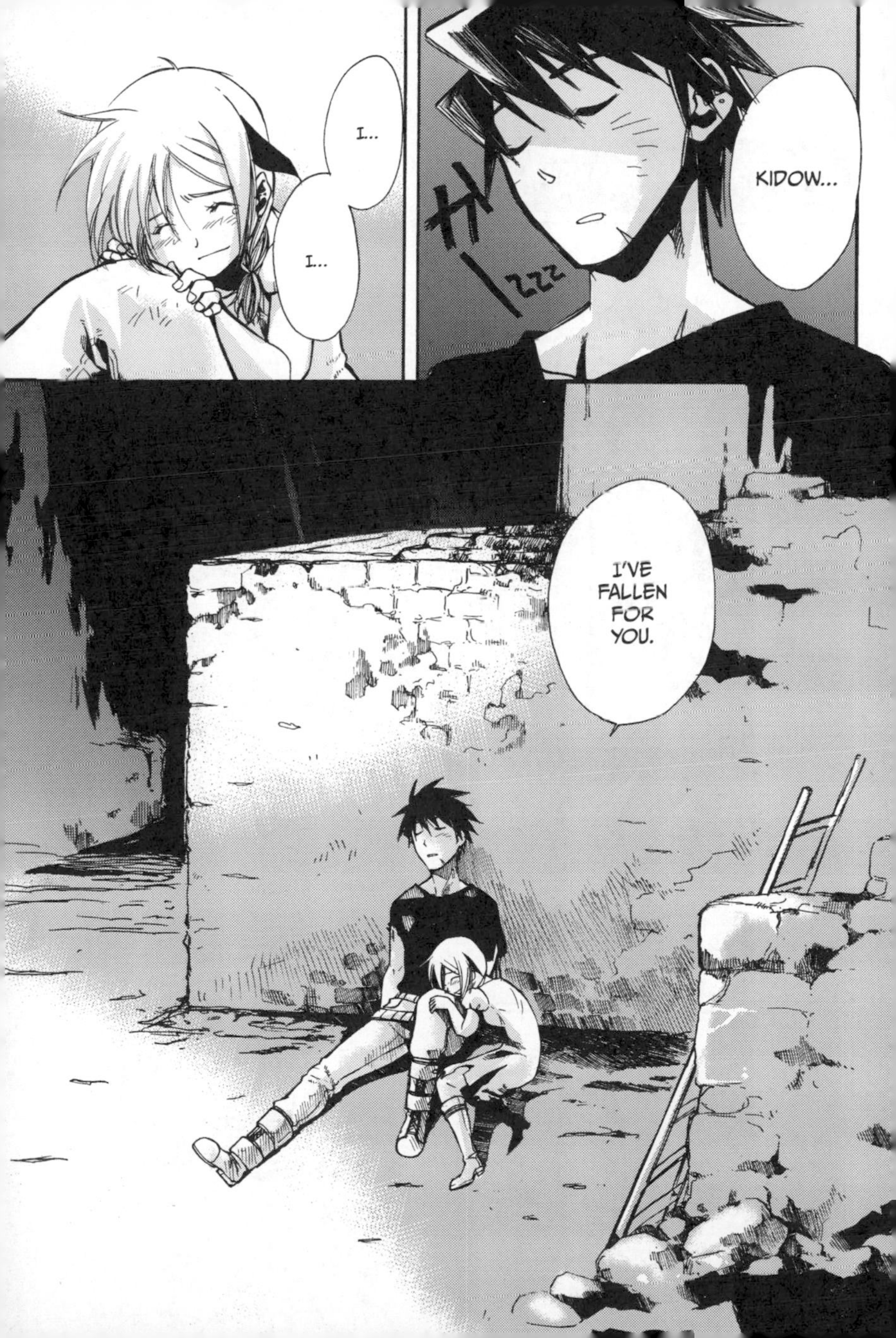
KIDOW...
ZZZ
I...
I...
I'VE FALLEN FOR YOU.

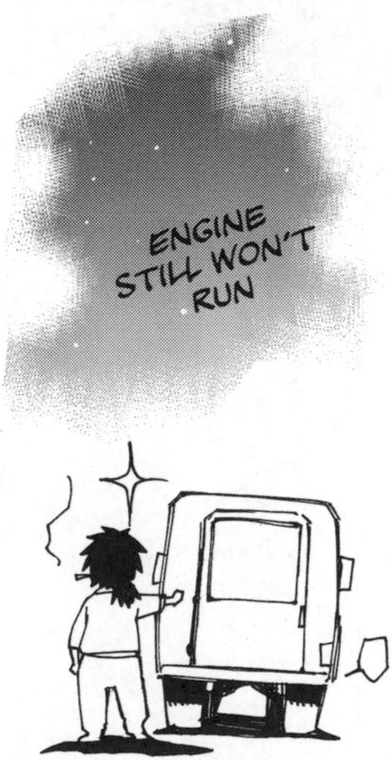
ENGINE STILL WON'T RUN

THE SLEEPING SCARY GUY.

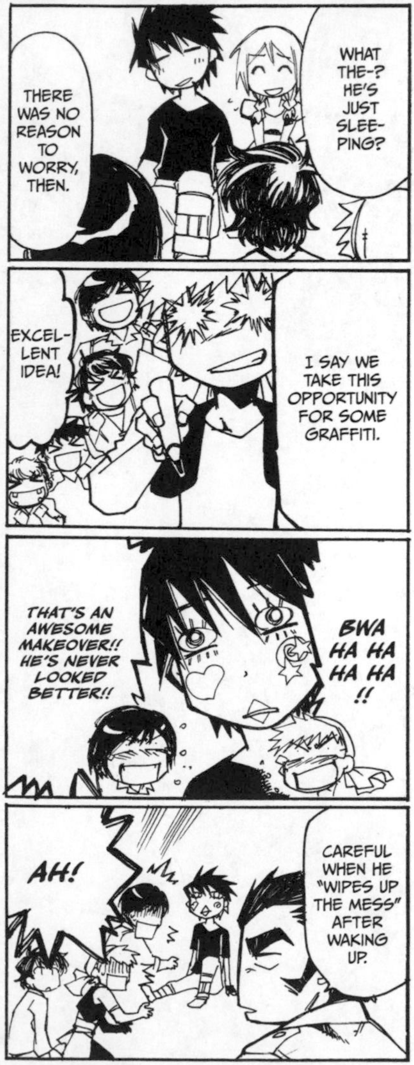
WHAT THE-? HE'S JUST SLEE-PING?
THERE WAS NO REASON TO WORRY, THEN.
I SAY WE TAKE THIS OPPORTUNITY FOR SOME GRAFFITI.
EXCEL-LENT IDEA!
BWA HA HA HA HA !!
THAT'S AN AWESOME MAKEOVER!! HE'S NEVER LOOKED BETTER!!
CAREFUL WHEN HE "WIPES UP THE MESS" AFTER WAKING UP.
AH!

...THAT CAN BE TAKEN MANY WAYS.

[CHAPTER 7]

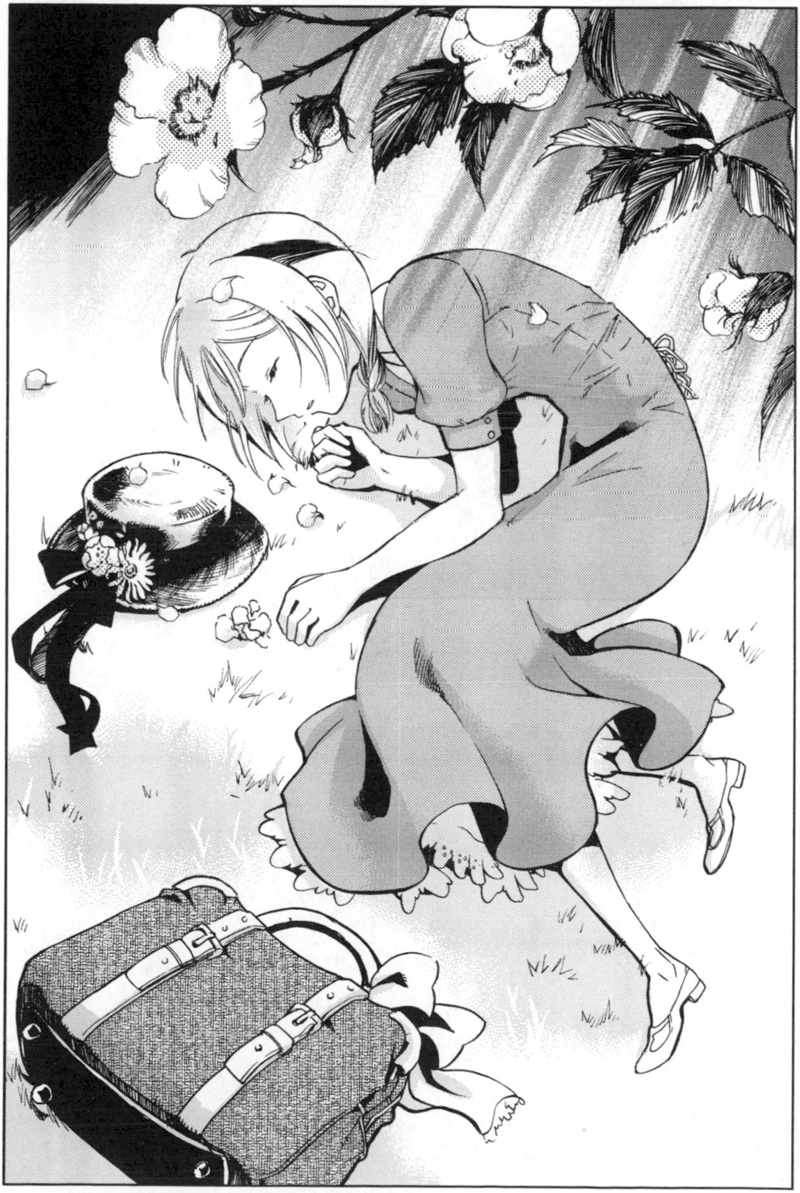

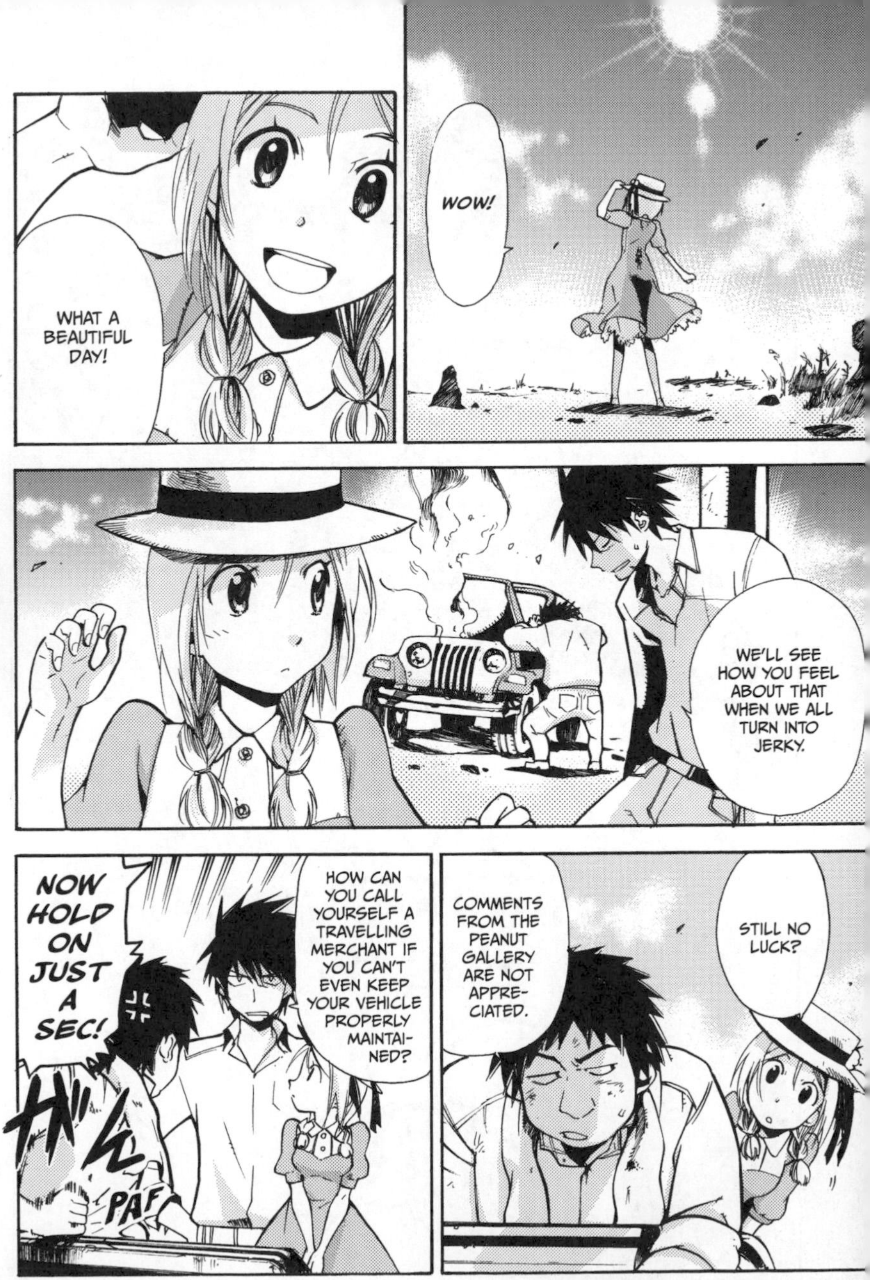
WOW!
WHAT A BEAUTIFUL DAY!
WE'LL SEE HOW YOU FEEL ABOUT THAT WHEN WE ALL TURN INTO JERKY.
STILL NO LUCK?
COMMENTS FROM THE PEANUT GALLERY ARE NOT APPRECIATED.
HOW CAN YOU CALL YOURSELF A TRAVELLING MERCHANT IF YOU CAN'T EVEN KEEP YOUR VEHICLE PROPERLY MAINTAINED?
NOW HOLD ON JUST A SEC!
PAF

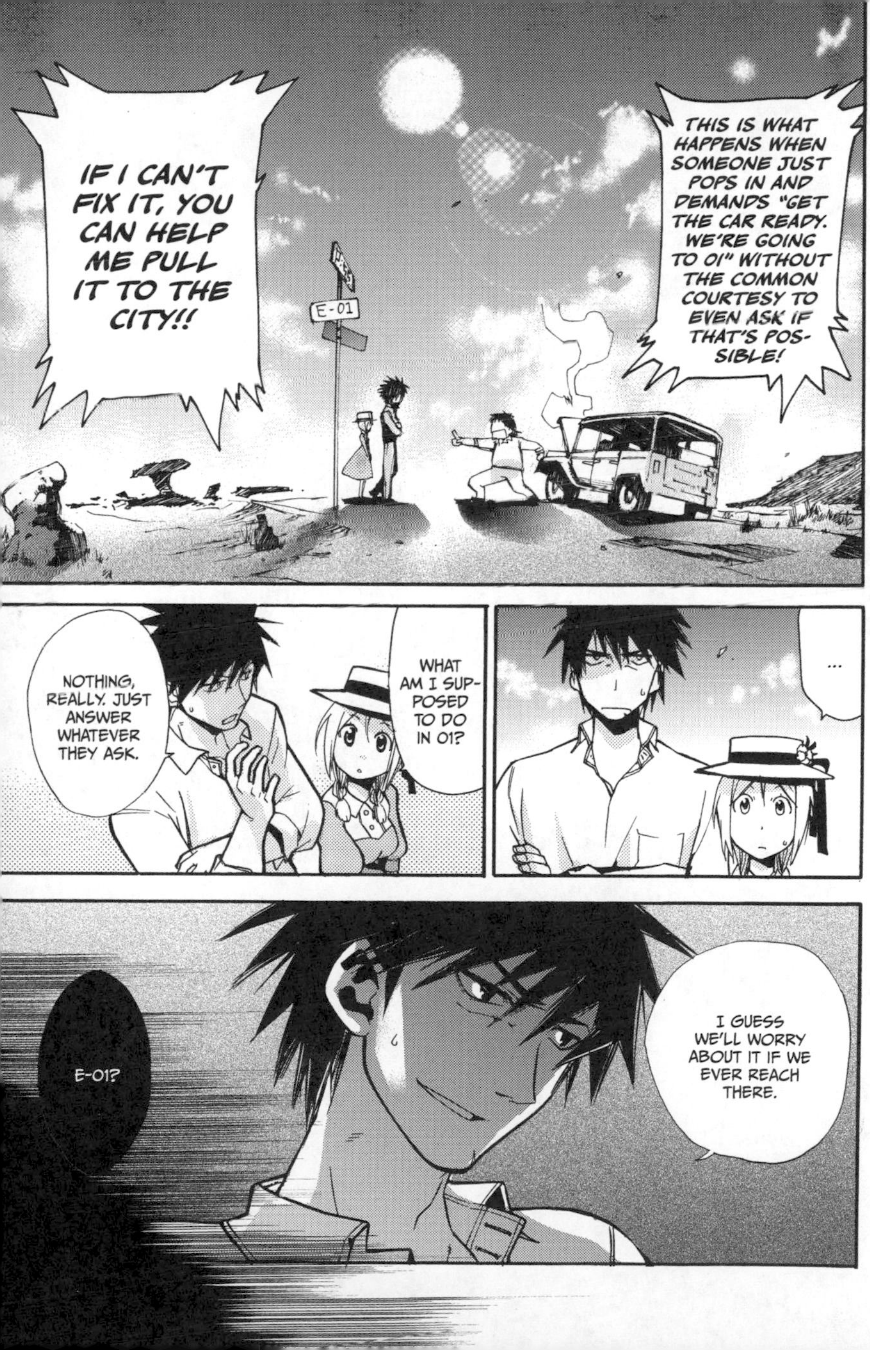
THIS IS WHAT HAPPENS WHEN SOMEONE JUST POPS IN AND DEMANDS "GET THE CAR READY. WE'RE GOING TO 01" WITHOUT THE COMMON COURTESY TO EVEN ASK IF THAT'S POSSIBLE!
E-01
IF I CAN'T FIX IT, YOU CAN HELP ME PULL IT TO THE CITY!!
...
WHAT AM I SUPPOSED TO DO IN 01?
NOTHING, REALLY. JUST ANSWER WHATEVER THEY ASK.
I GUESS WE'LL WORRY ABOUT IT IF WE EVER REACH THERE.
E-01?

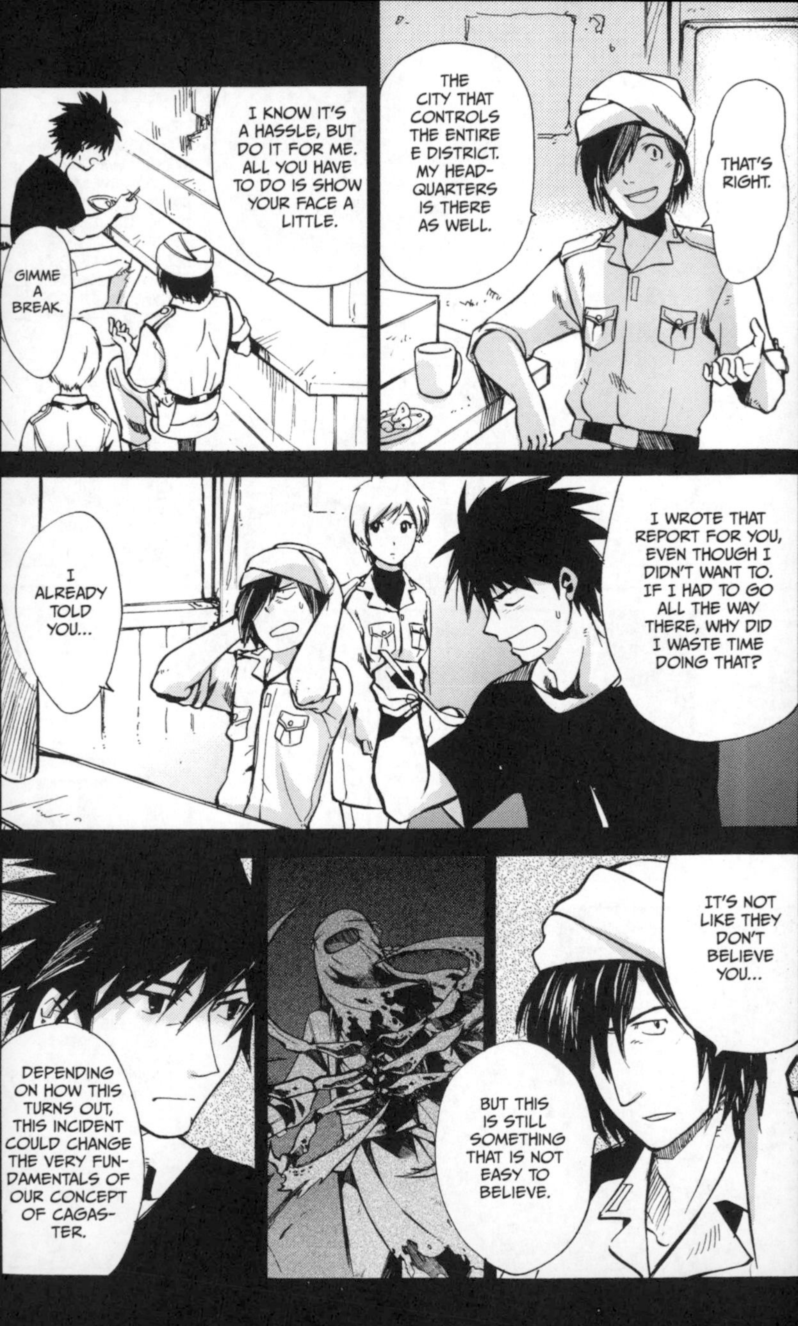
THAT'S RIGHT.
THE CITY THAT CONTROLS THE ENTIRE E DISTRICT. MY HEAD-QUARTERS IS THERE AS WELL.
I KNOW IT'S A HASSLE, BUT DO IT FOR ME. ALL YOU HAVE TO DO IS SHOW YOUR FACE A LITTLE.
GIMME A BREAK.
I WROTE THAT REPORT FOR YOU, EVEN THOUGH I DIDN'T WANT TO. IF I HAD TO GO ALL THE WAY THERE, WHY DID I WASTE TIME DOING THAT?
I ALREADY TOLD YOU...
IT'S NOT LIKE THEY DON'T BELIEVE YOU...
BUT THIS IS STILL SOMETHING THAT IS NOT EASY TO BELIEVE.
DEPENDING ON HOW THIS TURNS OUT, THIS INCIDENT COULD CHANGE THE VERY FUN-DAMENTALS OF OUR CONCEPT OF CAGAS-TER.

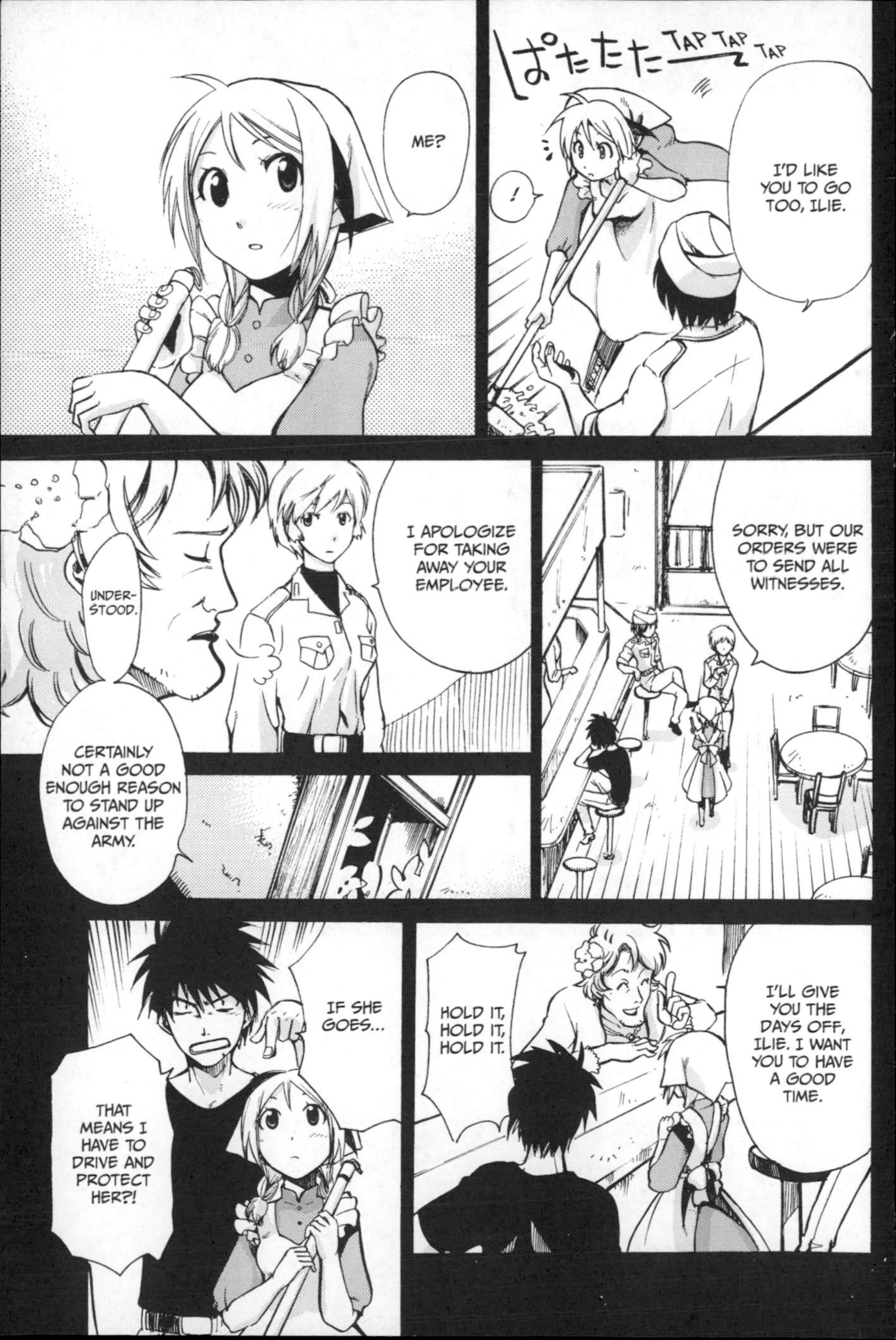
ぱたたた TAP TAP TAP
!
I'D LIKE YOU TO GO TOO, ILIE.
ME?
SORRY, BUT OUR ORDERS WERE TO SEND ALL WITNESSES.
I APOLOGIZE FOR TAKING AWAY YOUR EMPLOYEE.
UNDER-STOOD.
CERTAINLY NOT A GOOD ENOUGH REASON TO STAND UP AGAINST THE ARMY.
I'LL GIVE YOU THE DAYS OFF, ILIE. I WANT YOU TO HAVE A GOOD TIME.
HOLD IT, HOLD IT, HOLD IT.
IF SHE GOES...
THAT MEANS I HAVE TO DRIVE AND PROTECT HER?!

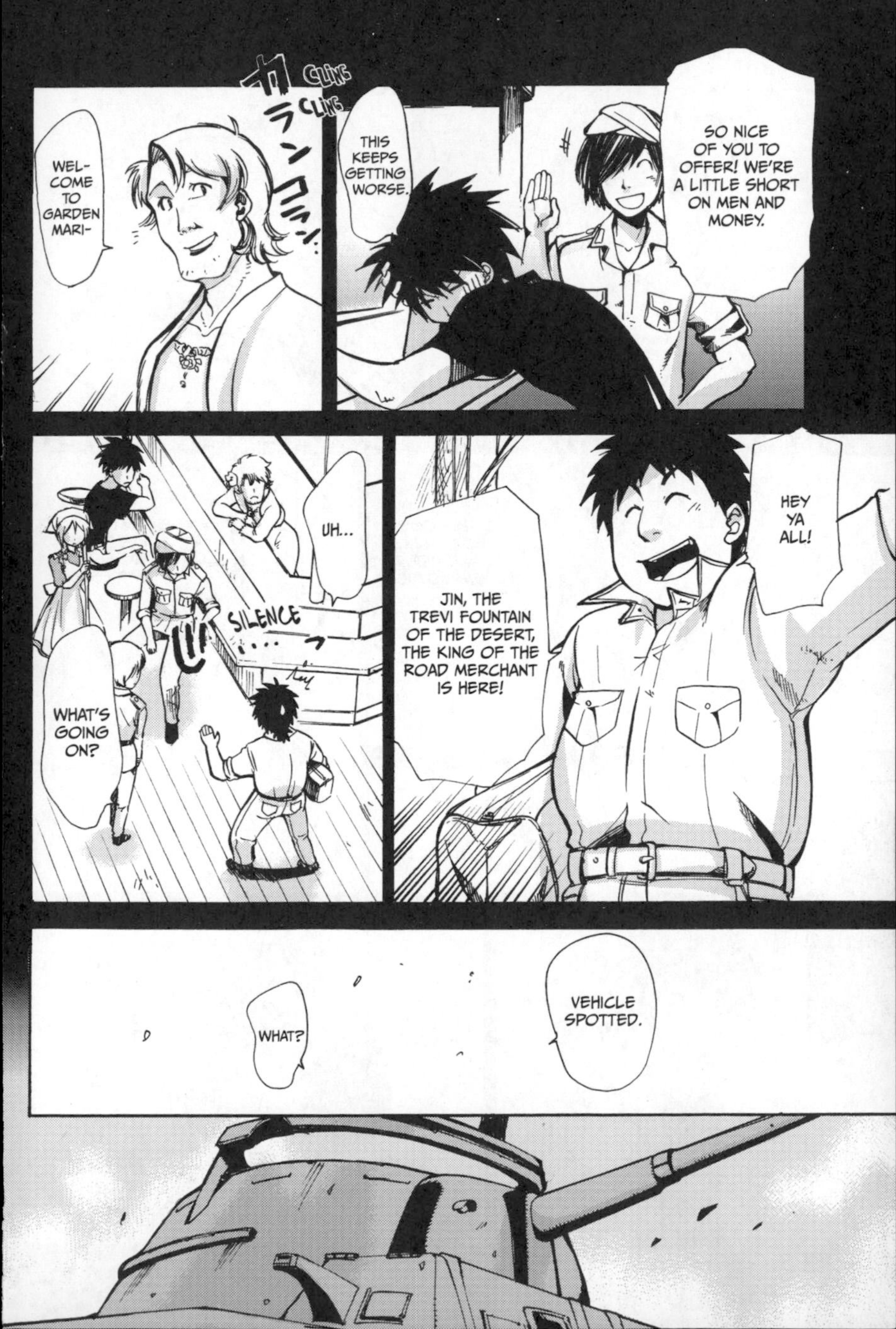
SO NICE OF YOU TO OFFER! WE'RE A LITTLE SHORT ON MEN AND MONEY.
THIS KEEPS GETTING WORSE.
カラン
CLING CLING
WEL-COME TO GARDEN MARI-
HEY YA ALL!
JIN, THE TREVI FOUNTAIN OF THE DESERT, THE KING OF THE ROAD MERCHANT IS HERE!
UH...
SILENCE
WHAT'S GOING ON?
VEHICLE SPOTTED.
WHAT?

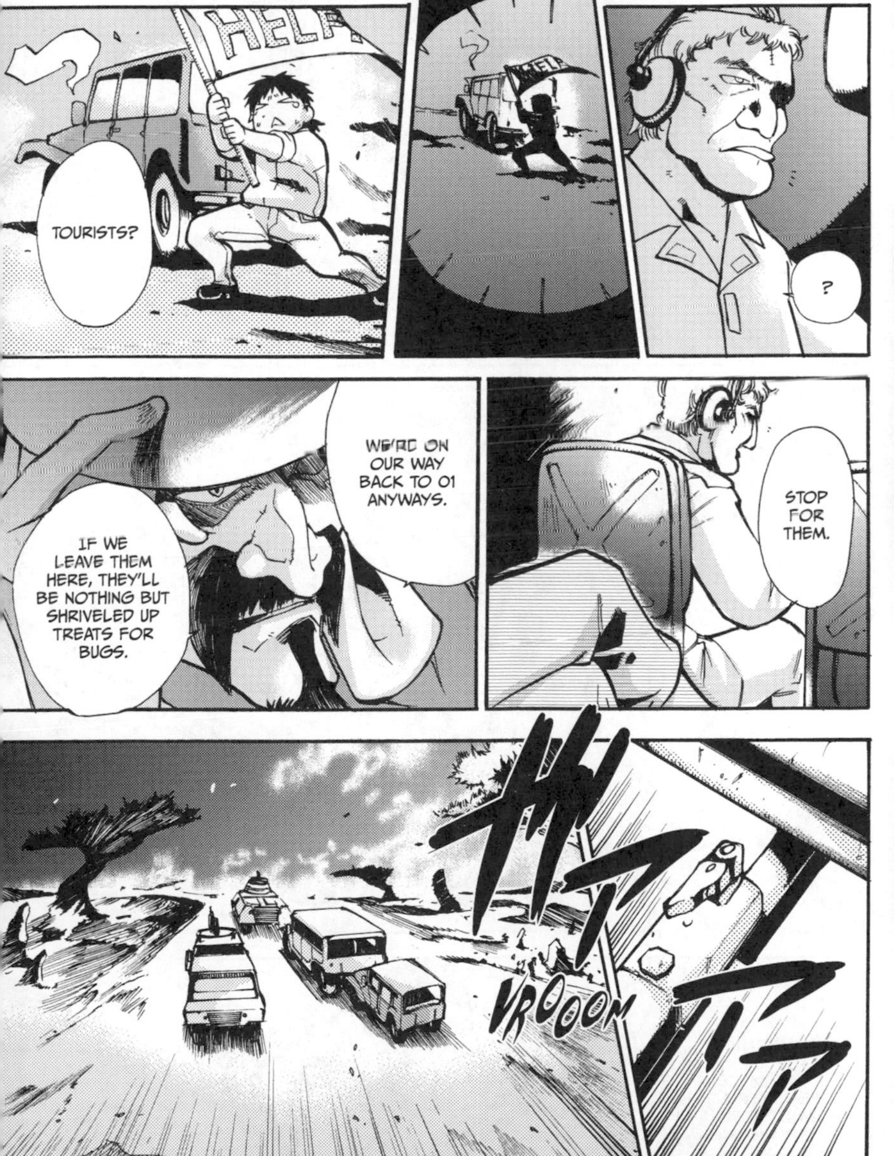
?
TOURISTS?
STOP FOR THEM.
WE'RE ON OUR WAY BACK TO 01 ANYWAYS.
IF WE LEAVE THEM HERE, THEY'LL BE NOTHING BUT SHRIVELED UP TREATS FOR BUGS.
VROOOM

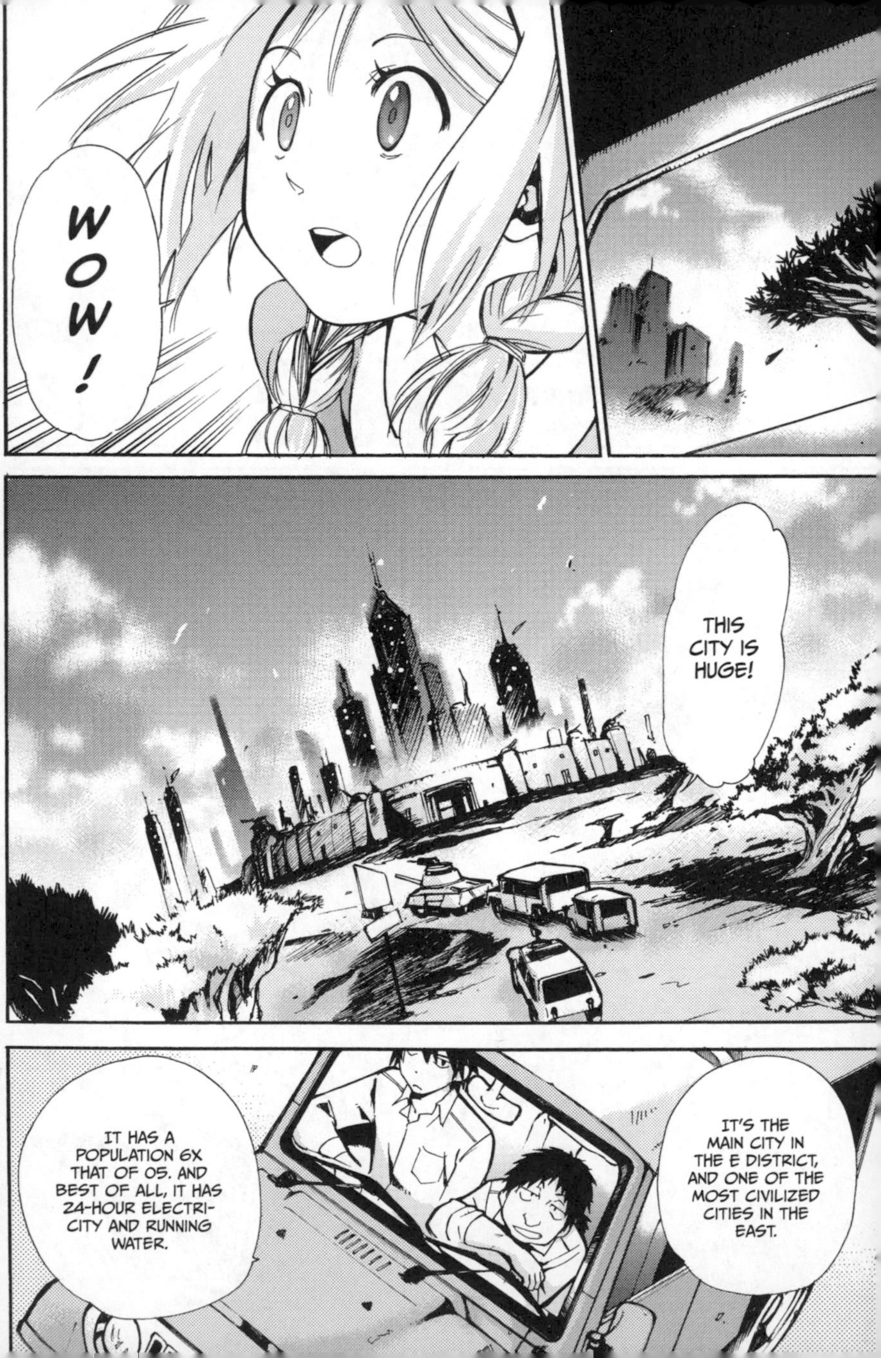
WOW!
THIS CITY IS HUGE!
IT'S THE MAIN CITY IN THE E DISTRICT, AND ONE OF THE MOST CIVILIZED CITIES IN THE EAST.
IT HAS A POPULATION 6X THAT OF 05. AND BEST OF ALL, IT HAS 24-HOUR ELECTRI-CITY AND RUNNING WATER.

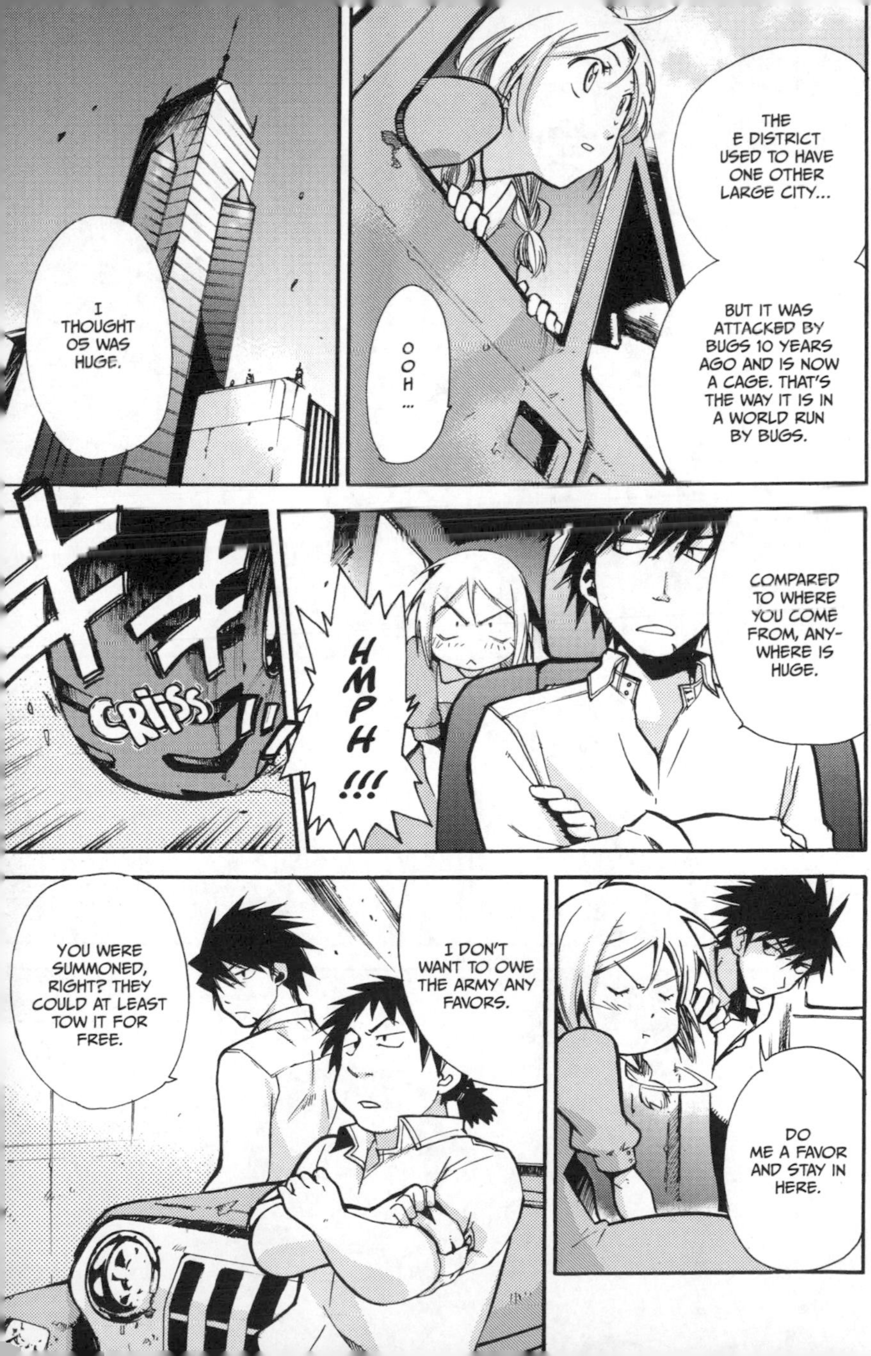
THE E DISTRICT USED TO HAVE ONE OTHER LARGE CITY...
BUT IT WAS ATTACKED BY BUGS 10 YEARS AGO AND IS NOW A CAGE. THAT'S THE WAY IT IS IN A WORLD RUN BY BUGS.
OOH...
I THOUGHT 05 WAS HUGE.
COMPARED TO WHERE YOU COME FROM, ANY-WHERE IS HUGE.
HMPH!!!
CRISS
DO ME A FAVOR AND STAY IN HERE.
I DON'T WANT TO OWE THE ARMY ANY FAVORS.
YOU WERE SUMMONED, RIGHT? THEY COULD AT LEAST TOW IT FOR FREE.

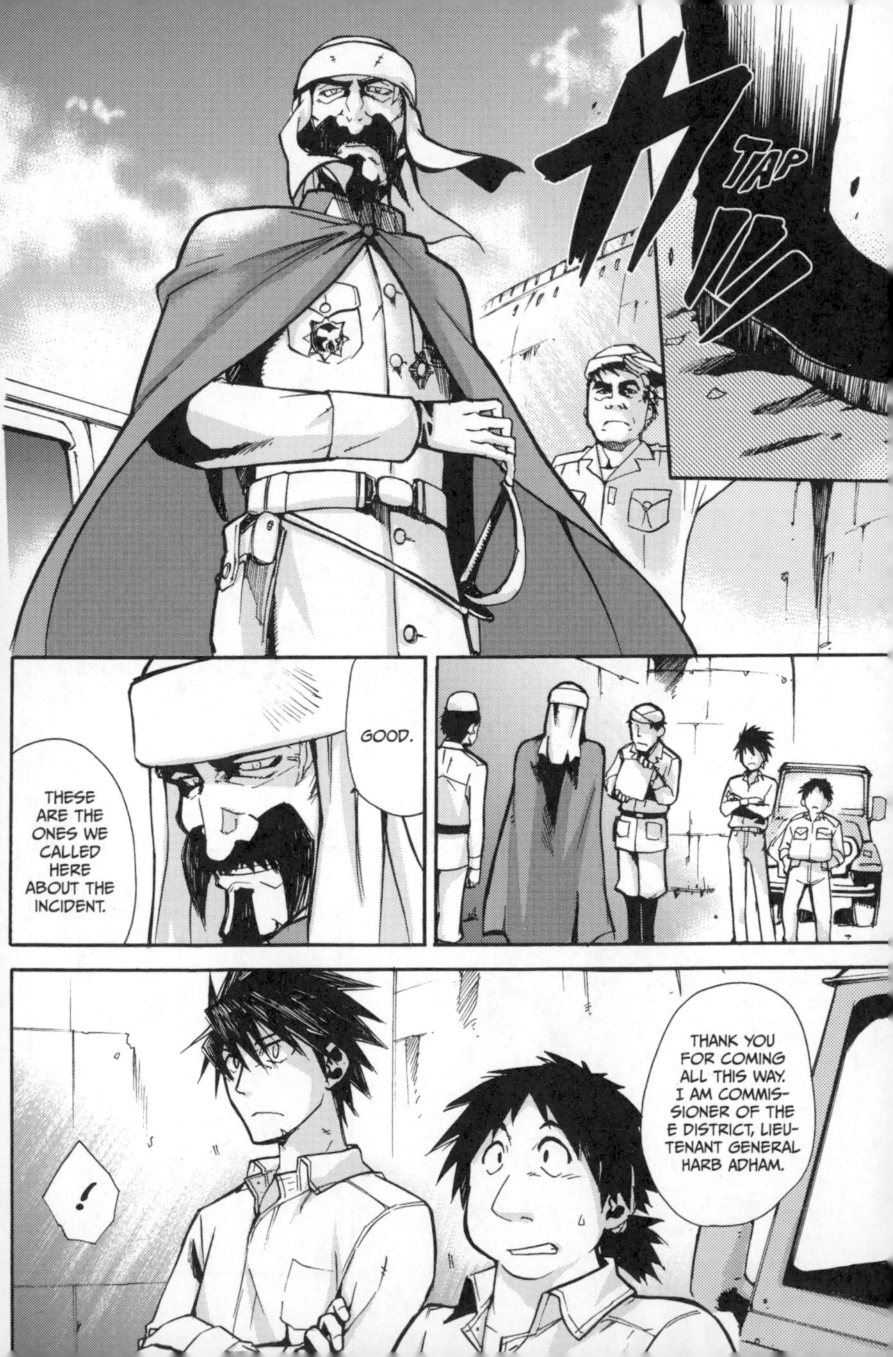
TAP
GOOD.
THESE ARE THE ONES WE CALLED HERE ABOUT THE INCIDENT.
THANK YOU FOR COMING ALL THIS WAY. I AM COMMISSIONER OF THE E DISTRICT, LIEUTENANT GENERAL HARB ADHAM.
!

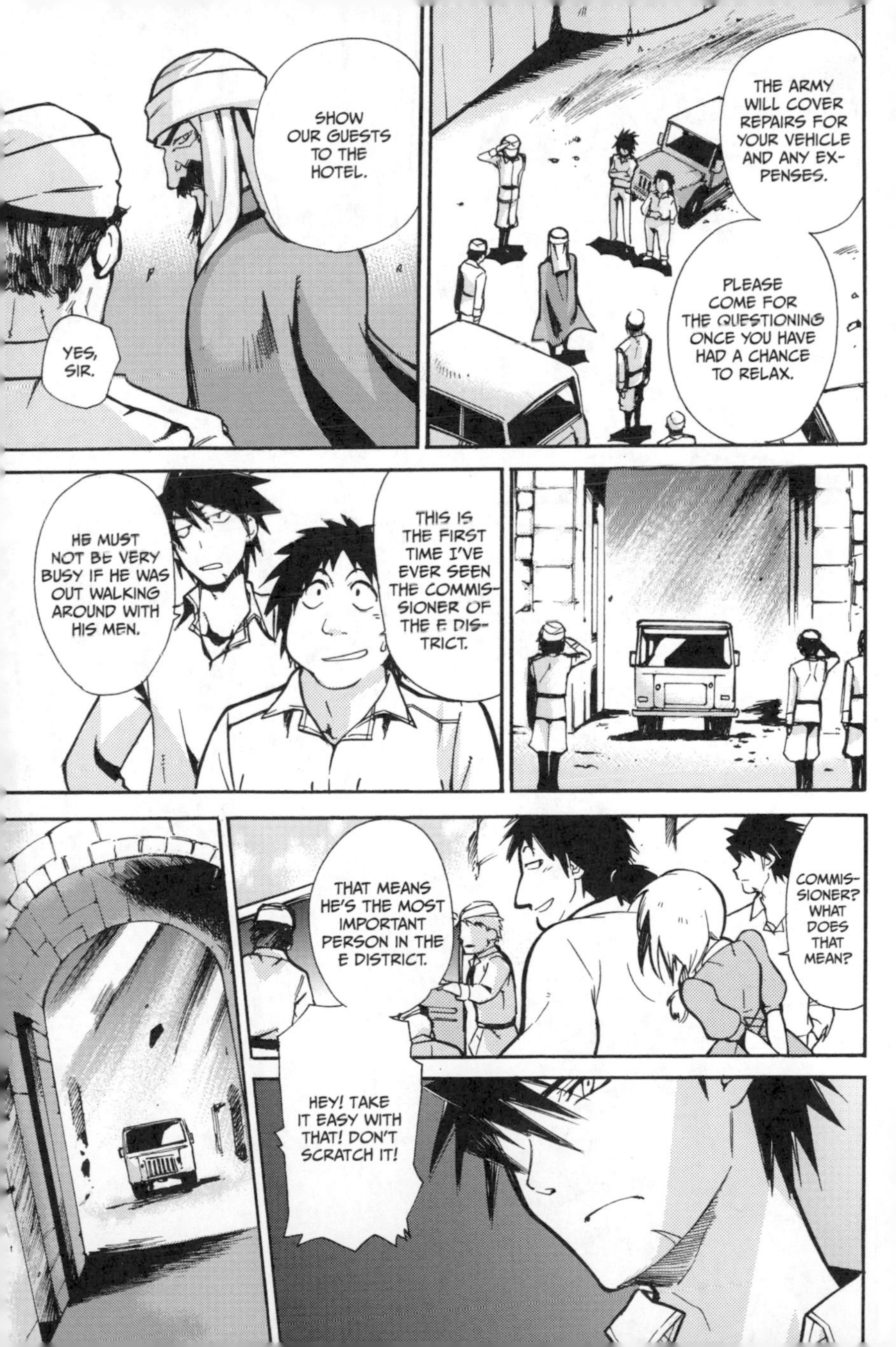
THE ARMY WILL COVER REPAIRS FOR YOUR VEHICLE AND ANY EX-PENSES.
PLEASE COME FOR THE QUESTIONING ONCE YOU HAVE HAD A CHANCE TO RELAX.
SHOW OUR GUESTS TO THE HOTEL.
YES, SIR.
THIS IS THE FIRST TIME I'VE EVER SEEN THE COMMIS-SIONER OF THE E DIS-TRICT.
HE MUST NOT BE VERY BUSY IF HE WAS OUT WALKING AROUND WITH HIS MEN.
COMMIS-SIONER? WHAT DOES THAT MEAN?
THAT MEANS HE'S THE MOST IMPORTANT PERSON IN THE E DISTRICT.
HEY! TAKE IT EASY WITH THAT! DON'T SCRATCH IT!

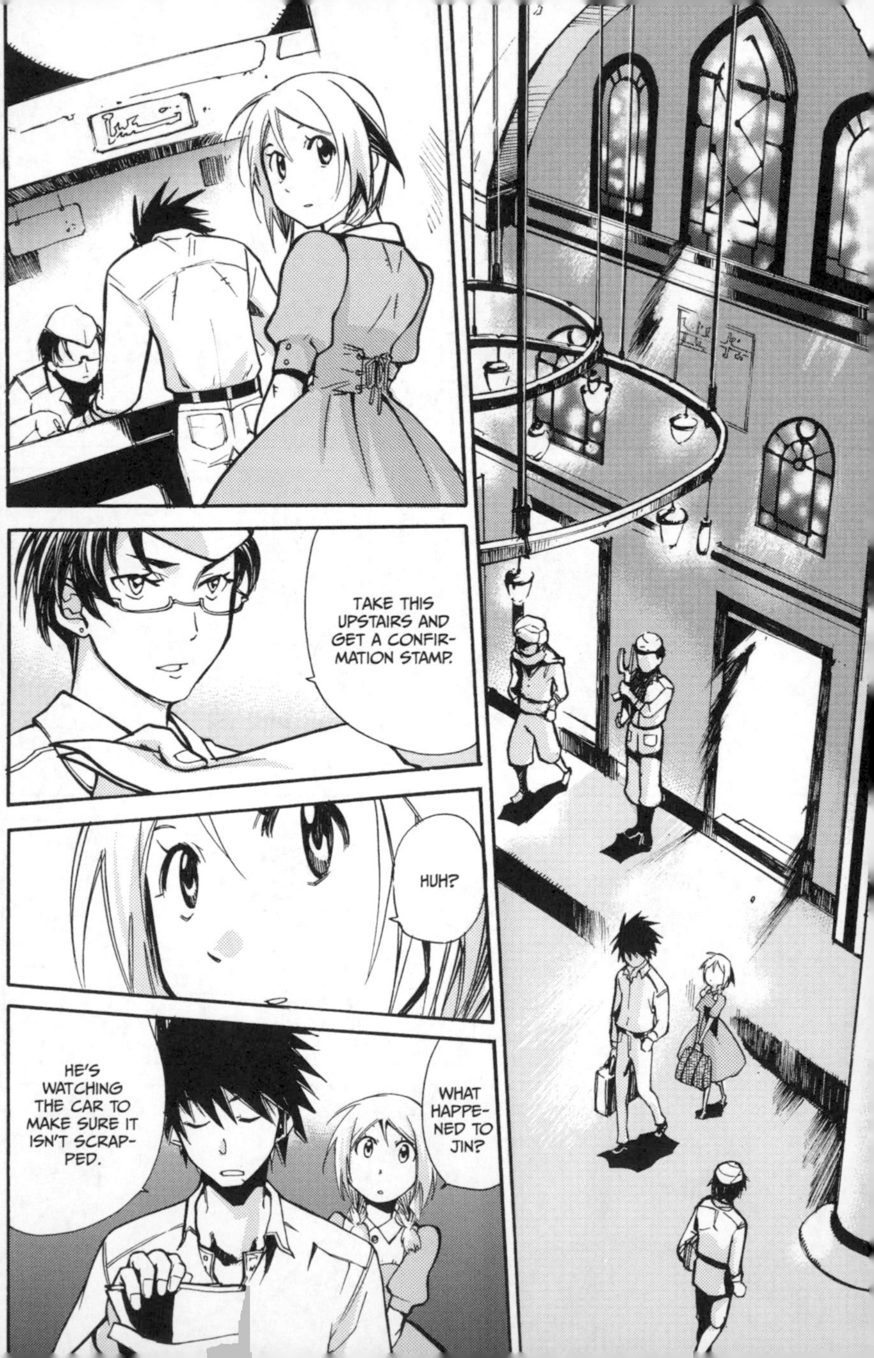
TAKE THIS UPSTAIRS AND GET A CONFIRMATION STAMP.
HUH?
WHAT HAPPENED TO JIN?
HE'S WATCHING THE CAR TO MAKE SURE IT ISN'T SCRAPPED.

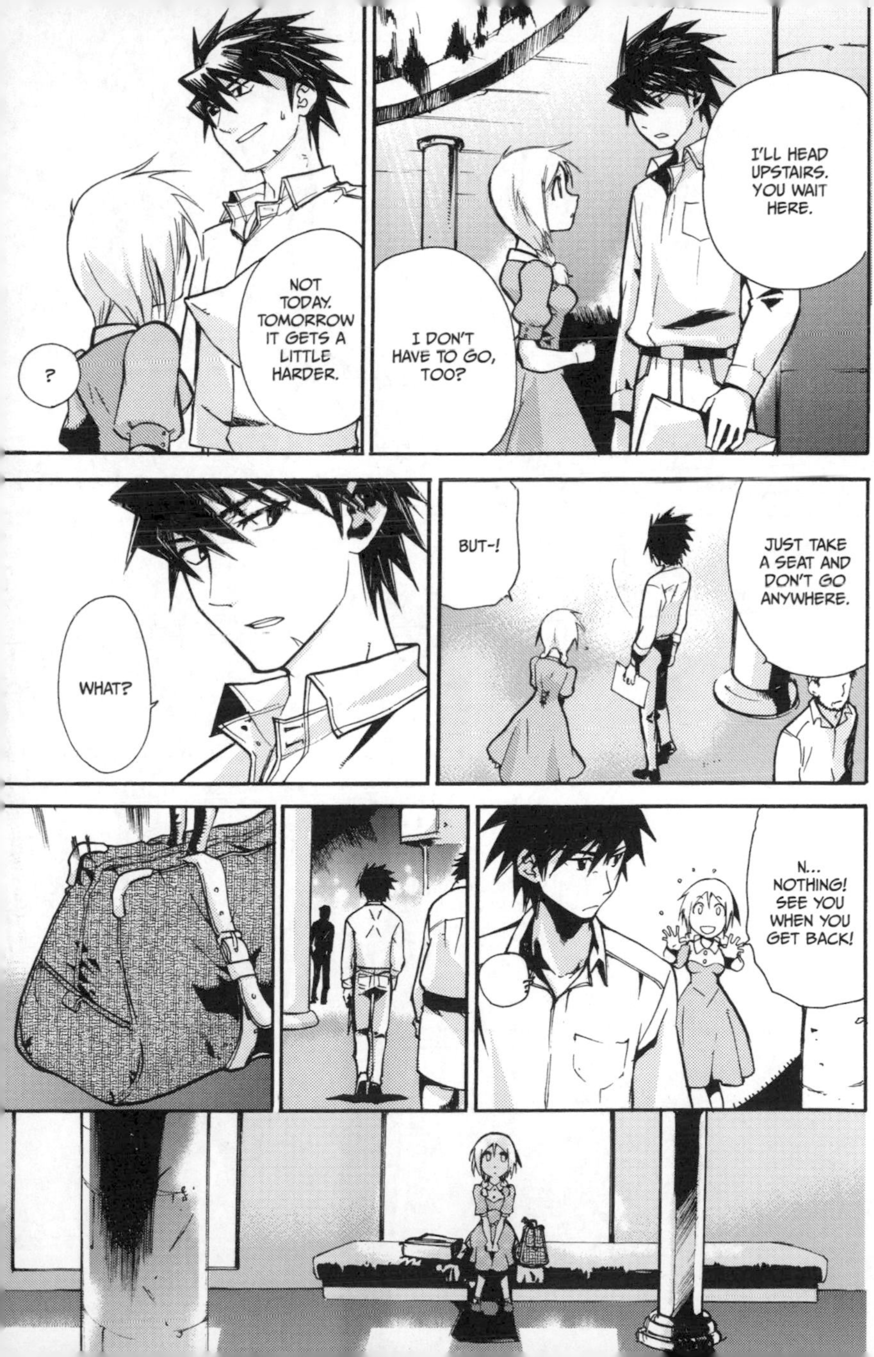
I'LL HEAD UPSTAIRS. YOU WAIT HERE.
I DON'T HAVE TO GO, TOO?
NOT TODAY. TOMORROW IT GETS A LITTLE HARDER.
?
JUST TAKE A SEAT AND DON'T GO ANYWHERE.
BUT-!
WHAT?
N... NOTHING! SEE YOU WHEN YOU GET BACK!

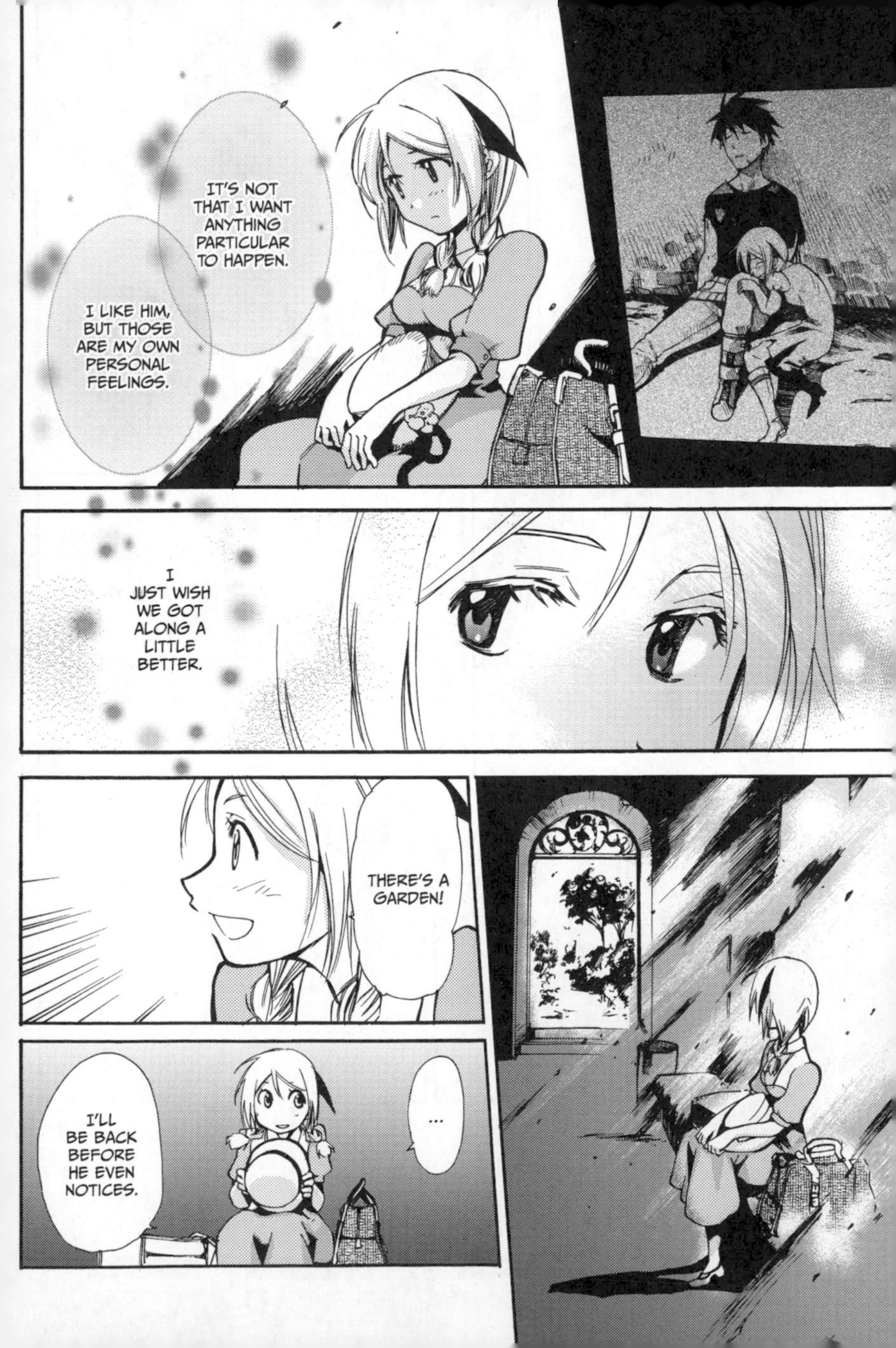
IT'S NOT THAT I WANT ANYTHING PARTICULAR TO HAPPEN.
I LIKE HIM, BUT THOSE ARE MY OWN PERSONAL FEELINGS.
I JUST WISH WE GOT ALONG A LITTLE BETTER.
THERE'S A GARDEN!
...
I'LL BE BACK BEFORE HE EVEN NOTICES.

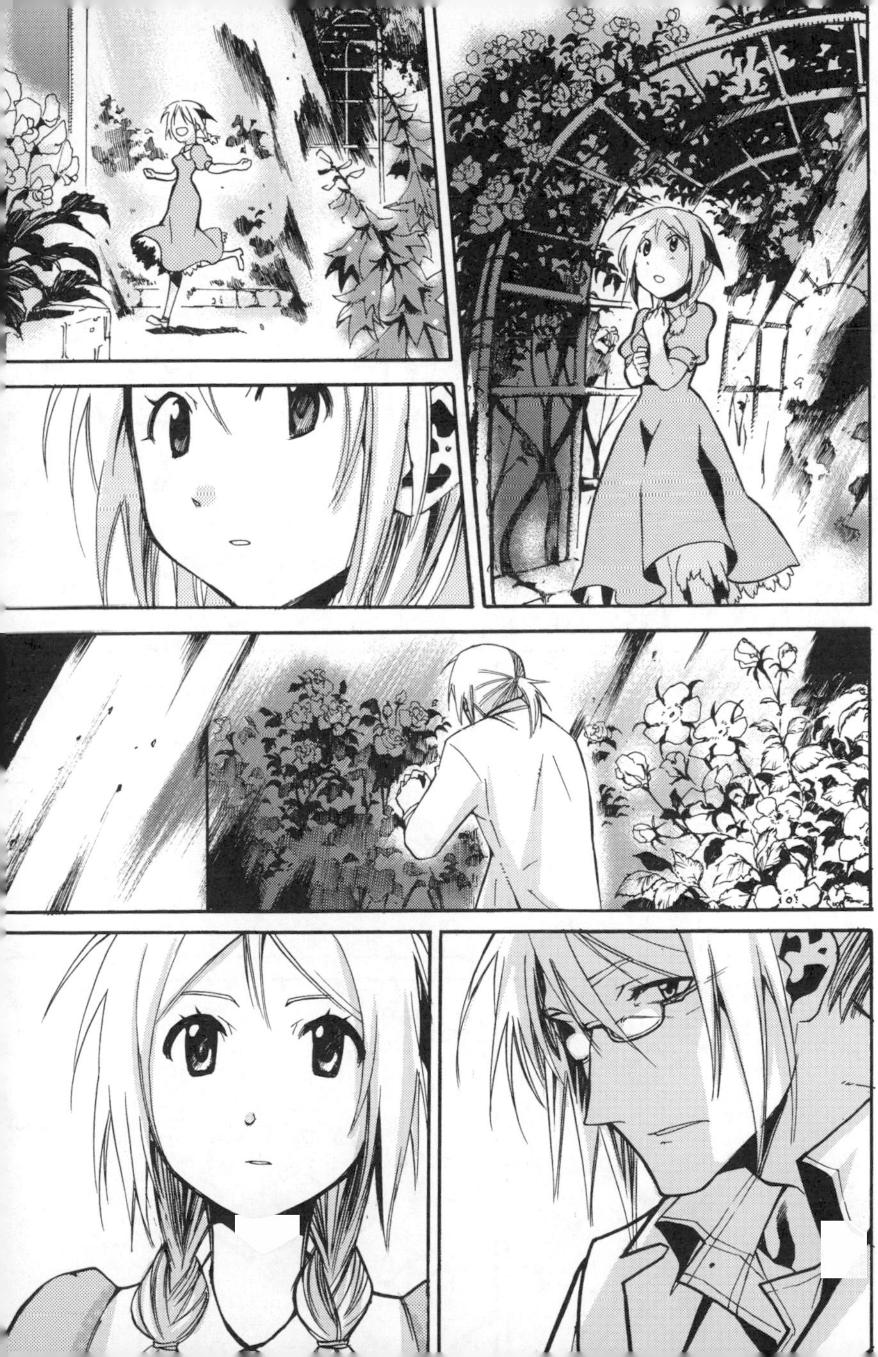

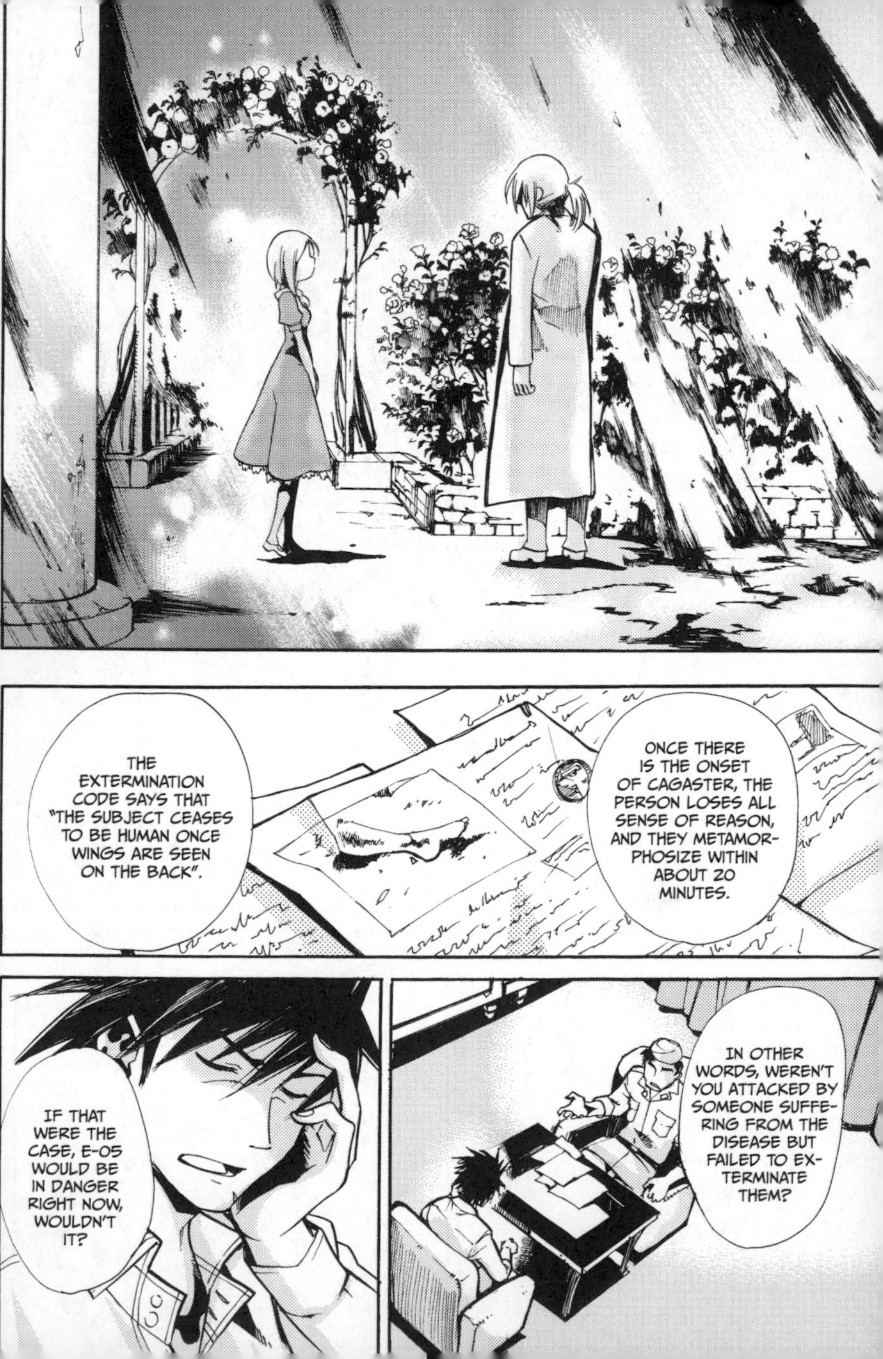
ONCE THERE IS THE ONSET OF CAGASTER, THE PERSON LOSES ALL SENSE OF REASON, AND THEY METAMOR-PHOSIZE WITHIN ABOUT 20 MINUTES.
THE EXTERMINATION CODE SAYS THAT "THE SUBJECT CEASES TO BE HUMAN ONCE WINGS ARE SEEN ON THE BACK".
IN OTHER WORDS, WEREN'T YOU ATTACKED BY SOMEONE SUFFE-RING FROM THE DISEASE BUT FAILED TO EX-TERMINATE THEM?
IF THAT WERE THE CASE, E-05 WOULD BE IN DANGER RIGHT NOW, WOULDN'T IT?

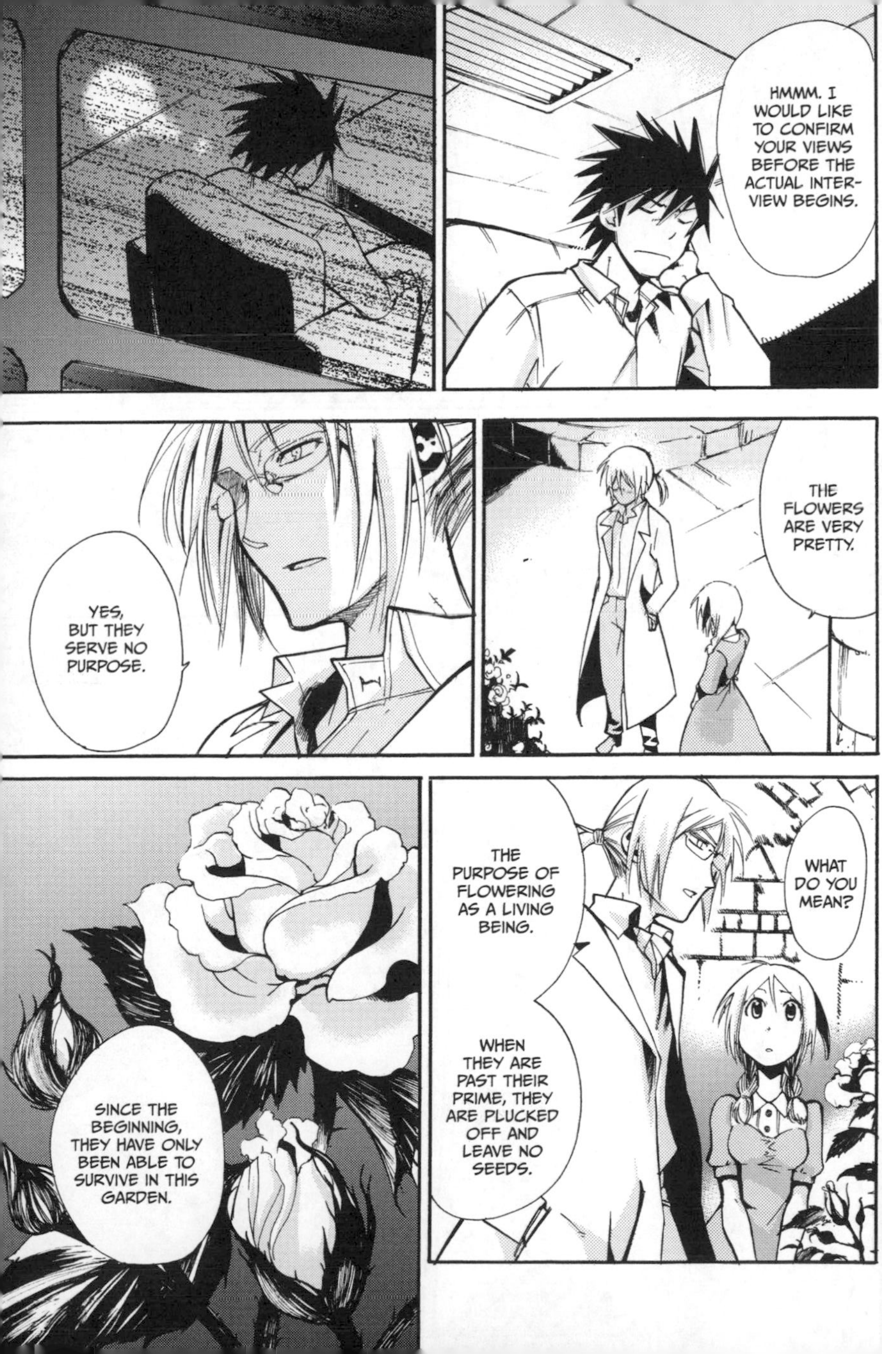
HMMM. I WOULD LIKE TO CONFIRM YOUR VIEWS BEFORE THE ACTUAL INTER-VIEW BEGINS.
THE FLOWERS ARE VERY PRETTY.
YES, BUT THEY SERVE NO PURPOSE.
WHAT DO YOU MEAN?
THE PURPOSE OF FLOWERING AS A LIVING BEING.
WHEN THEY ARE PAST THEIR PRIME, THEY ARE PLUCKED OFF AND LEAVE NO SEEDS.
SINCE THE BEGINNING, THEY HAVE ONLY BEEN ABLE TO SURVIVE IN THIS GARDEN.

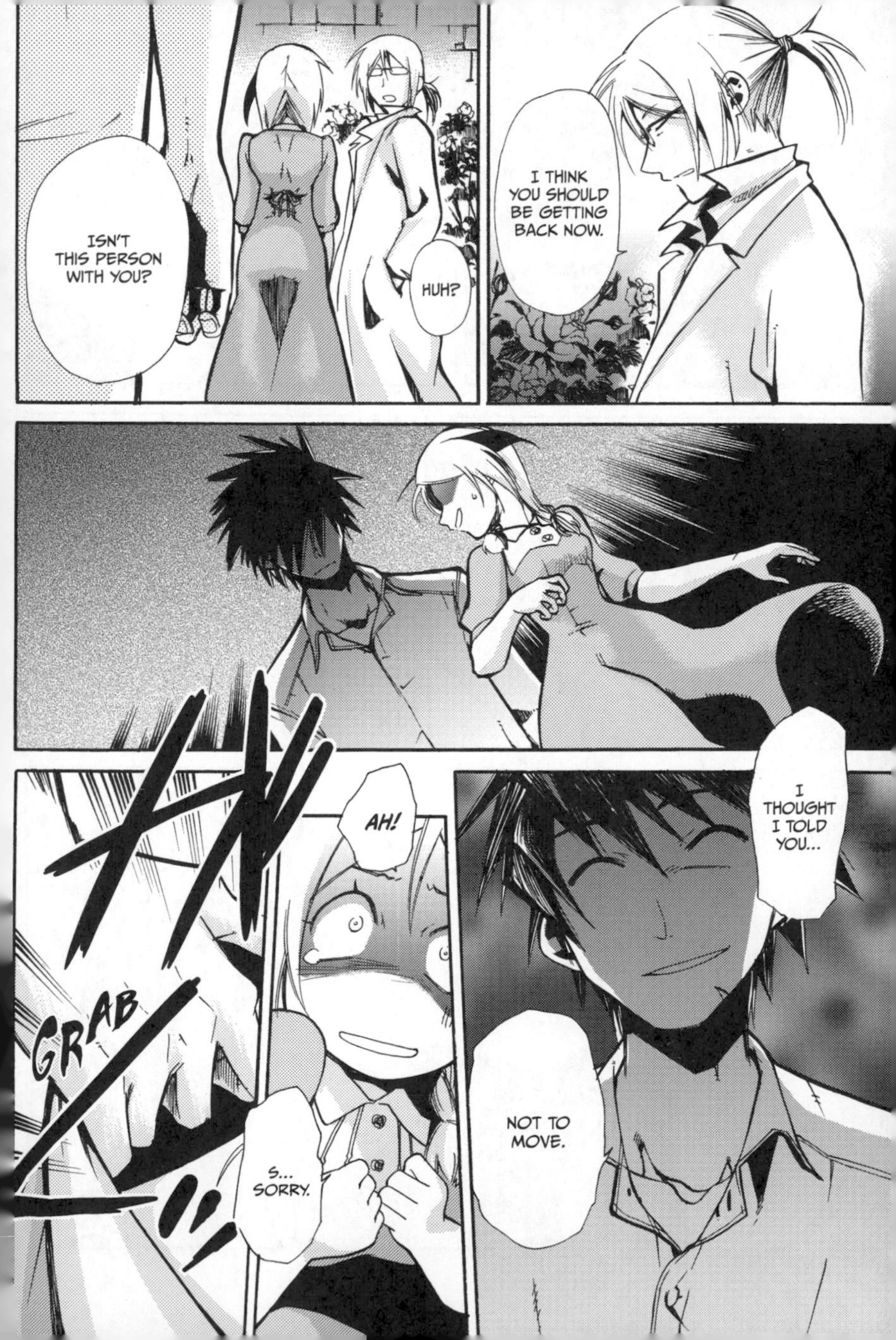
I THINK YOU SHOULD BE GETTING BACK NOW.
HUH?
ISN'T THIS PERSON WITH YOU?
I THOUGHT I TOLD YOU...
NOT TO MOVE.
AH!
GRAB
S... SORRY.

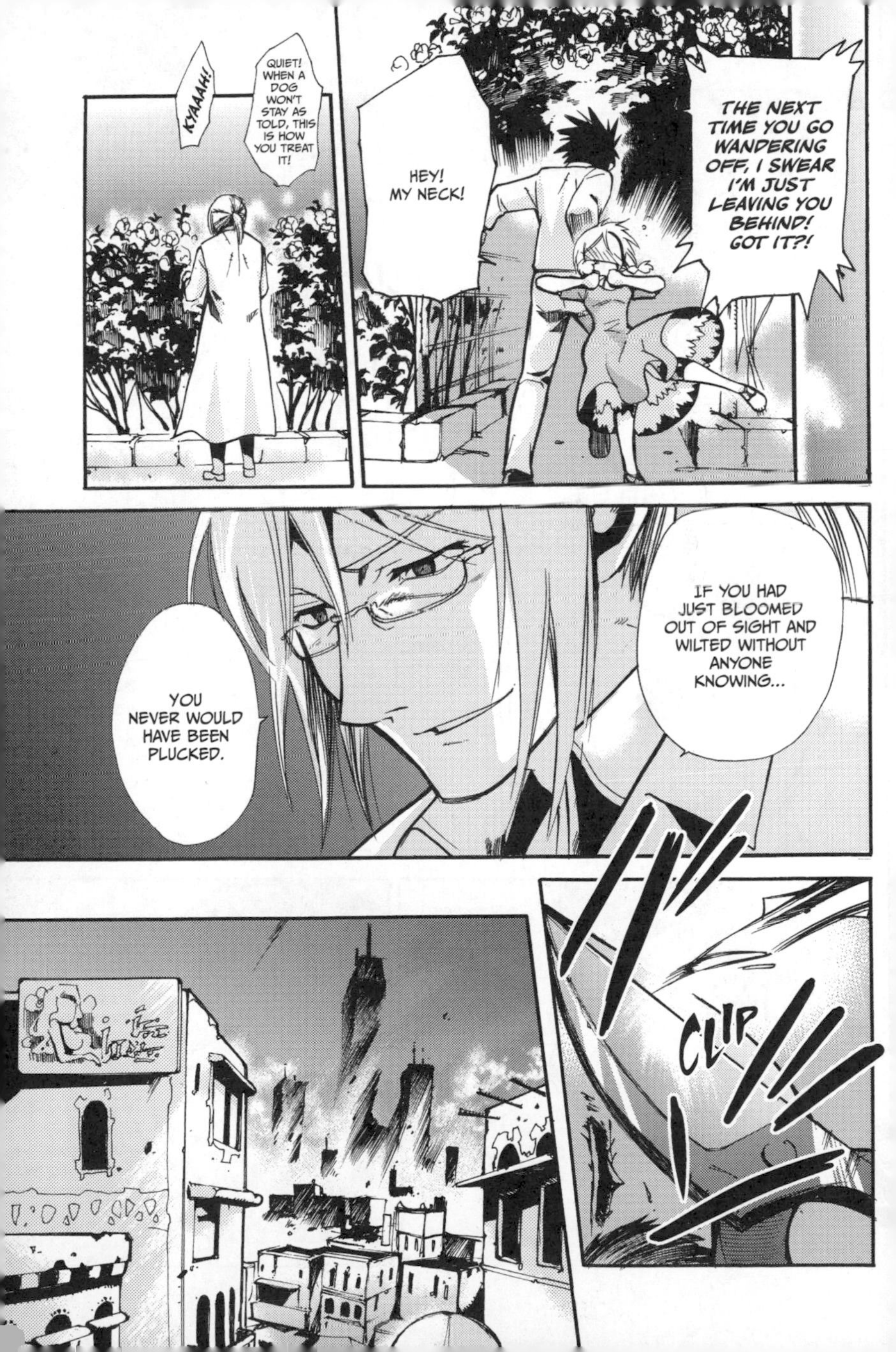
THE NEXT TIME YOU GO WANDERING OFF, I SWEAR I'M JUST LEAVING YOU BEHIND! GOT IT?!
HEY! MY NECK!
QUIET! WHEN A DOG WON'T STAY AS TOLD, THIS IS HOW YOU TREAT IT!
KYAAAH!
IF YOU HAD JUST BLOOMED OUT OF SIGHT AND WILTED WITHOUT ANYONE KNOWING...
YOU NEVER WOULD HAVE BEEN PLUCKED.
CLIP

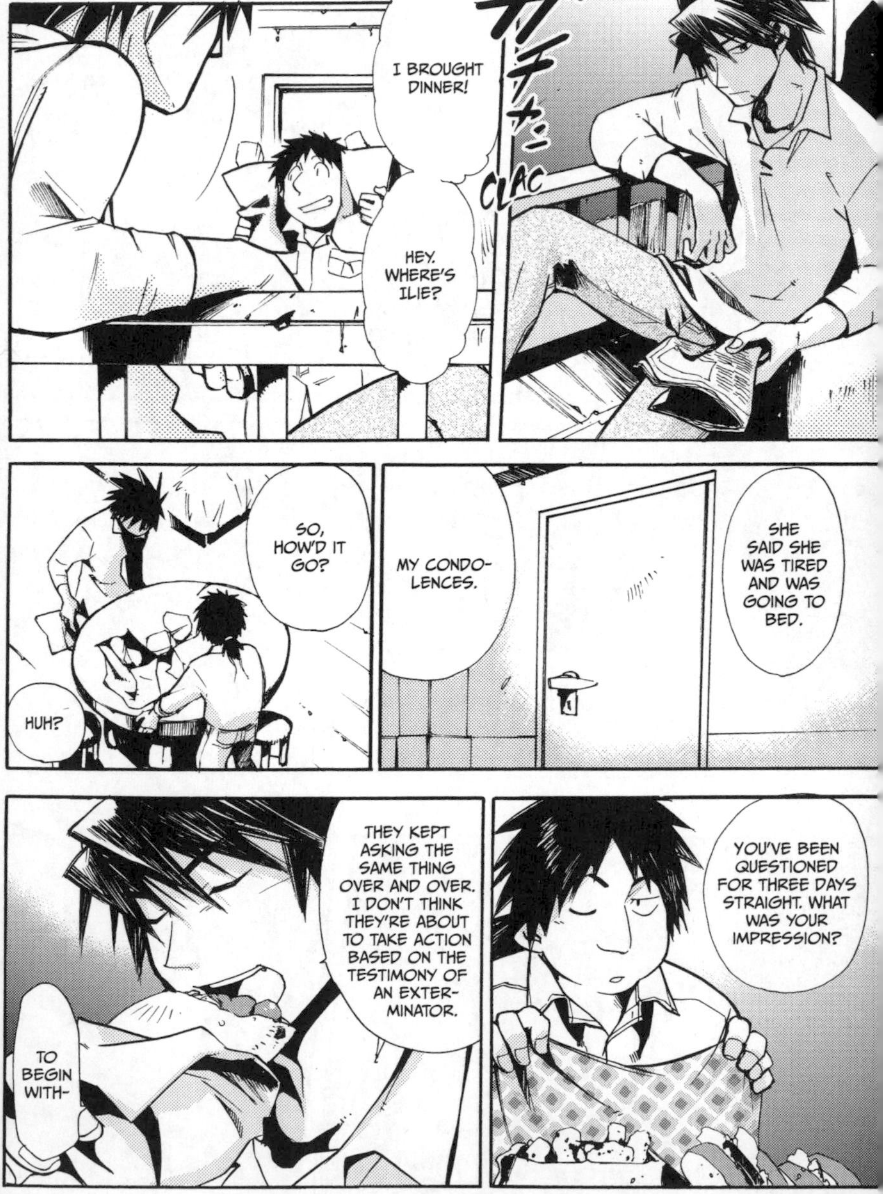
ガチャー
CLAC
I BROUGHT DINNER!
HEY. WHERE'S ILIE?
SHE SAID SHE WAS TIRED AND WAS GOING TO BED.
MY CONDO-LENCES.
SO, HOW'D IT GO?
HUH?
YOU'VE BEEN QUESTIONED FOR THREE DAYS STRAIGHT. WHAT WAS YOUR IMPRESSION?
THEY KEPT ASKING THE SAME THING OVER AND OVER. I DON'T THINK THEY'RE ABOUT TO TAKE ACTION BASED ON THE TESTIMONY OF AN EXTER-MINATOR.
TO BEGIN WITH-

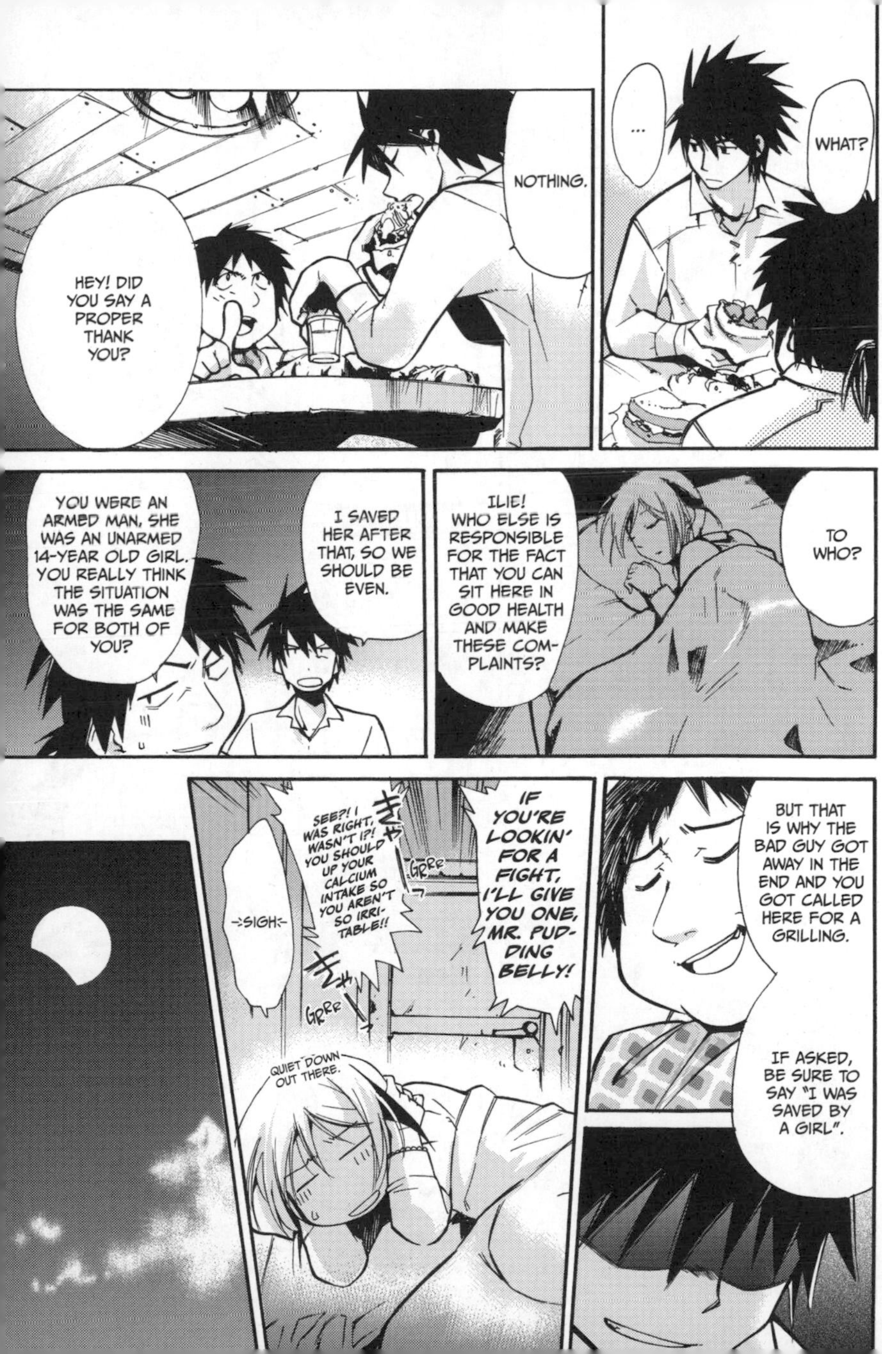
...
WHAT?
NOTHING.
HEY! DID YOU SAY A PROPER THANK YOU?
TO WHO?
ILIE! WHO ELSE IS RESPONSIBLE FOR THE FACT THAT YOU CAN SIT HERE IN GOOD HEALTH AND MAKE THESE COMPLAINTS?
I SAVED HER AFTER THAT, SO WE SHOULD BE EVEN.
YOU WERE AN ARMED MAN, SHE WAS AN UNARMED 14-YEAR OLD GIRL. YOU REALLY THINK THE SITUATION WAS THE SAME FOR BOTH OF YOU?
BUT THAT IS WHY THE BAD GUY GOT AWAY IN THE END AND YOU GOT CALLED HERE FOR A GRILLING.
IF ASKED, BE SURE TO SAY "I WAS SAVED BY A GIRL".
IF YOU'RE LOOKIN' FOR A FIGHT, I'LL GIVE YOU ONE, MR. PUDDING BELLY!
SEE?! I WAS RIGHT, WASN'T I?! YOU SHOULD UP YOUR CALCIUM INTAKE SO YOU AREN'T SO IRRITABLE!!
GRRR
GRRR
-SIGH-
QUIET DOWN OUT THERE.

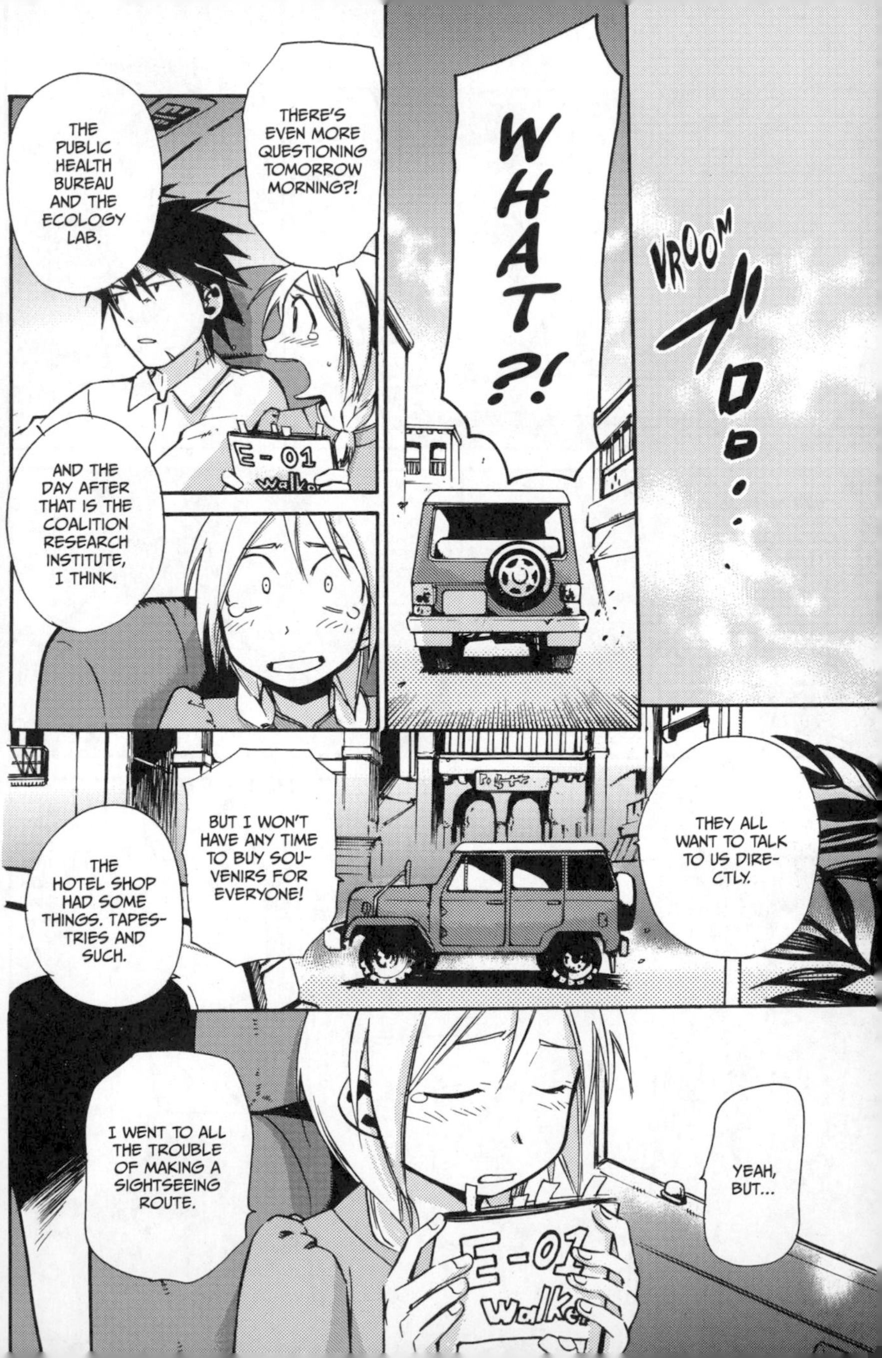
VROOM
WHAT?!
THERE'S EVEN MORE QUESTIONING TOMORROW MORNING?!
THE PUBLIC HEALTH BUREAU AND THE ECOLOGY LAB.
AND THE DAY AFTER THAT IS THE COALITION RESEARCH INSTITUTE, I THINK.
E-01 walker
THEY ALL WANT TO TALK TO US DIRECTLY.
BUT I WON'T HAVE ANY TIME TO BUY SOUVENIRS FOR EVERYONE!
THE HOTEL SHOP HAD SOME THINGS. TAPESTRIES AND SUCH.
YEAH, BUT...
I WENT TO ALL THE TROUBLE OF MAKING A SIGHTSEEING ROUTE.
E-01 walker

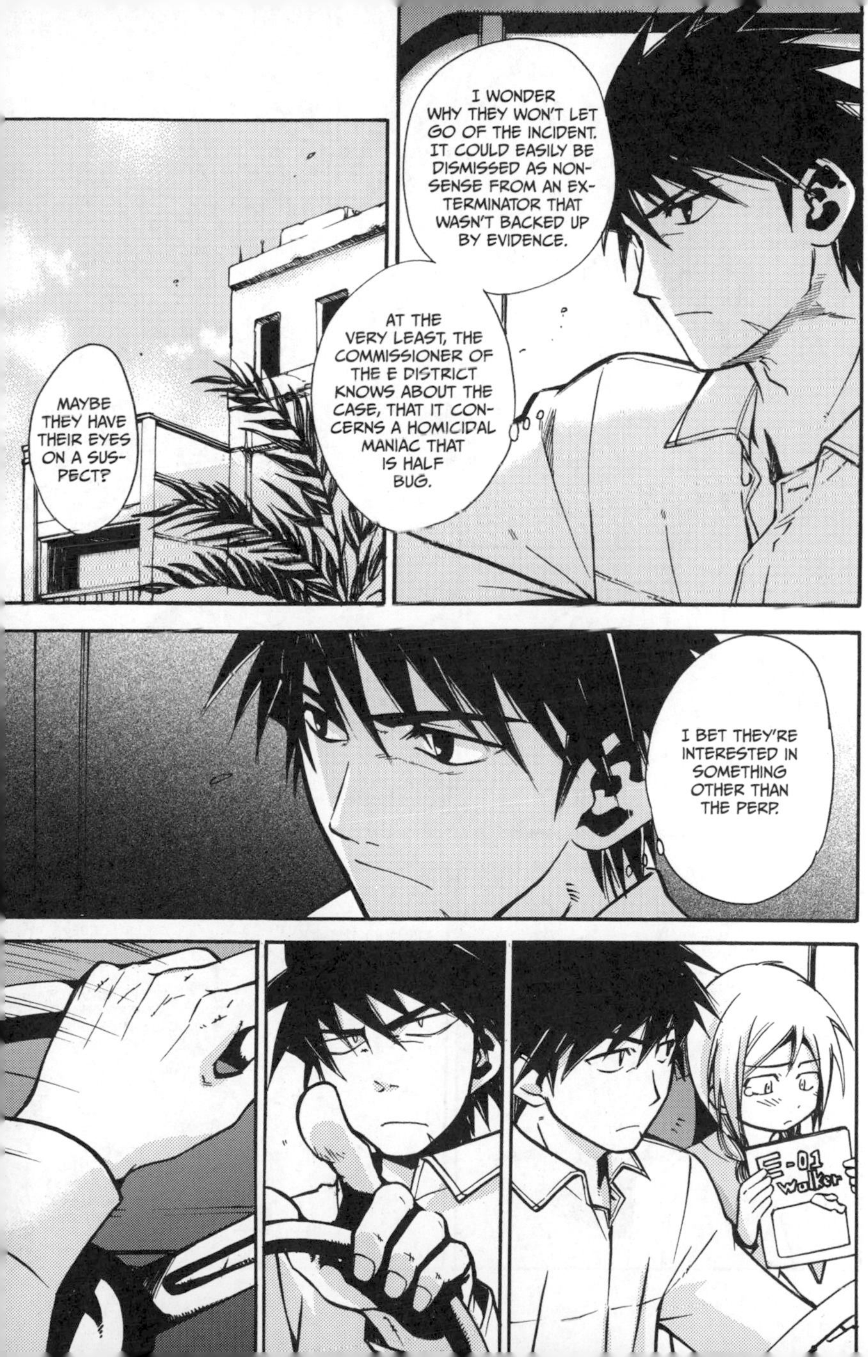
I WONDER WHY THEY WON'T LET GO OF THE INCIDENT. IT COULD EASILY BE DISMISSED AS NON-SENSE FROM AN EX-TERMINATOR THAT WASN'T BACKED UP BY EVIDENCE.
AT THE VERY LEAST, THE COMMISSIONER OF THE E DISTRICT KNOWS ABOUT THE CASE, THAT IT CON-CERNS A HOMICIDAL MANIAC THAT IS HALF BUG.
MAYBE THEY HAVE THEIR EYES ON A SUS-PECT?
I BET THEY'RE INTERESTED IN SOMETHING OTHER THAN THE PERP.
E-01 walker

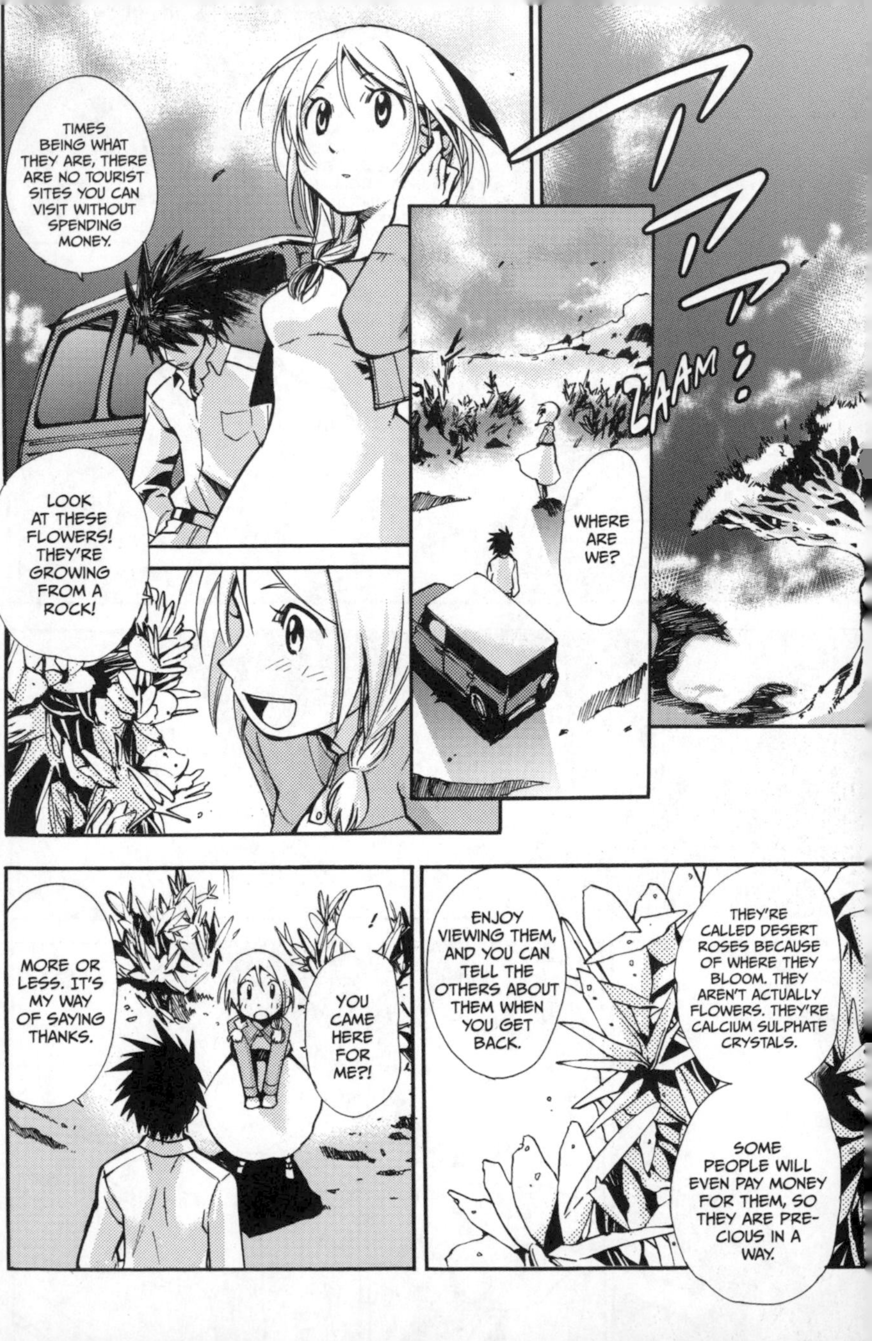
ZAAM
WHERE ARE WE?
TIMES BEING WHAT THEY ARE, THERE ARE NO TOURIST SITES YOU CAN VISIT WITHOUT SPENDING MONEY.
LOOK AT THESE FLOWERS! THEY'RE GROWING FROM A ROCK!
THEY'RE CALLED DESERT ROSES BECAUSE OF WHERE THEY BLOOM. THEY AREN'T ACTUALLY FLOWERS. THEY'RE CALCIUM SULPHATE CRYSTALS.
SOME PEOPLE WILL EVEN PAY MONEY FOR THEM, SO THEY ARE PRE-CIOUS IN A WAY.
ENJOY VIEWING THEM, AND YOU CAN TELL THE OTHERS ABOUT THEM WHEN YOU GET BACK.
!
YOU CAME HERE FOR ME?!
MORE OR LESS. IT'S MY WAY OF SAYING THANKS.

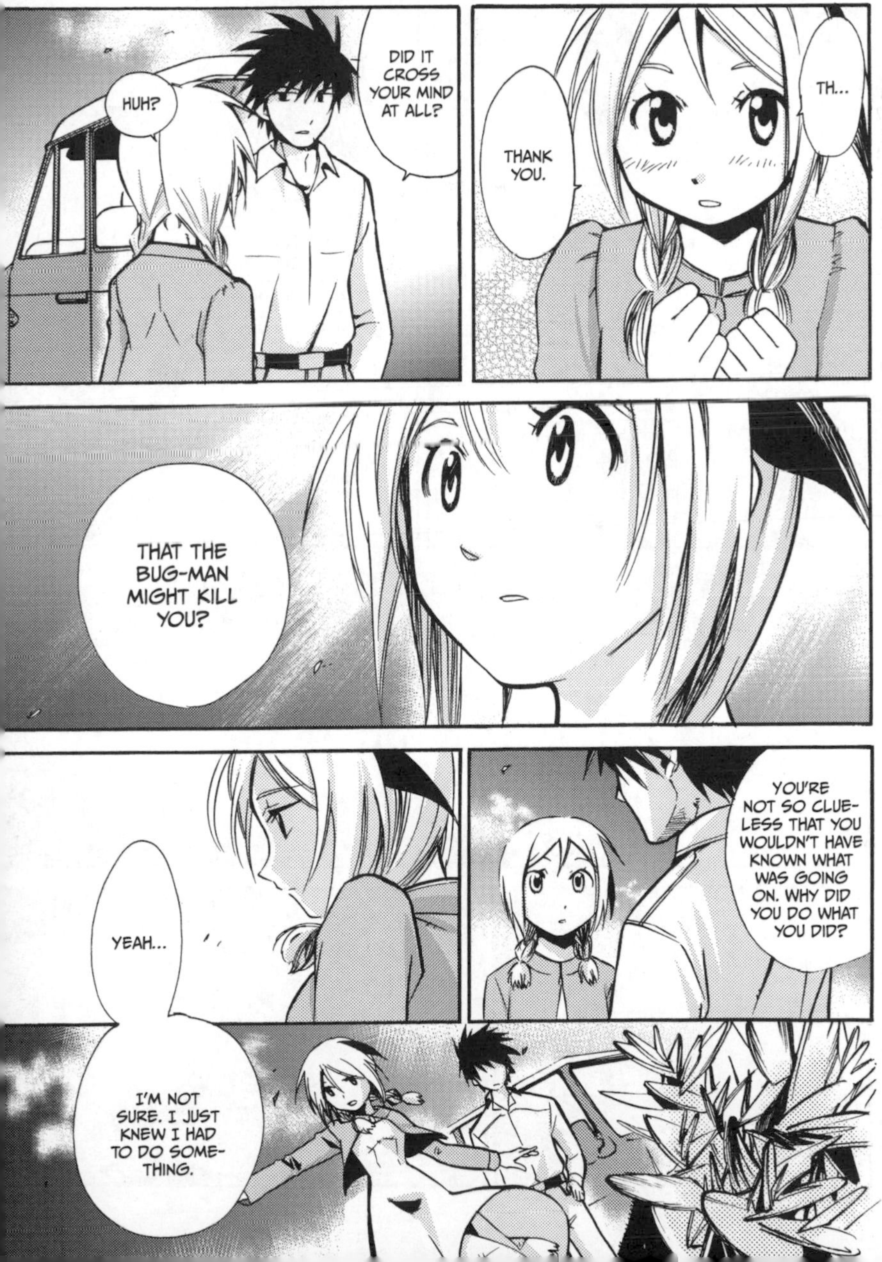
TH...
THANK YOU.
DID IT CROSS YOUR MIND AT ALL?
HUH?
THAT THE BUG-MAN MIGHT KILL YOU?
YOU'RE NOT SO CLUELESS THAT YOU WOULDN'T HAVE KNOWN WHAT WAS GOING ON. WHY DID YOU DO WHAT YOU DID?
YEAH...
I'M NOT SURE. I JUST KNEW I HAD TO DO SOMETHING.

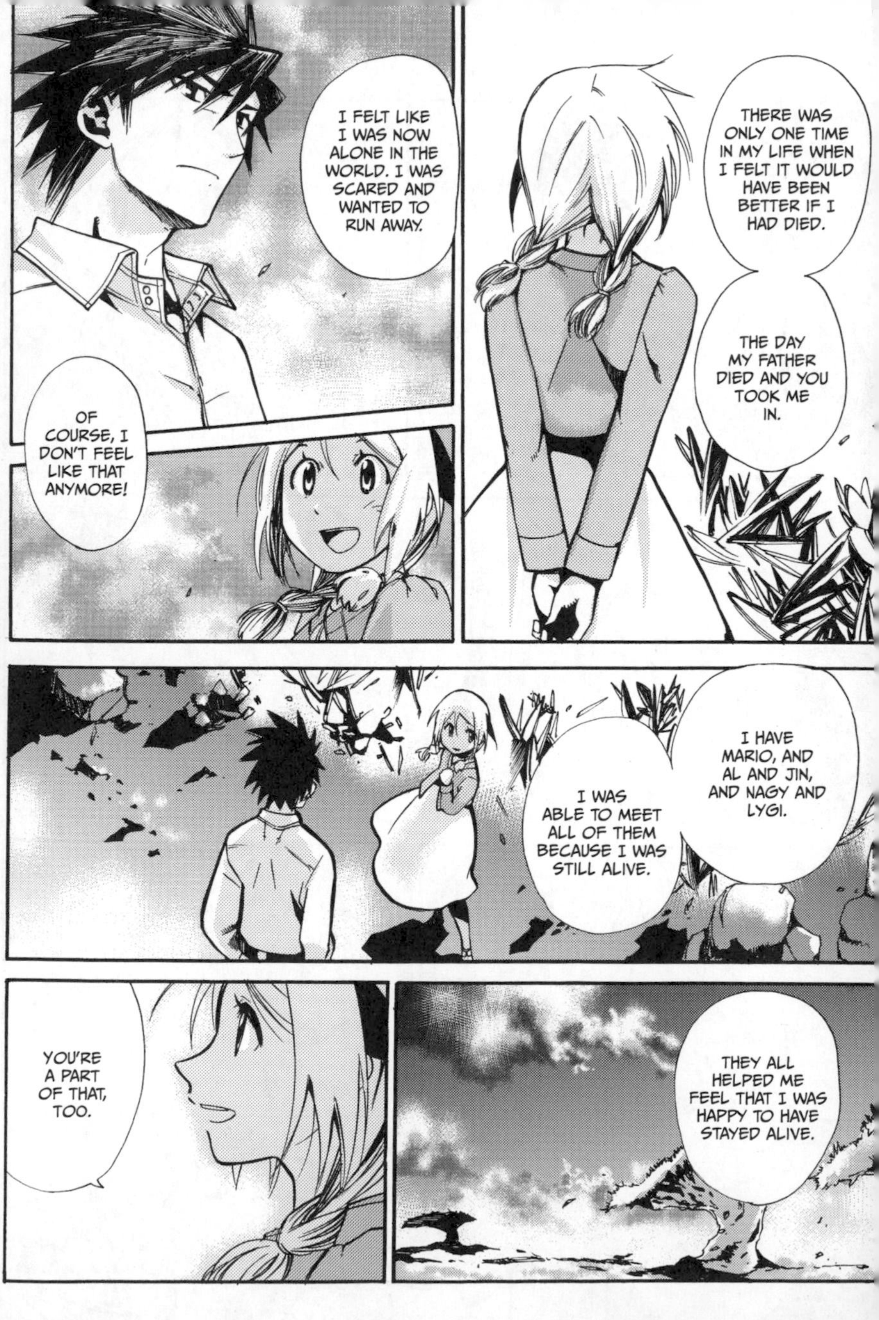
THERE WAS ONLY ONE TIME IN MY LIFE WHEN I FELT IT WOULD HAVE BEEN BETTER IF I HAD DIED.
THE DAY MY FATHER DIED AND YOU TOOK ME IN.
I FELT LIKE I WAS NOW ALONE IN THE WORLD. I WAS SCARED AND WANTED TO RUN AWAY.
OF COURSE, I DON'T FEEL LIKE THAT ANYMORE!
I HAVE MARIO, AND AL AND JIN, AND NAGY AND LYGI.
I WAS ABLE TO MEET ALL OF THEM BECAUSE I WAS STILL ALIVE.
THEY ALL HELPED ME FEEL THAT I WAS HAPPY TO HAVE STAYED ALIVE.
YOU'RE A PART OF THAT, TOO.

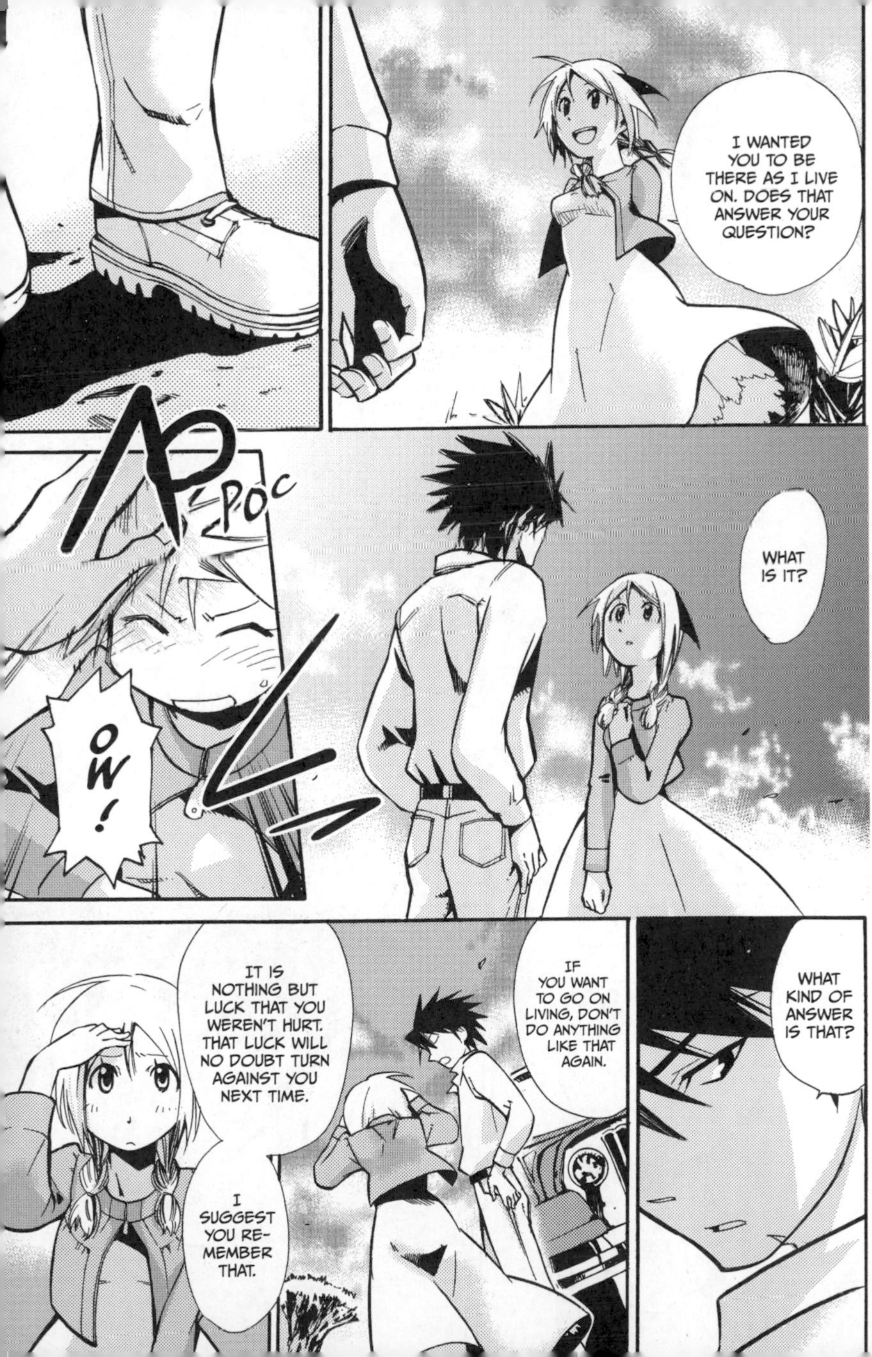

I WANTED YOU TO BE THERE AS I LIVE ON. DOES THAT ANSWER YOUR QUESTION?
WHAT IS IT?
POC
OW!
WHAT KIND OF ANSWER IS THAT?
IF YOU WANT TO GO ON LIVING, DON'T DO ANYTHING LIKE THAT AGAIN.
IT IS NOTHING BUT LUCK THAT YOU WEREN'T HURT. THAT LUCK WILL NO DOUBT TURN AGAINST YOU NEXT TIME.
I SUGGEST YOU RE-MEMBER THAT.

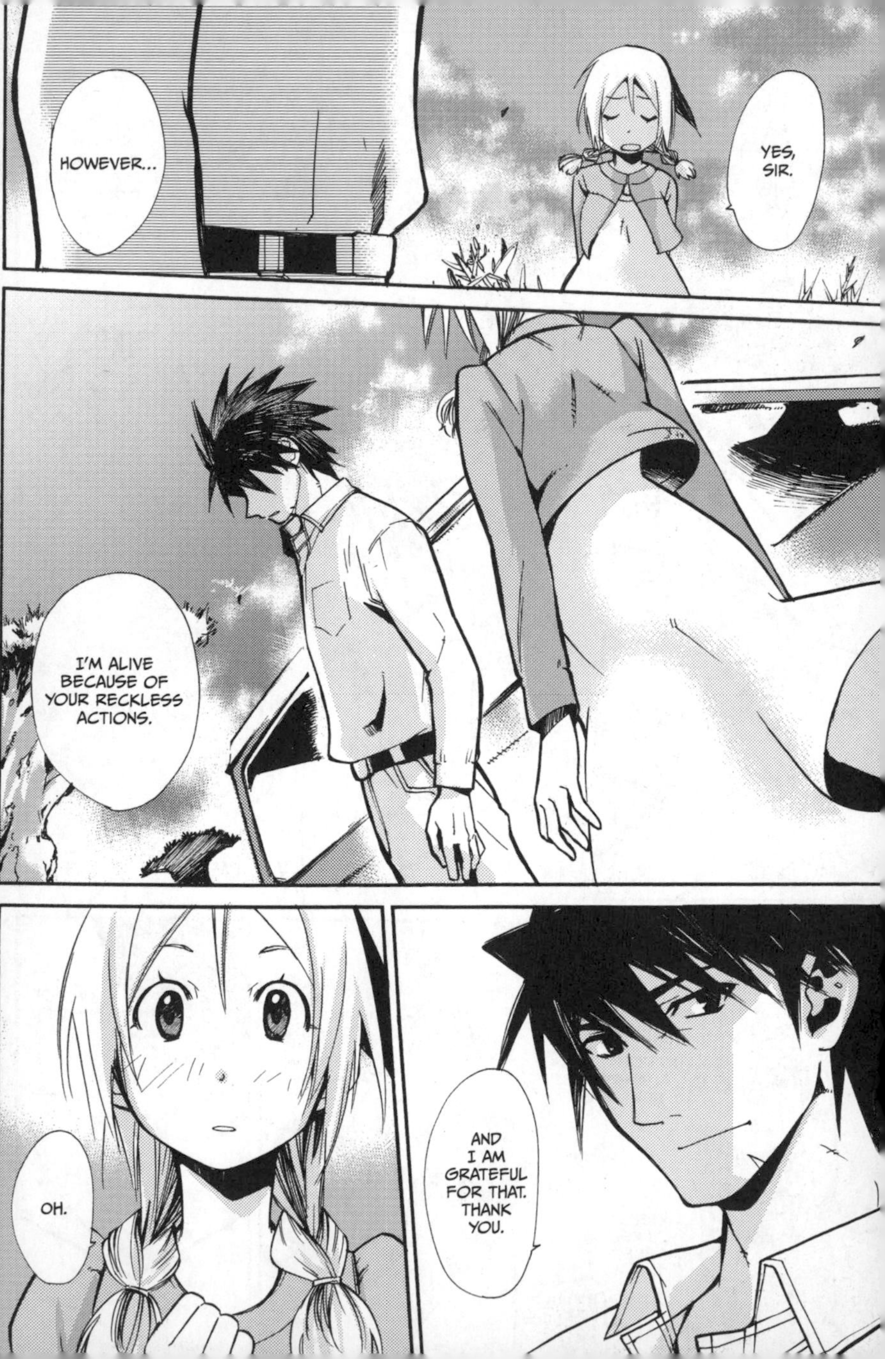
YES, SIR.
HOWEVER...
I'M ALIVE BECAUSE OF YOUR RECKLESS ACTIONS.
AND I AM GRATEFUL FOR THAT. THANK YOU.
OH.

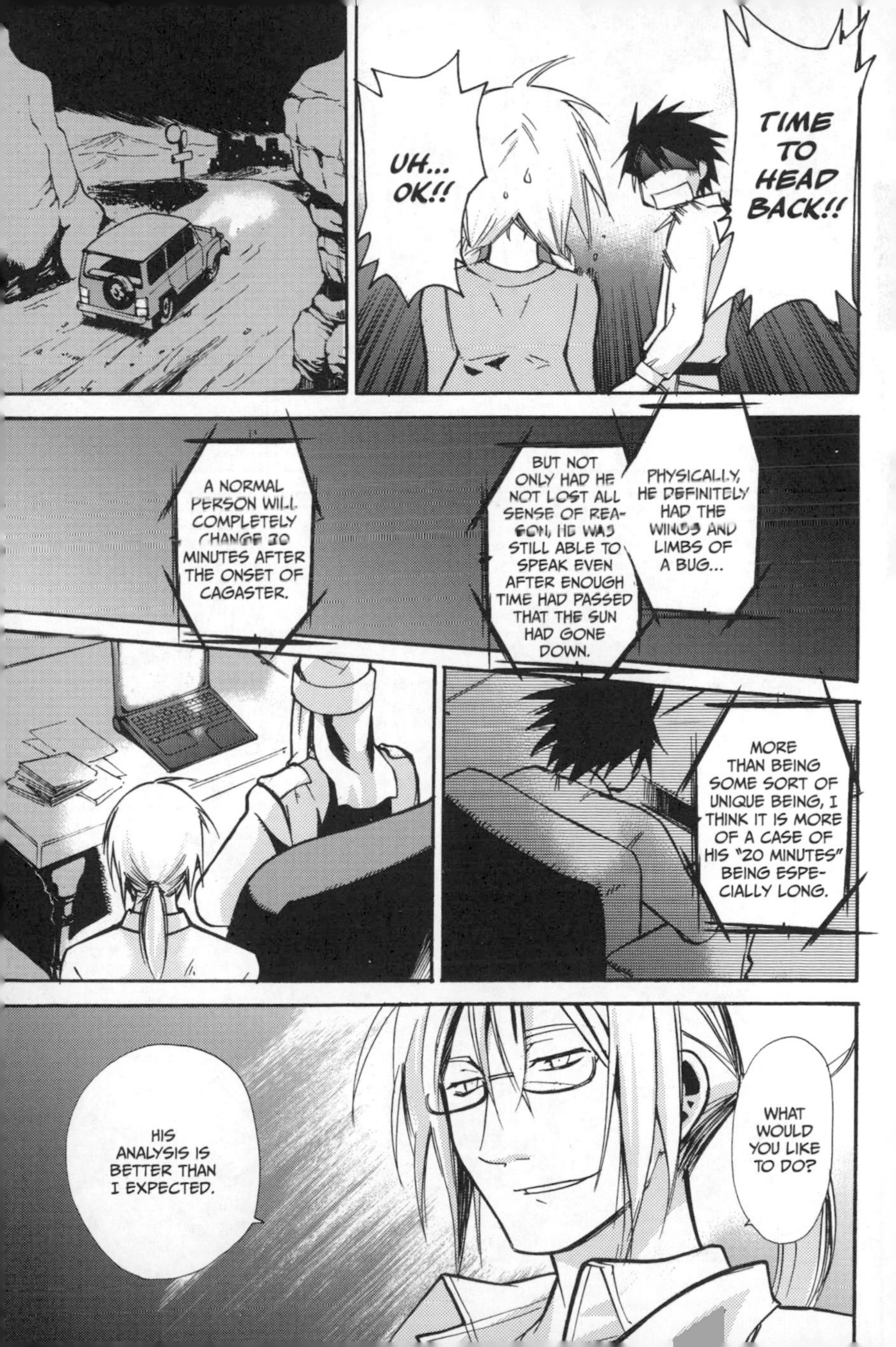
TIME TO HEAD BACK!!
UH... OK!!
PHYSICALLY, HE DEFINITELY HAD THE WINGS AND LIMBS OF A BUG...
BUT NOT ONLY HAD HE NOT LOST ALL SENSE OF REASON, HE WAS STILL ABLE TO SPEAK EVEN AFTER ENOUGH TIME HAD PASSED THAT THE SUN HAD GONE DOWN.
A NORMAL PERSON WILL COMPLETELY CHANGE 20 MINUTES AFTER THE ONSET OF CAGASTER.
MORE THAN BEING SOME SORT OF UNIQUE BEING, I THINK IT IS MORE OF A CASE OF HIS "20 MINUTES" BEING ESPECIALLY LONG.
WHAT WOULD YOU LIKE TO DO?
HIS ANALYSIS IS BETTER THAN I EXPECTED.

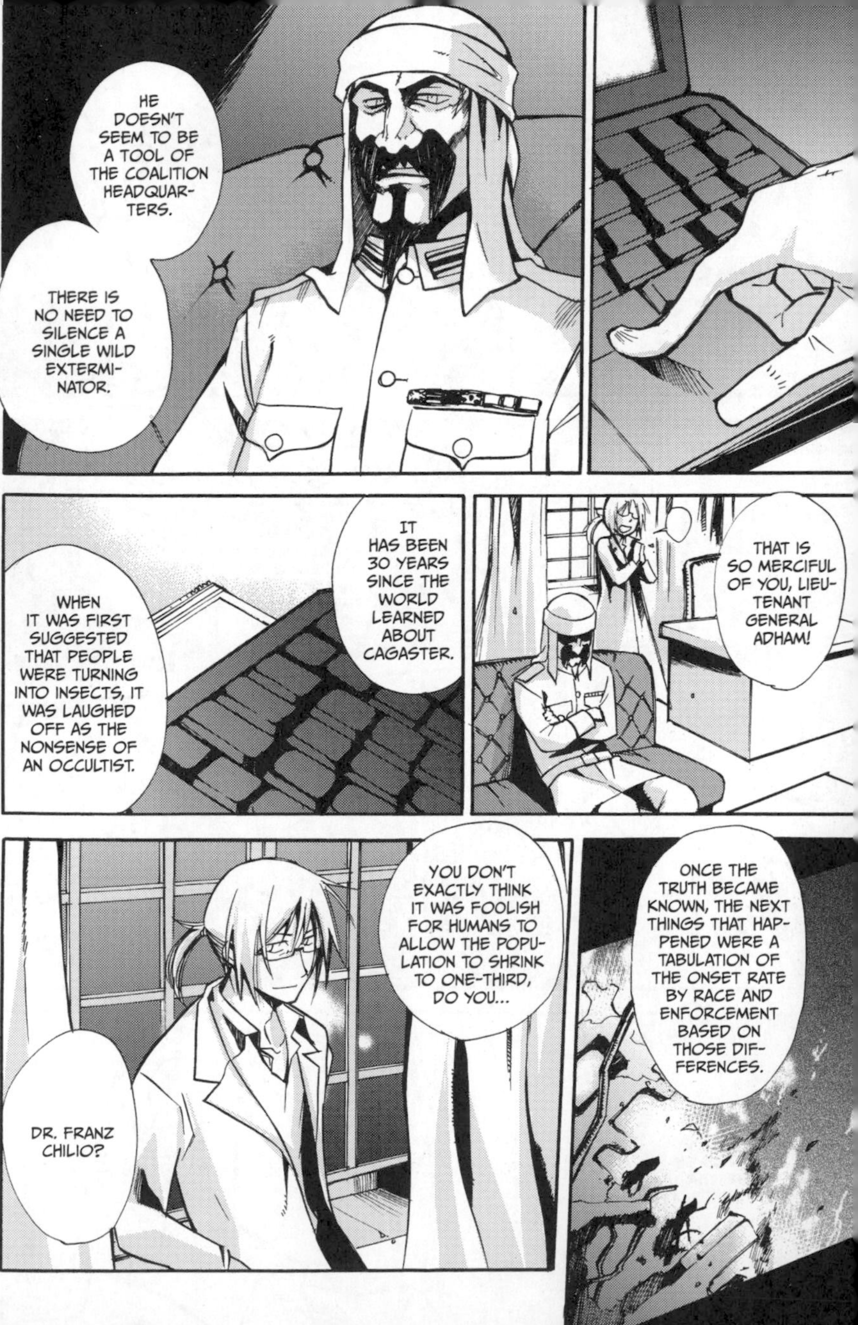
HE DOESN'T SEEM TO BE A TOOL OF THE COALITION HEADQUARTERS.
THERE IS NO NEED TO SILENCE A SINGLE WILD EXTERMINATOR.
THAT IS SO MERCIFUL OF YOU, LIEUTENANT GENERAL ADHAM!
IT HAS BEEN 30 YEARS SINCE THE WORLD LEARNED ABOUT CAGASTER.
WHEN IT WAS FIRST SUGGESTED THAT PEOPLE WERE TURNING INTO INSECTS, IT WAS LAUGHED OFF AS THE NONSENSE OF AN OCCULTIST.
ONCE THE TRUTH BECAME KNOWN, THE NEXT THINGS THAT HAPPENED WERE A TABULATION OF THE ONSET RATE BY RACE AND ENFORCEMENT BASED ON THOSE DIFFERENCES.
YOU DON'T EXACTLY THINK IT WAS FOOLISH FOR HUMANS TO ALLOW THE POPULATION TO SHRINK TO ONE-THIRD, DO YOU...
DR. FRANZ CHILIO?

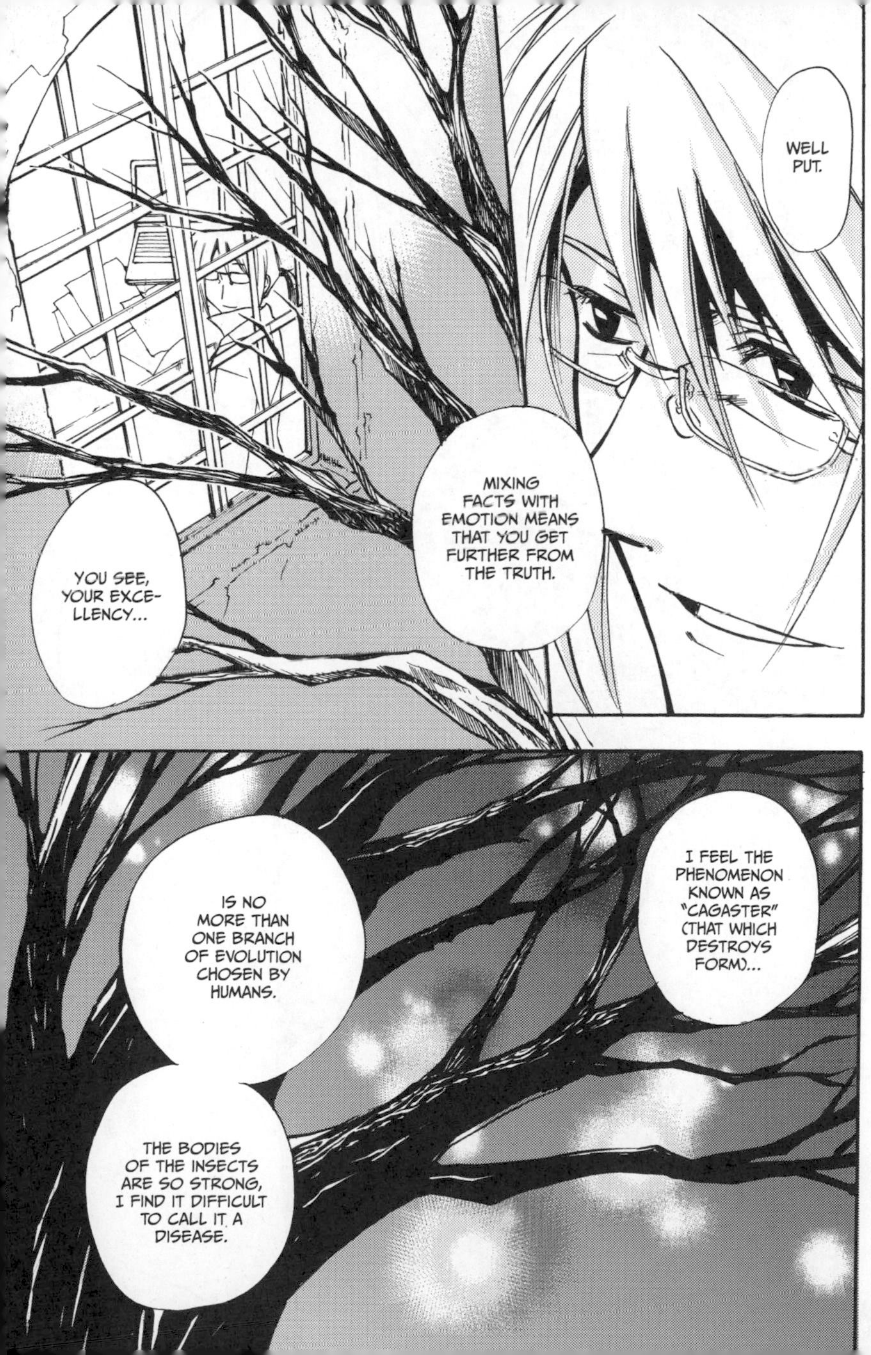
WELL PUT.
MIXING FACTS WITH EMOTION MEANS THAT YOU GET FURTHER FROM THE TRUTH.
YOU SEE, YOUR EXCE-LLENCY...
I FEEL THE PHENOMENON KNOWN AS "CAGASTER" (THAT WHICH DESTROYS FORM)...
IS NO MORE THAN ONE BRANCH OF EVOLUTION CHOSEN BY HUMANS.
THE BODIES OF THE INSECTS ARE SO STRONG, I FIND IT DIFFICULT TO CALL IT A DISEASE.

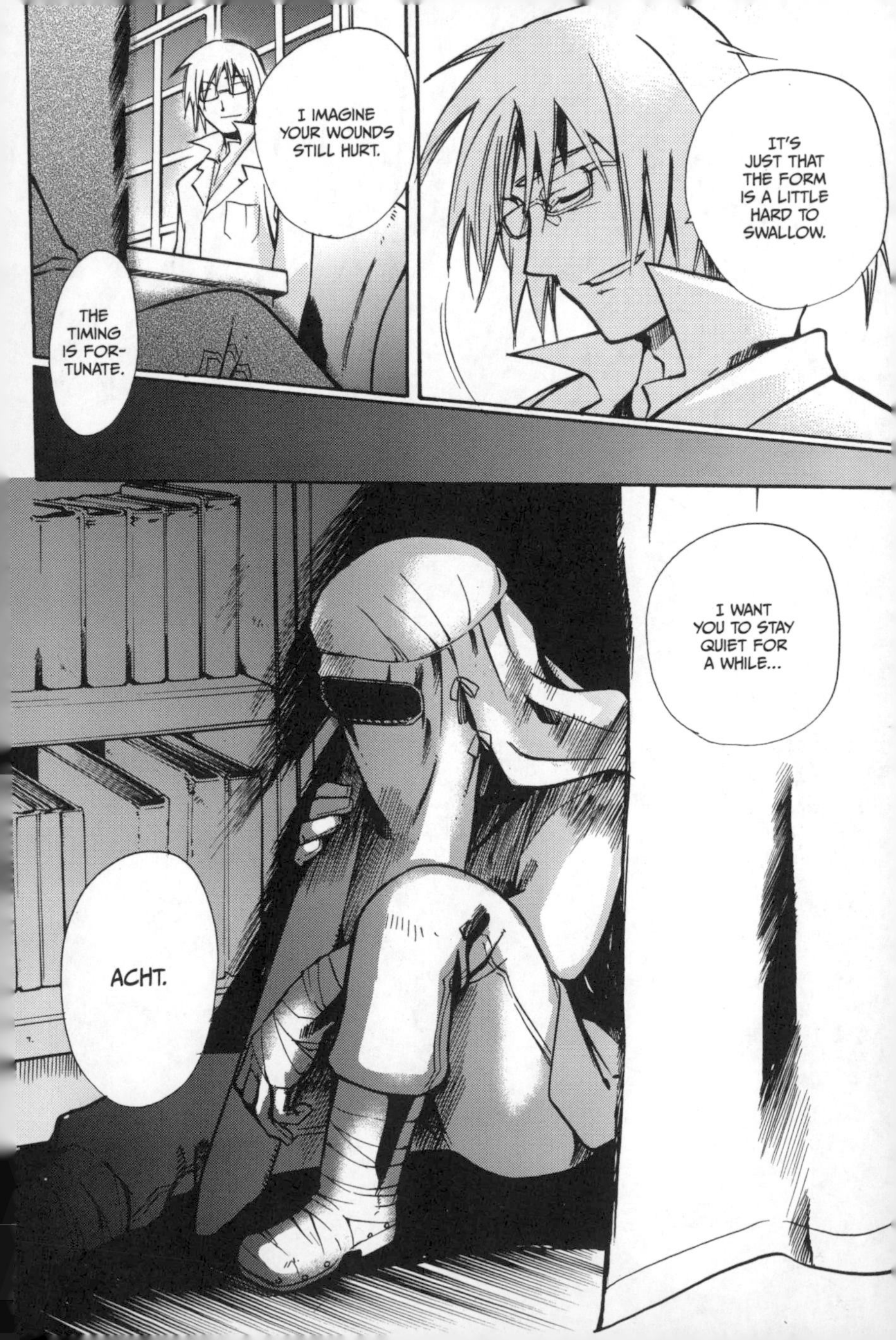
IT'S JUST THAT THE FORM IS A LITTLE HARD TO SWALLOW.
I IMAGINE YOUR WOUNDS STILL HURT.
THE TIMING IS FOR-TUNATE.
I WANT YOU TO STAY QUIET FOR A WHILE...
ACHT.

[CHAPTER 8]

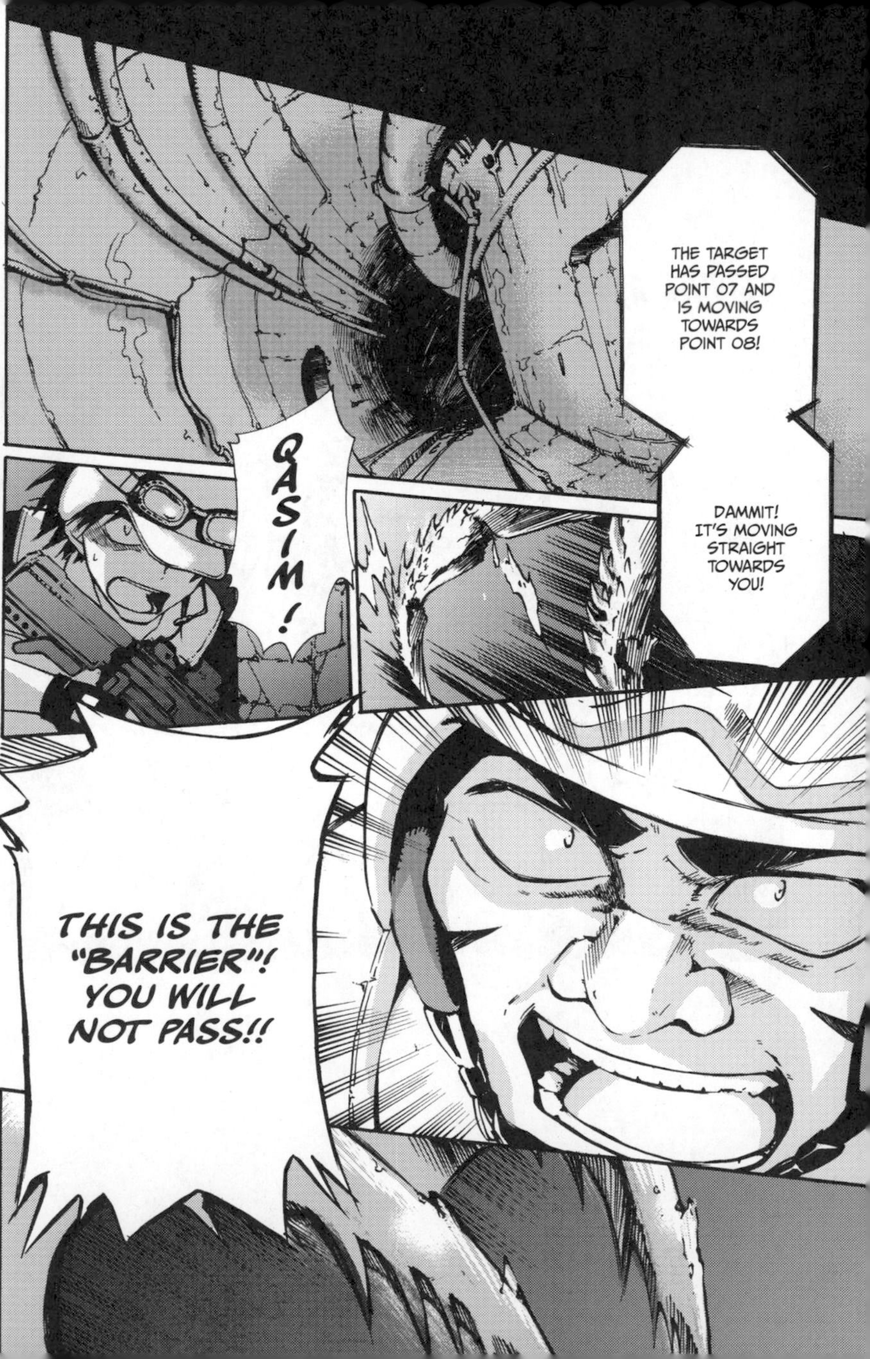
THE TARGET HAS PASSED POINT 07 AND IS MOVING TOWARDS POINT 08!
DAMMIT! IT'S MOVING STRAIGHT TOWARDS YOU!
QASIM!
THIS IS THE "BARRIER"! YOU WILL NOT PASS!!

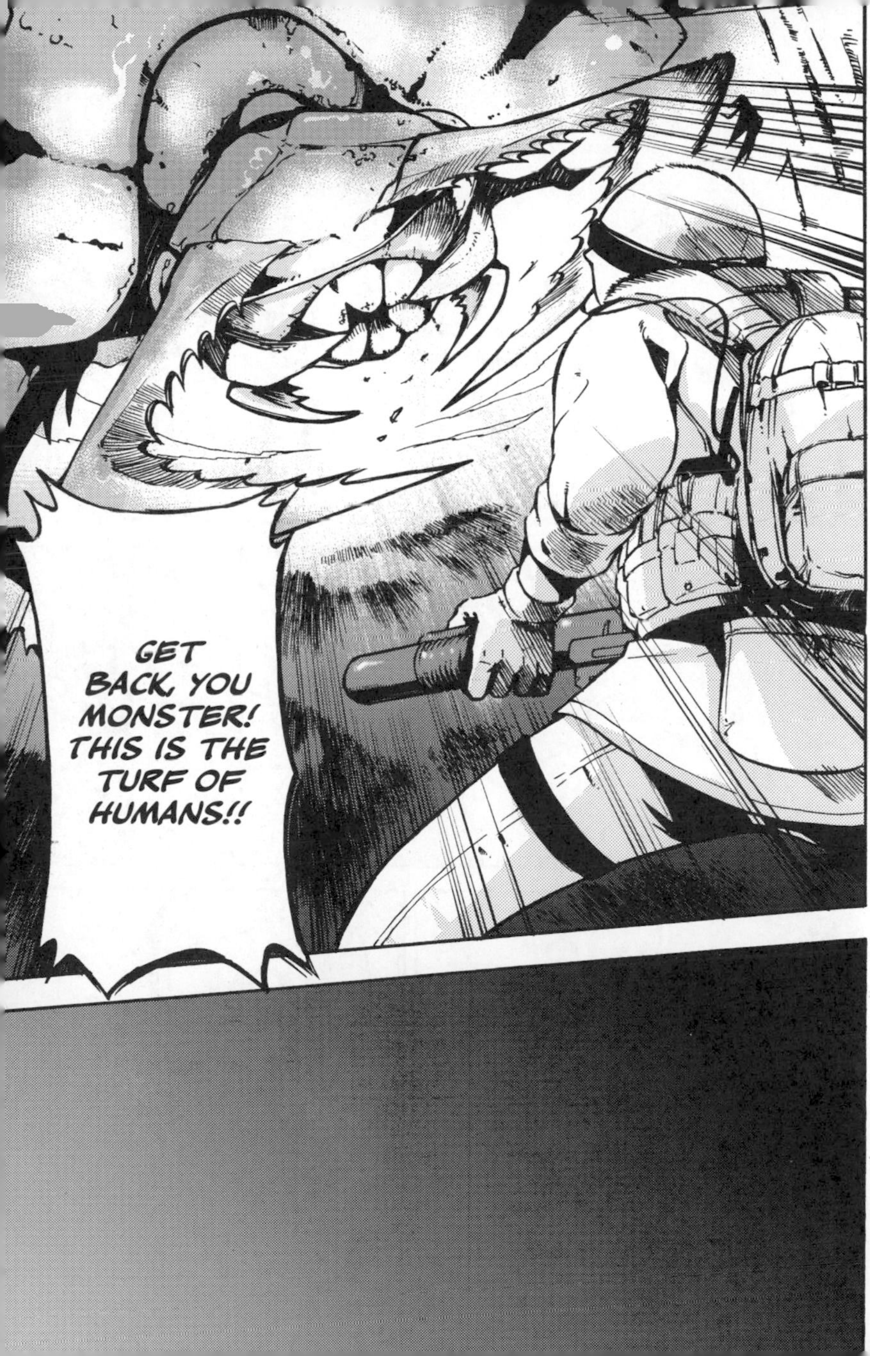
GET BACK, YOU MONSTER! THIS IS THE TURF OF HUMANS!!

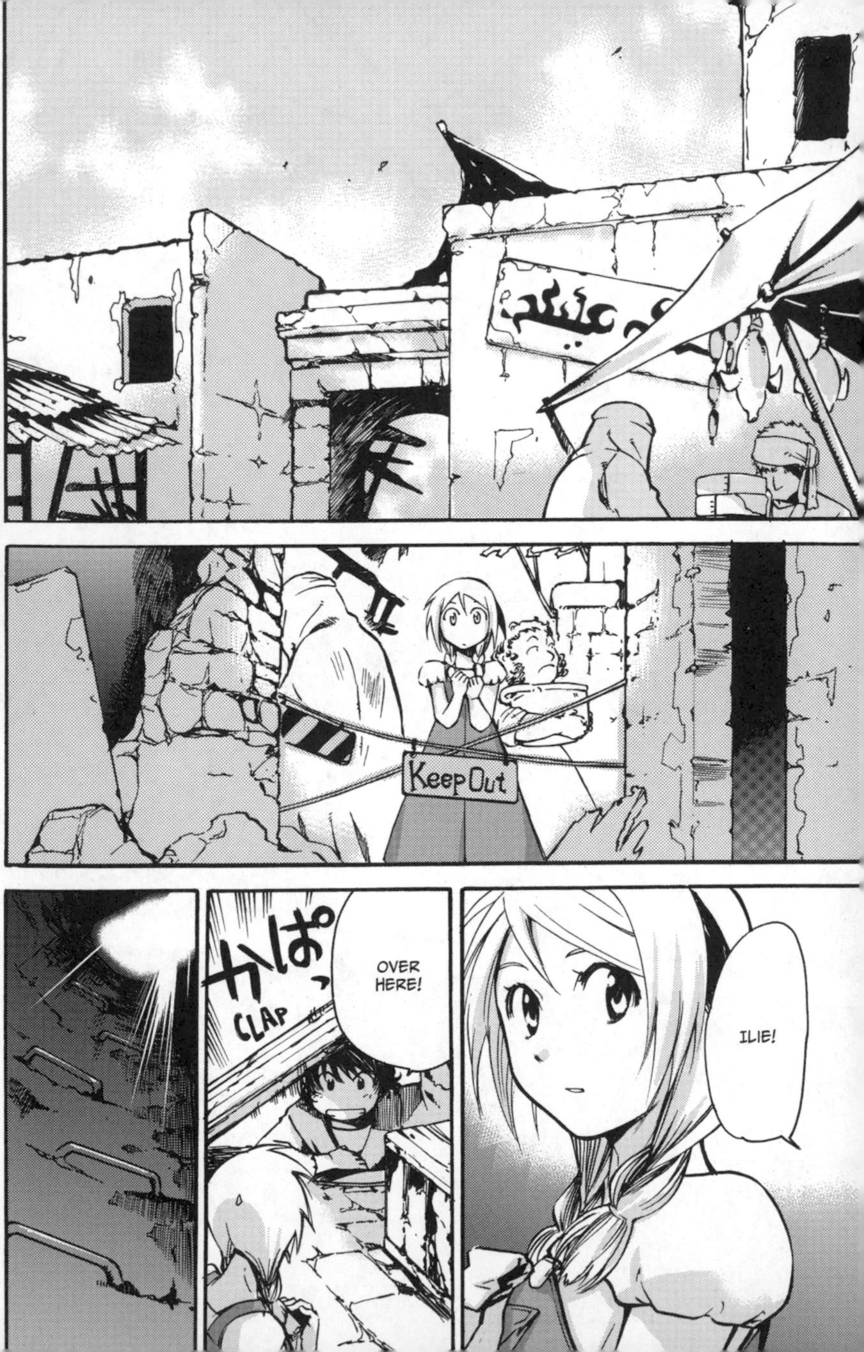
Keep Out
ILIE!
かぱっ
CLAP
OVER HERE!

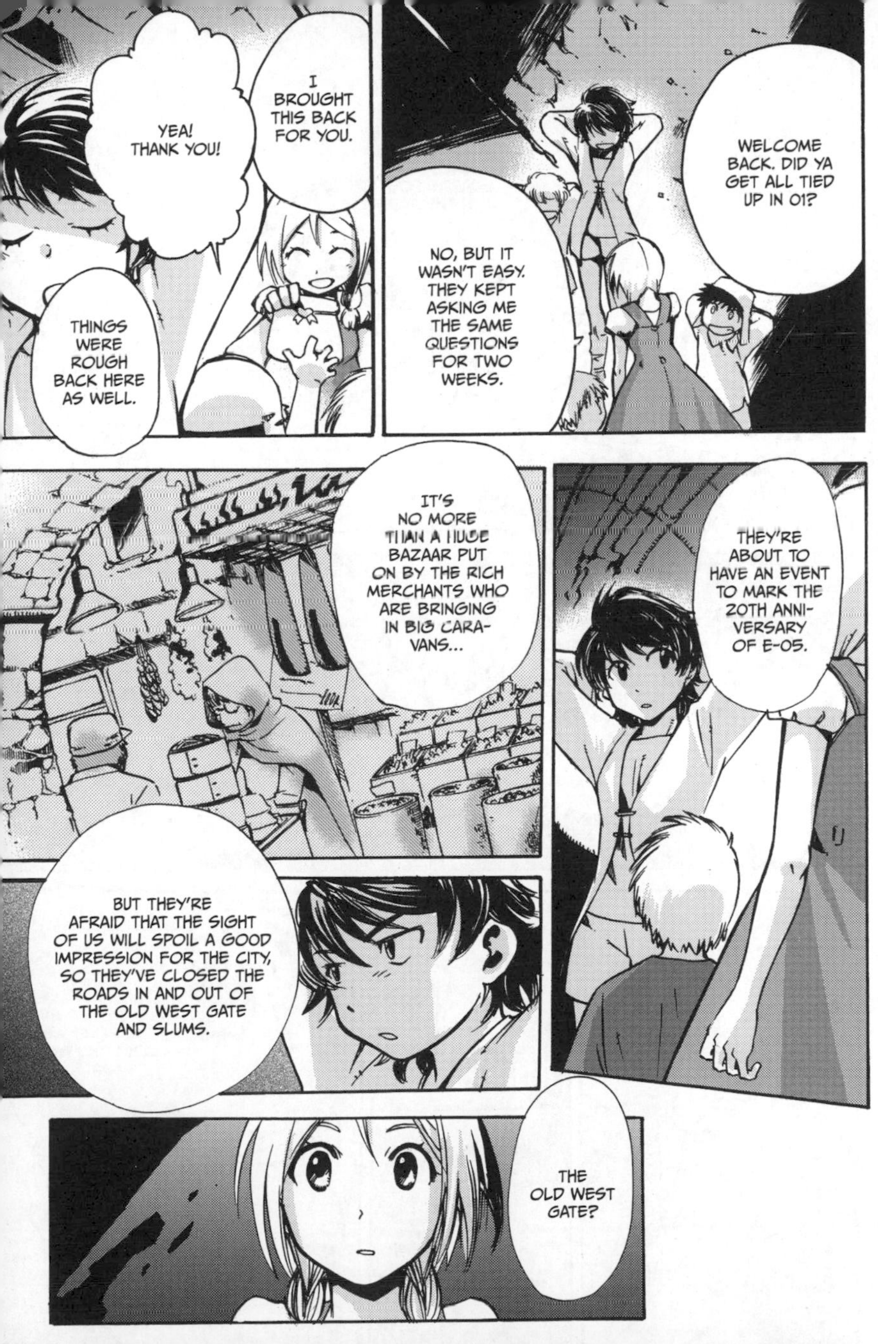

WELCOME BACK. DID YA GET ALL TIED UP IN 01?
NO, BUT IT WASN'T EASY. THEY KEPT ASKING ME THE SAME QUESTIONS FOR TWO WEEKS.
I BROUGHT THIS BACK FOR YOU.
YEA! THANK YOU!
THINGS WERE ROUGH BACK HERE AS WELL.
THEY'RE ABOUT TO HAVE AN EVENT TO MARK THE 20TH ANNI-VERSARY OF E-05.
IT'S NO MORE THAN A HUGE BAZAAR PUT ON BY THE RICH MERCHANTS WHO ARE BRINGING IN BIG CARA-VANS...
BUT THEY'RE AFRAID THAT THE SIGHT OF US WILL SPOIL A GOOD IMPRESSION FOR THE CITY, SO THEY'VE CLOSED THE ROADS IN AND OUT OF THE OLD WEST GATE AND SLUMS.
THE OLD WEST GATE?

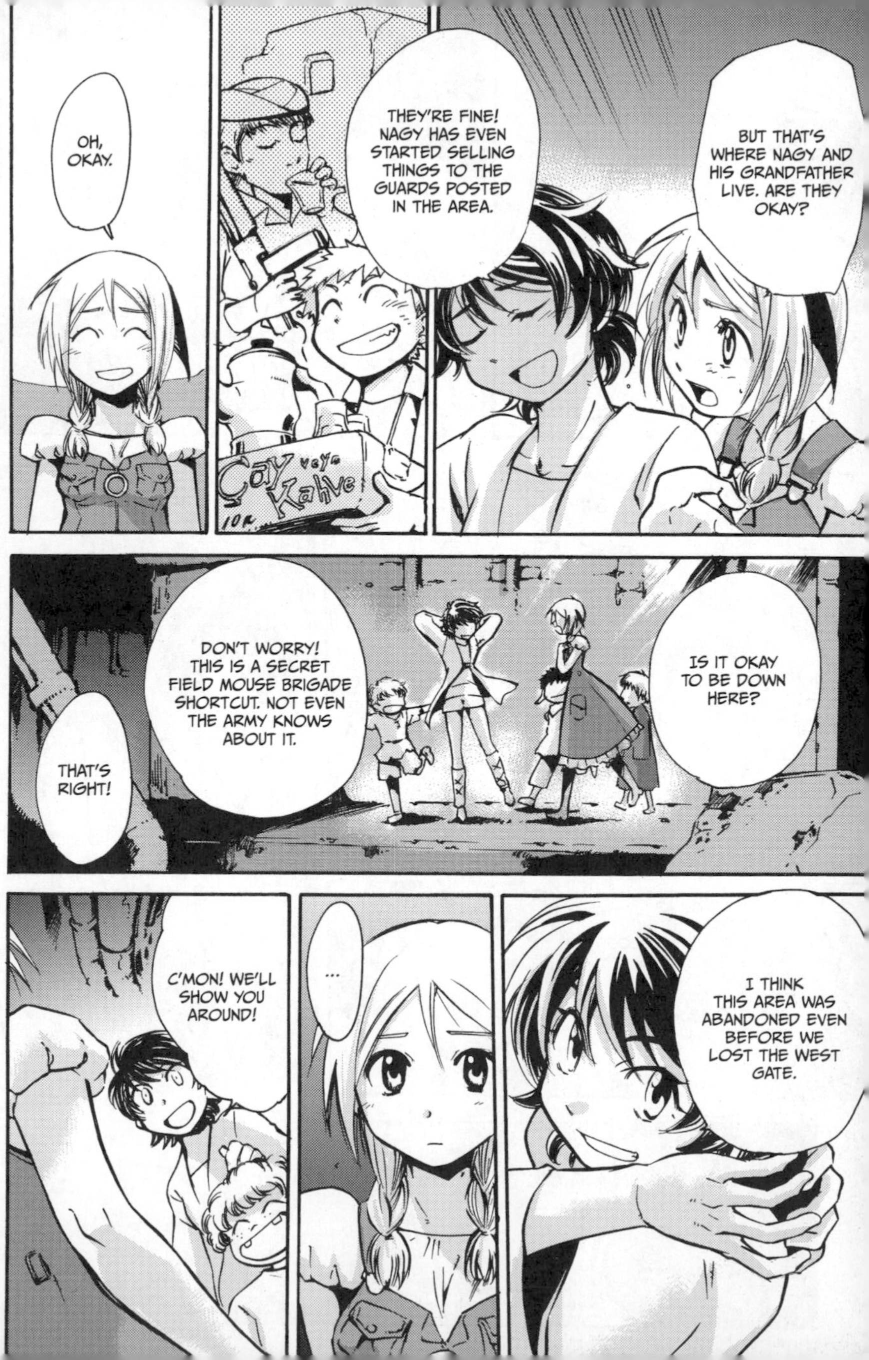
BUT THAT'S WHERE NAGY AND HIS GRANDFATHER LIVE. ARE THEY OKAY?
THEY'RE FINE! NAGY HAS EVEN STARTED SELLING THINGS TO THE GUARDS POSTED IN THE AREA.
Çay veya Kahve
OH, OKAY.
IS IT OKAY TO BE DOWN HERE?
DON'T WORRY! THIS IS A SECRET FIELD MOUSE BRIGADE SHORTCUT. NOT EVEN THE ARMY KNOWS ABOUT IT.
THAT'S RIGHT!
I THINK THIS AREA WAS ABANDONED EVEN BEFORE WE LOST THE WEST GATE.
...
C'MON! WE'LL SHOW YOU AROUND!

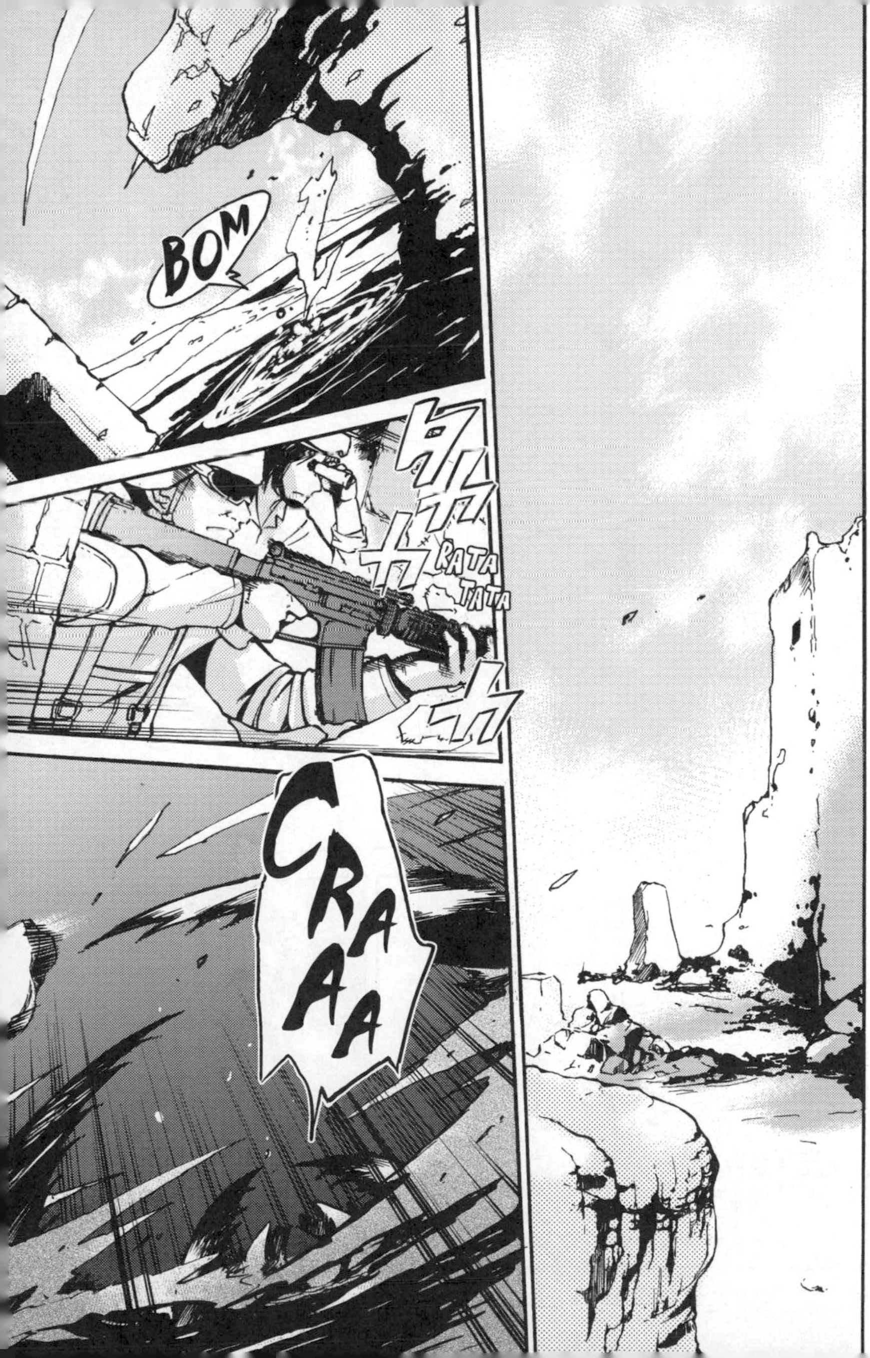
BOM
RATA TATA
CRAAA

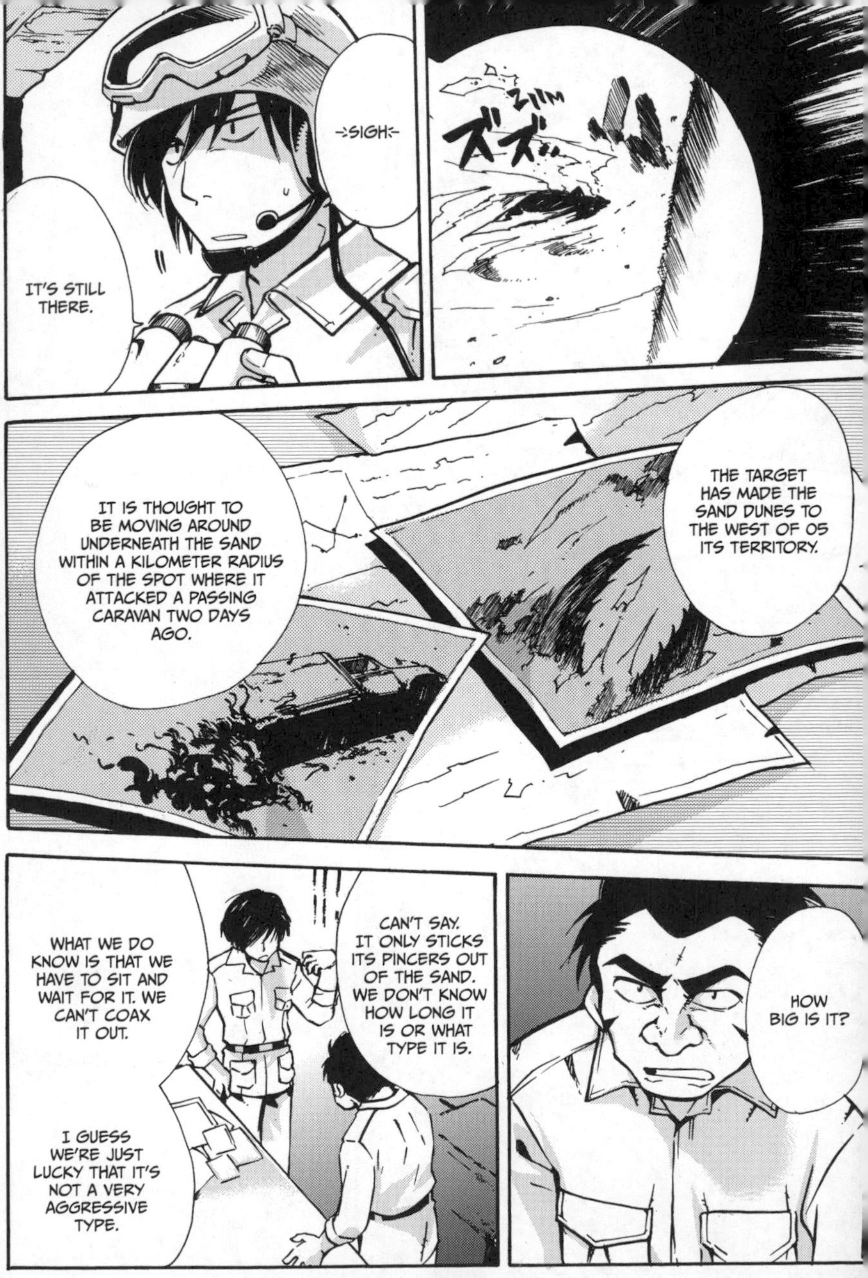

ズズ
-SIGH-
IT'S STILL THERE.
THE TARGET HAS MADE THE SAND DUNES TO THE WEST OF 05 ITS TERRITORY.
IT IS THOUGHT TO BE MOVING AROUND UNDERNEATH THE SAND WITHIN A KILOMETER RADIUS OF THE SPOT WHERE IT ATTACKED A PASSING CARAVAN TWO DAYS AGO.
HOW BIG IS IT?
CAN'T SAY. IT ONLY STICKS ITS PINCERS OUT OF THE SAND. WE DON'T KNOW HOW LONG IT IS OR WHAT TYPE IT IS.
WHAT WE DO KNOW IS THAT WE HAVE TO SIT AND WAIT FOR IT. WE CAN'T COAX IT OUT.
I GUESS WE'RE JUST LUCKY THAT IT'S NOT A VERY AGGRESSIVE TYPE.

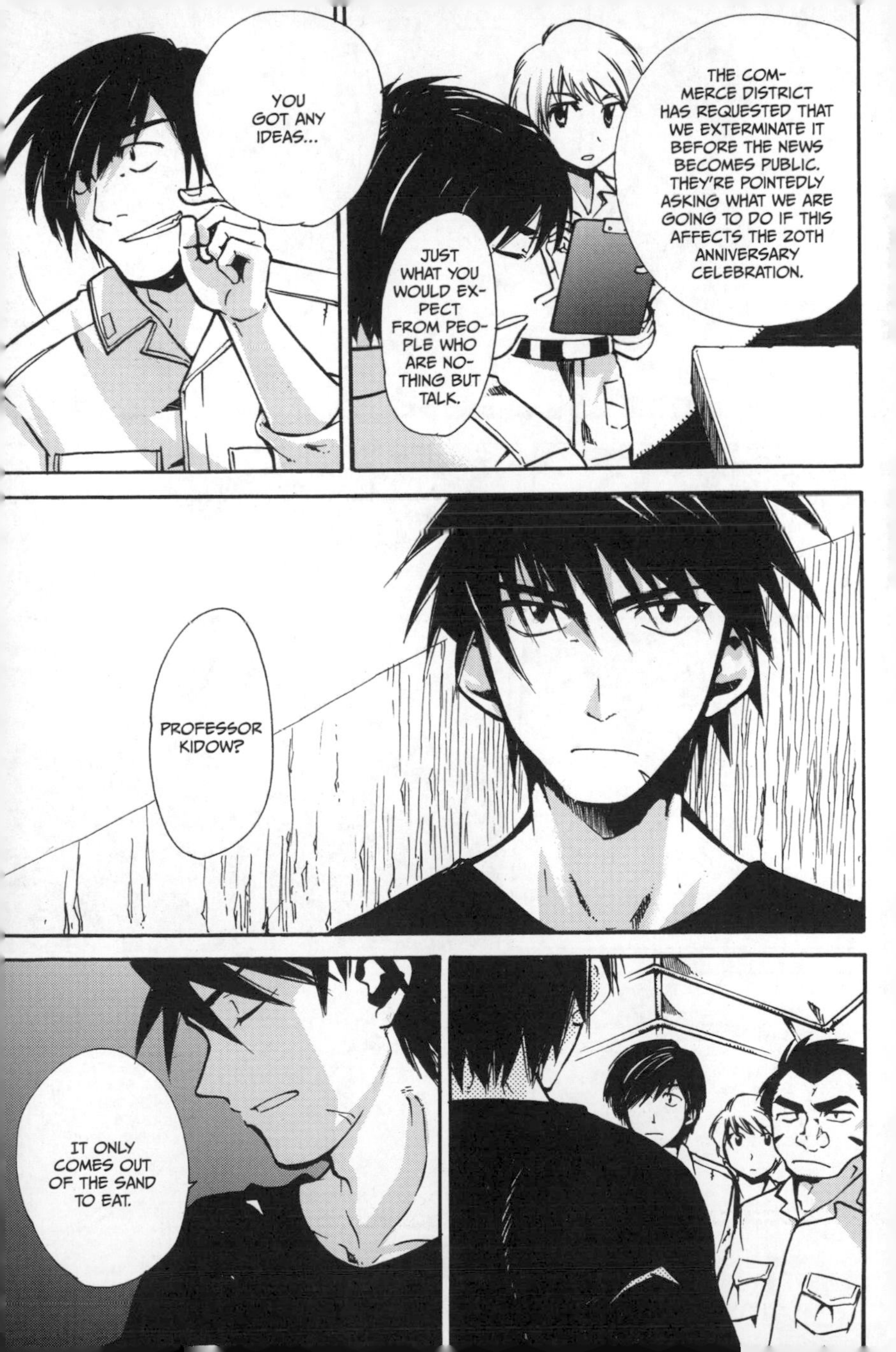
THE COM-MERCE DISTRICT HAS REQUESTED THAT WE EXTERMINATE IT BEFORE THE NEWS BECOMES PUBLIC. THEY'RE POINTEDLY ASKING WHAT WE ARE GOING TO DO IF THIS AFFECTS THE 20TH ANNIVERSARY CELEBRATION.
JUST WHAT YOU WOULD EX-PECT FROM PEO-PLE WHO ARE NO-THING BUT TALK.
YOU GOT ANY IDEAS...
PROFESSOR KIDOW?
IT ONLY COMES OUT OF THE SAND TO EAT.

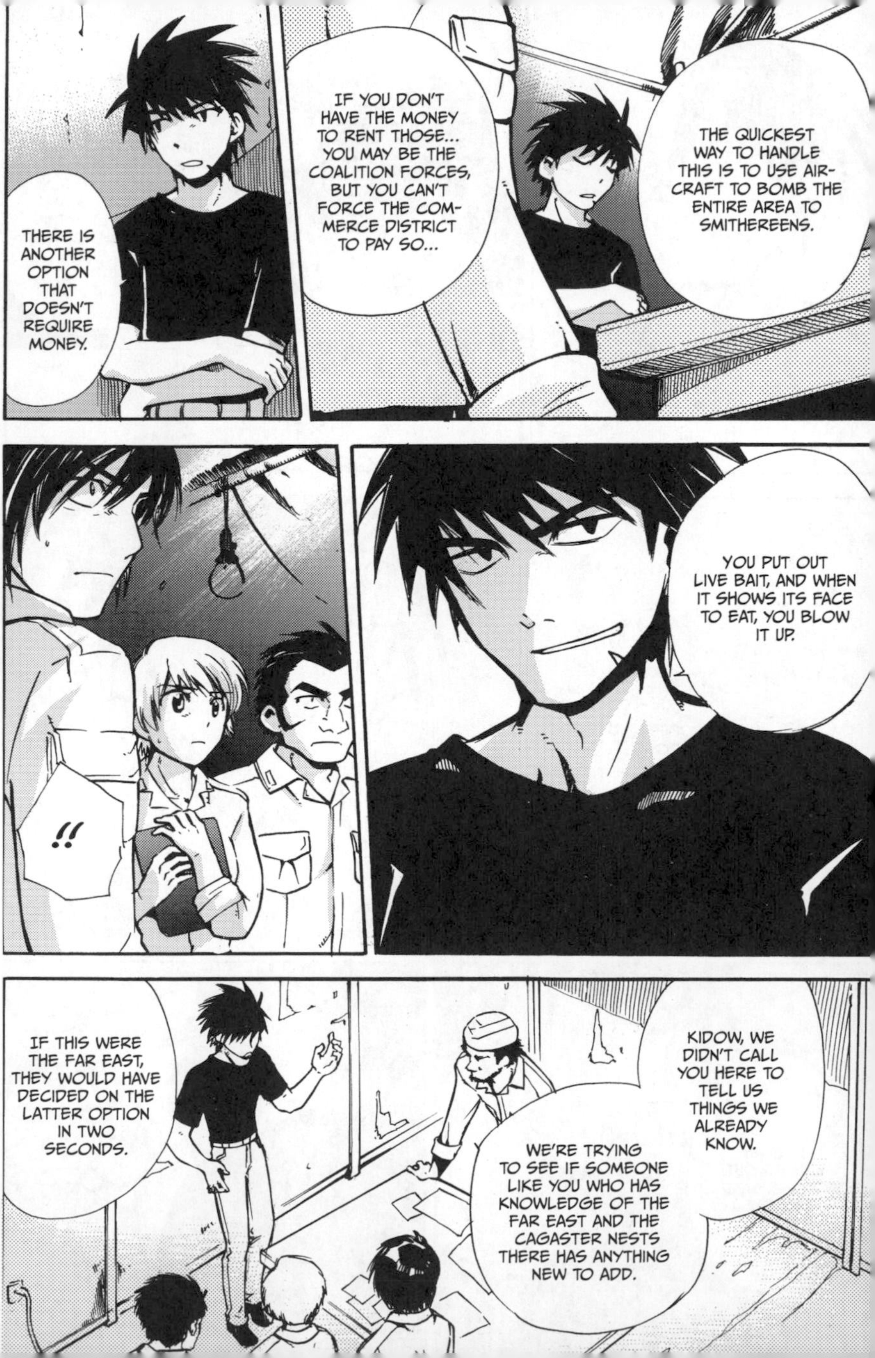
THE QUICKEST WAY TO HANDLE THIS IS TO USE AIR-CRAFT TO BOMB THE ENTIRE AREA TO SMITHEREENS.
IF YOU DON'T HAVE THE MONEY TO RENT THOSE... YOU MAY BE THE COALITION FORCES, BUT YOU CAN'T FORCE THE COM-MERCE DISTRICT TO PAY SO...
THERE IS ANOTHER OPTION THAT DOESN'T REQUIRE MONEY.
YOU PUT OUT LIVE BAIT, AND WHEN IT SHOWS ITS FACE TO EAT, YOU BLOW IT UP.
!!
KIDOW, WE DIDN'T CALL YOU HERE TO TELL US THINGS WE ALREADY KNOW.
WE'RE TRYING TO SEE IF SOMEONE LIKE YOU WHO HAS KNOWLEDGE OF THE FAR EAST AND THE CAGASTER NESTS THERE HAS ANYTHING NEW TO ADD.
IF THIS WERE THE FAR EAST, THEY WOULD HAVE DECIDED ON THE LATTER OPTION IN TWO SECONDS.

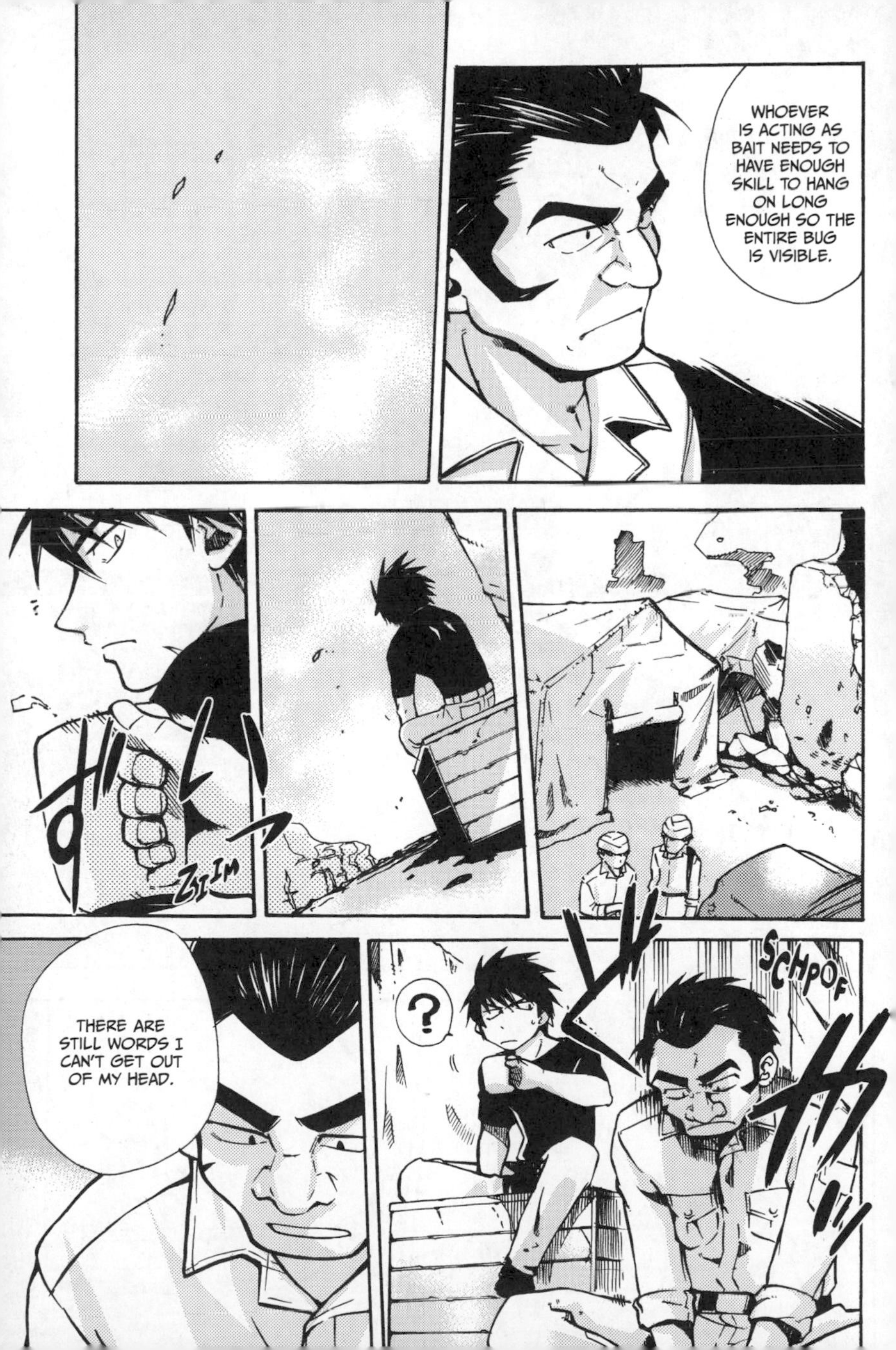
WHOEVER IS ACTING AS BAIT NEEDS TO HAVE ENOUGH SKILL TO HANG ON LONG ENOUGH SO THE ENTIRE BUG IS VISIBLE.
ZIIM
SCHPOF
?
THERE ARE STILL WORDS I CAN'T GET OUT OF MY HEAD.

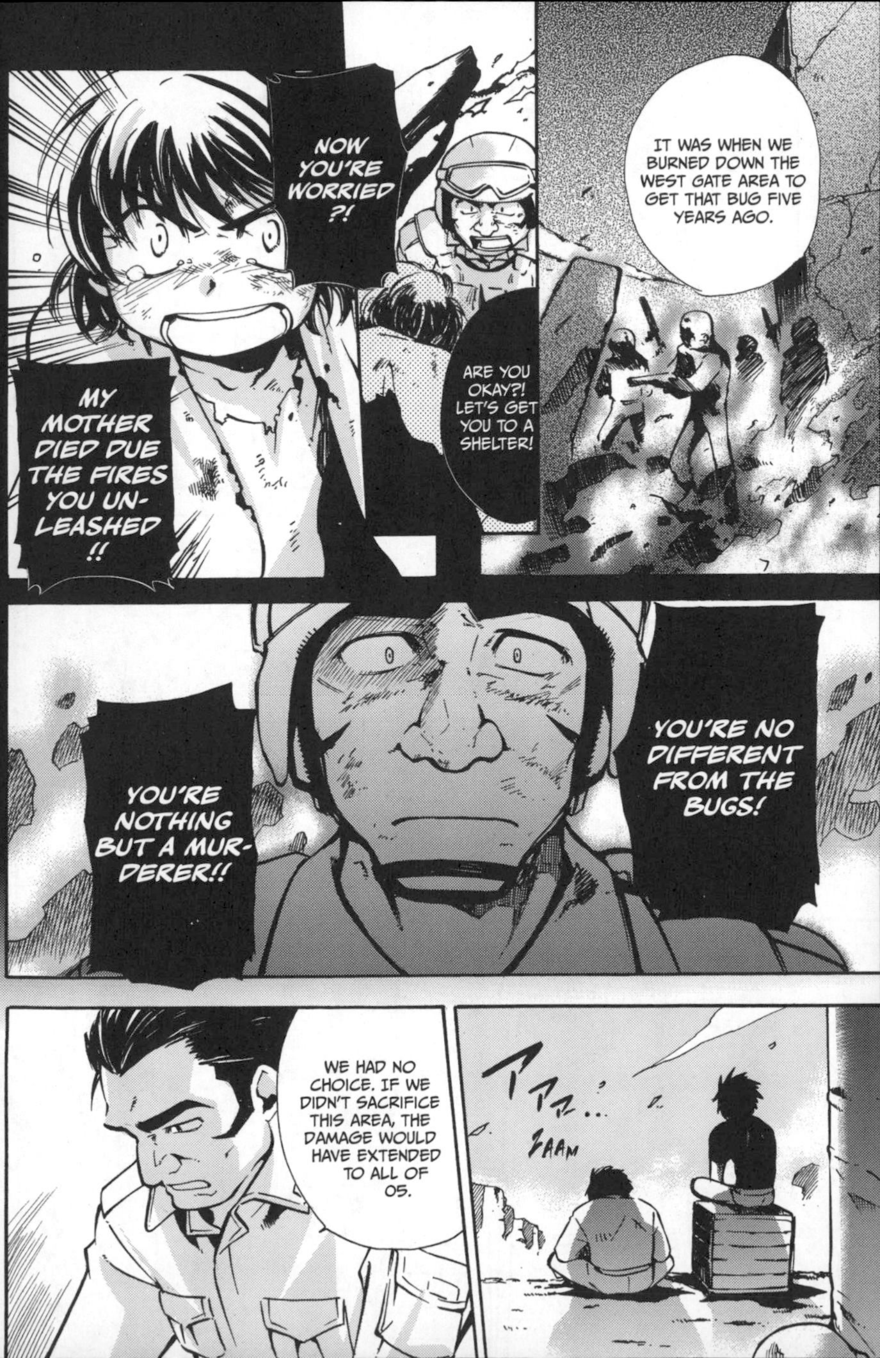
IT WAS WHEN WE BURNED DOWN THE WEST GATE AREA TO GET THAT BUG FIVE YEARS AGO.
ARE YOU OKAY?! LET'S GET YOU TO A SHELTER!
NOW YOU'RE WORRIED ?!
MY MOTHER DIED DUE THE FIRES YOU UN-LEASHED !!
YOU'RE NO DIFFERENT FROM THE BUGS!
YOU'RE NOTHING BUT A MUR-DERER!!
ZAAN
WE HAD NO CHOICE. IF WE DIDN'T SACRIFICE THIS AREA, THE DAMAGE WOULD HAVE EXTENDED TO ALL OF O5.

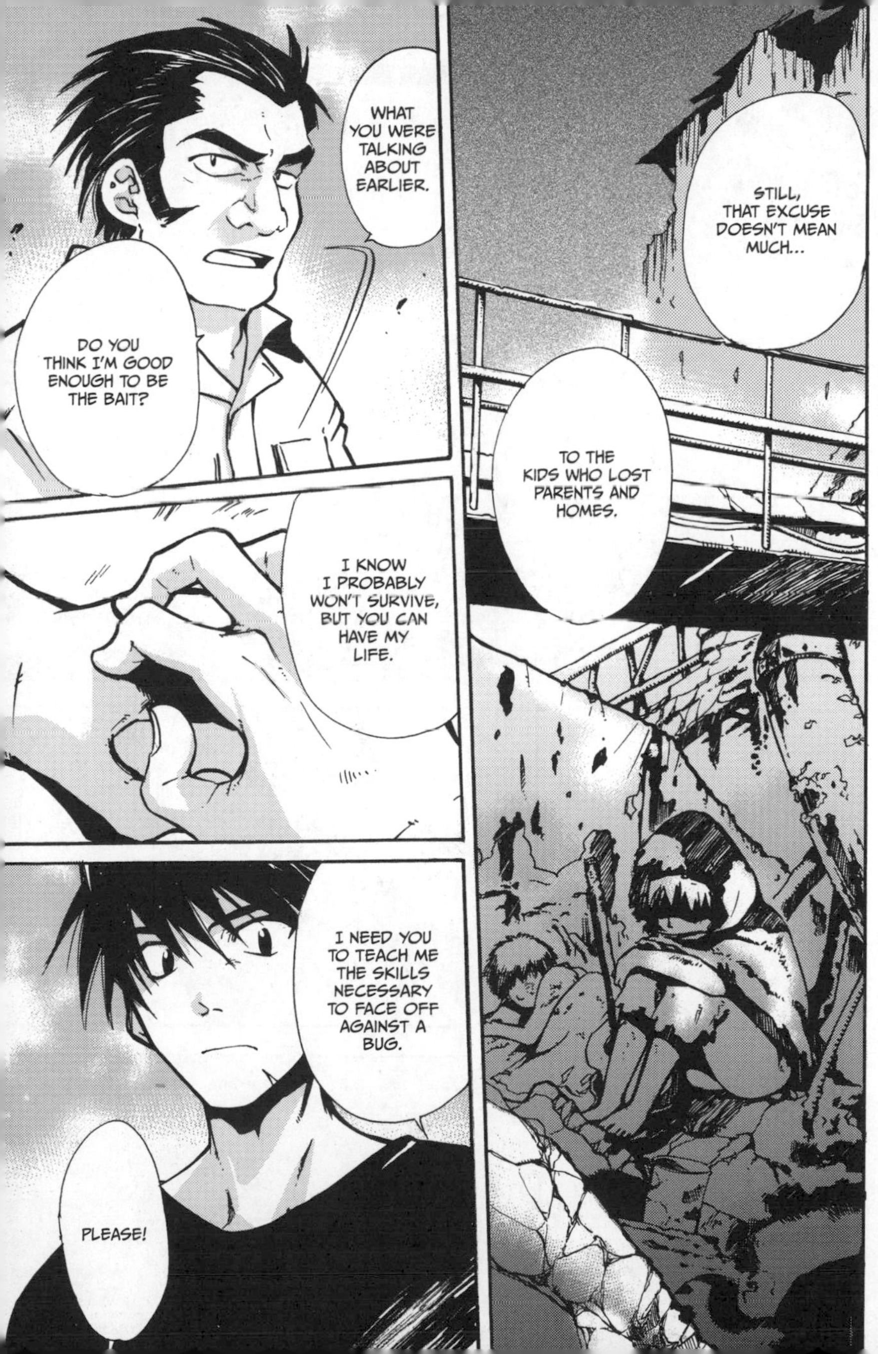
STILL, THAT EXCUSE DOESN'T MEAN MUCH...
TO THE KIDS WHO LOST PARENTS AND HOMES.
WHAT YOU WERE TALKING ABOUT EARLIER.
DO YOU THINK I'M GOOD ENOUGH TO BE THE BAIT?
I KNOW I PROBABLY WON'T SURVIVE, BUT YOU CAN HAVE MY LIFE.
I NEED YOU TO TEACH ME THE SKILLS NECESSARY TO FACE OFF AGAINST A BUG.
PLEASE!

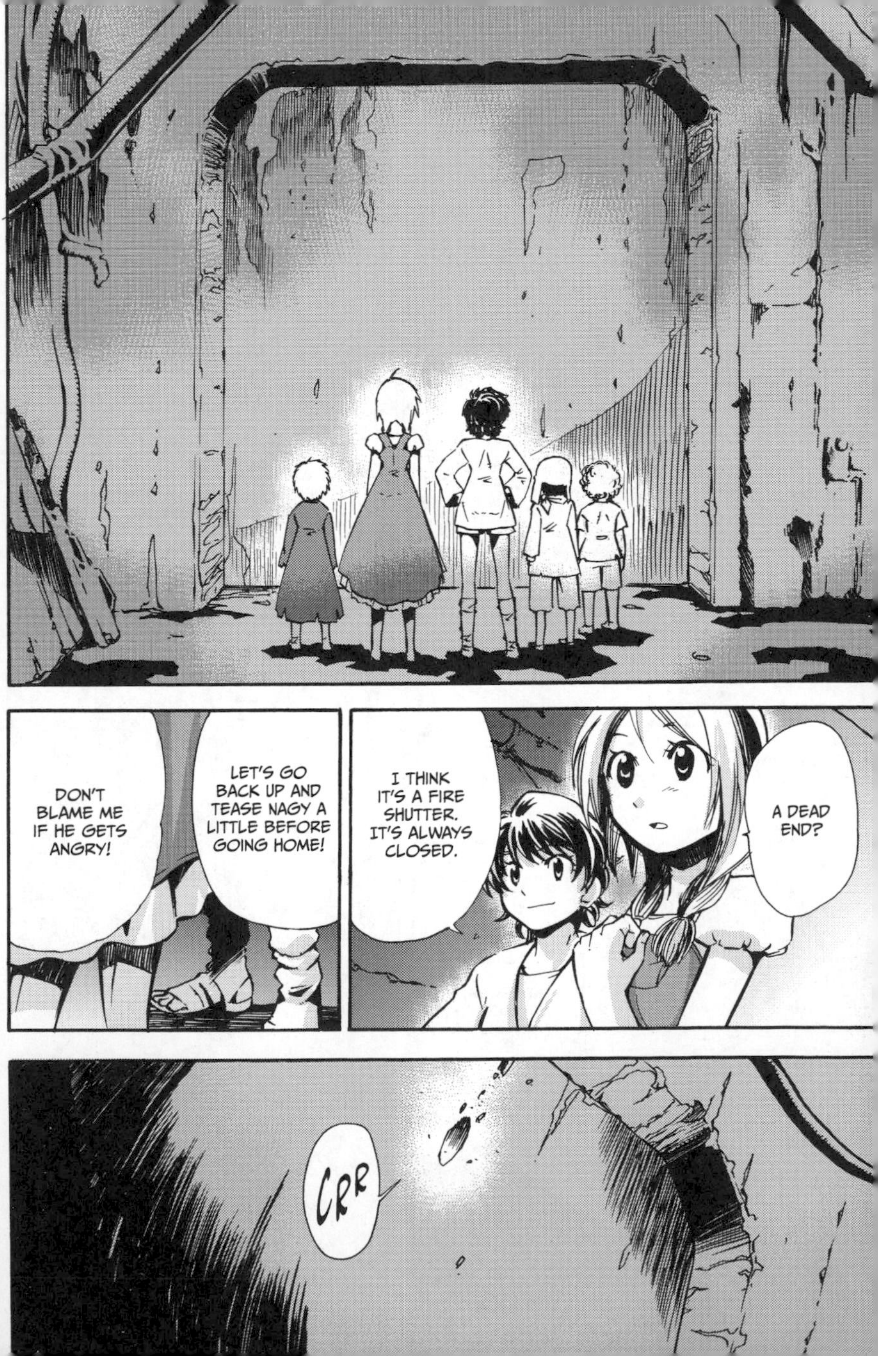
A DEAD END?
I THINK IT'S A FIRE SHUTTER. IT'S ALWAYS CLOSED.
LET'S GO BACK UP AND TEASE NAGY A LITTLE BEFORE GOING HOME!
DON'T BLAME ME IF HE GETS ANGRY!
CRR

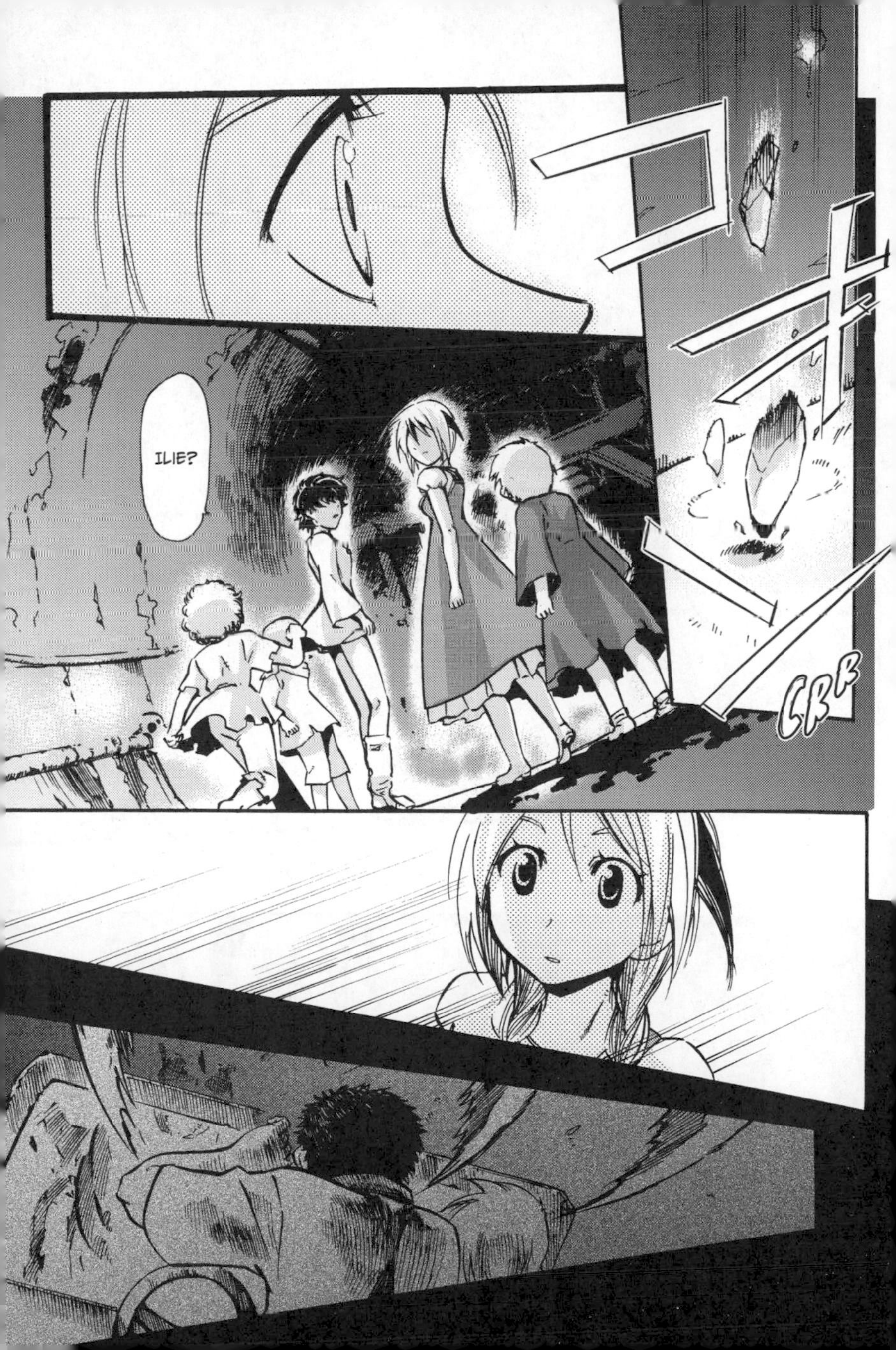
CRR
ILIE?

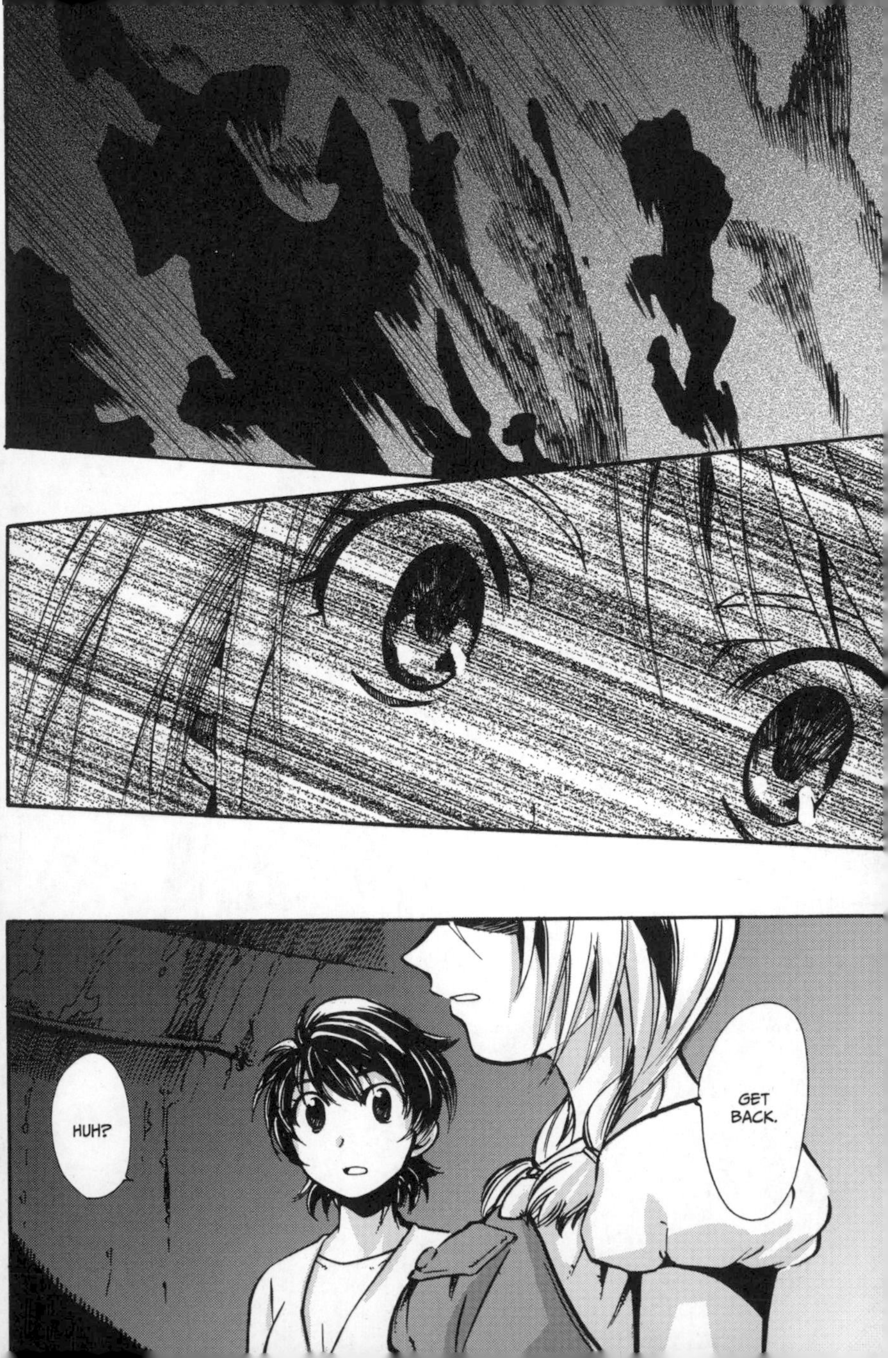
GET BACK.
HUH?

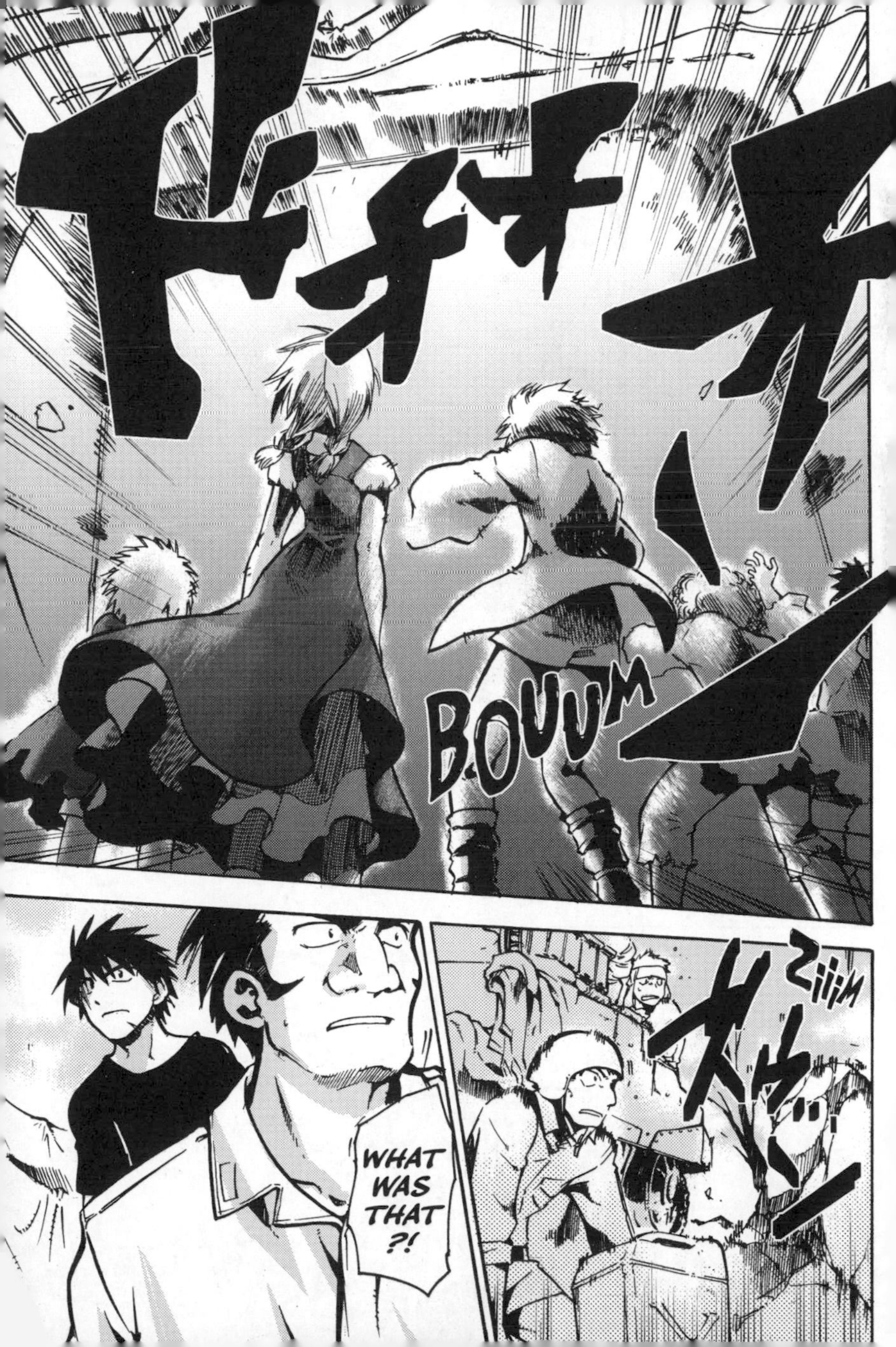
BOUUM
ZIIIM
WHAT WAS THAT ?!

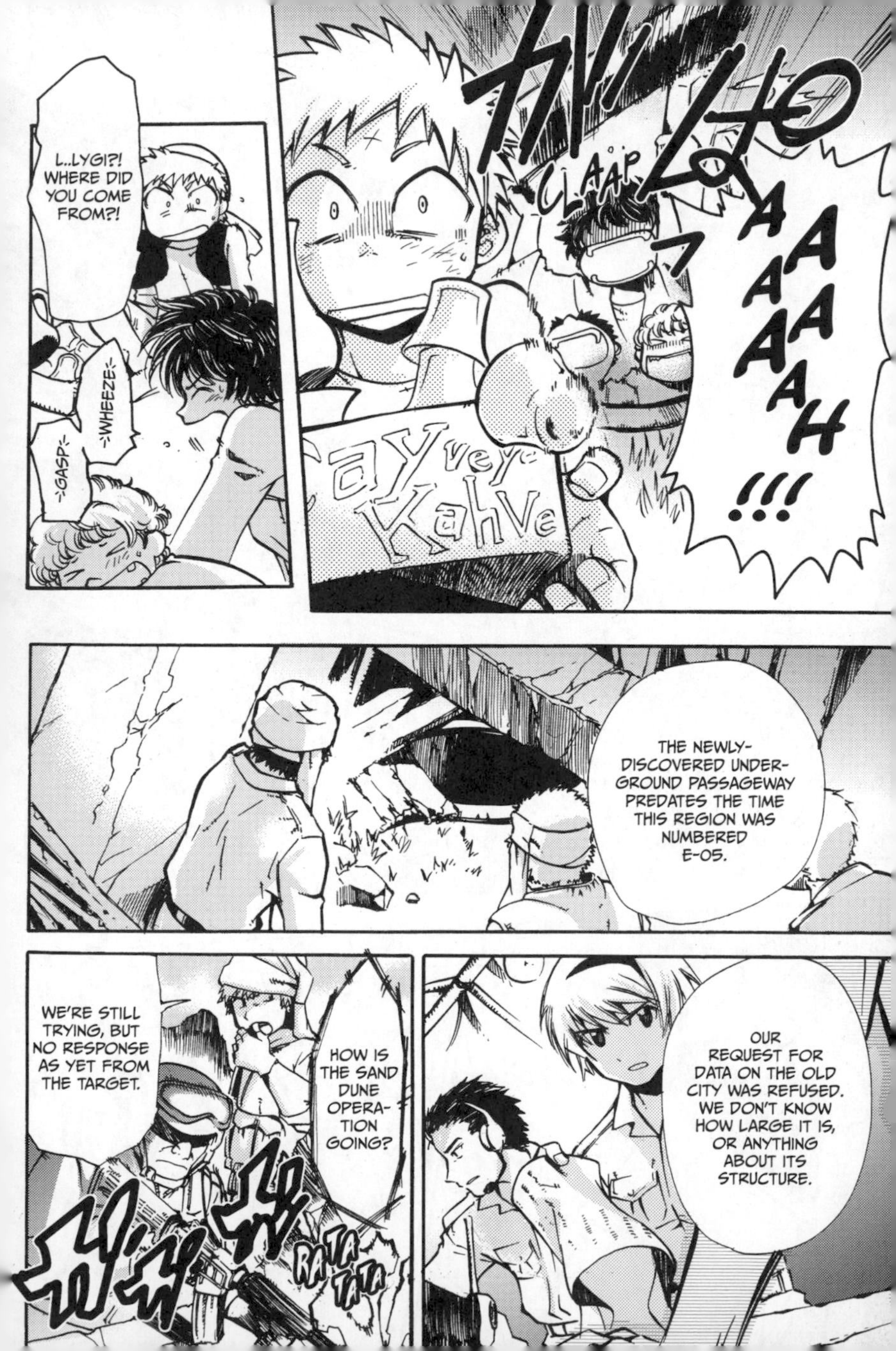
CLAAP
AAAAAAAH!!!
L..LYGI?! WHERE DID YOU COME FROM?!
-WHEEZE-
-GASP-
THE NEWLY-DISCOVERED UNDER-GROUND PASSAGEWAY PREDATES THE TIME THIS REGION WAS NUMBERED E-05.
OUR REQUEST FOR DATA ON THE OLD CITY WAS REFUSED. WE DON'T KNOW HOW LARGE IT IS, OR ANYTHING ABOUT ITS STRUCTURE.
HOW IS THE SAND DUNE OPERATION GOING?
WE'RE STILL TRYING, BUT NO RESPONSE AS YET FROM THE TARGET.
RATATATA

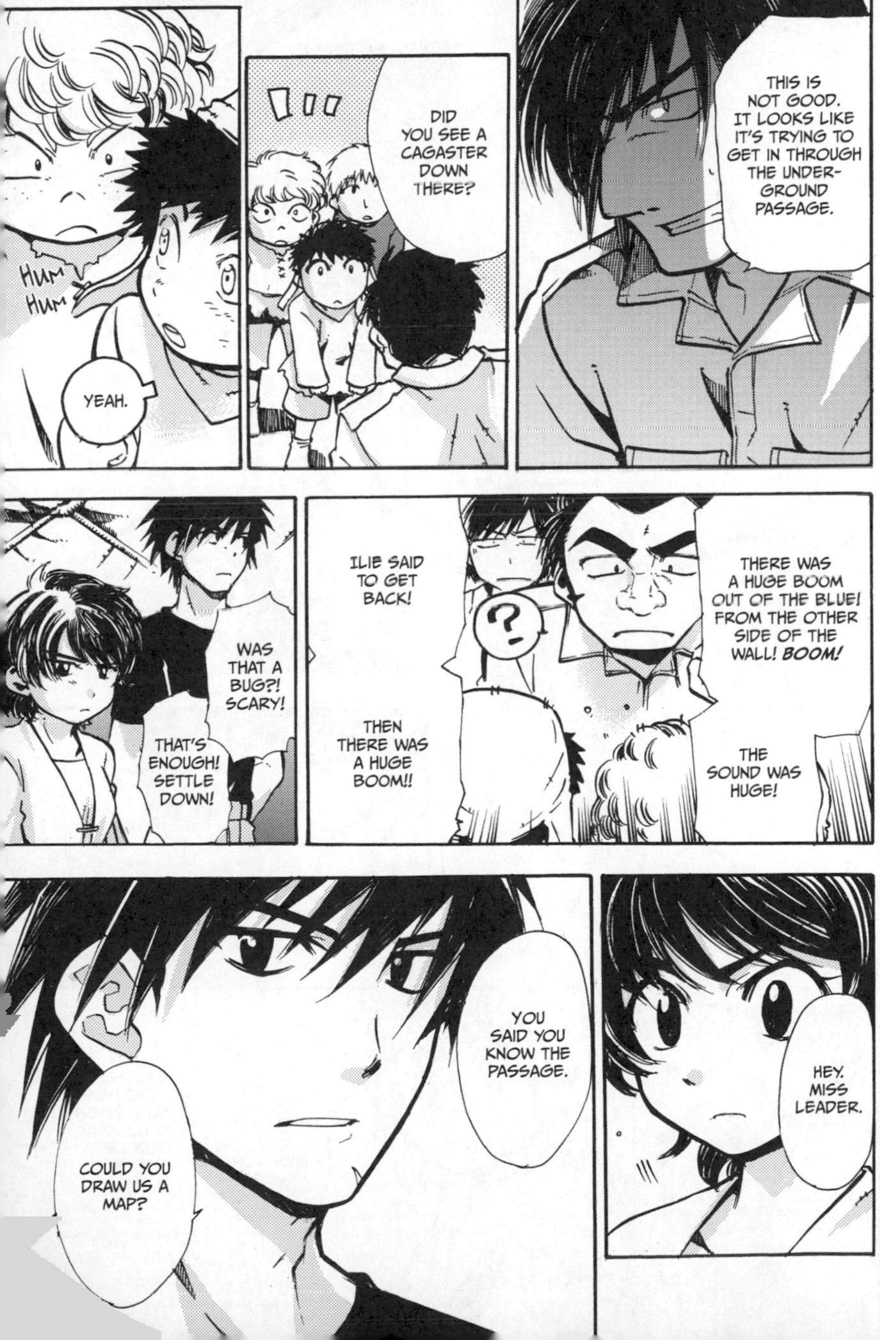
THIS IS NOT GOOD. IT LOOKS LIKE IT'S TRYING TO GET IN THROUGH THE UNDER-GROUND PASSAGE.
DID YOU SEE A CAGASTER DOWN THERE?
HUM HUM
YEAH.
THERE WAS A HUGE BOOM OUT OF THE BLUE! FROM THE OTHER SIDE OF THE WALL! *BOOM!*
ILIE SAID TO GET BACK!
?
THE SOUND WAS HUGE!
THEN THERE WAS A HUGE BOOM!!
WAS THAT A BUG?! SCARY!
THAT'S ENOUGH! SETTLE DOWN!
HEY. MISS LEADER.
YOU SAID YOU KNOW THE PASSAGE.
COULD YOU DRAW US A MAP?

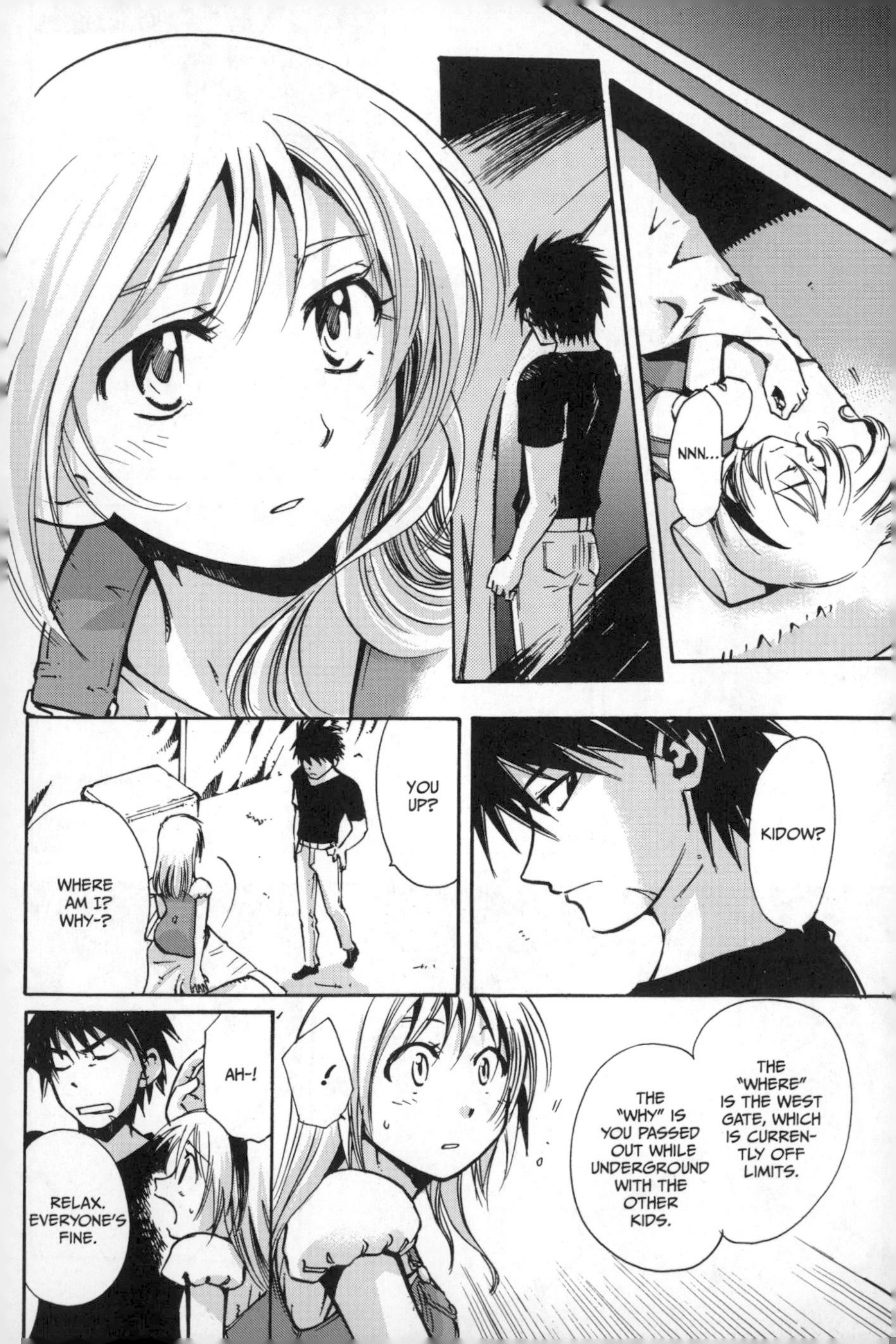
NNN...
KIDOW?
YOU UP?
WHERE AM I? WHY-?
THE "WHERE" IS THE WEST GATE, WHICH IS CURRENTLY OFF LIMITS.
THE "WHY" IS YOU PASSED OUT WHILE UNDERGROUND WITH THE OTHER KIDS.
!
AH-!
RELAX. EVERYONE'S FINE.

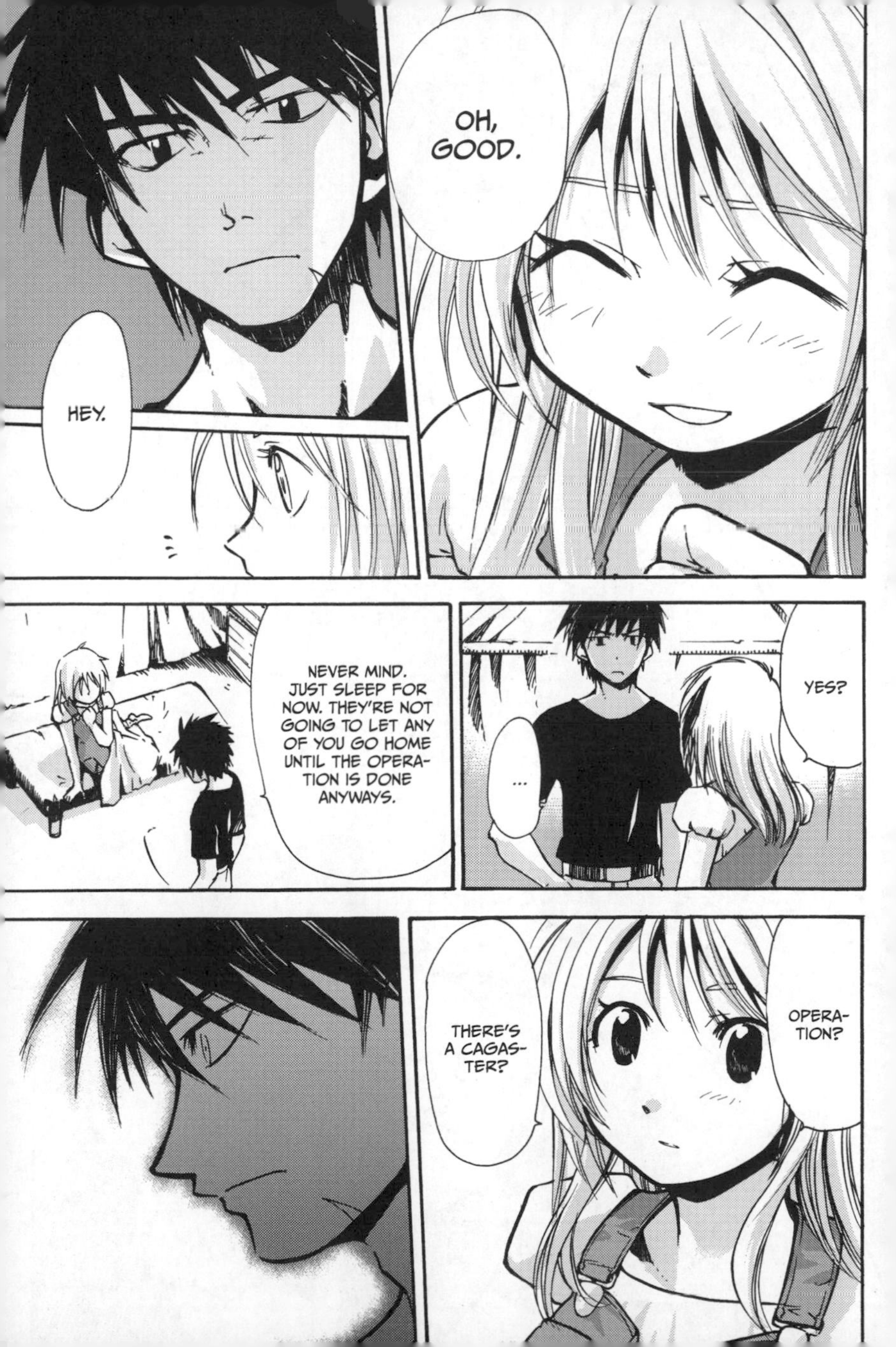
OH, GOOD.
HEY.
YES?
...
NEVER MIND. JUST SLEEP FOR NOW. THEY'RE NOT GOING TO LET ANY OF YOU GO HOME UNTIL THE OPERATION IS DONE ANYWAYS.
OPERATION?
THERE'S A CAGASTER?

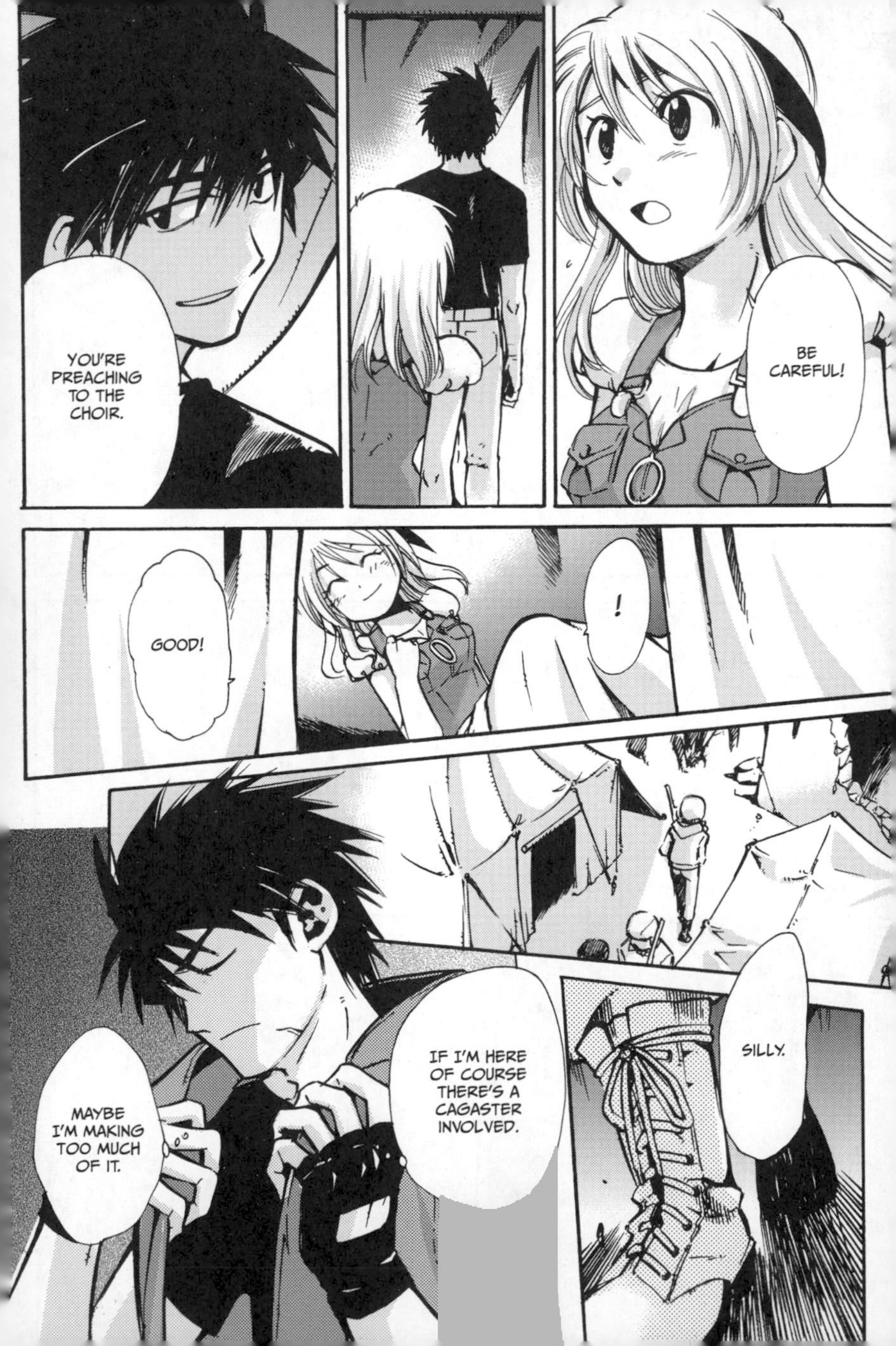
BE CAREFUL!
YOU'RE PREACHING TO THE CHOIR.
!
GOOD!
SILLY.
IF I'M HERE OF COURSE THERE'S A CAGASTER INVOLVED.
MAYBE I'M MAKING TOO MUCH OF IT.

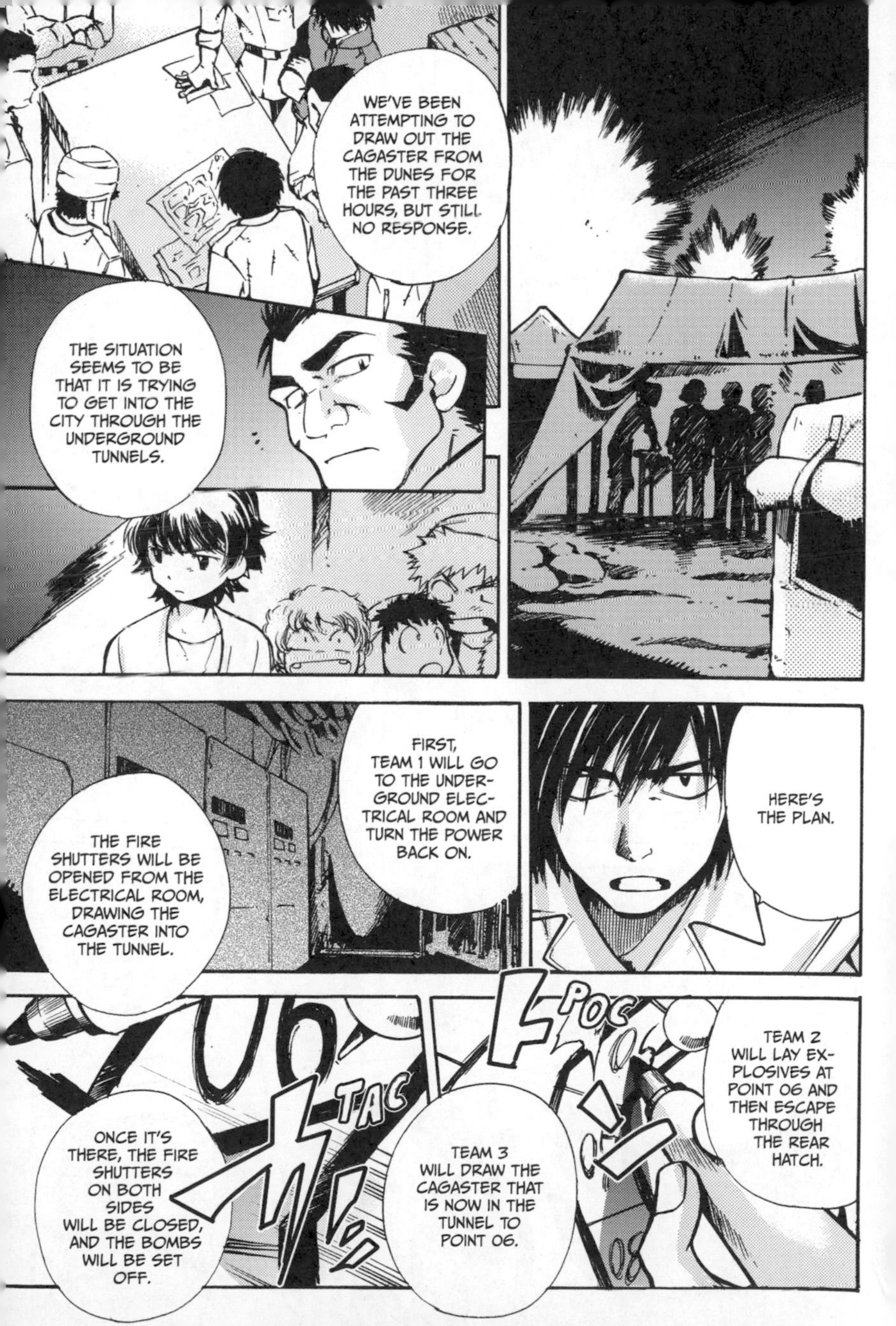
WE'VE BEEN ATTEMPTING TO DRAW OUT THE CAGASTER FROM THE DUNES FOR THE PAST THREE HOURS, BUT STILL NO RESPONSE.
THE SITUATION SEEMS TO BE THAT IT IS TRYING TO GET INTO THE CITY THROUGH THE UNDERGROUND TUNNELS.
HERE'S THE PLAN.
FIRST, TEAM 1 WILL GO TO THE UNDER-GROUND ELEC-TRICAL ROOM AND TURN THE POWER BACK ON.
THE FIRE SHUTTERS WILL BE OPENED FROM THE ELECTRICAL ROOM, DRAWING THE CAGASTER INTO THE TUNNEL.
POC
TEAM 2 WILL LAY EX-PLOSIVES AT POINT 06 AND THEN ESCAPE THROUGH THE REAR HATCH.
TEAM 3 WILL DRAW THE CAGASTER THAT IS NOW IN THE TUNNEL TO POINT 06.
TAC
ONCE IT'S THERE, THE FIRE SHUTTERS ON BOTH SIDES WILL BE CLOSED, AND THE BOMBS WILL BE SET OFF.

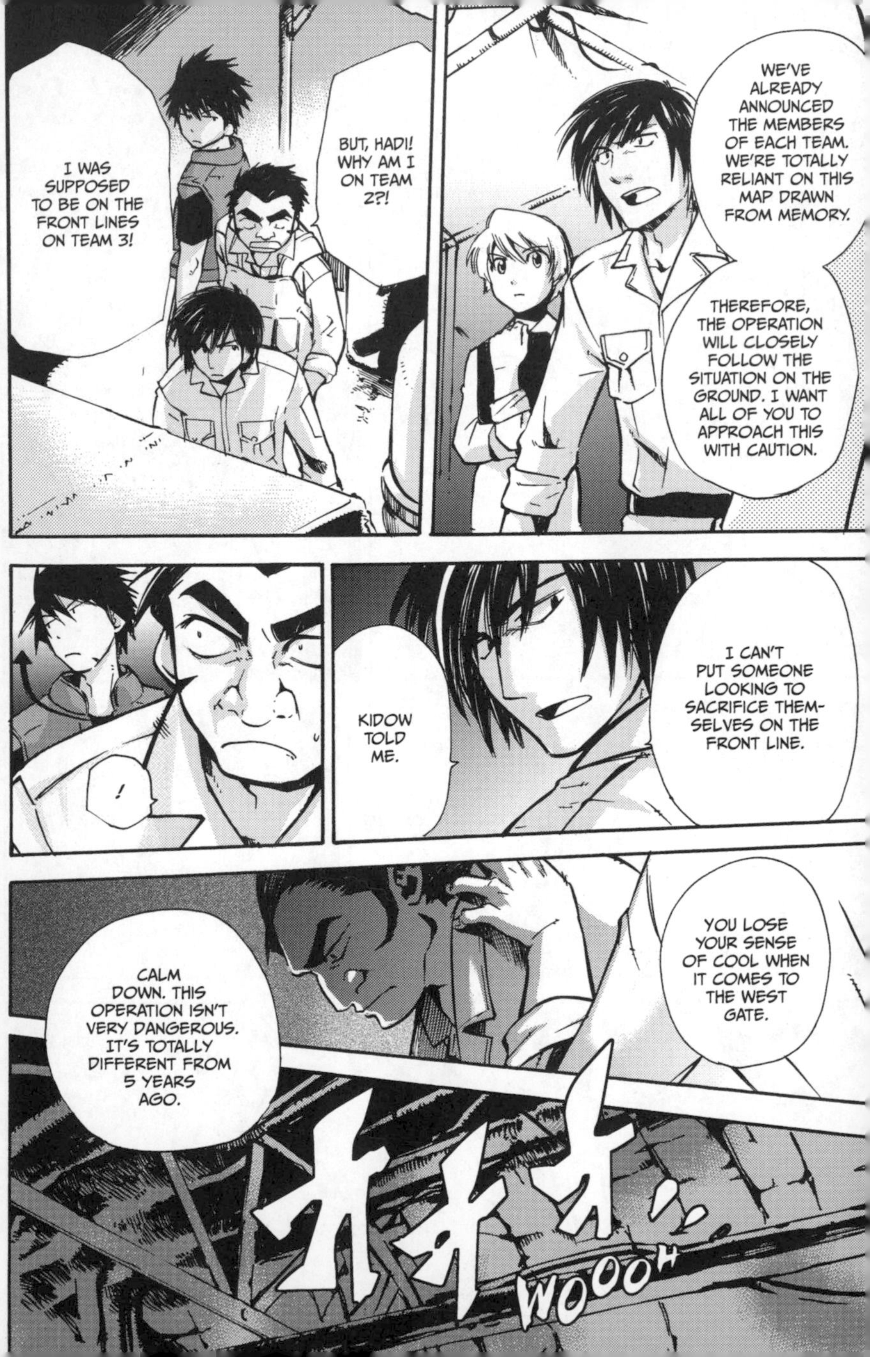
WE'VE ALREADY ANNOUNCED THE MEMBERS OF EACH TEAM. WE'RE TOTALLY RELIANT ON THIS MAP DRAWN FROM MEMORY.
THEREFORE, THE OPERATION WILL CLOSELY FOLLOW THE SITUATION ON THE GROUND. I WANT ALL OF YOU TO APPROACH THIS WITH CAUTION.
BUT, HADI! WHY AM I ON TEAM 2?!
I WAS SUPPOSED TO BE ON THE FRONT LINES ON TEAM 3!
I CAN'T PUT SOMEONE LOOKING TO SACRIFICE THEM-SELVES ON THE FRONT LINE.
KIDOW TOLD ME.
!
YOU LOSE YOUR SENSE OF COOL WHEN IT COMES TO THE WEST GATE.
CALM DOWN. THIS OPERATION ISN'T VERY DANGEROUS. IT'S TOTALLY DIFFERENT FROM 5 YEARS AGO.
WOOOH

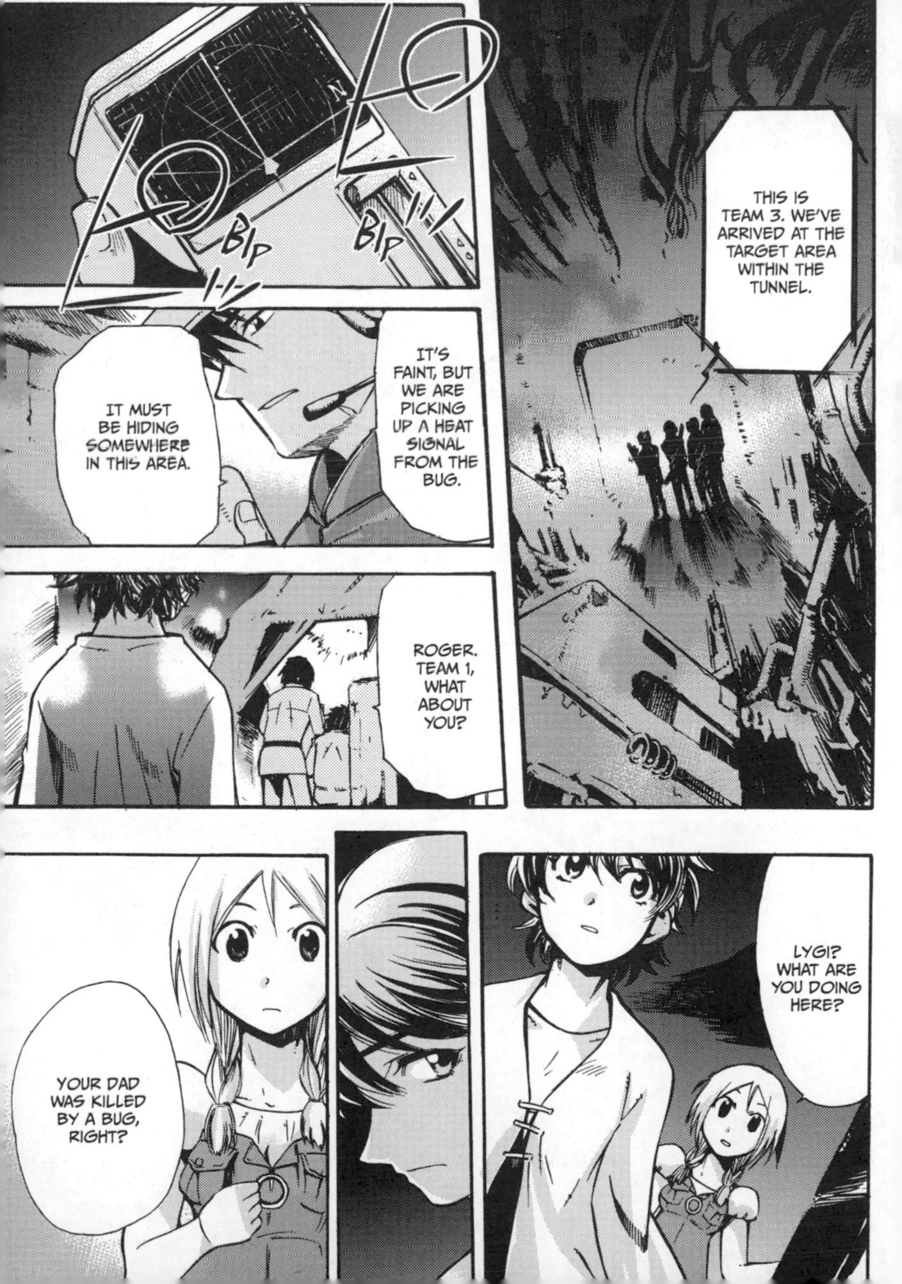
THIS IS TEAM 3. WE'VE ARRIVED AT THE TARGET AREA WITHIN THE TUNNEL.
BIP
BIP
IT'S FAINT, BUT WE ARE PICKING UP A HEAT SIGNAL FROM THE BUG.
IT MUST BE HIDING SOMEWHERE IN THIS AREA.
ROGER. TEAM 1, WHAT ABOUT YOU?
LYGI? WHAT ARE YOU DOING HERE?
YOUR DAD WAS KILLED BY A BUG, RIGHT?

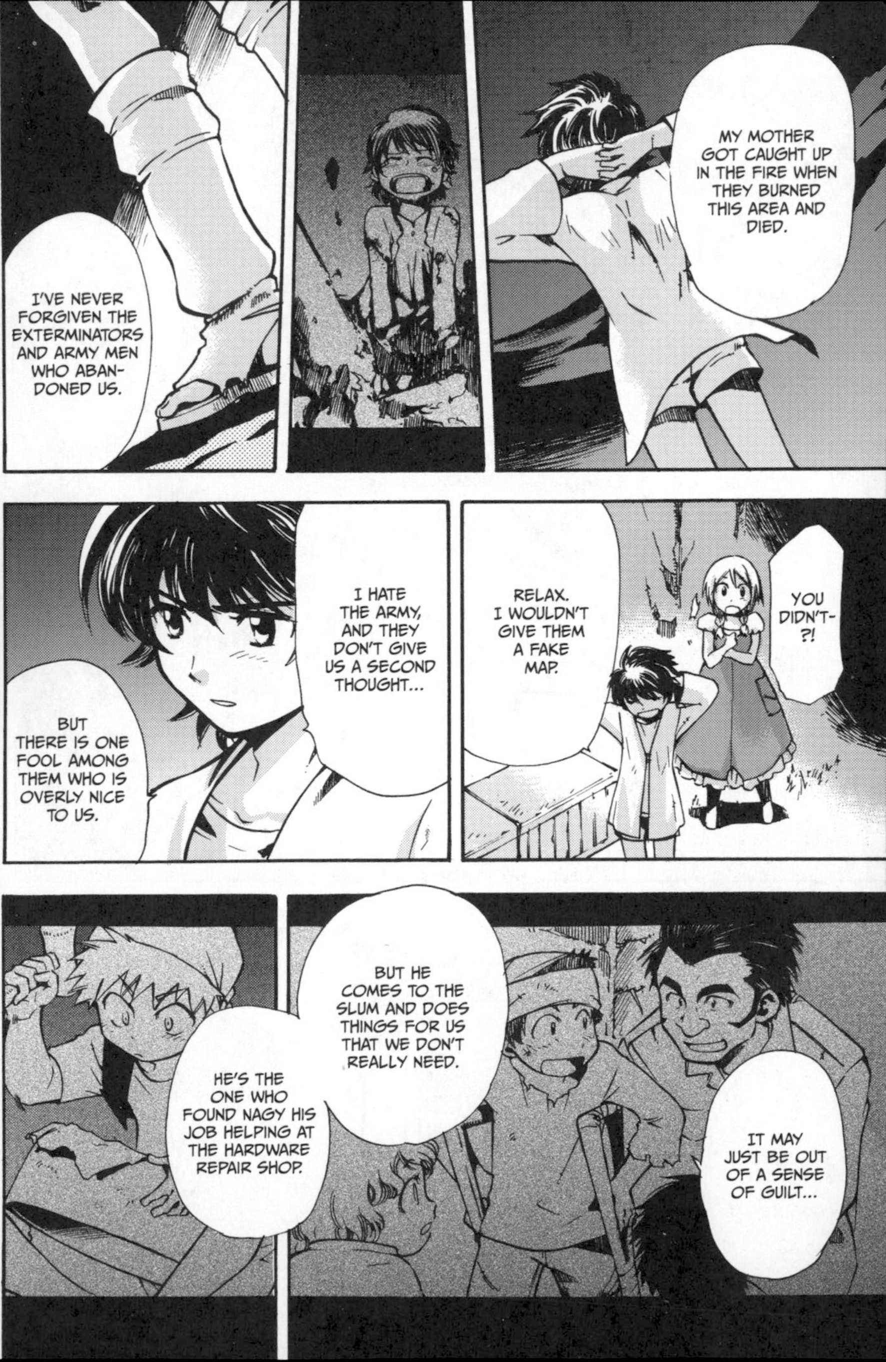
MY MOTHER GOT CAUGHT UP IN THE FIRE WHEN THEY BURNED THIS AREA AND DIED.
I'VE NEVER FORGIVEN THE EXTERMINATORS AND ARMY MEN WHO ABAN-DONED US.
YOU DIDN'T-?!
RELAX. I WOULDN'T GIVE THEM A FAKE MAP.
I HATE THE ARMY, AND THEY DON'T GIVE US A SECOND THOUGHT...
BUT THERE IS ONE FOOL AMONG THEM WHO IS OVERLY NICE TO US.
BUT HE COMES TO THE SLUM AND DOES THINGS FOR US THAT WE DON'T REALLY NEED.
HE'S THE ONE WHO FOUND NAGY HIS JOB HELPING AT THE HARDWARE REPAIR SHOP.
IT MAY JUST BE OUT OF A SENSE OF GUILT...

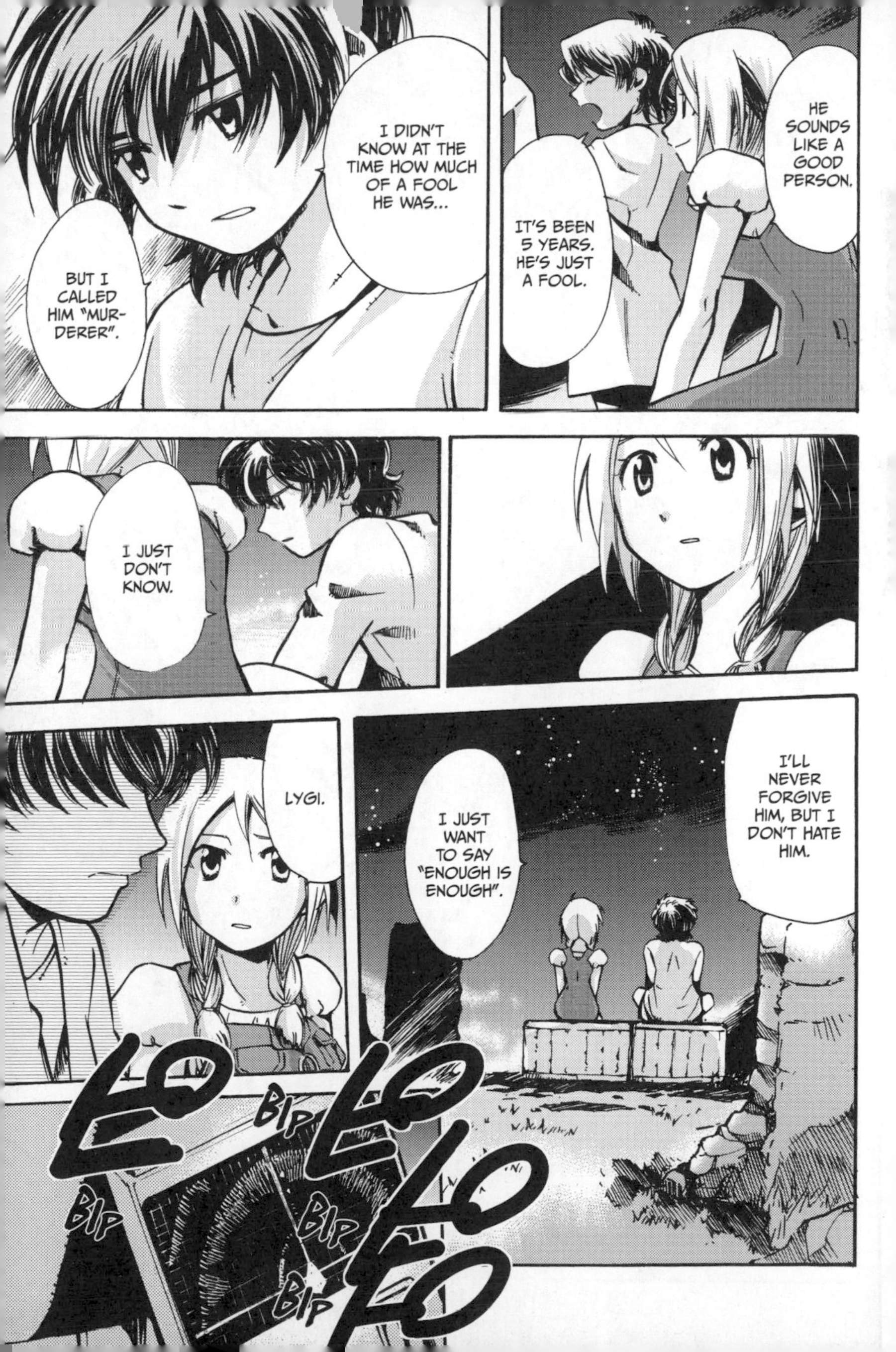
HE SOUNDS LIKE A GOOD PERSON.
IT'S BEEN 5 YEARS. HE'S JUST A FOOL.
I DIDN'T KNOW AT THE TIME HOW MUCH OF A FOOL HE WAS...
BUT I CALLED HIM "MUR-DERER".
I JUST DON'T KNOW.
I'LL NEVER FORGIVE HIM, BUT I DON'T HATE HIM.
I JUST WANT TO SAY "ENOUGH IS ENOUGH".
LYGI.
LO LO LO LO
BIP BIP BIP BIP BIP

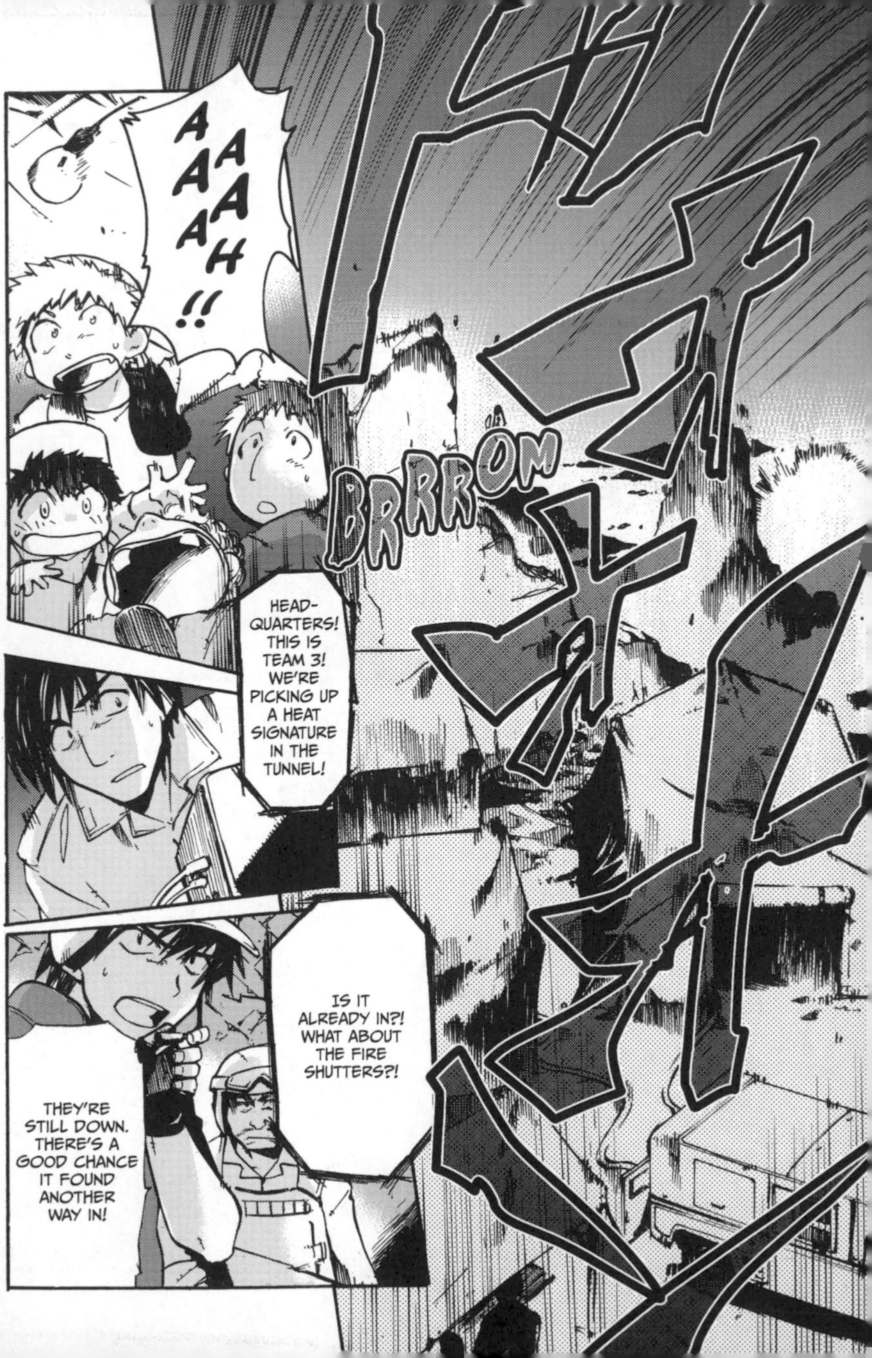
BRRROM
AAAAAH!!
HEAD-QUARTERS! THIS IS TEAM 3! WE'RE PICKING UP A HEAT SIGNATURE IN THE TUNNEL!
IS IT ALREADY IN?! WHAT ABOUT THE FIRE SHUTTERS?!
THEY'RE STILL DOWN. THERE'S A GOOD CHANCE IT FOUND ANOTHER WAY IN!

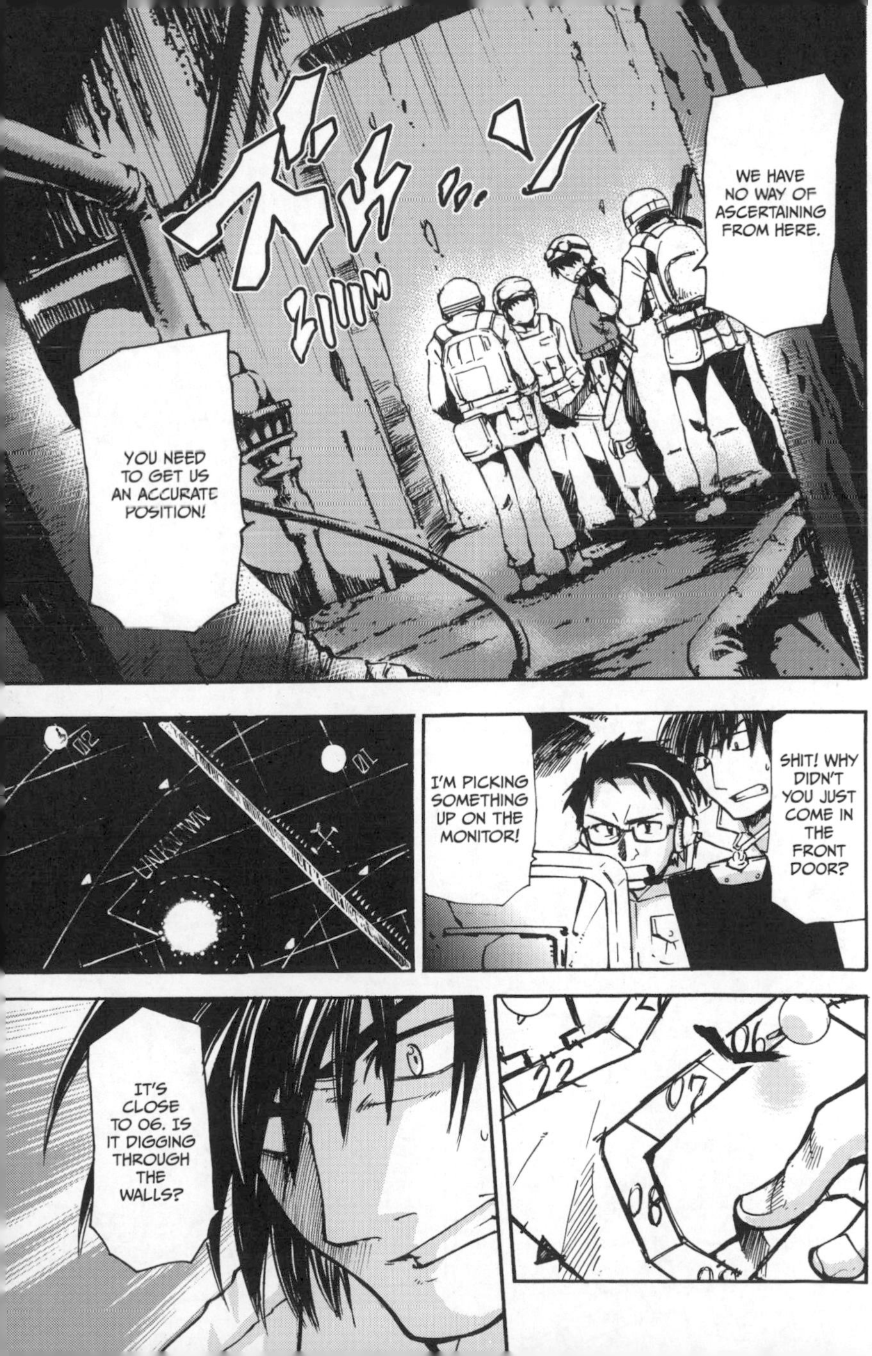
WE HAVE NO WAY OF ASCERTAINING FROM HERE.
ZIIIM
YOU NEED TO GET US AN ACCURATE POSITION!
SHIT! WHY DIDN'T YOU JUST COME IN THE FRONT DOOR?
I'M PICKING SOMETHING UP ON THE MONITOR!
01
02
06
22
07
08
IT'S CLOSE TO 06. IS IT DIGGING THROUGH THE WALLS?

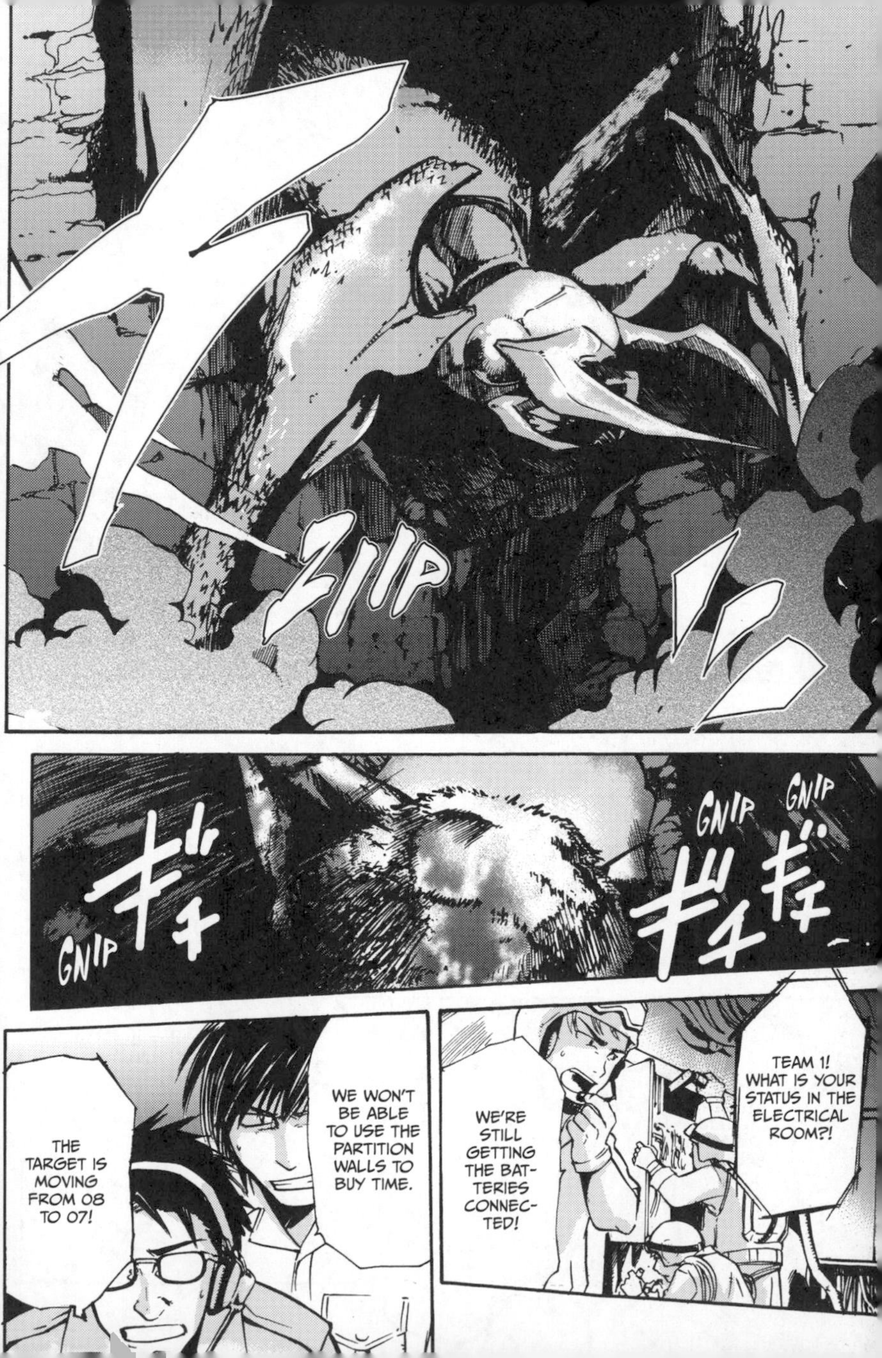
ZIP
GNIP
GNIP
GNIP
TEAM 1! WHAT IS YOUR STATUS IN THE ELECTRICAL ROOM?!
WE'RE STILL GETTING THE BAT-TERIES CONNEC-TED!
WE WON'T BE ABLE TO USE THE PARTITION WALLS TO BUY TIME.
THE TARGET IS MOVING FROM 08 TO 07!

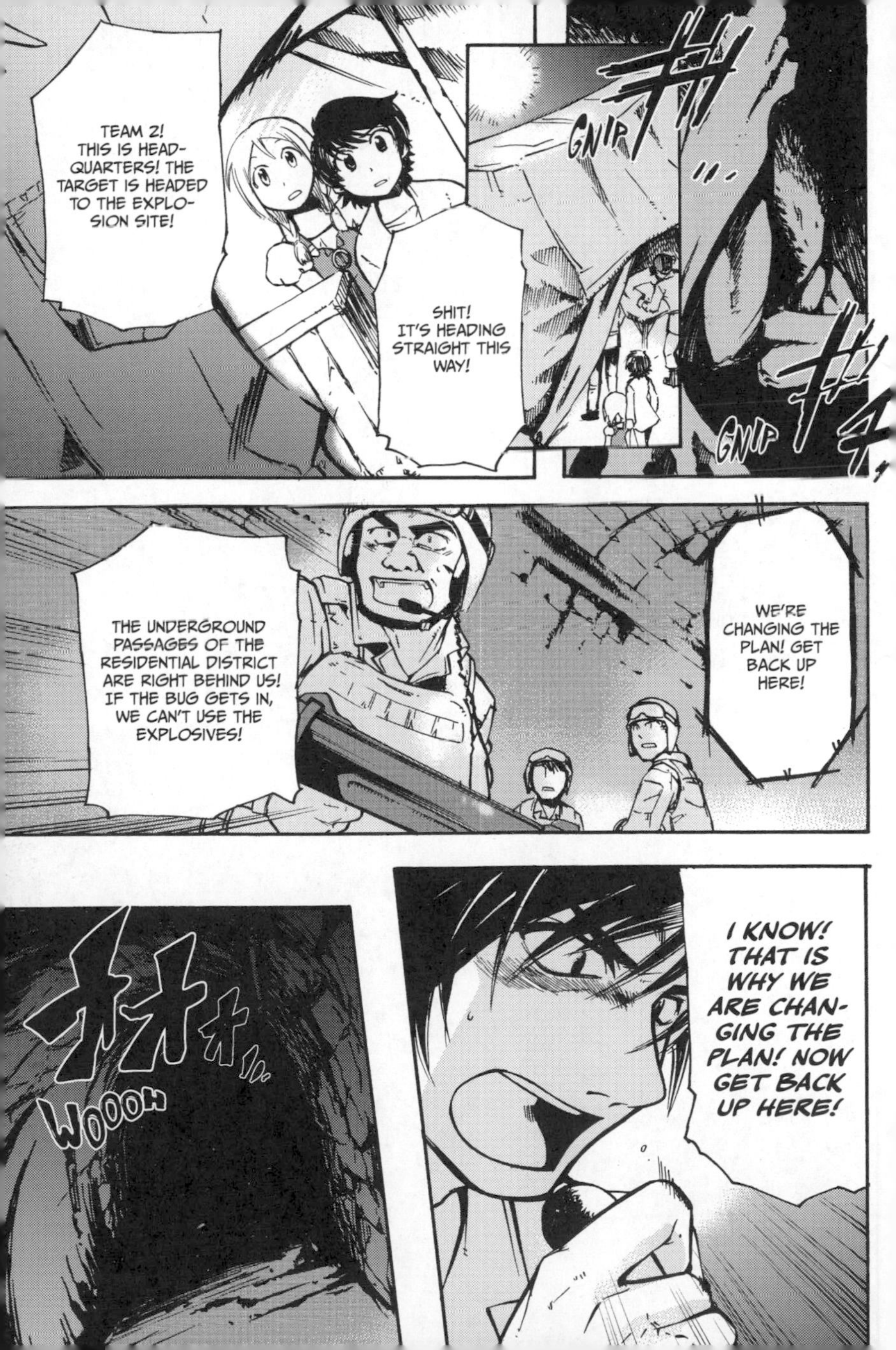
GNIP
GNIP
TEAM 2! THIS IS HEAD-QUARTERS! THE TARGET IS HEADED TO THE EXPLO-SION SITE!
SHIT! IT'S HEADING STRAIGHT THIS WAY!
WE'RE CHANGING THE PLAN! GET BACK UP HERE!
THE UNDERGROUND PASSAGES OF THE RESIDENTIAL DISTRICT ARE RIGHT BEHIND US! IF THE BUG GETS IN, WE CAN'T USE THE EXPLOSIVES!
I KNOW! THAT IS WHY WE ARE CHAN-GING THE PLAN! NOW GET BACK UP HERE!
WOOOH

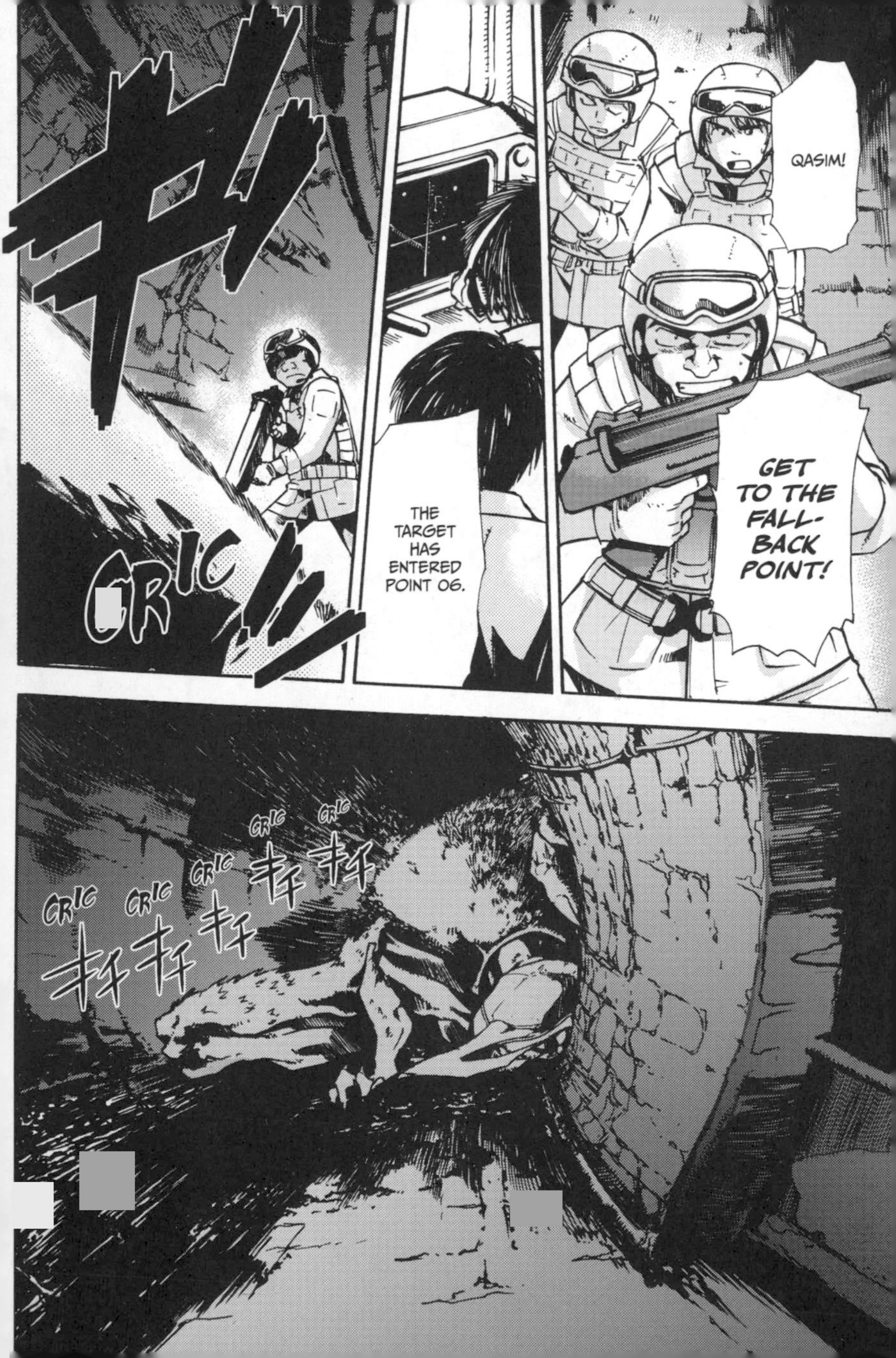
QASIM!
GET TO THE FALL-BACK POINT!
THE TARGET HAS ENTERED POINT 06.
CRIC!!
CRIC
CRIC
CRIC
CRIC
CRIC

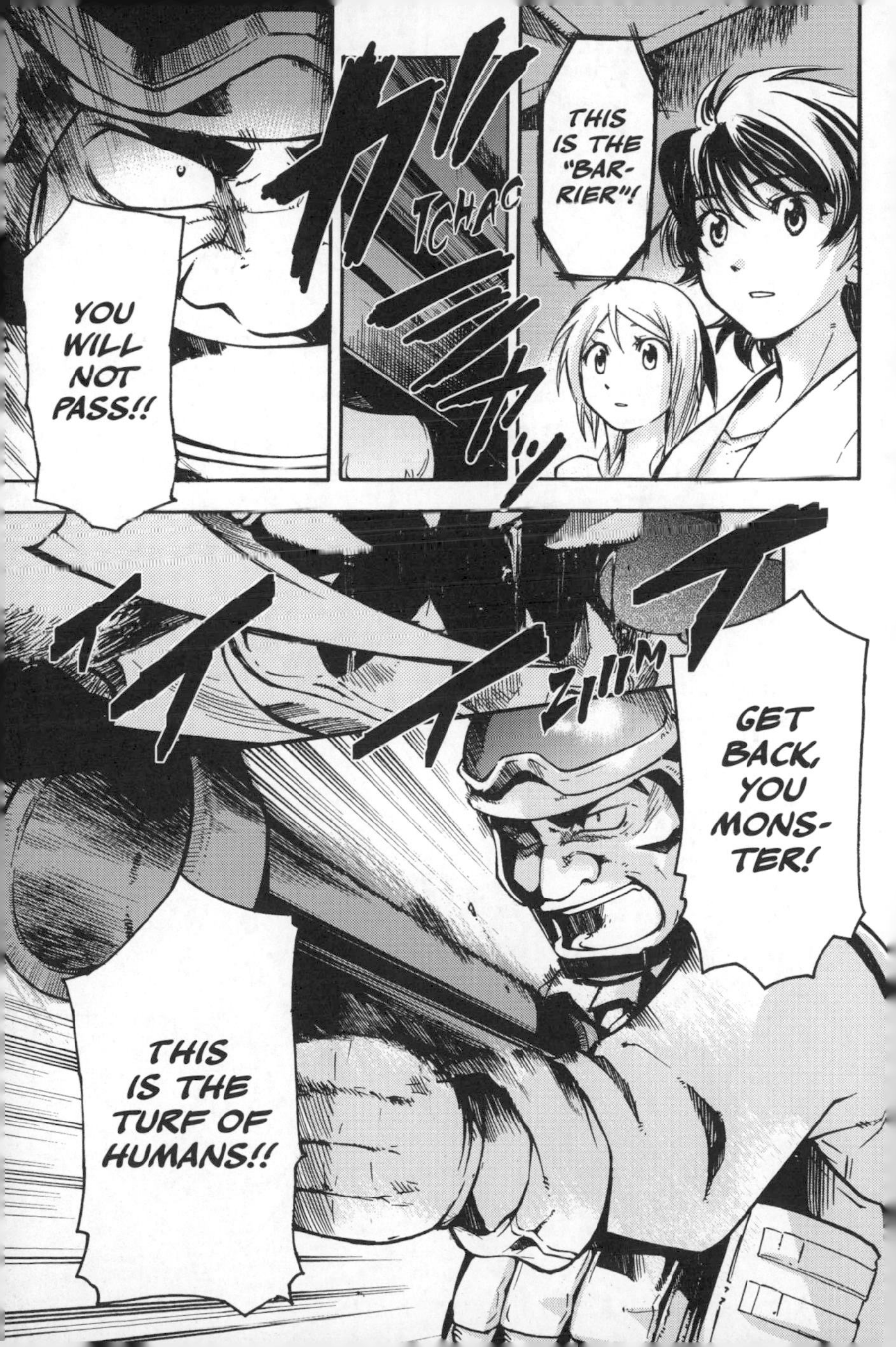
THIS IS THE "BAR-RIER"!
TCHAC
YOU WILL NOT PASS!!
GET BACK, YOU MONS-TER!
ZIIIM
THIS IS THE TURF OF HUMANS!!

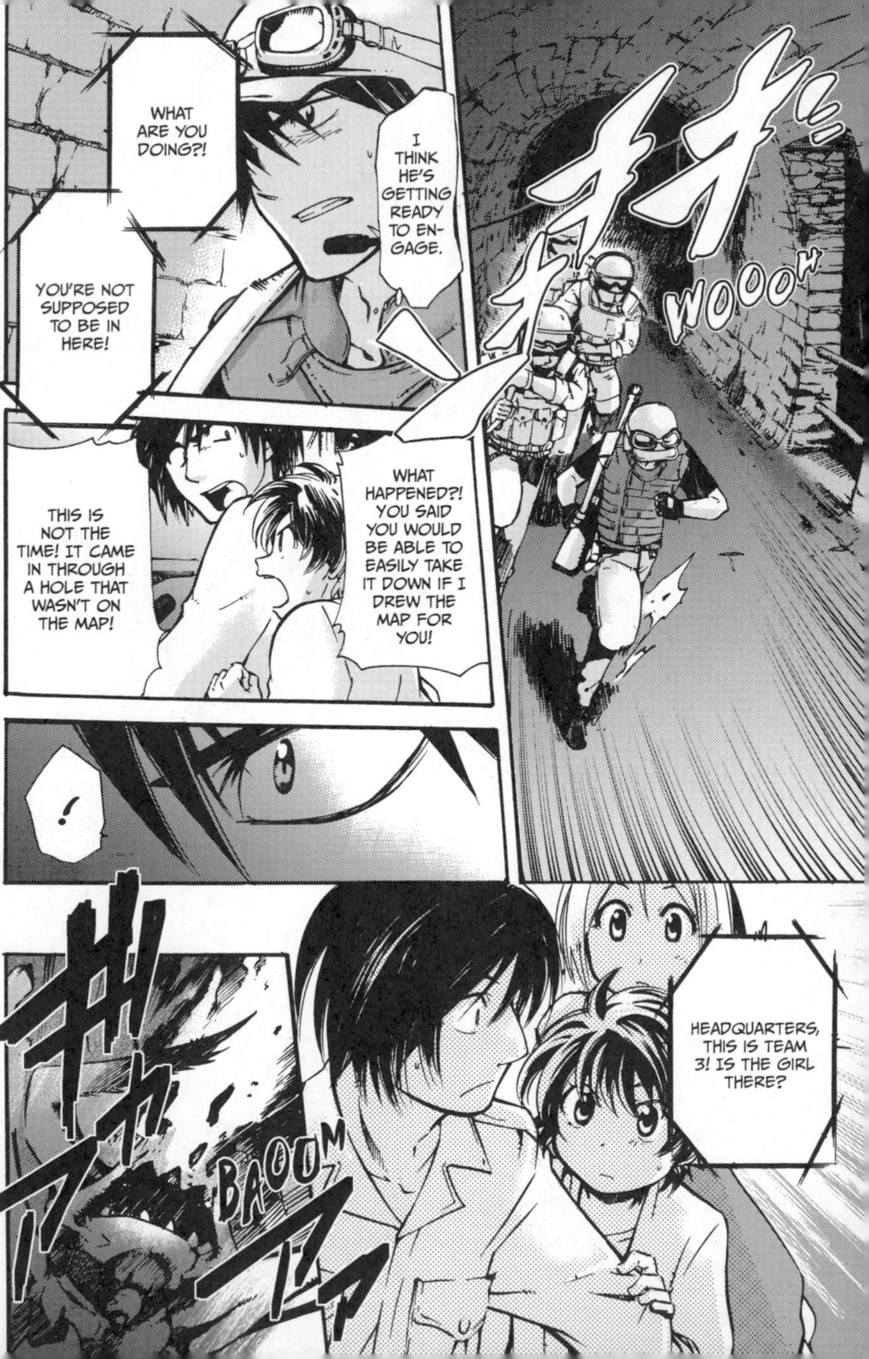
WOOOOH
I THINK HE'S GETTING READY TO EN-GAGE.
WHAT ARE YOU DOING?!
YOU'RE NOT SUPPOSED TO BE IN HERE!
WHAT HAPPENED?! YOU SAID YOU WOULD BE ABLE TO EASILY TAKE IT DOWN IF I DREW THE MAP FOR YOU!
THIS IS NOT THE TIME! IT CAME IN THROUGH A HOLE THAT WASN'T ON THE MAP!
!
HEADQUARTERS, THIS IS TEAM 3! IS THE GIRL THERE?
BAOOM

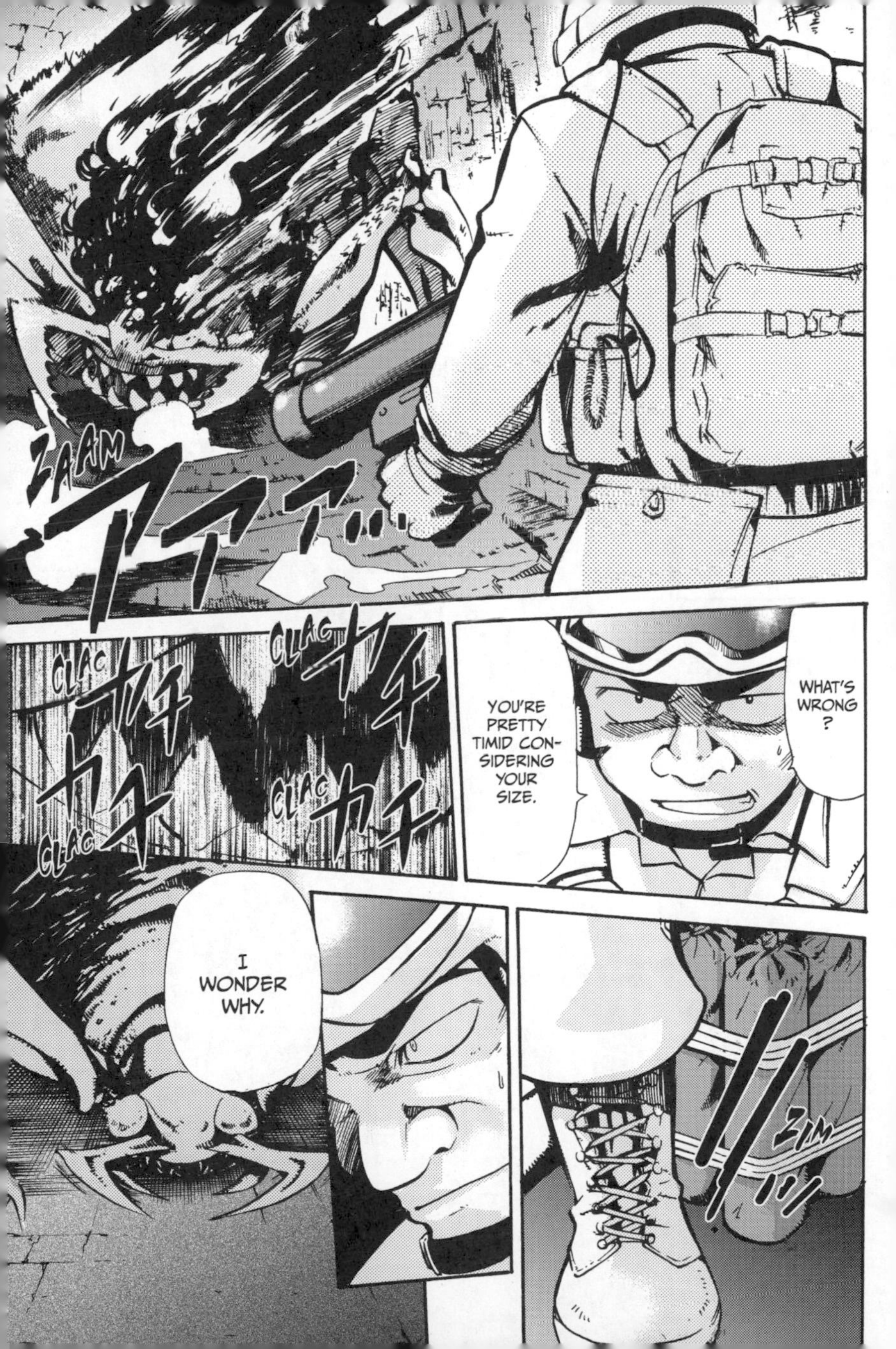

ZAAM
アアア…
WHAT'S WRONG?
YOU'RE PRETTY TIMID CONSIDERING YOUR SIZE.
CLAC CLAC CLAC CLAC
カチカチカチカチ
ZIM
I WONDER WHY.

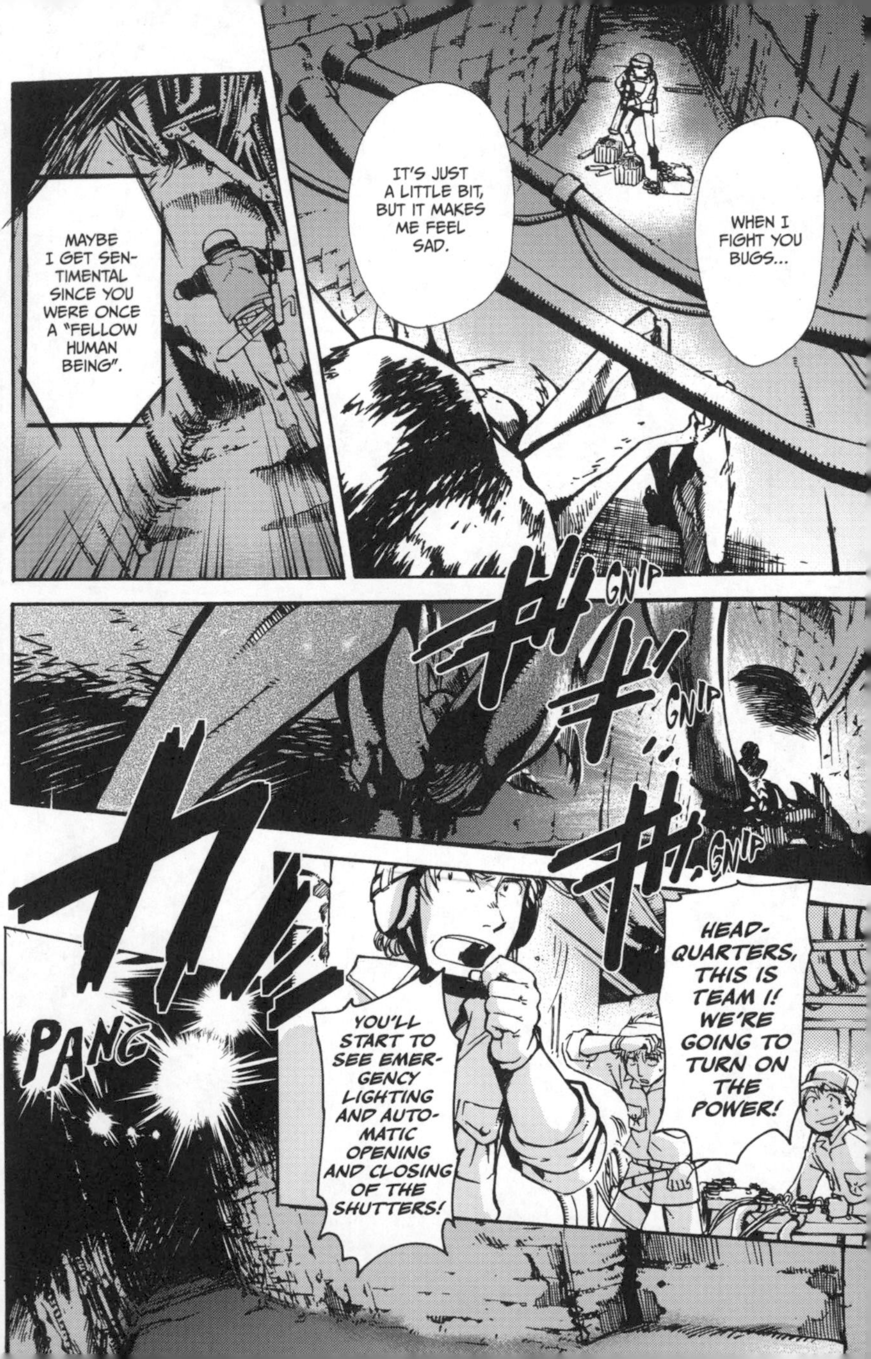
WHEN I FIGHT YOU BUGS...
IT'S JUST A LITTLE BIT, BUT IT MAKES ME FEEL SAD.
MAYBE I GET SEN-TIMENTAL SINCE YOU WERE ONCE A "FELLOW HUMAN BEING".
GNIP
GNIP
GNIP
PANG
HEAD-QUARTERS, THIS IS TEAM I! WE'RE GOING TO TURN ON THE POWER!
YOU'LL START TO SEE EMER-GENCY LIGHTING AND AUTO-MATIC OPENING AND CLOSING OF THE SHUTTERS!

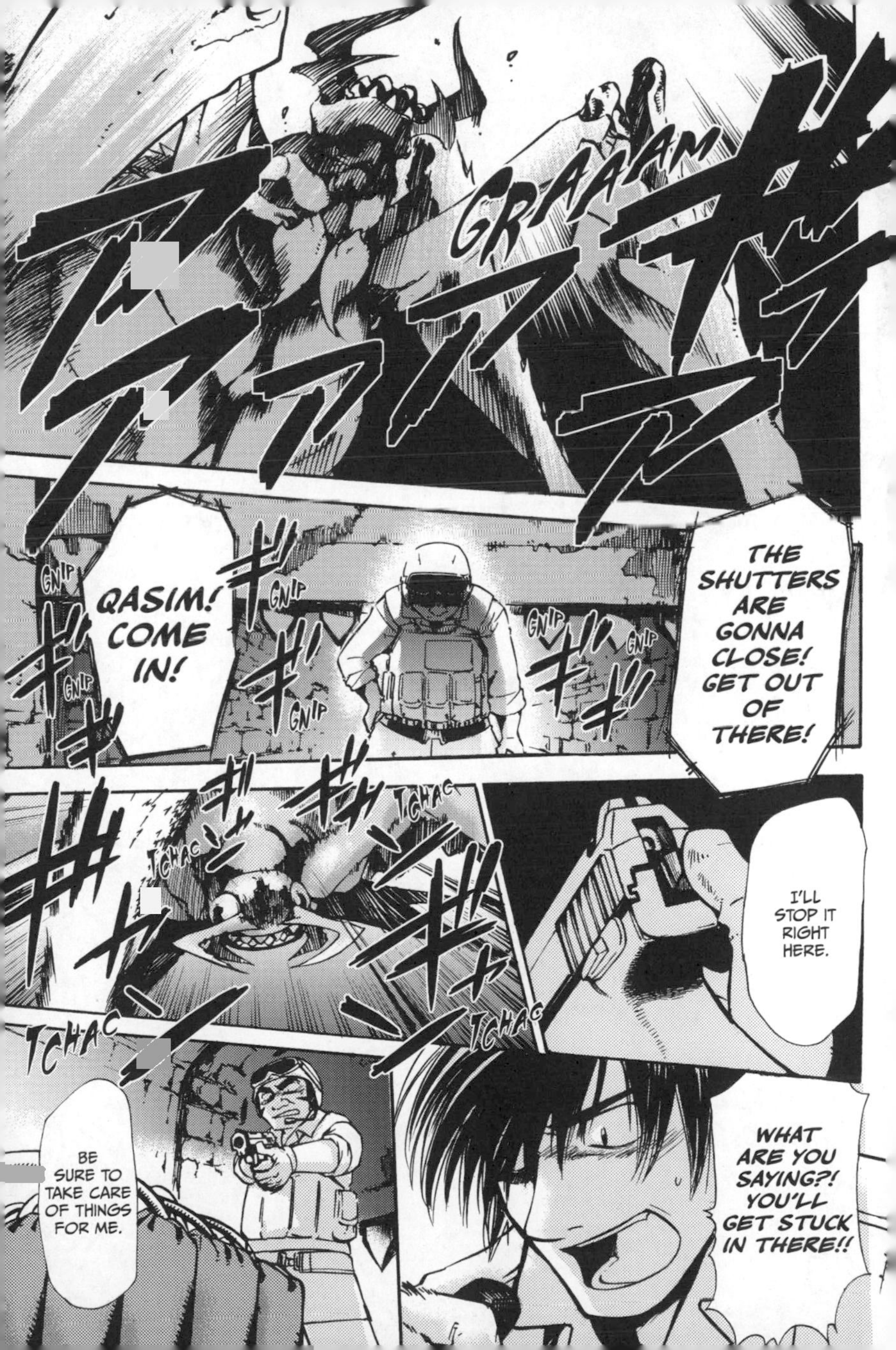
GRAAAAM
THE SHUTTERS ARE GONNA CLOSE! GET OUT OF THERE!
GNIP
GNIP
QASIM! COME IN!
GNIP
GNIP
GNIP
I'LL STOP IT RIGHT HERE.
TCHAC
TCHAC
TCHAC
TCHAC
WHAT ARE YOU SAYING?! YOU'LL GET STUCK IN THERE!!
BE SURE TO TAKE CARE OF THINGS FOR ME.

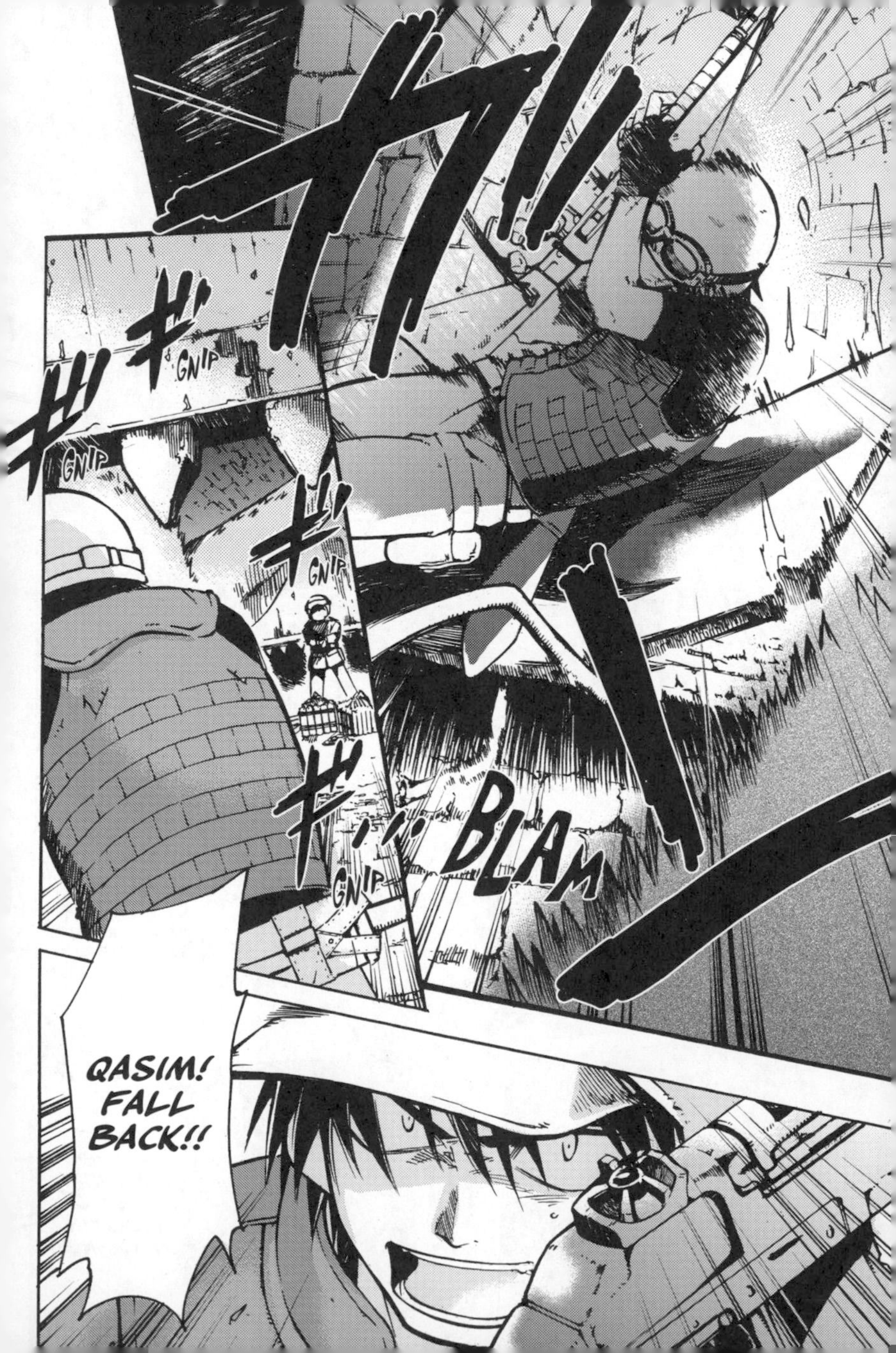
GNIP
GNIP
GNIP
GNIP
BLAM
QASIM! FALL BACK!!

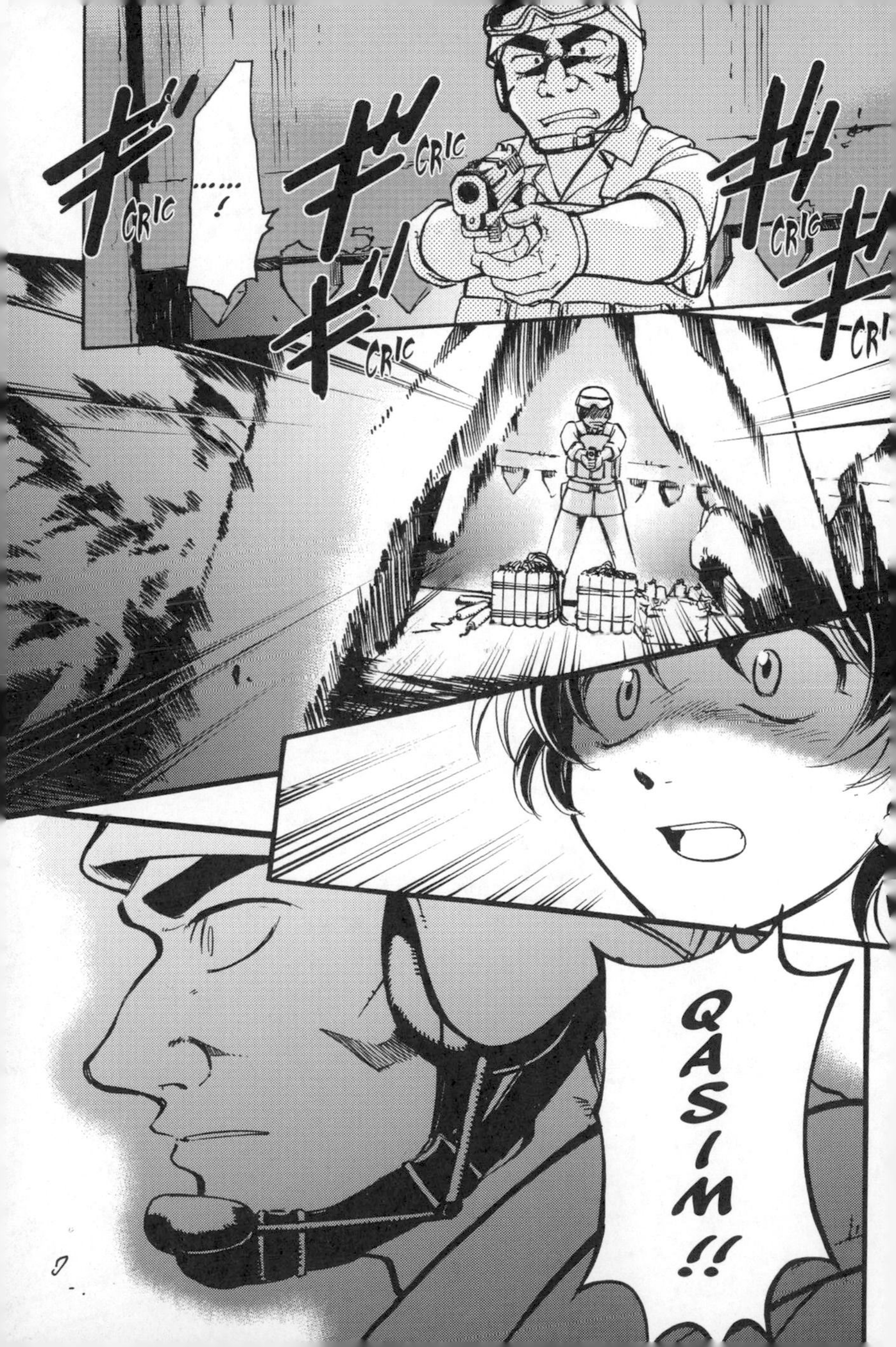

CRIC
CRI
CRIC
CRIC
......!
CRIC
QASIM!!

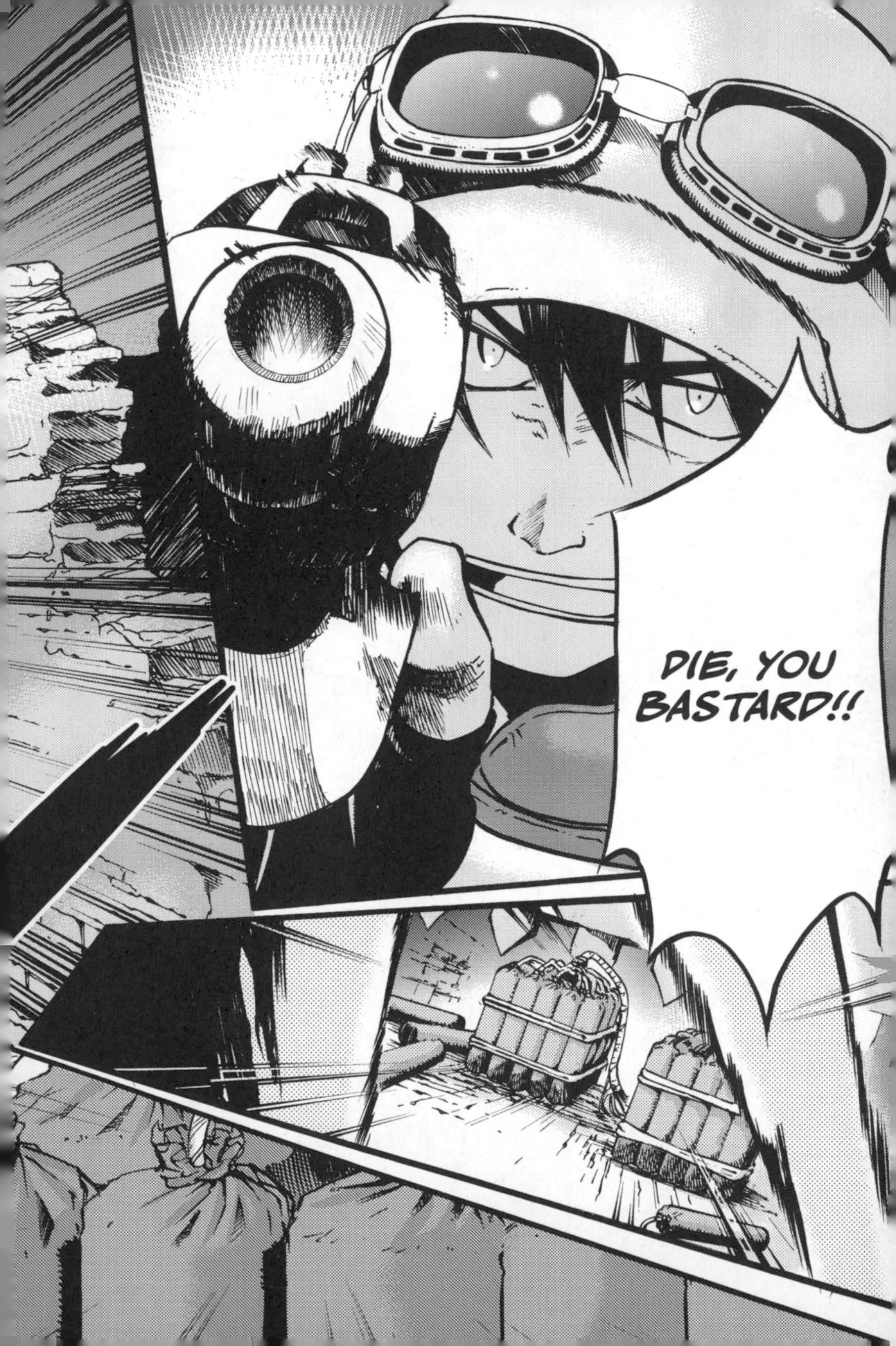
DIE, YOU BASTARD!!

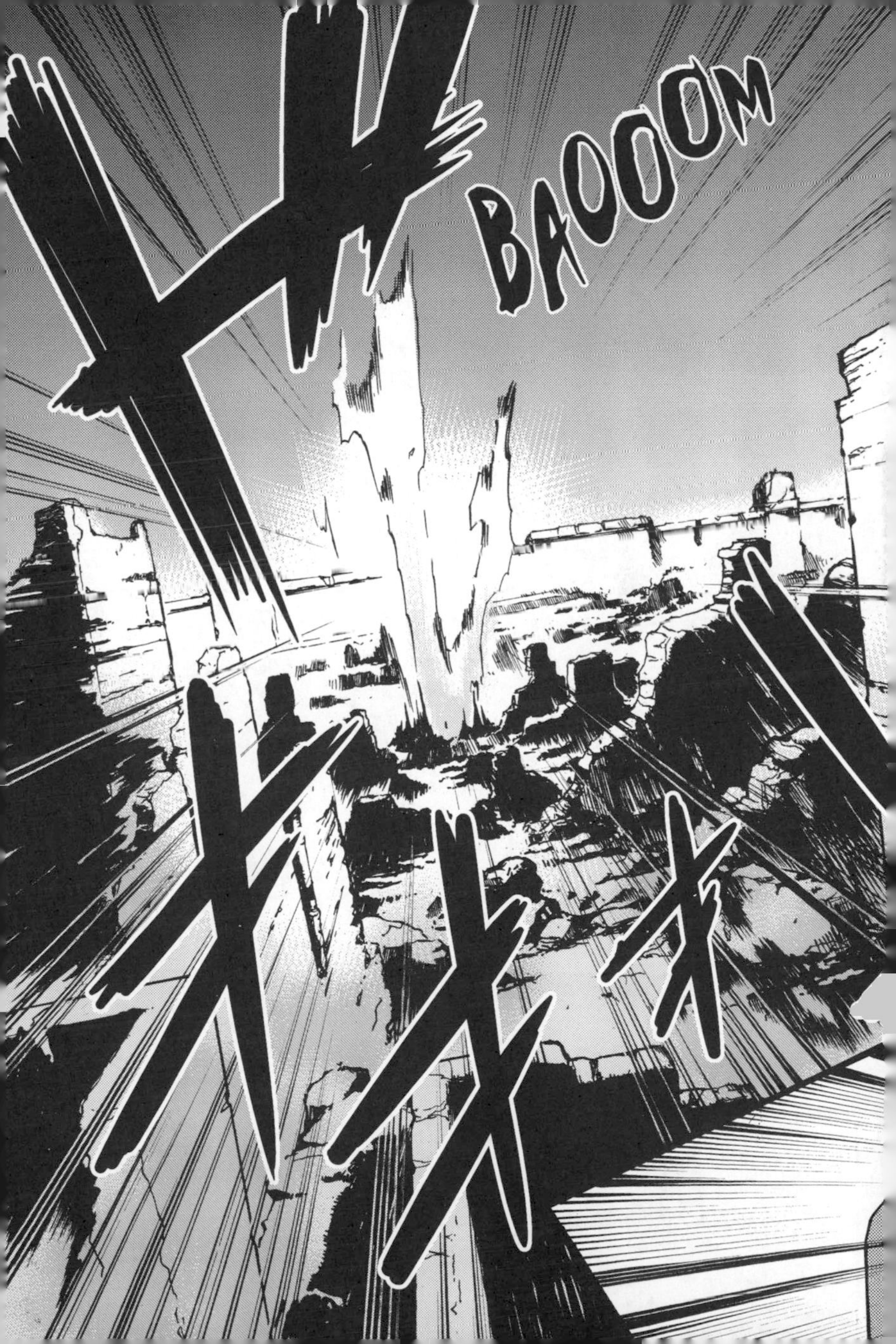
BAOOOM

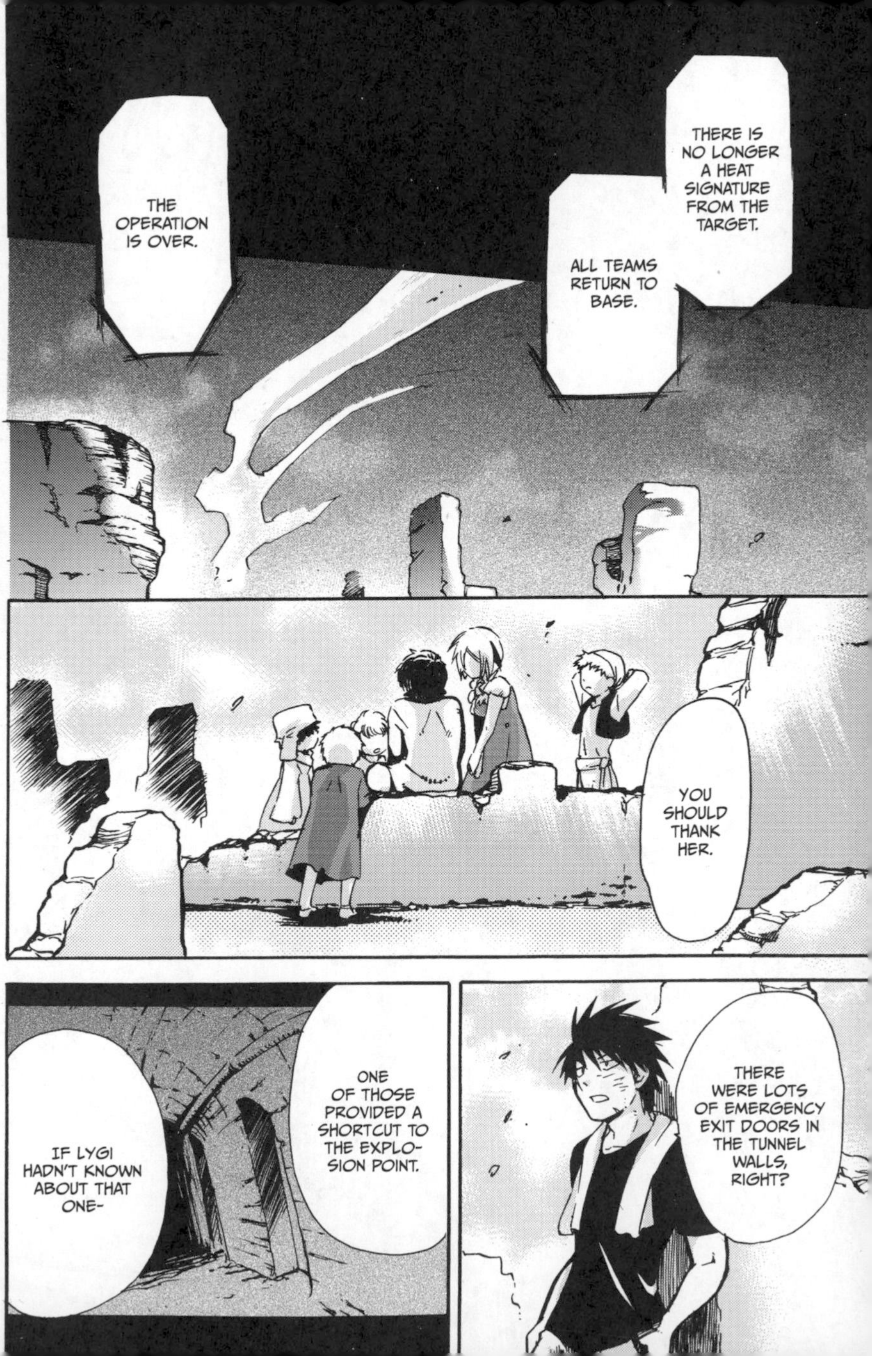
THERE IS NO LONGER A HEAT SIGNATURE FROM THE TARGET.
ALL TEAMS RETURN TO BASE.
THE OPERATION IS OVER.
YOU SHOULD THANK HER.
THERE WERE LOTS OF EMERGENCY EXIT DOORS IN THE TUNNEL WALLS, RIGHT?
ONE OF THOSE PROVIDED A SHORTCUT TO THE EXPLO-SION POINT.
IF LYGI HADN'T KNOWN ABOUT THAT ONE-

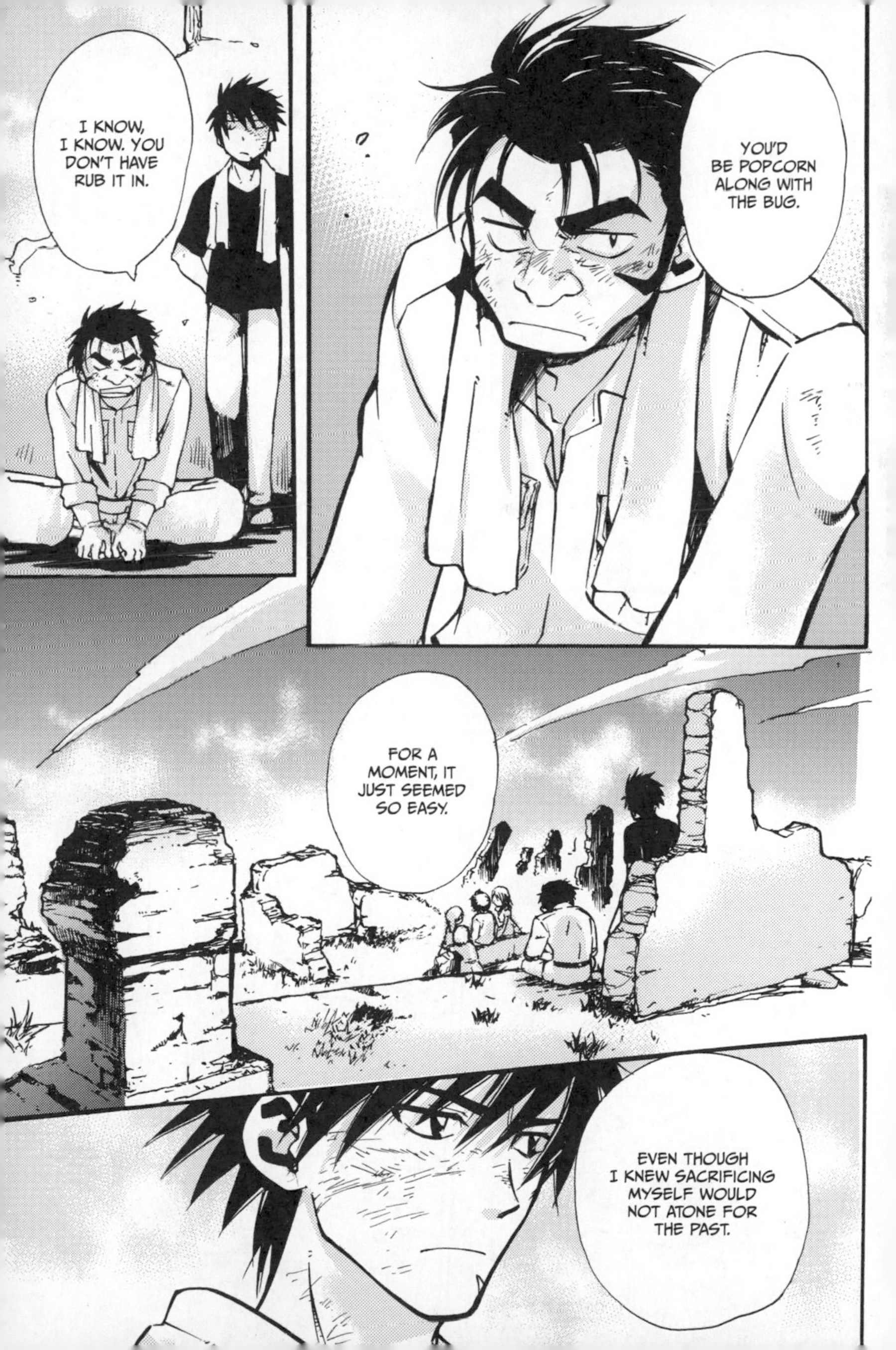
YOU'D BE POPCORN ALONG WITH THE BUG.
I KNOW, I KNOW. YOU DON'T HAVE RUB IT IN.
FOR A MOMENT, IT JUST SEEMED SO EASY.
EVEN THOUGH I KNEW SACRIFICING MYSELF WOULD NOT ATONE FOR THE PAST.

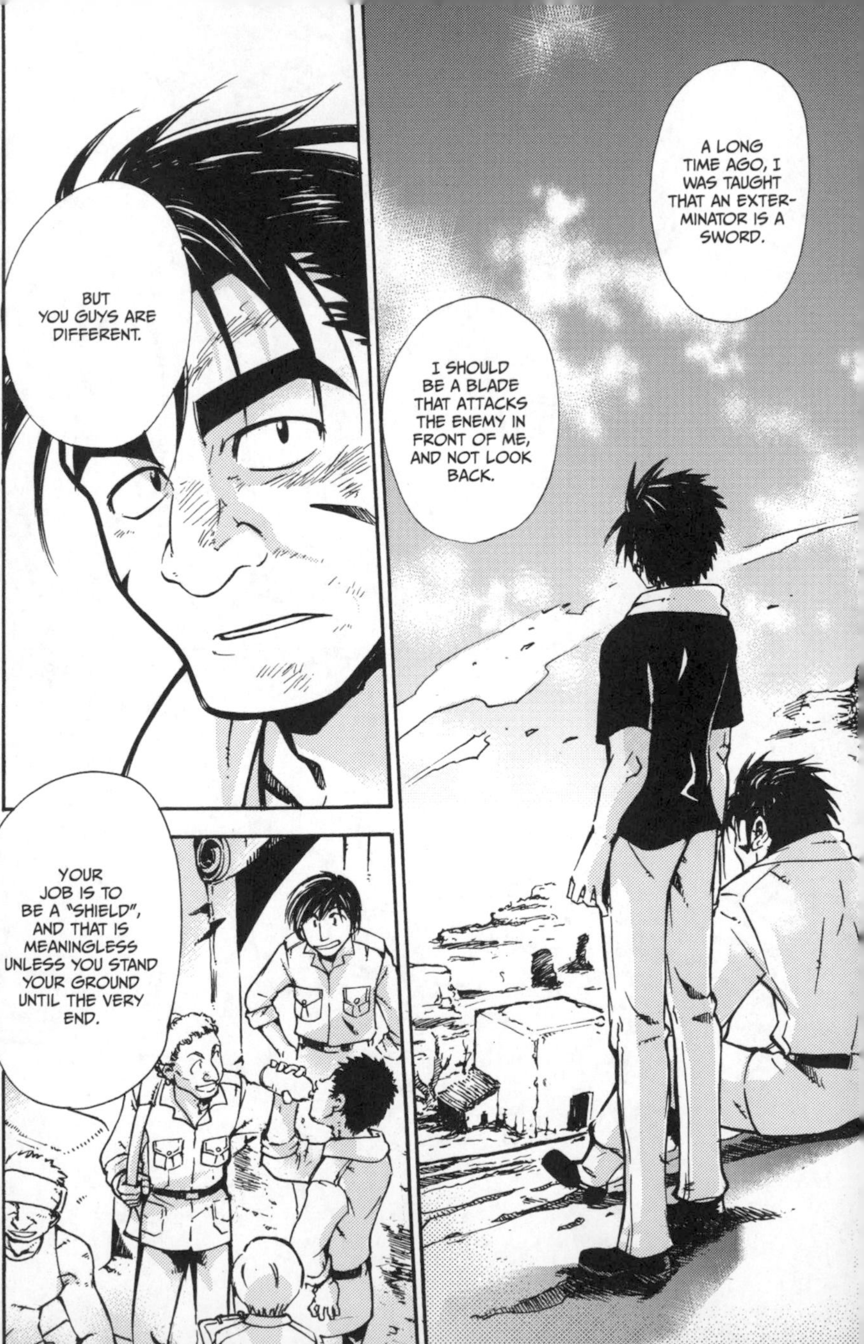
A LONG TIME AGO, I WAS TAUGHT THAT AN EXTER- MINATOR IS A SWORD.
I SHOULD BE A BLADE THAT ATTACKS THE ENEMY IN FRONT OF ME, AND NOT LOOK BACK.
BUT YOU GUYS ARE DIFFERENT.
YOUR JOB IS TO BE A "SHIELD", AND THAT IS MEANINGLESS UNLESS YOU STAND YOUR GROUND UNTIL THE VERY END.

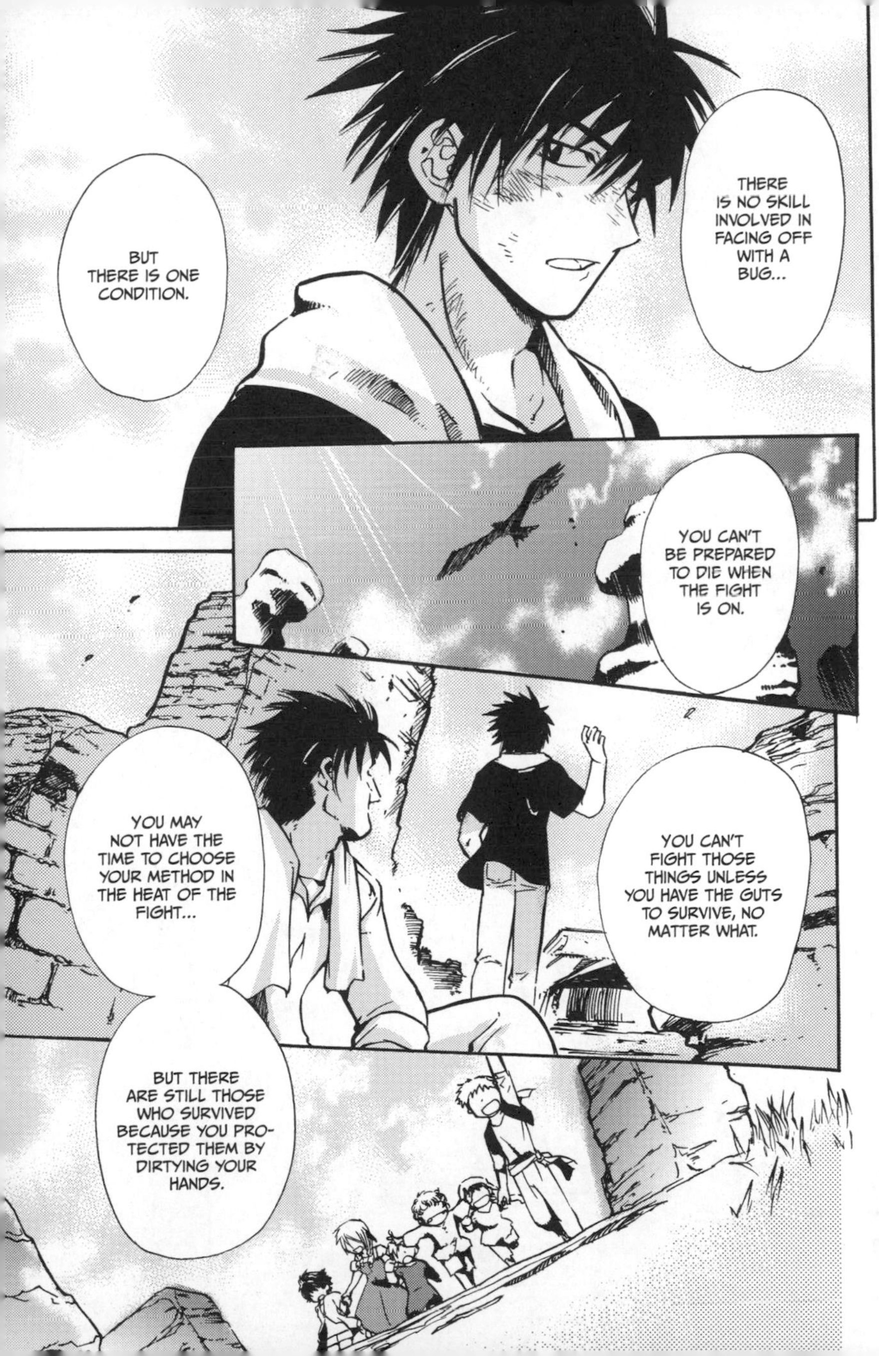
THERE IS NO SKILL INVOLVED IN FACING OFF WITH A BUG...
BUT THERE IS ONE CONDITION.
YOU CAN'T BE PREPARED TO DIE WHEN THE FIGHT IS ON.
YOU CAN'T FIGHT THOSE THINGS UNLESS YOU HAVE THE GUTS TO SURVIVE, NO MATTER WHAT.
YOU MAY NOT HAVE THE TIME TO CHOOSE YOUR METHOD IN THE HEAT OF THE FIGHT...
BUT THERE ARE STILL THOSE WHO SURVIVED BECAUSE YOU PRO-TECTED THEM BY DIRTYING YOUR HANDS.

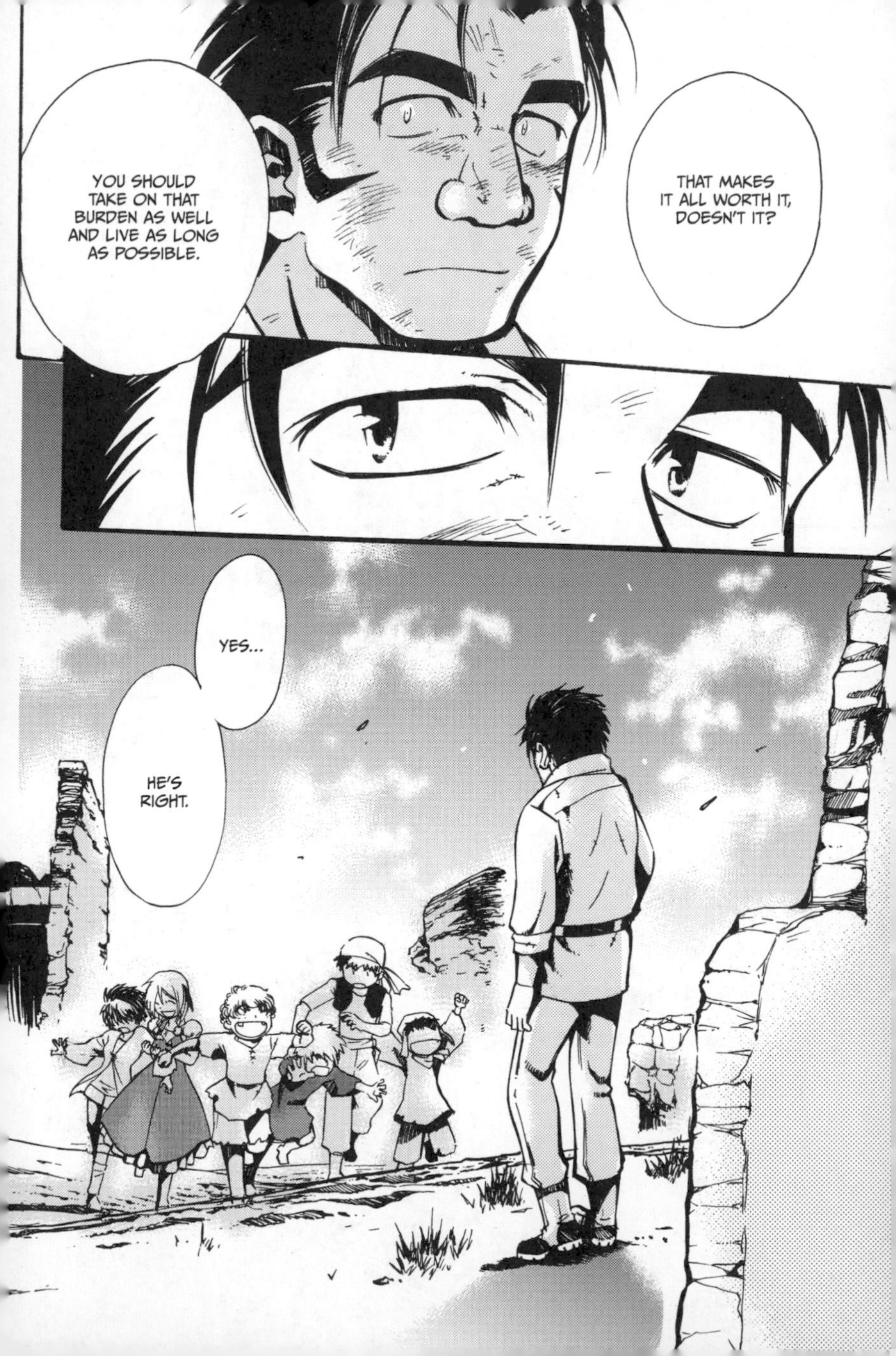
THAT MAKES IT ALL WORTH IT, DOESN'T IT?
YOU SHOULD TAKE ON THAT BURDEN AS WELL AND LIVE AS LONG AS POSSIBLE.
YES...
HE'S RIGHT.

[CHAPTER 9]

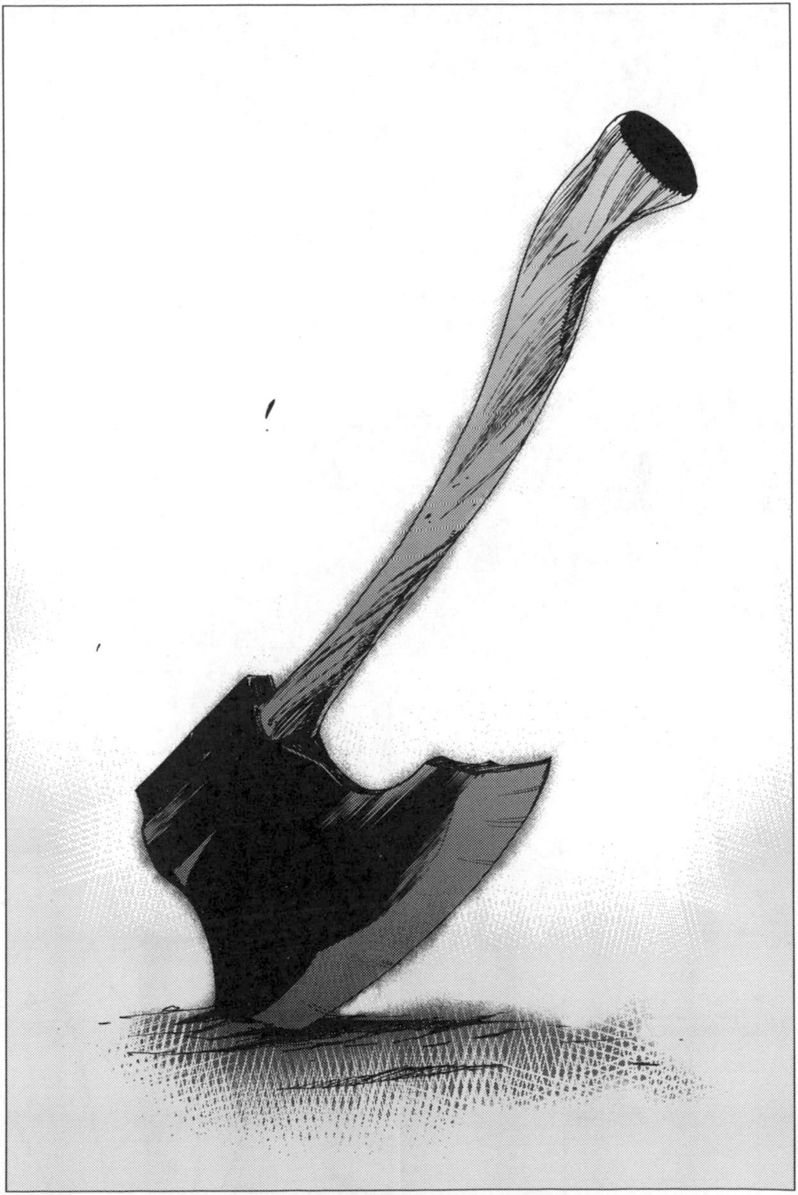

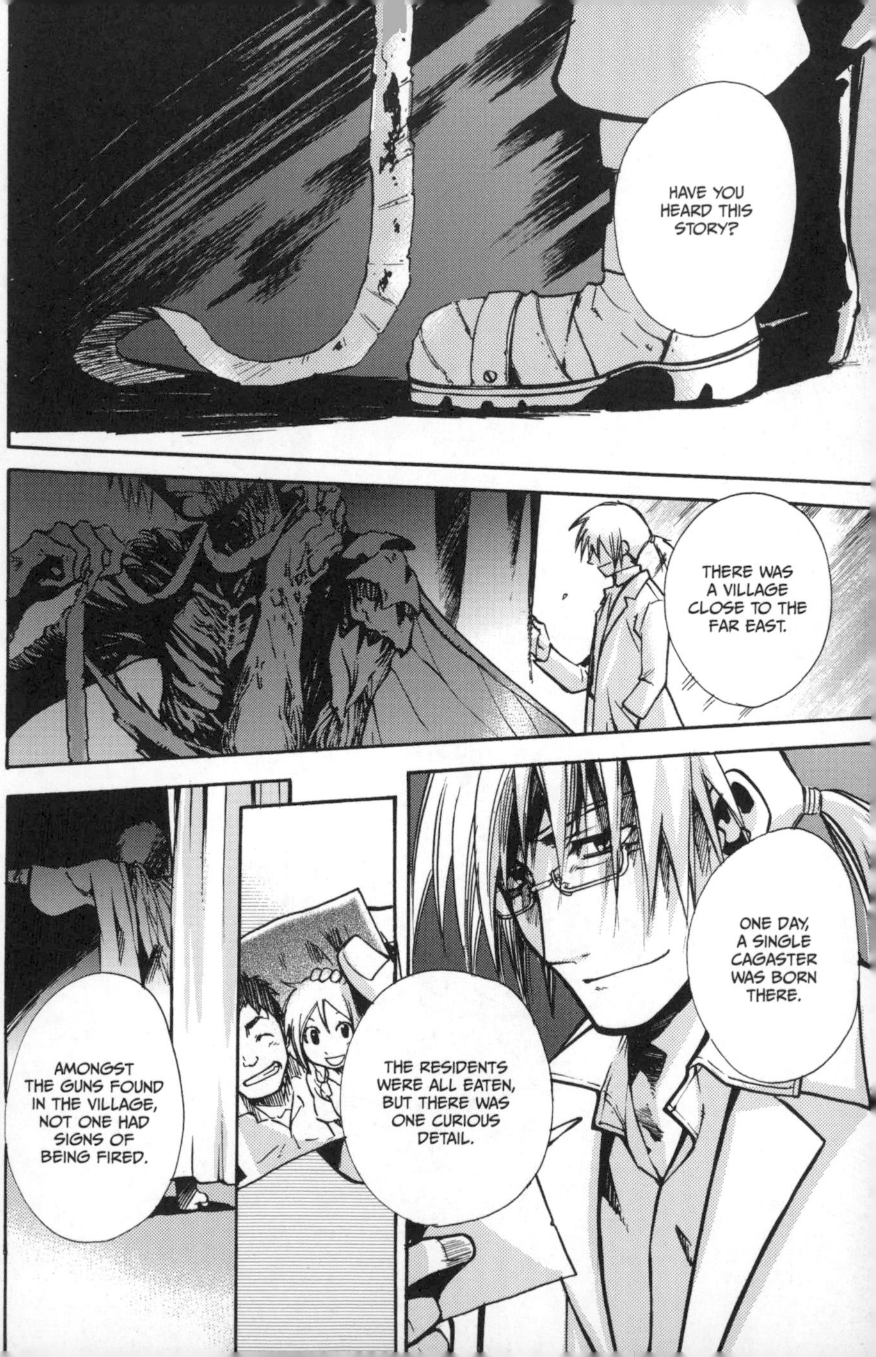
HAVE YOU HEARD THIS STORY?
THERE WAS A VILLAGE CLOSE TO THE FAR EAST.
ONE DAY, A SINGLE CAGASTER WAS BORN THERE.
THE RESIDENTS WERE ALL EATEN, BUT THERE WAS ONE CURIOUS DETAIL.
AMONGST THE GUNS FOUND IN THE VILLAGE, NOT ONE HAD SIGNS OF BEING FIRED.

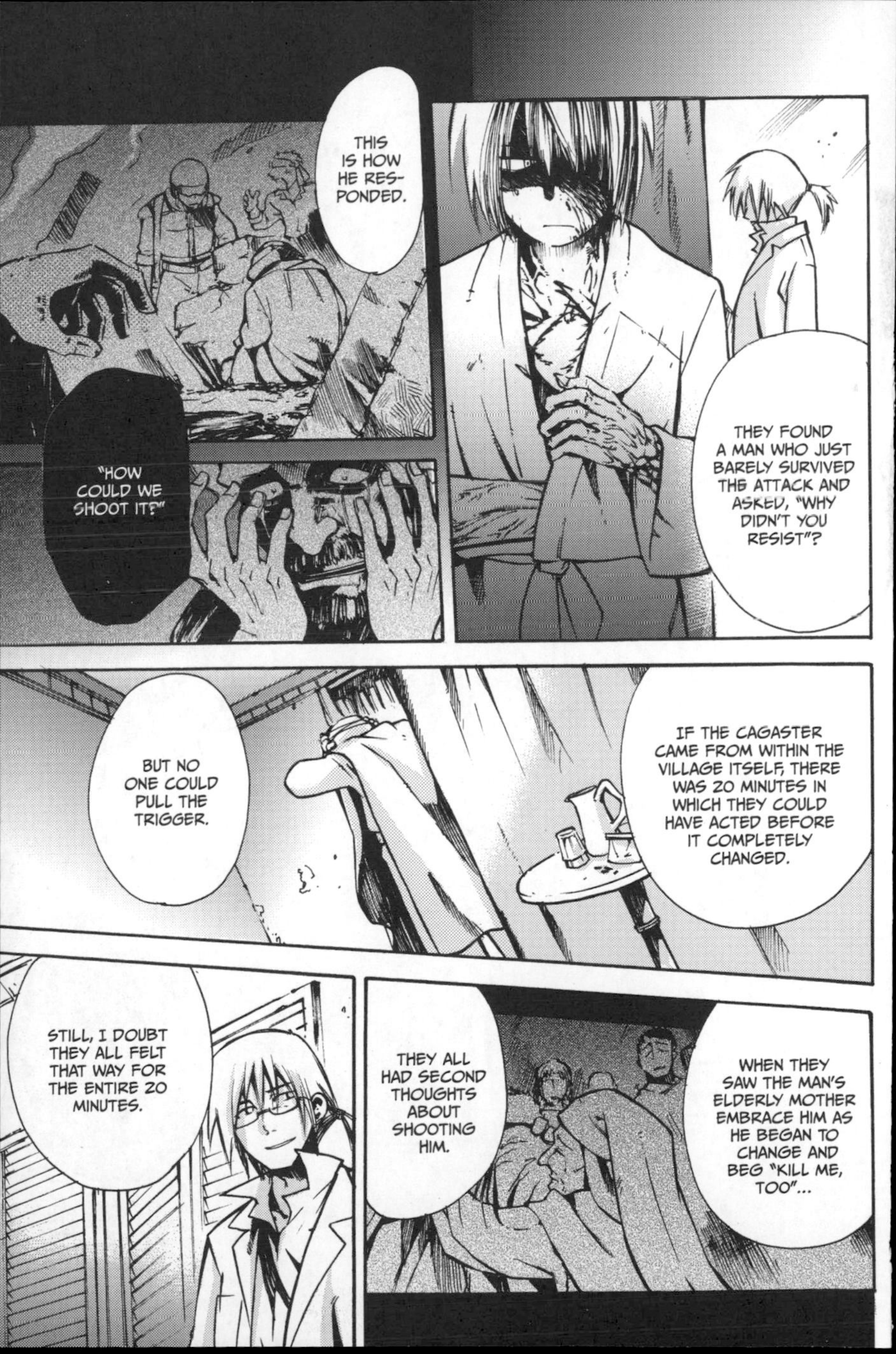
THEY FOUND A MAN WHO JUST BARELY SURVIVED THE ATTACK AND ASKED, "WHY DIDN'T YOU RESIST"?
THIS IS HOW HE RES-PONDED.
"HOW COULD WE SHOOT IT?"
IF THE CAGASTER CAME FROM WITHIN THE VILLAGE ITSELF, THERE WAS 20 MINUTES IN WHICH THEY COULD HAVE ACTED BEFORE IT COMPLETELY CHANGED.
BUT NO ONE COULD PULL THE TRIGGER.
WHEN THEY SAW THE MAN'S ELDERLY MOTHER EMBRACE HIM AS HE BEGAN TO CHANGE AND BEG "KILL ME, TOO"...
THEY ALL HAD SECOND THOUGHTS ABOUT SHOOTING HIM.
STILL, I DOUBT THEY ALL FELT THAT WAY FOR THE ENTIRE 20 MINUTES.

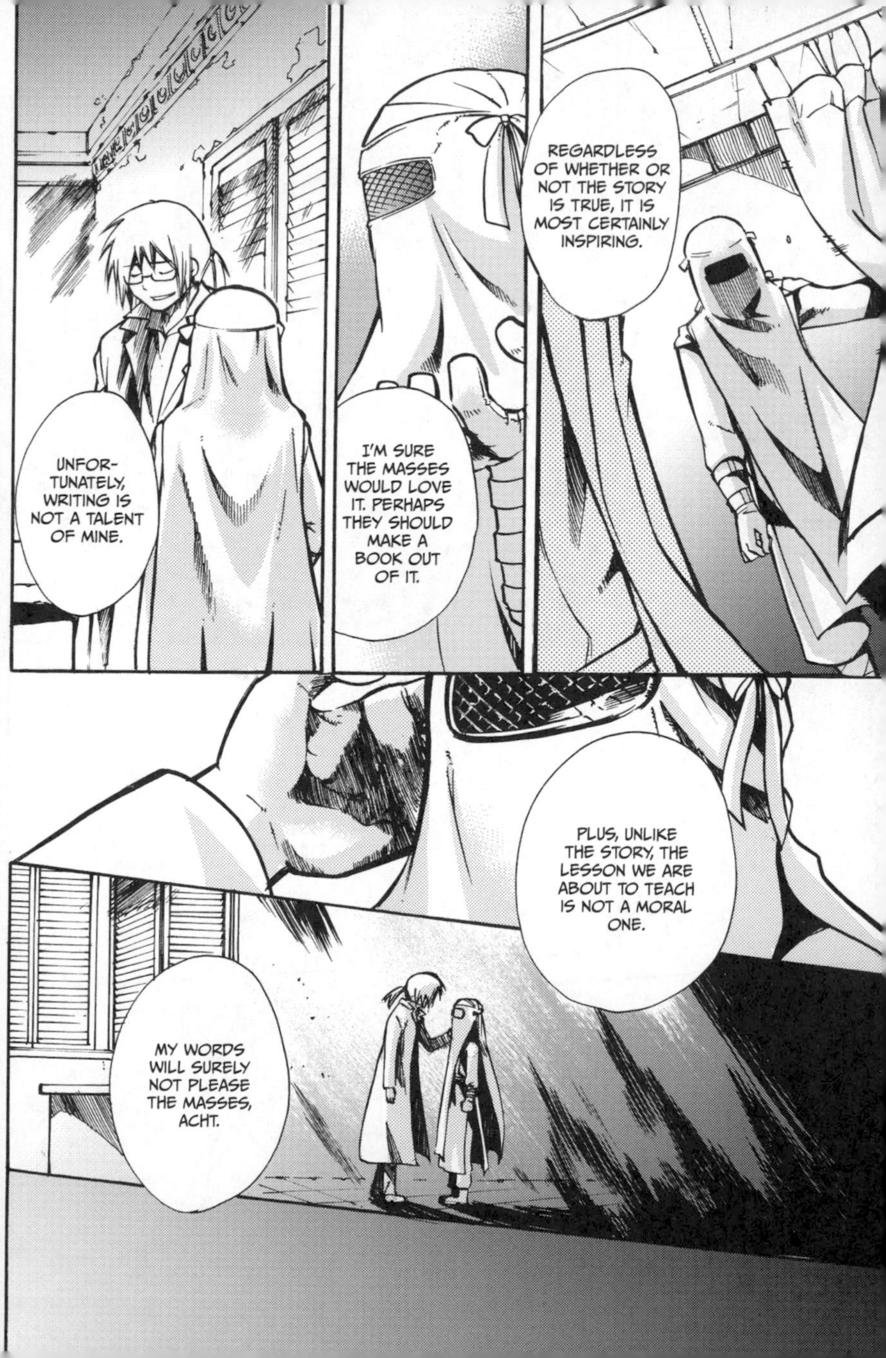
REGARDLESS OF WHETHER OR NOT THE STORY IS TRUE, IT IS MOST CERTAINLY INSPIRING.
I'M SURE THE MASSES WOULD LOVE IT. PERHAPS THEY SHOULD MAKE A BOOK OUT OF IT.
UNFOR-TUNATELY, WRITING IS NOT A TALENT OF MINE.
PLUS, UNLIKE THE STORY, THE LESSON WE ARE ABOUT TO TEACH IS NOT A MORAL ONE.
MY WORDS WILL SURELY NOT PLEASE THE MASSES, ACHT.

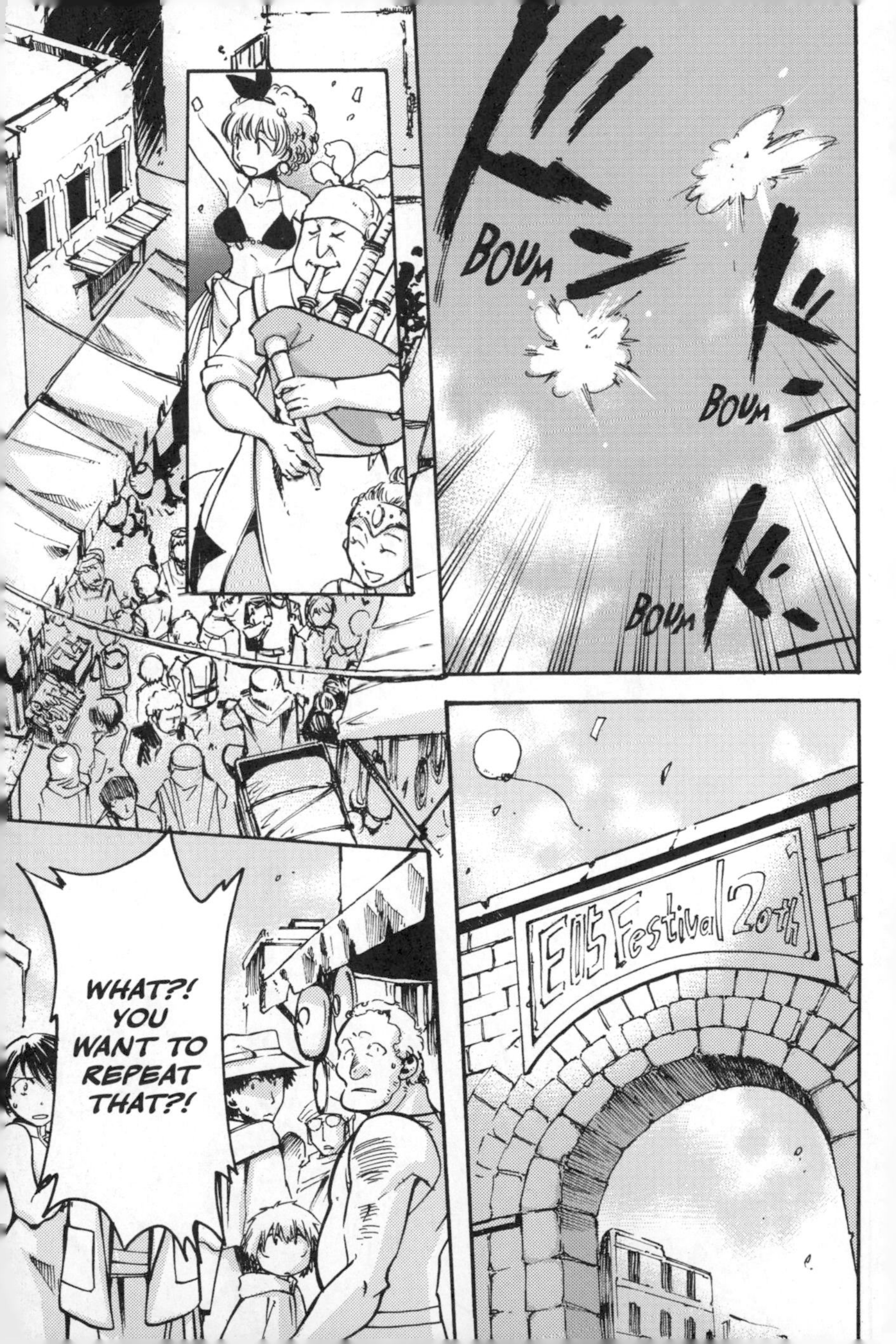
BOUM
BOUM
BOUM
Elis Festival 20th
WHAT?! YOU WANT TO REPEAT THAT?!

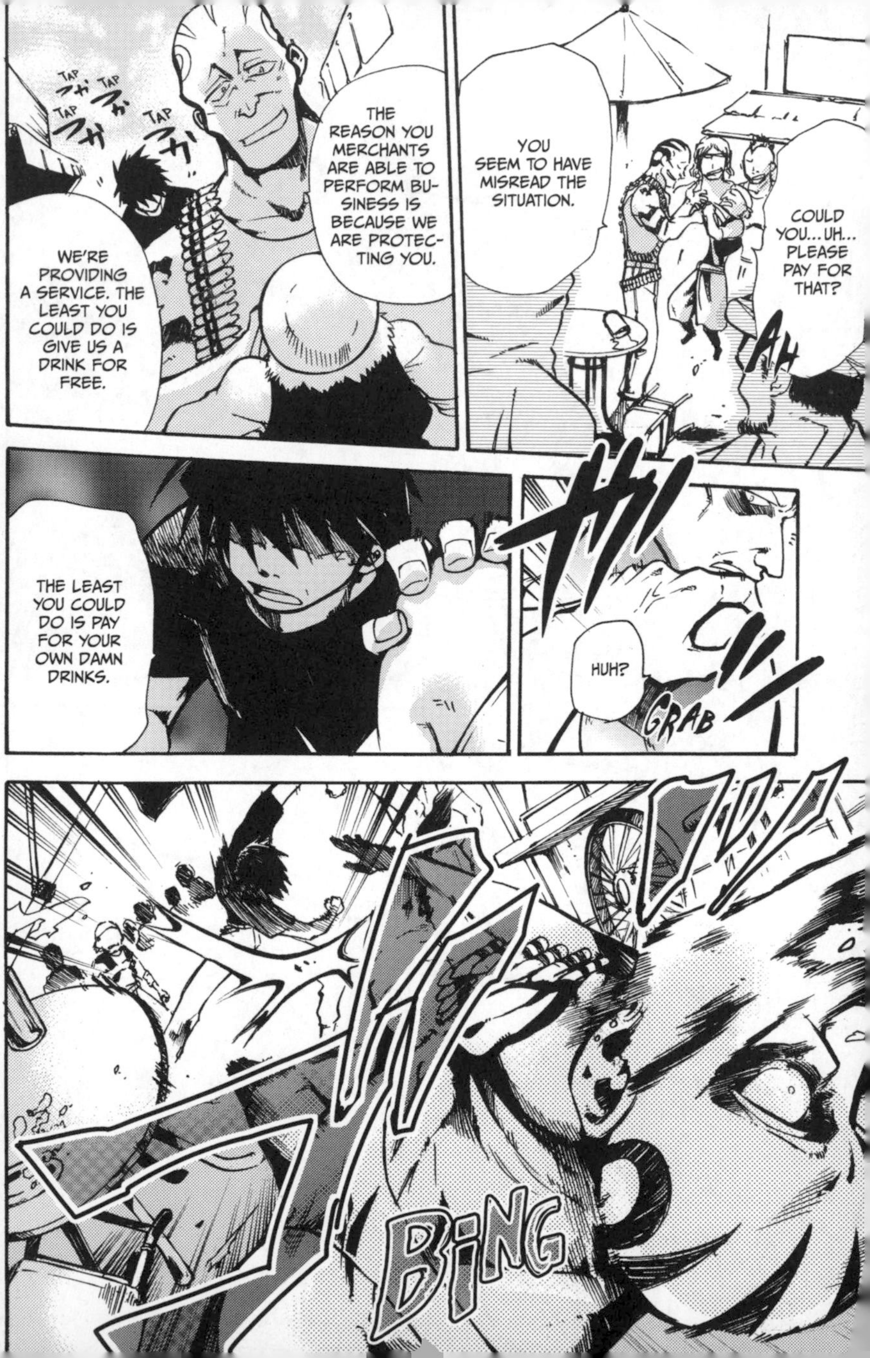
AH
COULD YOU...UH... PLEASE PAY FOR THAT?
YOU SEEM TO HAVE MISREAD THE SITUATION.
TAP TAP TAP TAP
THE REASON YOU MERCHANTS ARE ABLE TO PERFORM BUSINESS IS BECAUSE WE ARE PROTECTING YOU.
WE'RE PROVIDING A SERVICE. THE LEAST YOU COULD DO IS GIVE US A DRINK FOR FREE.
HUH?
GRAB
THE LEAST YOU COULD DO IS PAY FOR YOUR OWN DAMN DRINKS.
BING

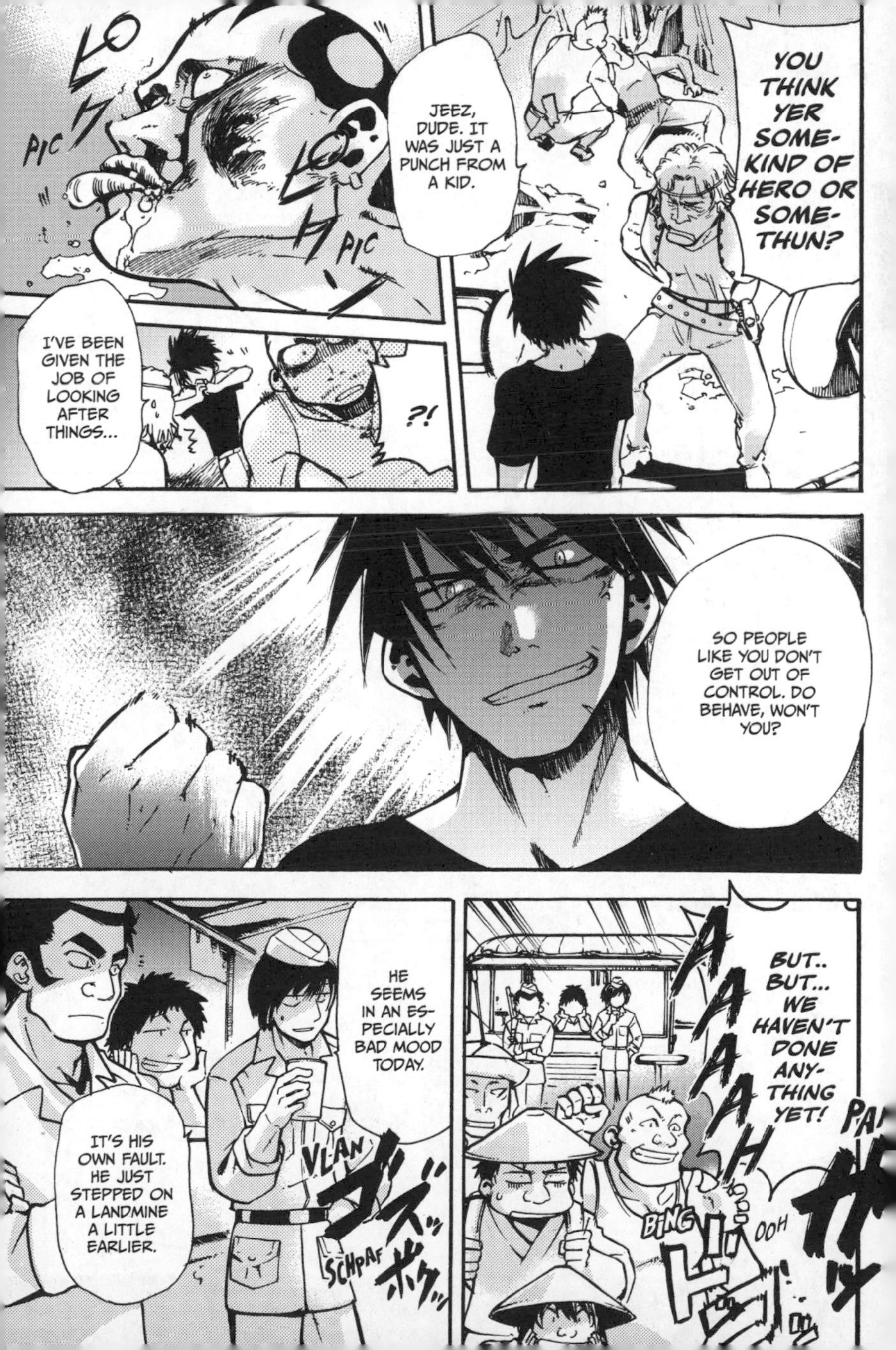

YOU THINK YER SOME-KIND OF HERO OR SOME-THUN?
PIC
PIC
JEEZ, DUDE. IT WAS JUST A PUNCH FROM A KID.
I'VE BEEN GIVEN THE JOB OF LOOKING AFTER THINGS...
?!
SO PEOPLE LIKE YOU DON'T GET OUT OF CONTROL. DO BEHAVE, WON'T YOU?
PA
AAAAAH
BUT.. BUT... WE HAVEN'T DONE ANY-THING YET!
OOH
BING
HE SEEMS IN AN ES-PECIALLY BAD MOOD TODAY.
VLAN
IT'S HIS OWN FAULT. HE JUST STEPPED ON A LANDMINE A LITTLE EARLIER.
SCHPAF

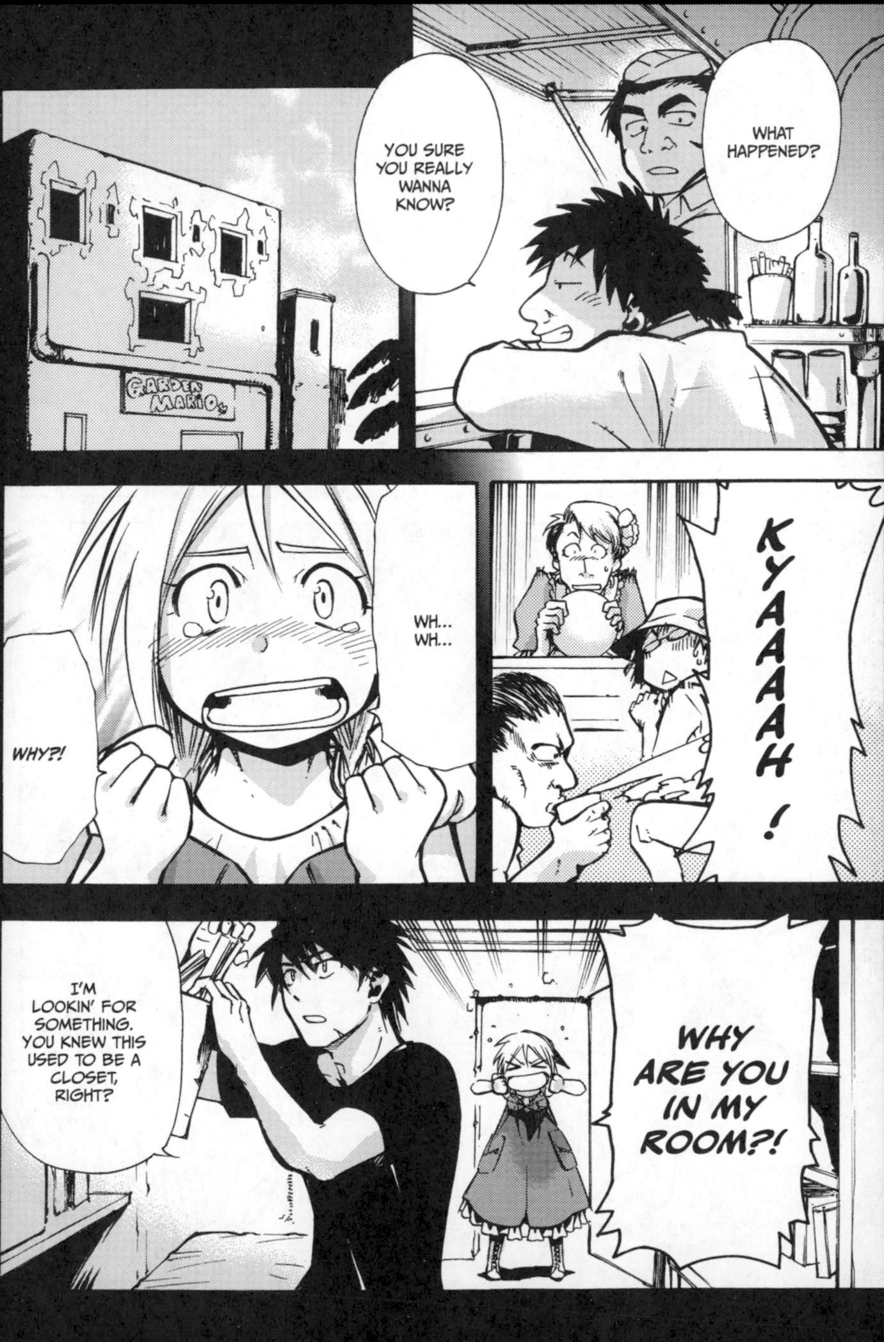
WHAT HAPPENED?
YOU SURE YOU REALLY WANNA KNOW?
GARDEN MARIO
KYAAAAAH!
WH... WH...
WHY?!
WHY ARE YOU IN MY ROOM?!
I'M LOOKIN' FOR SOMETHING. YOU KNEW THIS USED TO BE A CLOSET, RIGHT?

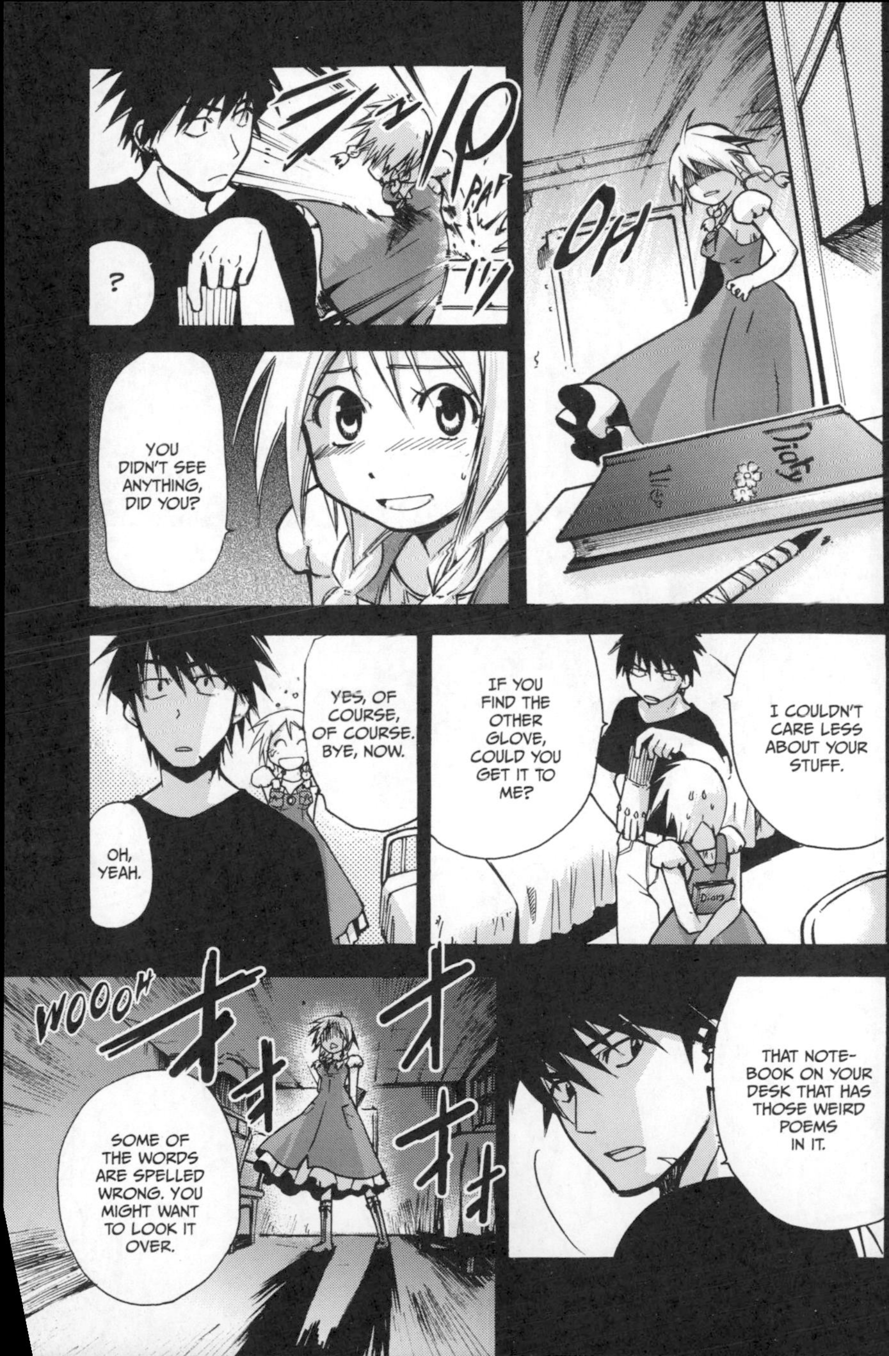
OH
Diary
PAF
?
YOU DIDN'T SEE ANYTHING, DID YOU?
I COULDN'T CARE LESS ABOUT YOUR STUFF.
IF YOU FIND THE OTHER GLOVE, COULD YOU GET IT TO ME?
YES, OF COURSE, OF COURSE. BYE, NOW.
OH, YEAH.
THAT NOTE-BOOK ON YOUR DESK THAT HAS THOSE WEIRD POEMS IN IT.
WOOOH
SOME OF THE WORDS ARE SPELLED WRONG. YOU MIGHT WANT TO LOOK IT OVER.

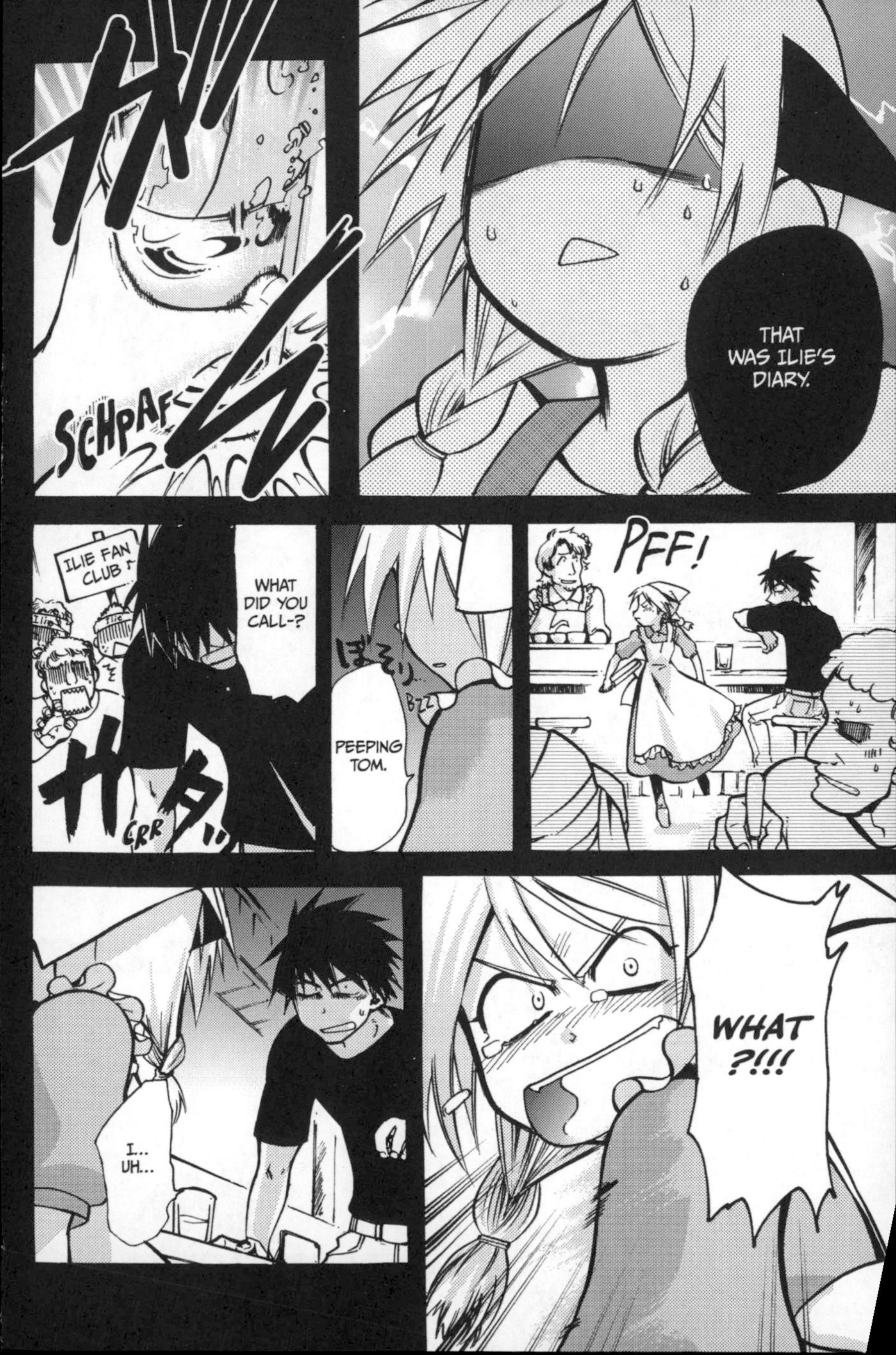

THAT WAS ILIE'S DIARY.
SCHPAF
PFF!
ぼそり
BZZ
PEEPING TOM.
ILIE FAN CLUB
WHAT DID YOU CALL-?
GRR
WHAT ?!!!
I... UH...

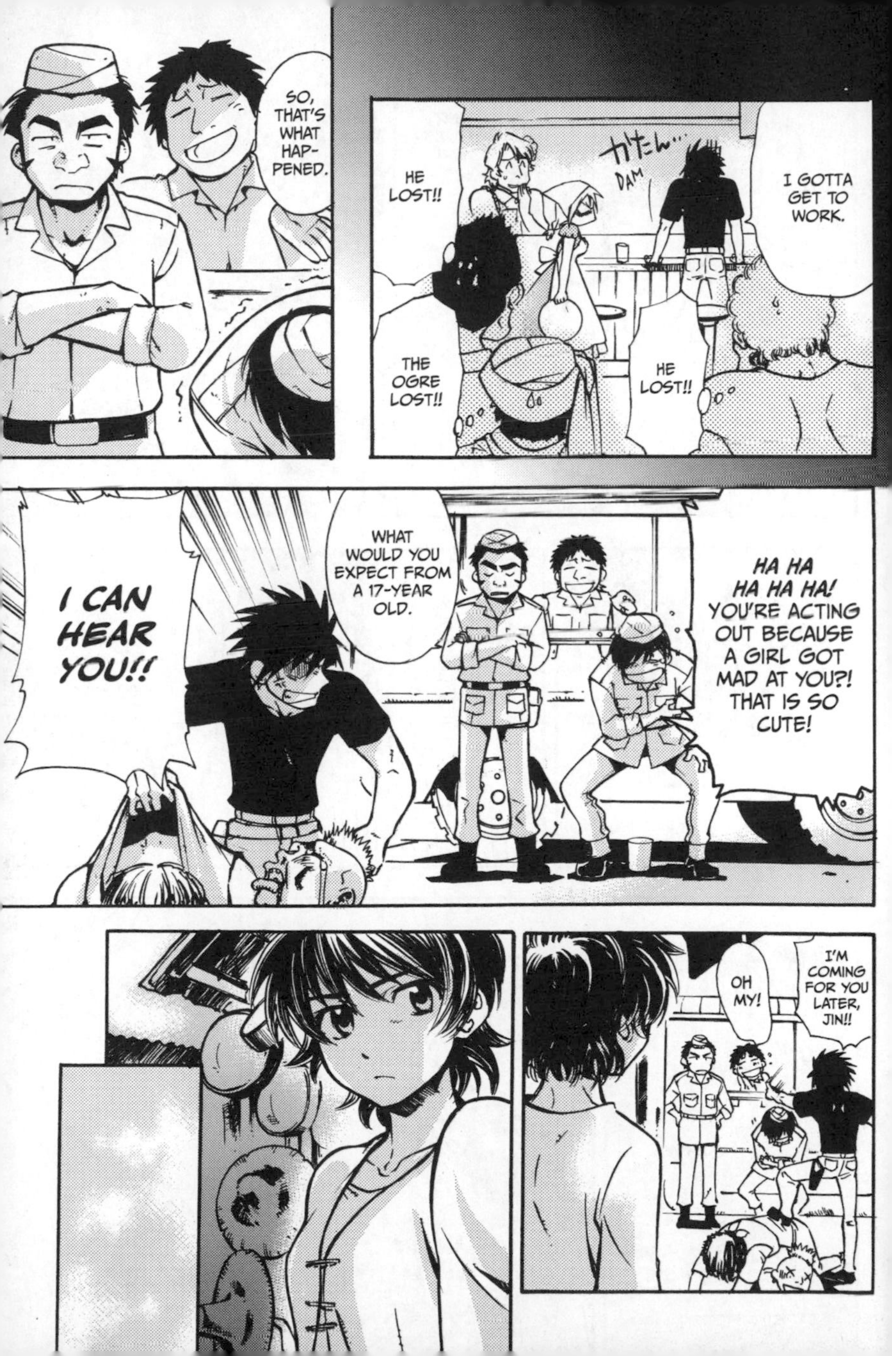
I GOTTA GET TO WORK.
かたん… DAM
HE LOST!!
HE LOST!!
THE OGRE LOST!!
SO, THAT'S WHAT HAP-PENED.
HA HA HA HA HA! YOU'RE ACTING OUT BECAUSE A GIRL GOT MAD AT YOU?! THAT IS SO CUTE!
WHAT WOULD YOU EXPECT FROM A 17-YEAR OLD.
I CAN HEAR YOU!!
I'M COMING FOR YOU LATER, JIN!!
OH MY!

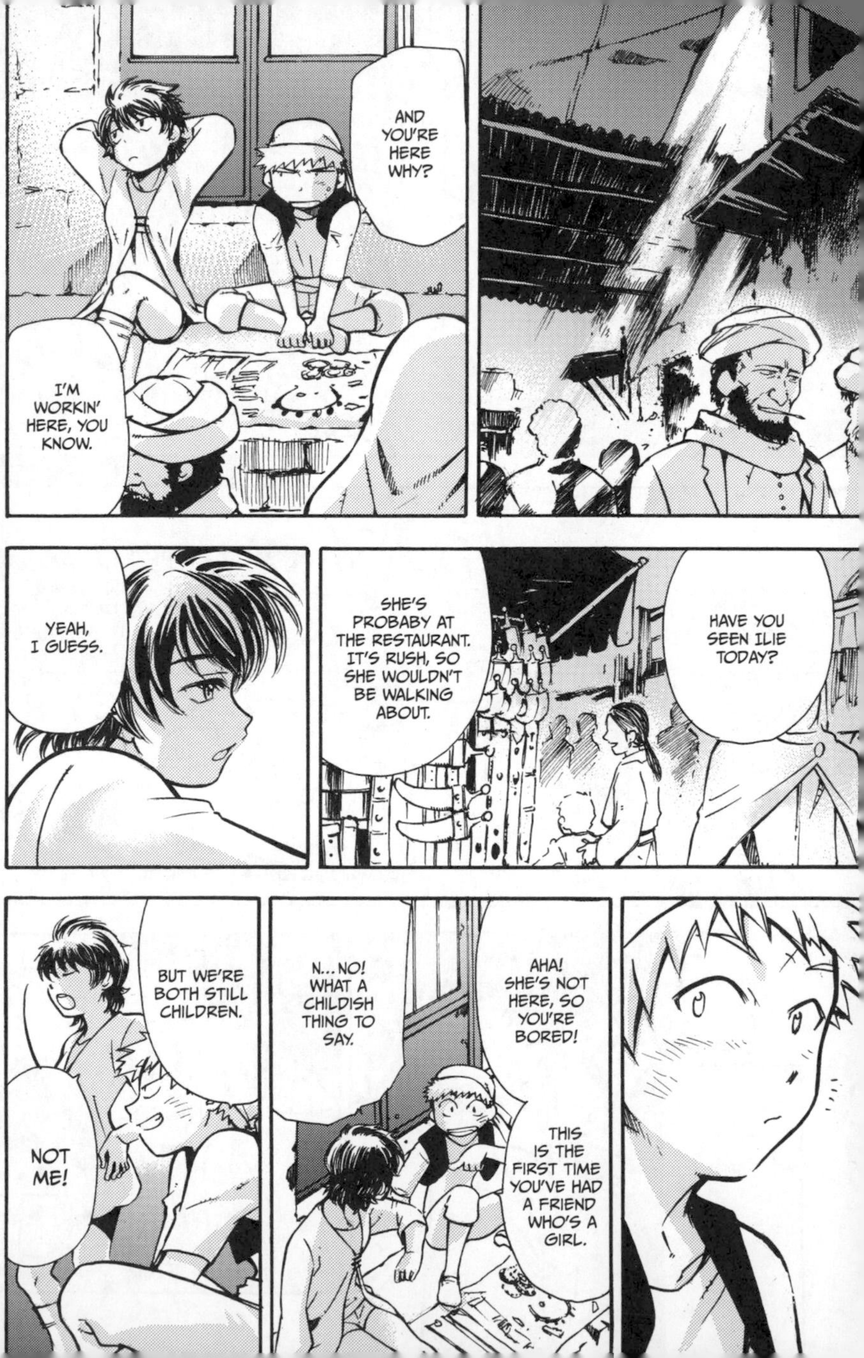
AND YOU'RE HERE WHY?
I'M WORKIN' HERE, YOU KNOW.
HAVE YOU SEEN ILIE TODAY?
SHE'S PROBABY AT THE RESTAURANT. IT'S RUSH, SO SHE WOULDN'T BE WALKING ABOUT.
YEAH, I GUESS.
AHA! SHE'S NOT HERE, SO YOU'RE BORED!
THIS IS THE FIRST TIME YOU'VE HAD A FRIEND WHO'S A GIRL.
N...NO! WHAT A CHILDISH THING TO SAY.
BUT WE'RE BOTH STILL CHILDREN.
NOT ME!

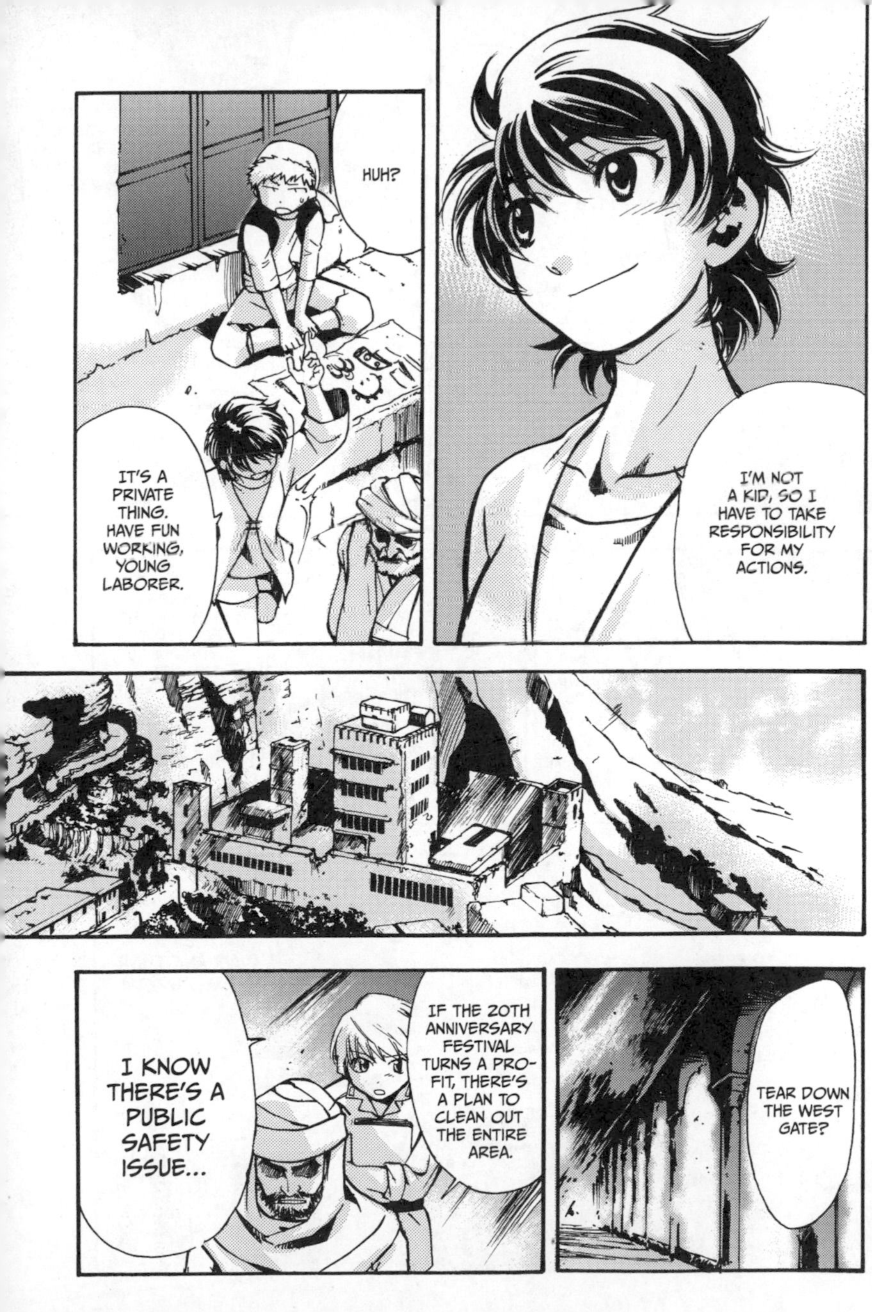
I'M NOT A KID, SO I HAVE TO TAKE RESPONSIBILITY FOR MY ACTIONS.
HUH?
IT'S A PRIVATE THING. HAVE FUN WORKING, YOUNG LABORER.
TEAR DOWN THE WEST GATE?
IF THE 20TH ANNIVERSARY FESTIVAL TURNS A PRO-FIT, THERE'S A PLAN TO CLEAN OUT THE ENTIRE AREA.
I KNOW THERE'S A PUBLIC SAFETY ISSUE...

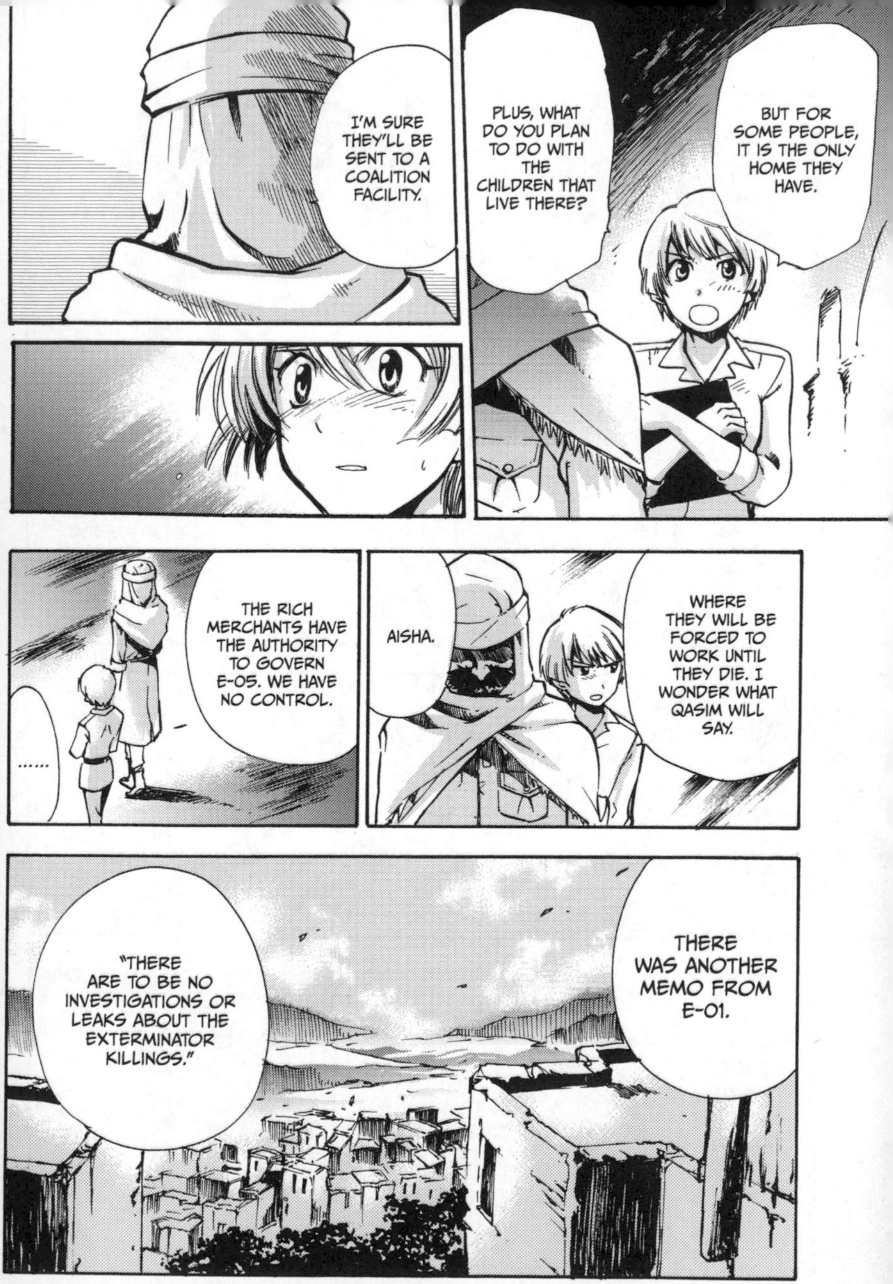
BUT FOR SOME PEOPLE, IT IS THE ONLY HOME THEY HAVE.
PLUS, WHAT DO YOU PLAN TO DO WITH THE CHILDREN THAT LIVE THERE?
I'M SURE THEY'LL BE SENT TO A COALITION FACILITY.
WHERE THEY WILL BE FORCED TO WORK UNTIL THEY DIE. I WONDER WHAT QASIM WILL SAY.
AISHA.
THE RICH MERCHANTS HAVE THE AUTHORITY TO GOVERN E-05. WE HAVE NO CONTROL.
......
THERE WAS ANOTHER MEMO FROM E-01.
"THERE ARE TO BE NO INVESTIGATIONS OR LEAKS ABOUT THE EXTERMINATOR KILLINGS."

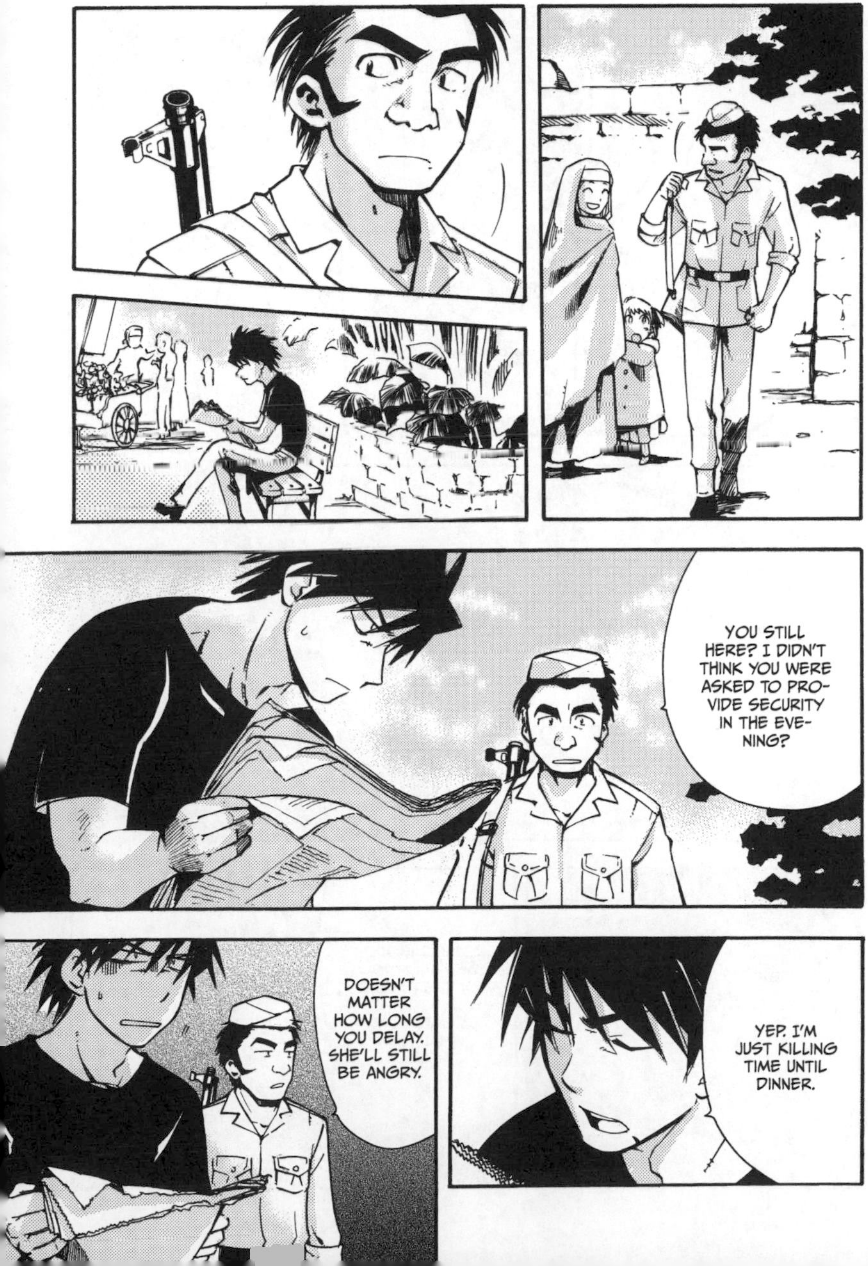
YOU STILL HERE? I DIDN'T THINK YOU WERE ASKED TO PRO- VIDE SECURITY IN THE EVE- NING?
YEP. I'M JUST KILLING TIME UNTIL DINNER.
DOESN'T MATTER HOW LONG YOU DELAY. SHE'LL STILL BE ANGRY.

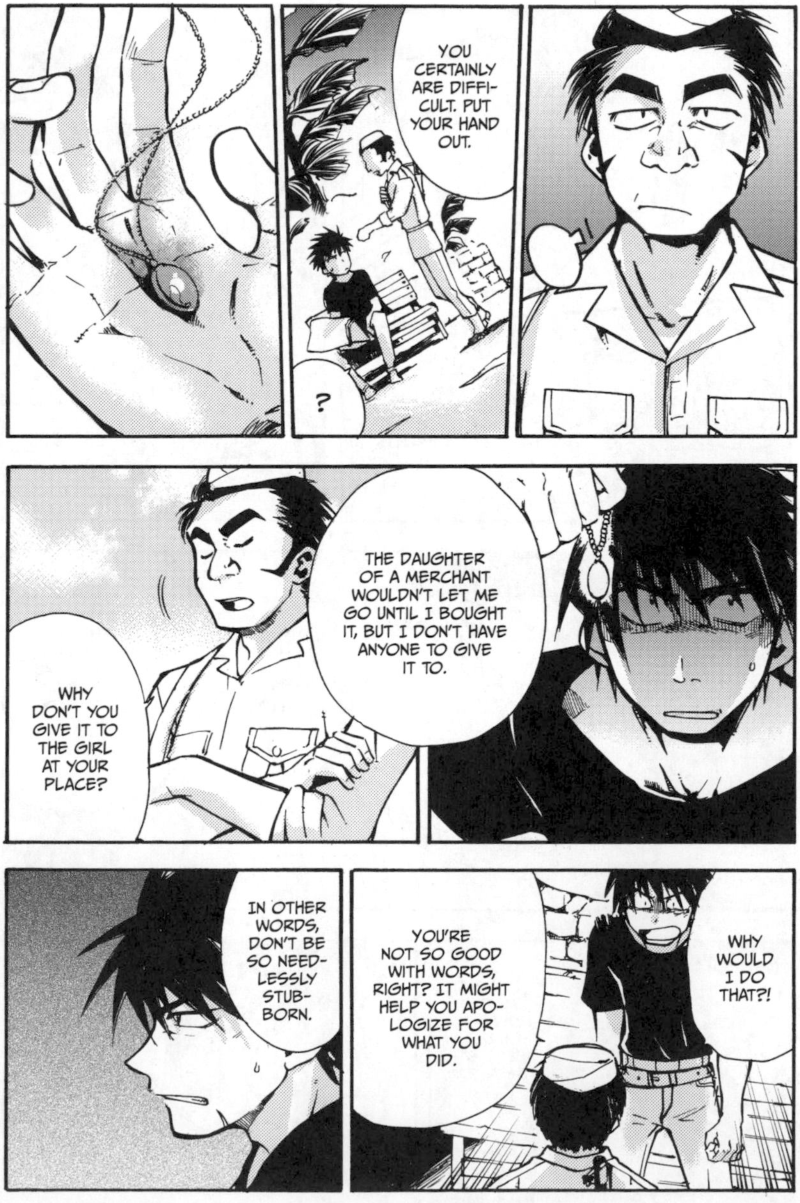
YOU CERTAINLY ARE DIFFI-CULT. PUT YOUR HAND OUT.
?
THE DAUGHTER OF A MERCHANT WOULDN'T LET ME GO UNTIL I BOUGHT IT, BUT I DON'T HAVE ANYONE TO GIVE IT TO.
WHY DON'T YOU GIVE IT TO THE GIRL AT YOUR PLACE?
WHY WOULD I DO THAT?!
YOU'RE NOT SO GOOD WITH WORDS, RIGHT? IT MIGHT HELP YOU APO-LOGIZE FOR WHAT YOU DID.
IN OTHER WORDS, DON'T BE SO NEED-LESSLY STUB-BORN.

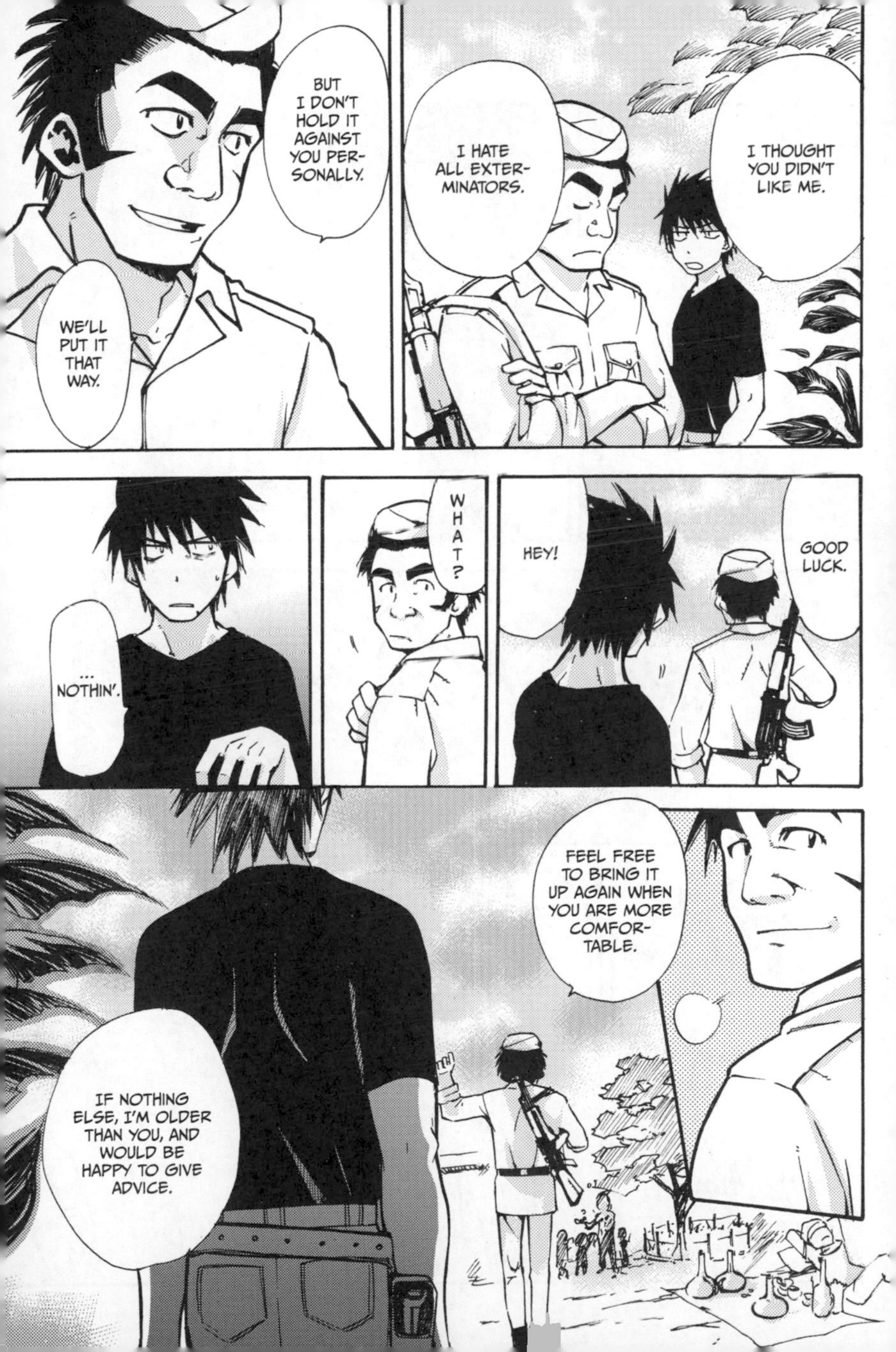
I THOUGHT YOU DIDN'T LIKE ME.
I HATE ALL EXTERMINATORS.
BUT I DON'T HOLD IT AGAINST YOU PERSONALLY.
WE'LL PUT IT THAT WAY.
GOOD LUCK.
HEY!
WHAT?
... NOTHIN'.
FEEL FREE TO BRING IT UP AGAIN WHEN YOU ARE MORE COMFORTABLE.
IF NOTHING ELSE, I'M OLDER THAN YOU, AND WOULD BE HAPPY TO GIVE ADVICE.

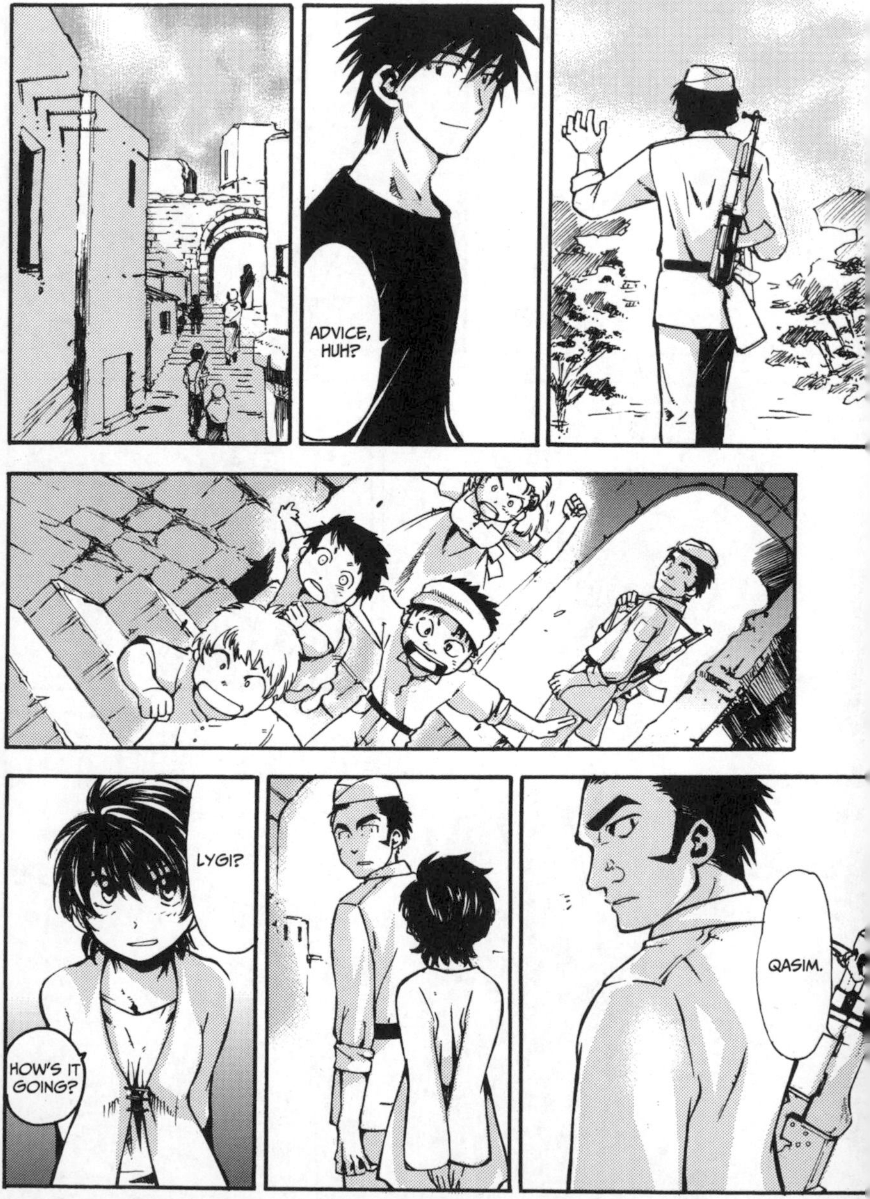
ADVICE, HUH?
QASIM.
LYGI?
HOW'S IT GOING?

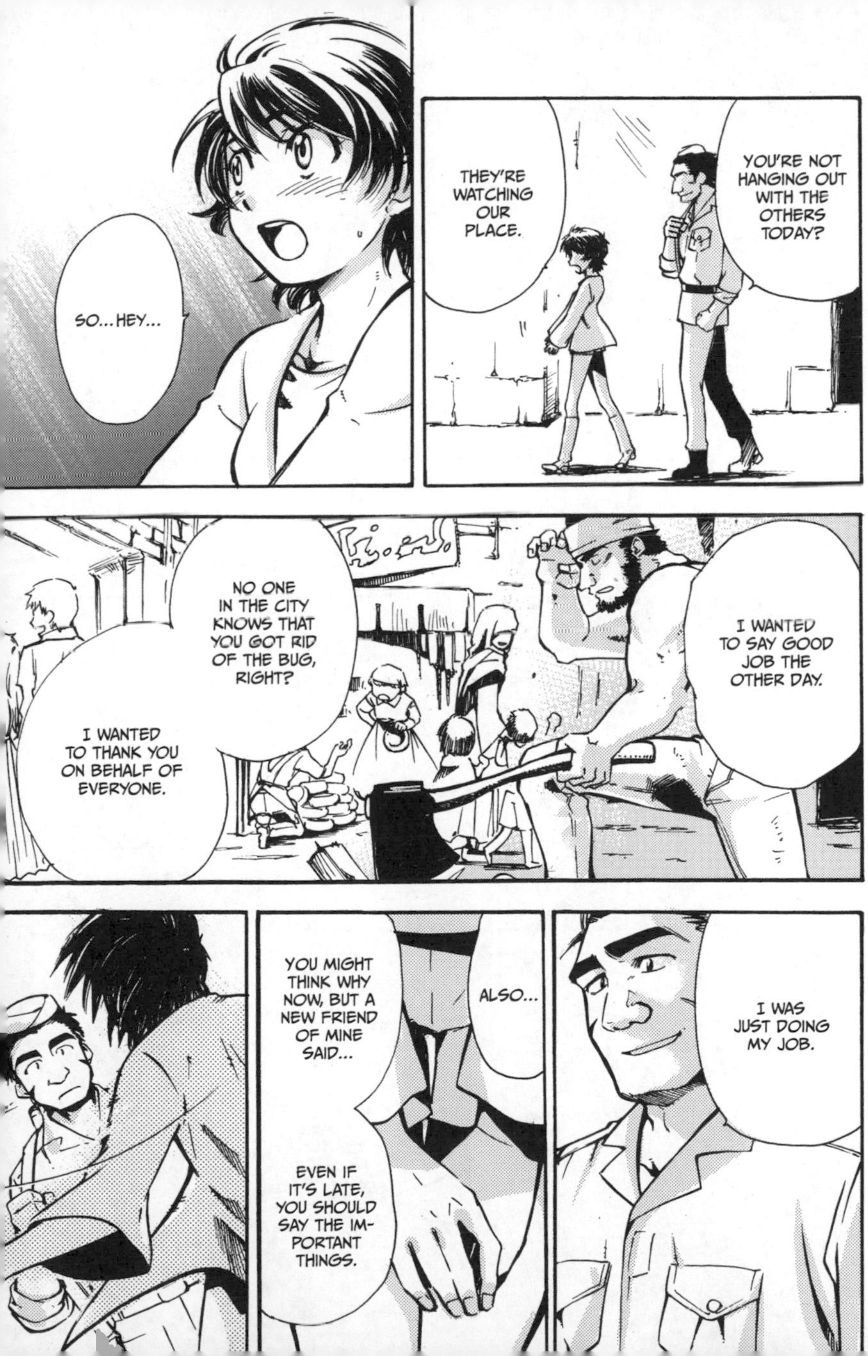
YOU'RE NOT HANGING OUT WITH THE OTHERS TODAY?
THEY'RE WATCHING OUR PLACE.
SO...HEY...
I WANTED TO SAY GOOD JOB THE OTHER DAY.
NO ONE IN THE CITY KNOWS THAT YOU GOT RID OF THE BUG, RIGHT?
I WANTED TO THANK YOU ON BEHALF OF EVERYONE.
I WAS JUST DOING MY JOB.
ALSO...
YOU MIGHT THINK WHY NOW, BUT A NEW FRIEND OF MINE SAID...
EVEN IF IT'S LATE, YOU SHOULD SAY THE IM-PORTANT THINGS.

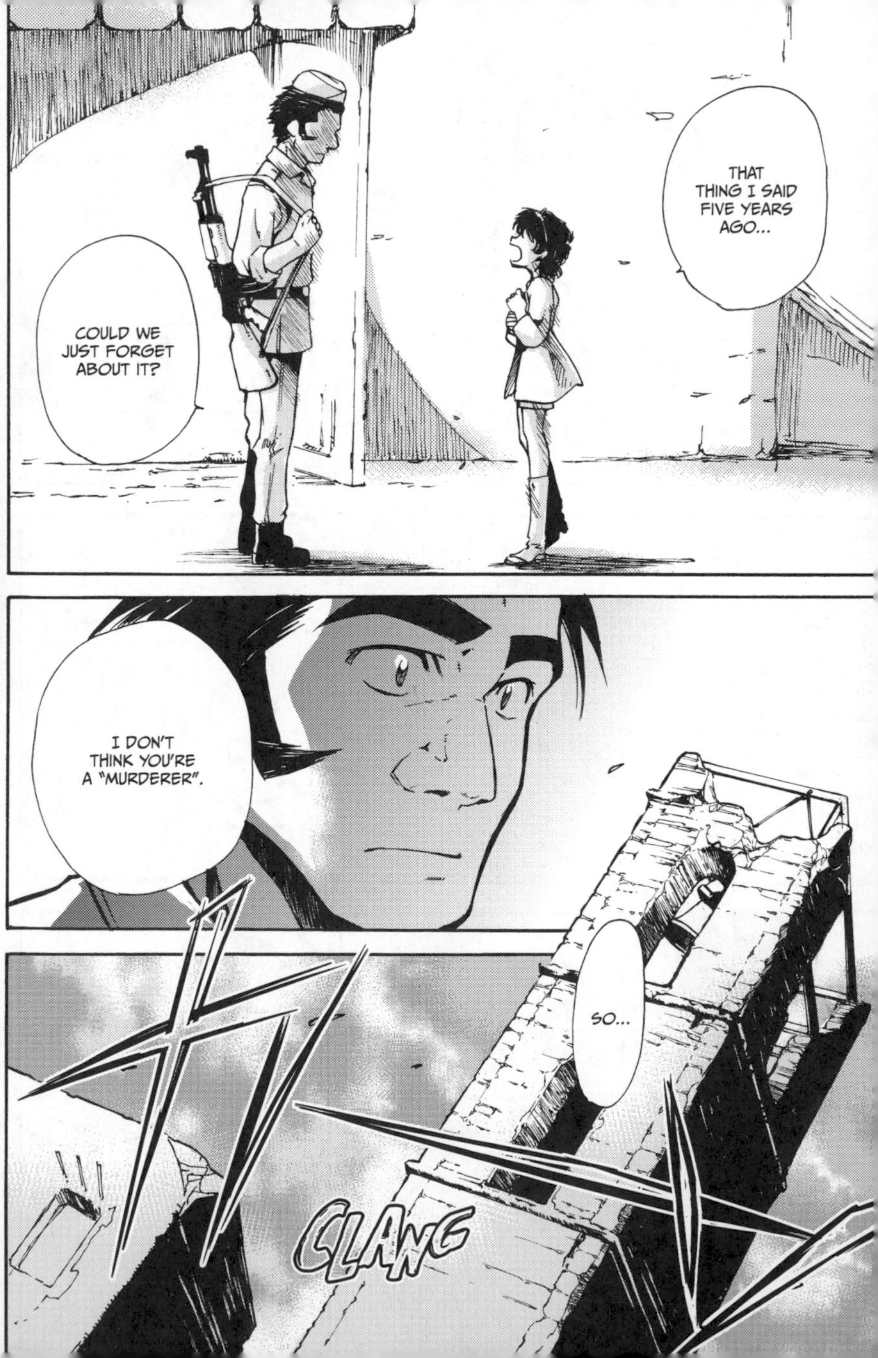
THAT THING I SAID FIVE YEARS AGO...
COULD WE JUST FORGET ABOUT IT?
I DON'T THINK YOU'RE A "MURDERER".
SO...
CLANG

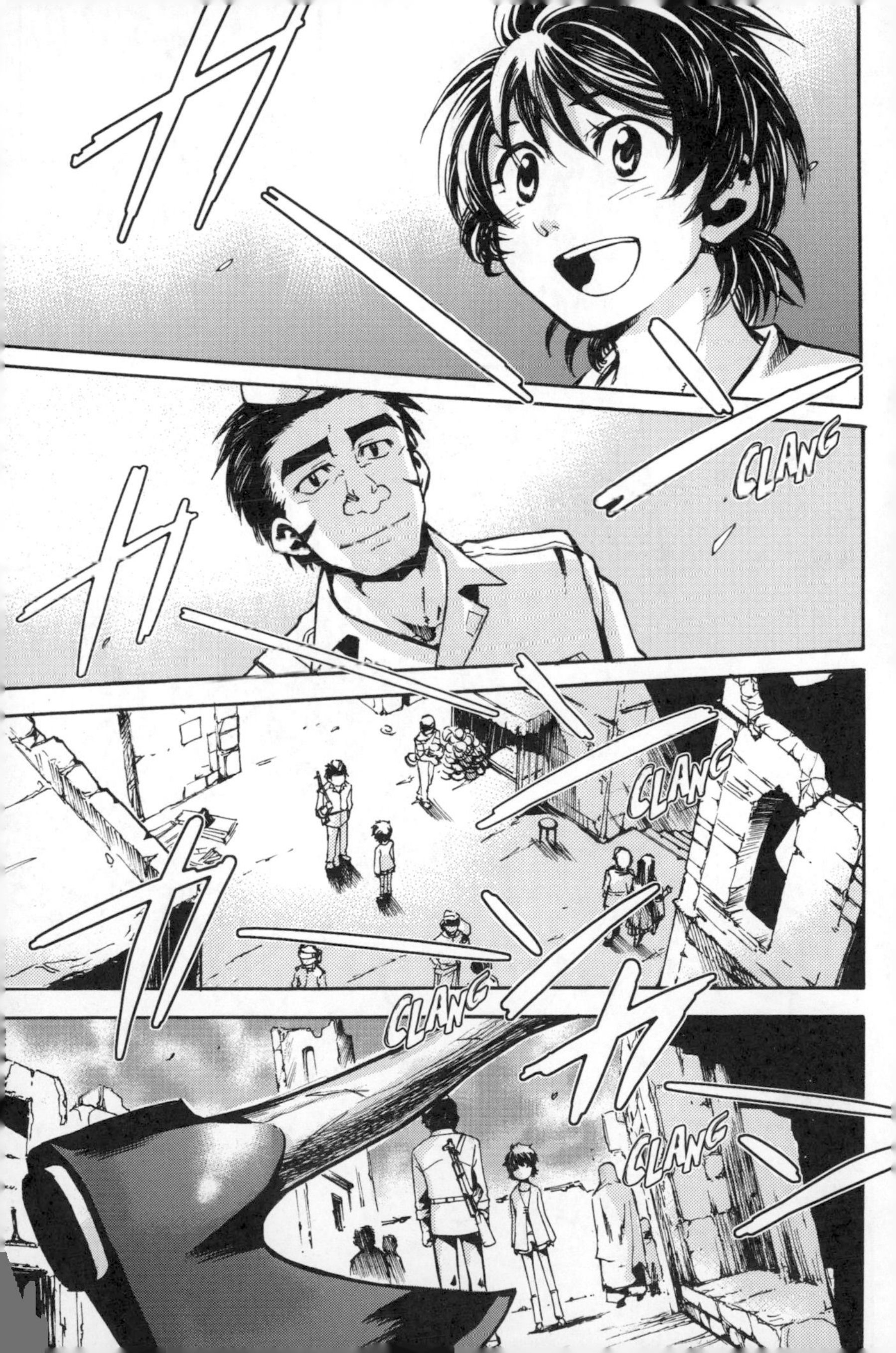
CLANG
CLANG
CLANG
CLANG

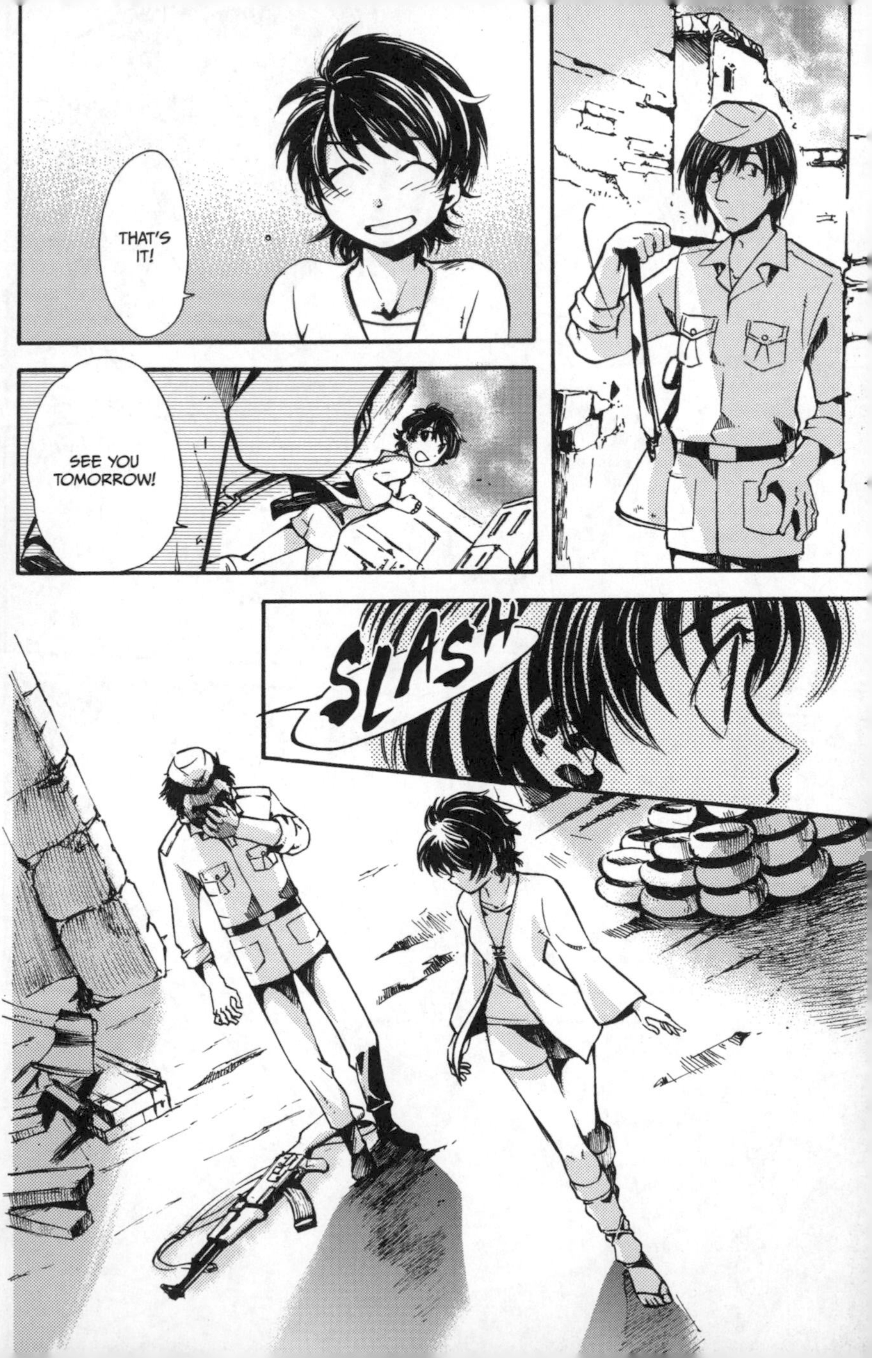
THAT'S IT!
SEE YOU TOMORROW!
SLASH

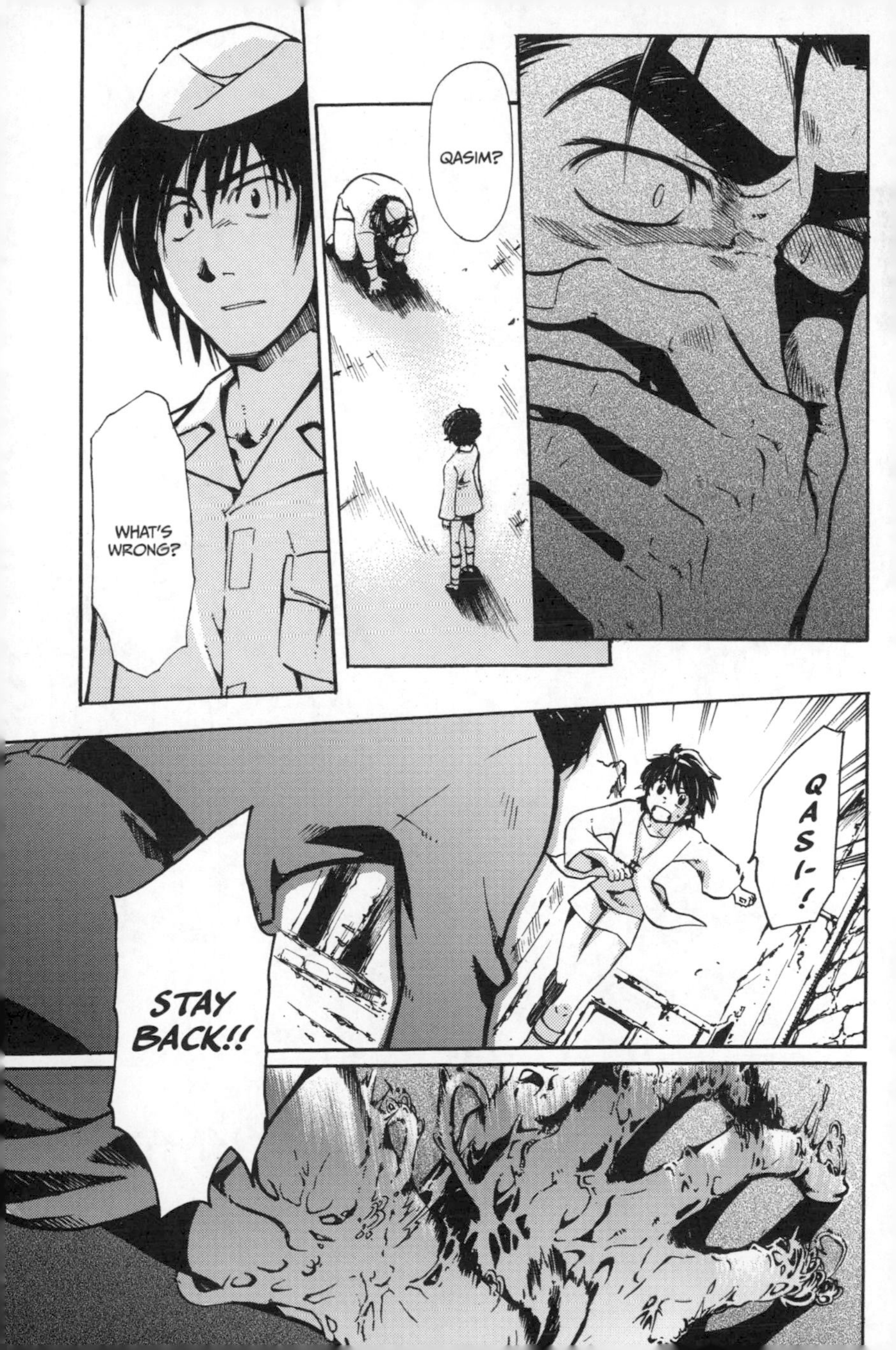
QASIM?
WHAT'S WRONG?
QASI-!
STAY BACK!!

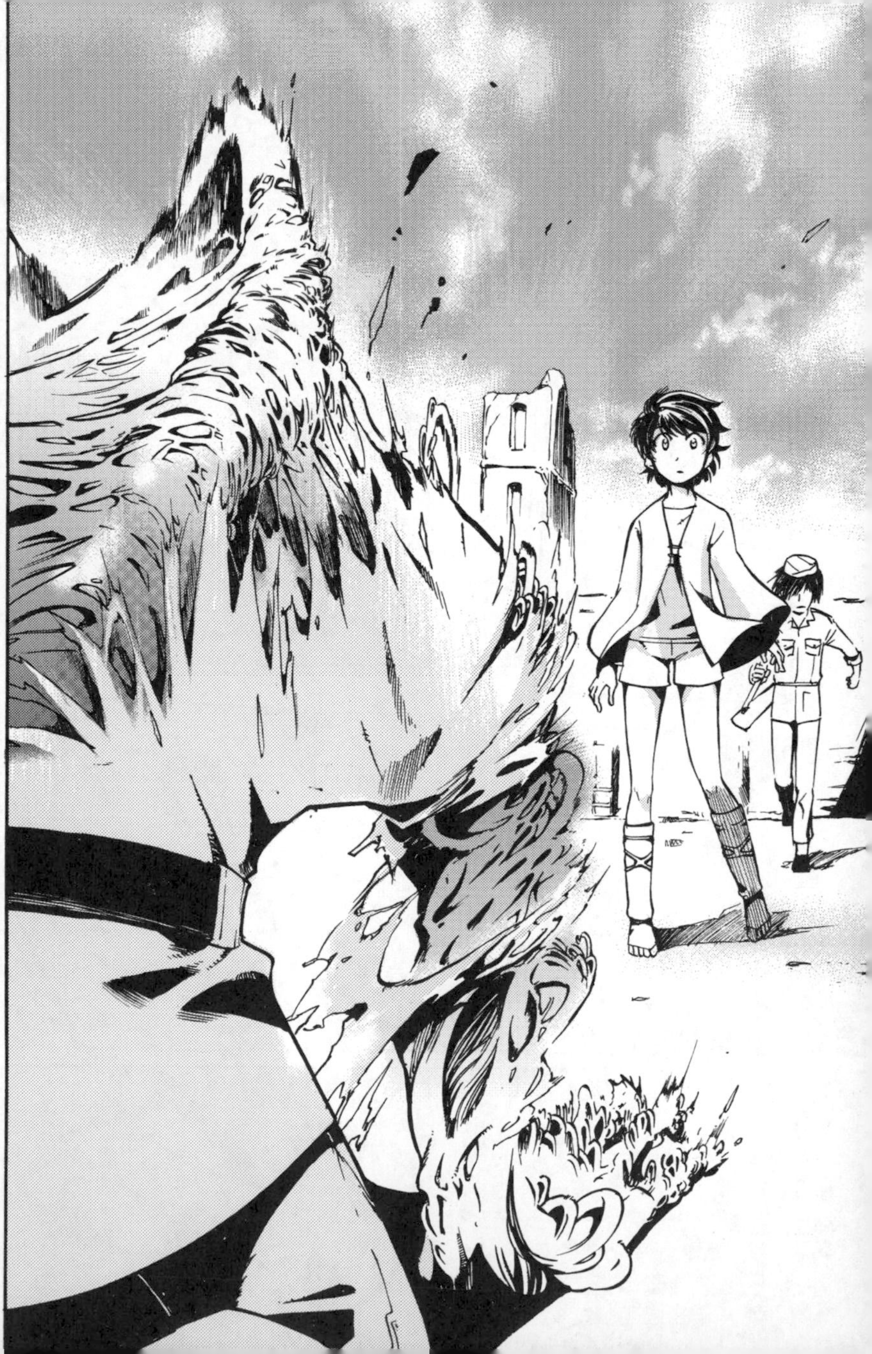

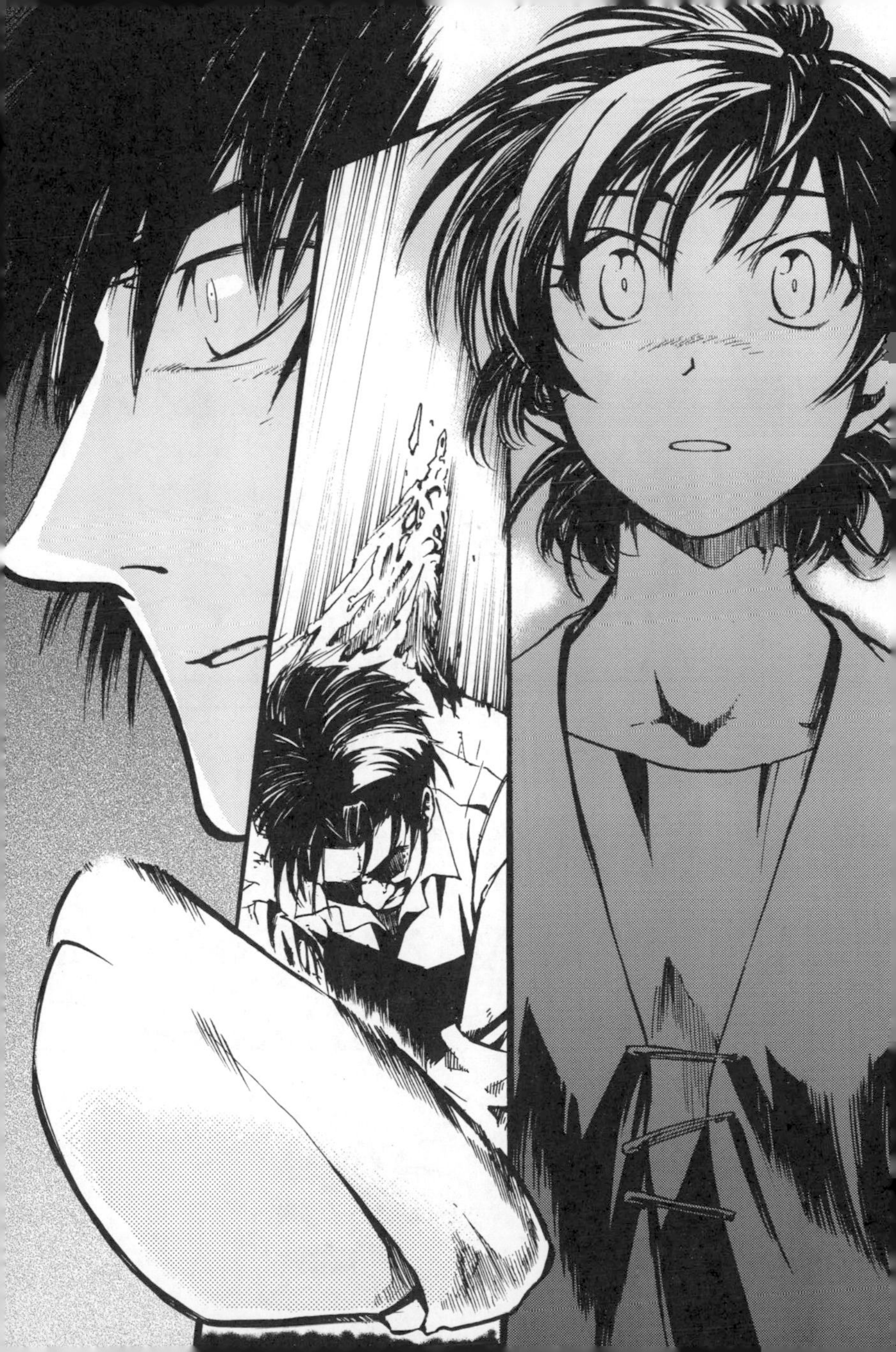

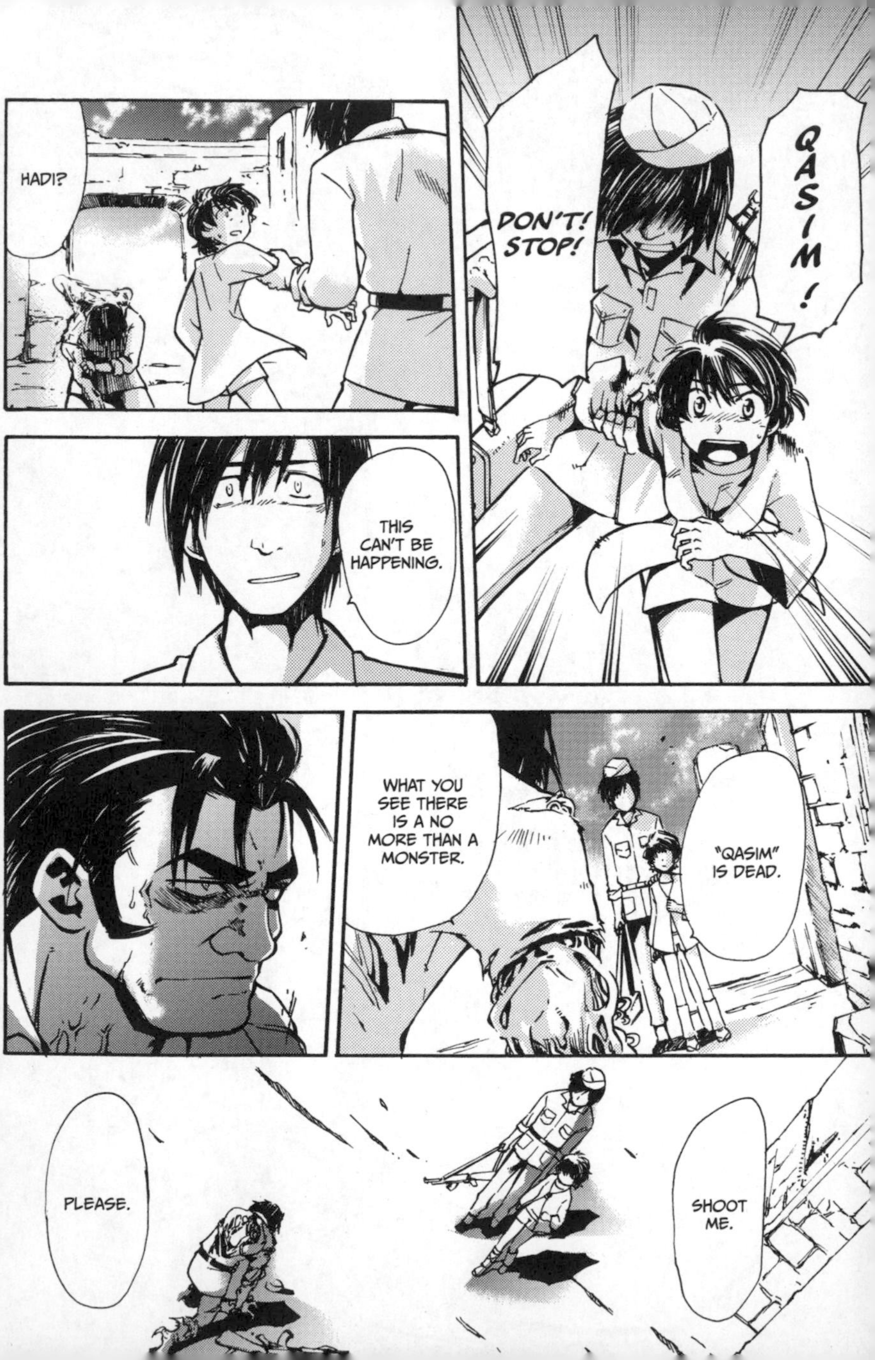
QASIM!
DON'T! STOP!
HADI?
THIS CAN'T BE HAPPENING.
"QASIM" IS DEAD.
WHAT YOU SEE THERE IS A NO MORE THAN A MONSTER.
SHOOT ME.
PLEASE.

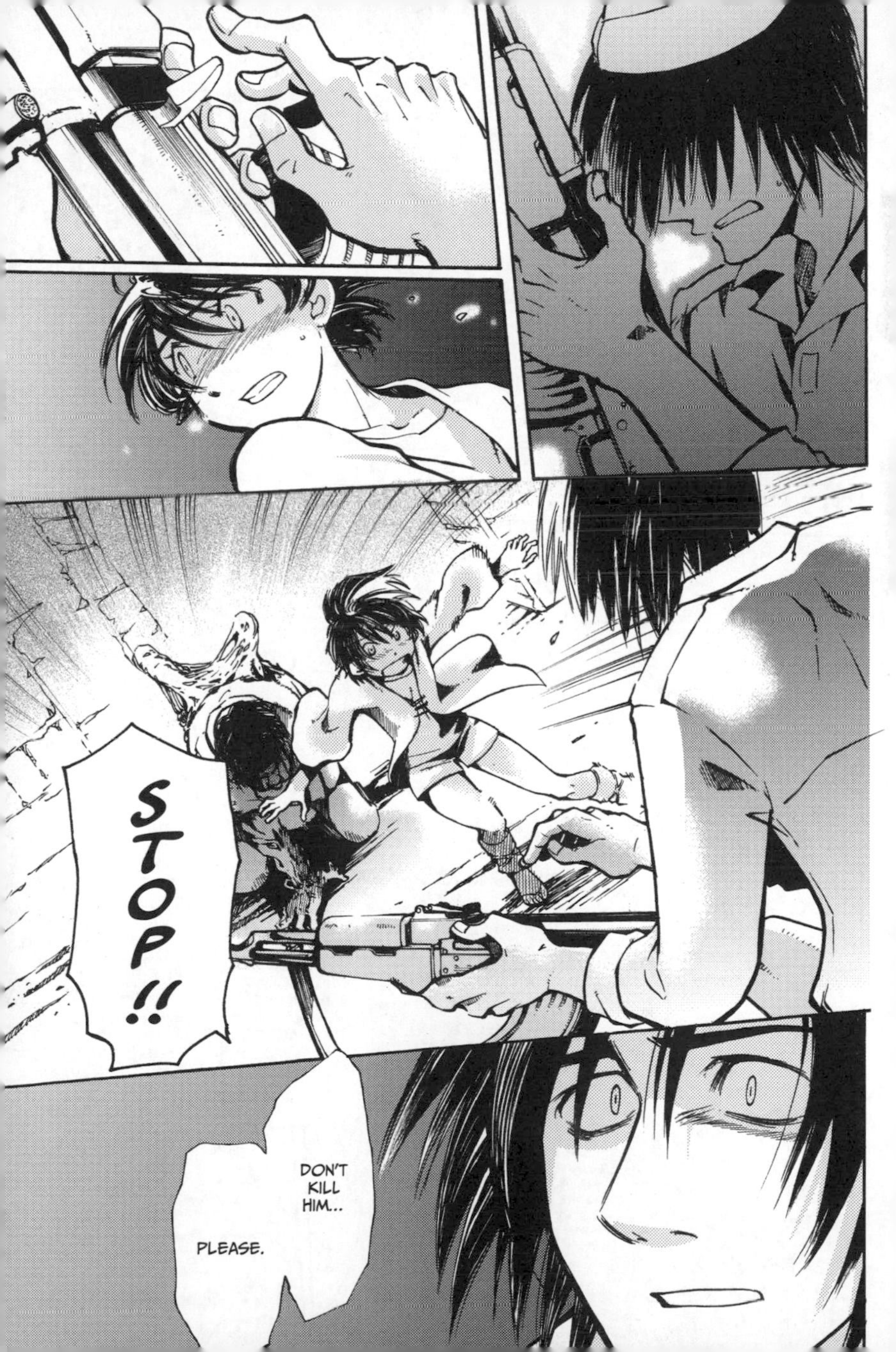
STOP!!
DON'T KILL HIM...
PLEASE.

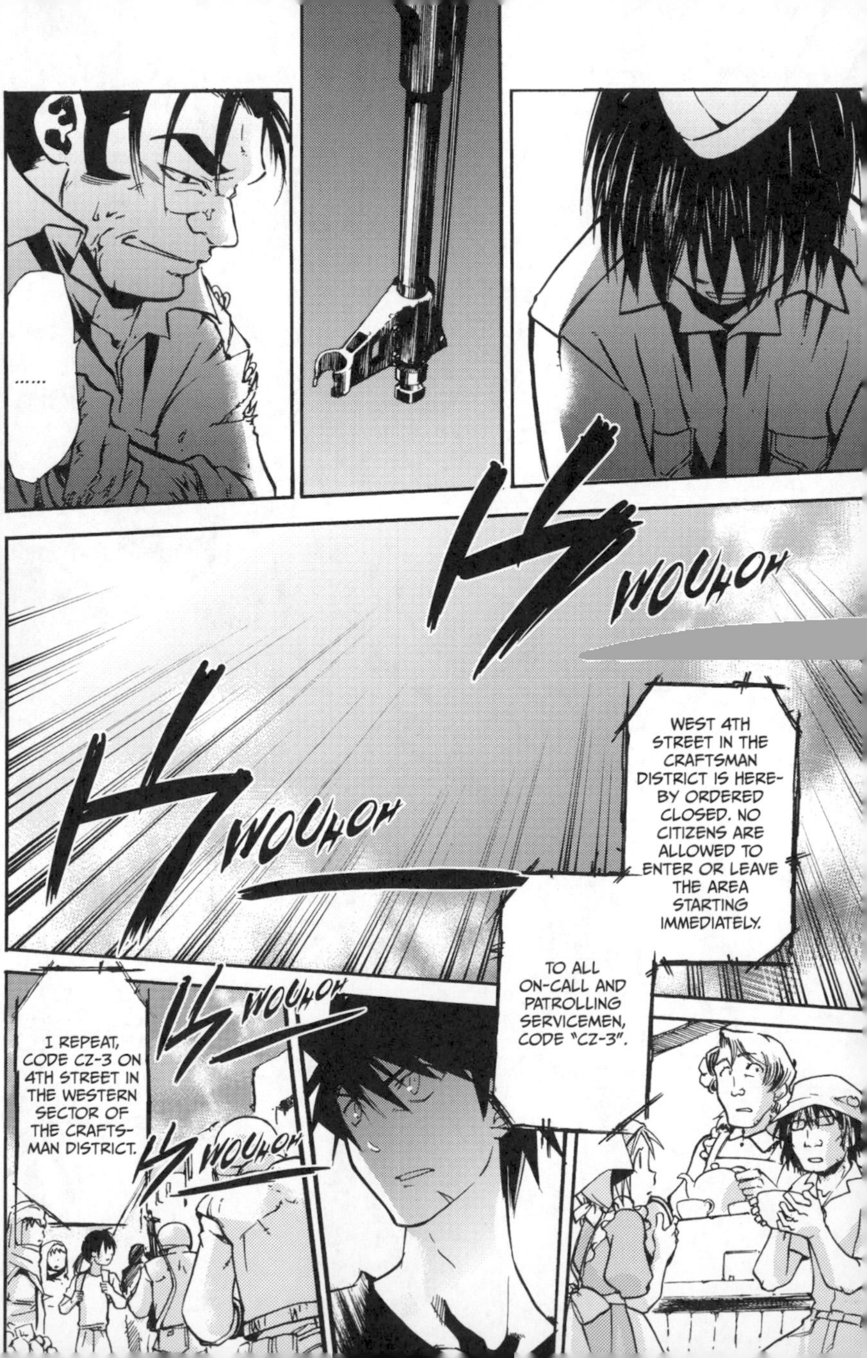
……
WOUHOH
WOUHOH
WEST 4TH STREET IN THE CRAFTSMAN DISTRICT IS HEREBY ORDERED CLOSED. NO CITIZENS ARE ALLOWED TO ENTER OR LEAVE THE AREA STARTING IMMEDIATELY.
TO ALL ON-CALL AND PATROLLING SERVICEMEN, CODE "CZ-3".
WOUHOH
I REPEAT, CODE CZ-3 ON 4TH STREET IN THE WESTERN SECTOR OF THE CRAFTSMAN DISTRICT.
WOUHOH

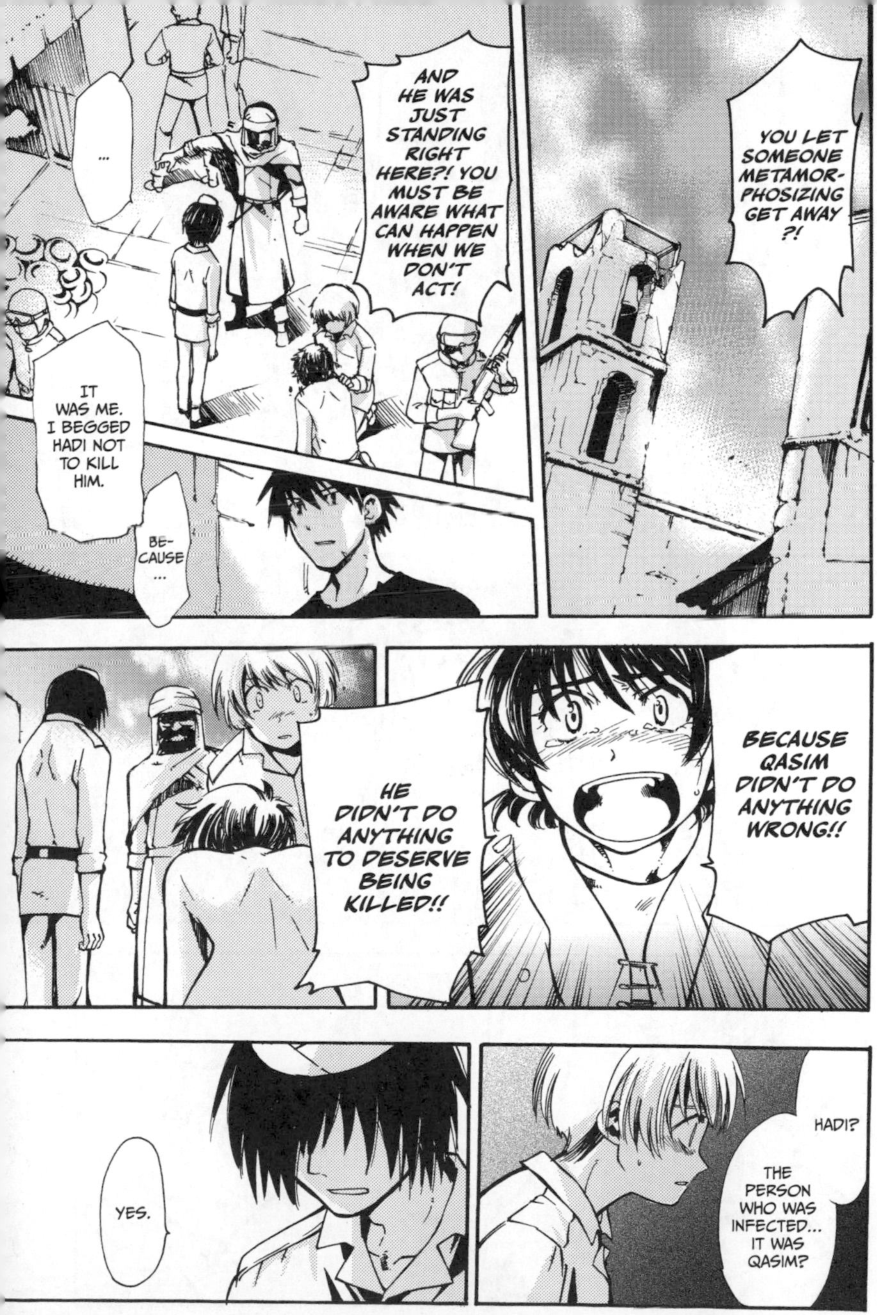
YOU LET SOMEONE METAMORPHOSIZING GET AWAY?!
AND HE WAS JUST STANDING RIGHT HERE?! YOU MUST BE AWARE WHAT CAN HAPPEN WHEN WE DON'T ACT!
...
IT WAS ME. I BEGGED HADI NOT TO KILL HIM.
BE-CAUSE ...
BECAUSE QASIM DIDN'T DO ANYTHING WRONG!!
HE DIDN'T DO ANYTHING TO DESERVE BEING KILLED!!
HADI?
THE PERSON WHO WAS INFECTED... IT WAS QASIM?
YES.

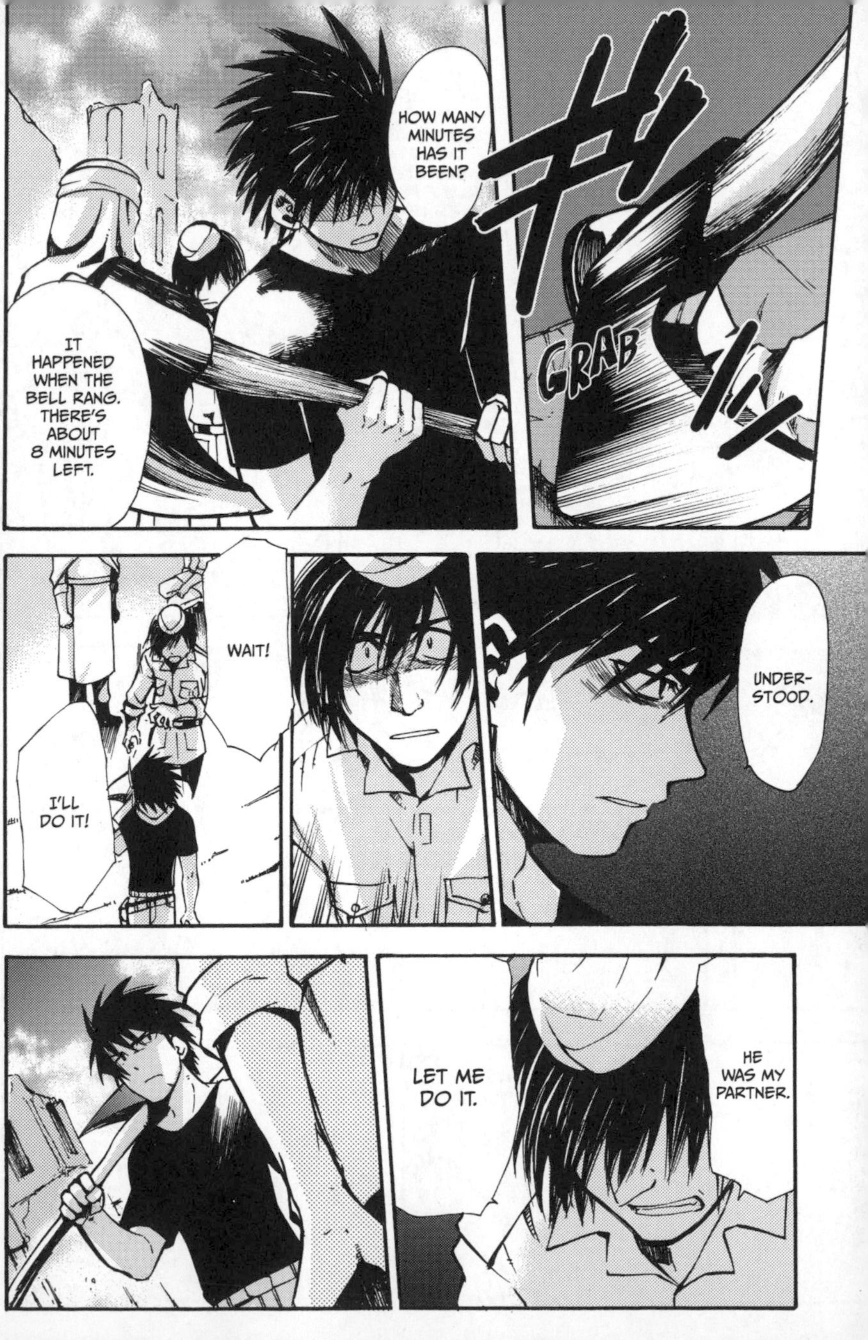
GRAB
HOW MANY MINUTES HAS IT BEEN?
IT HAPPENED WHEN THE BELL RANG. THERE'S ABOUT 8 MINUTES LEFT.
UNDER-STOOD.
WAIT!
I'LL DO IT!
HE WAS MY PARTNER.
LET ME DO IT.

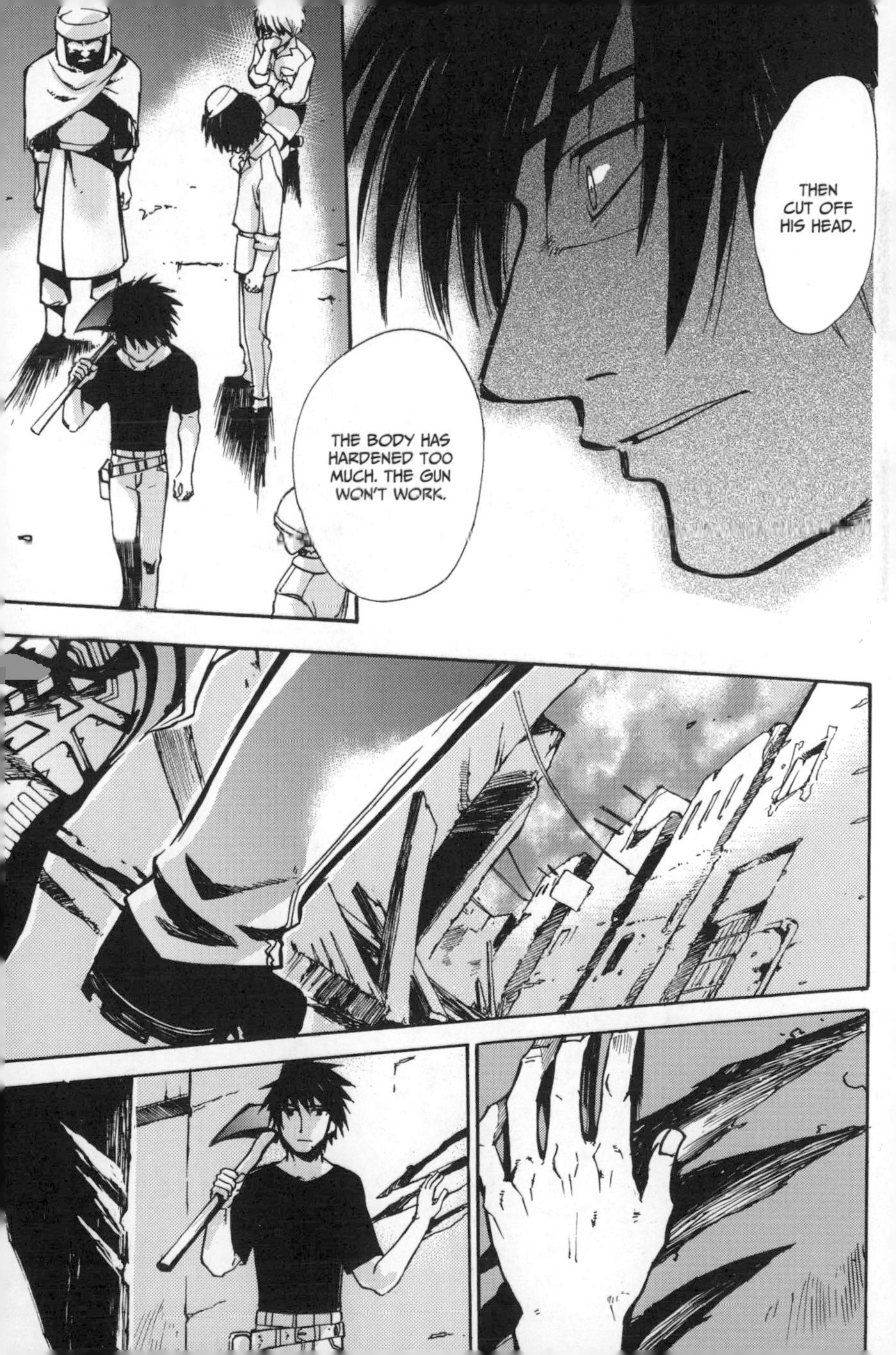
THE BODY HAS HARDENED TOO MUCH. THE GUN WON'T WORK.
THEN CUT OFF HIS HEAD.

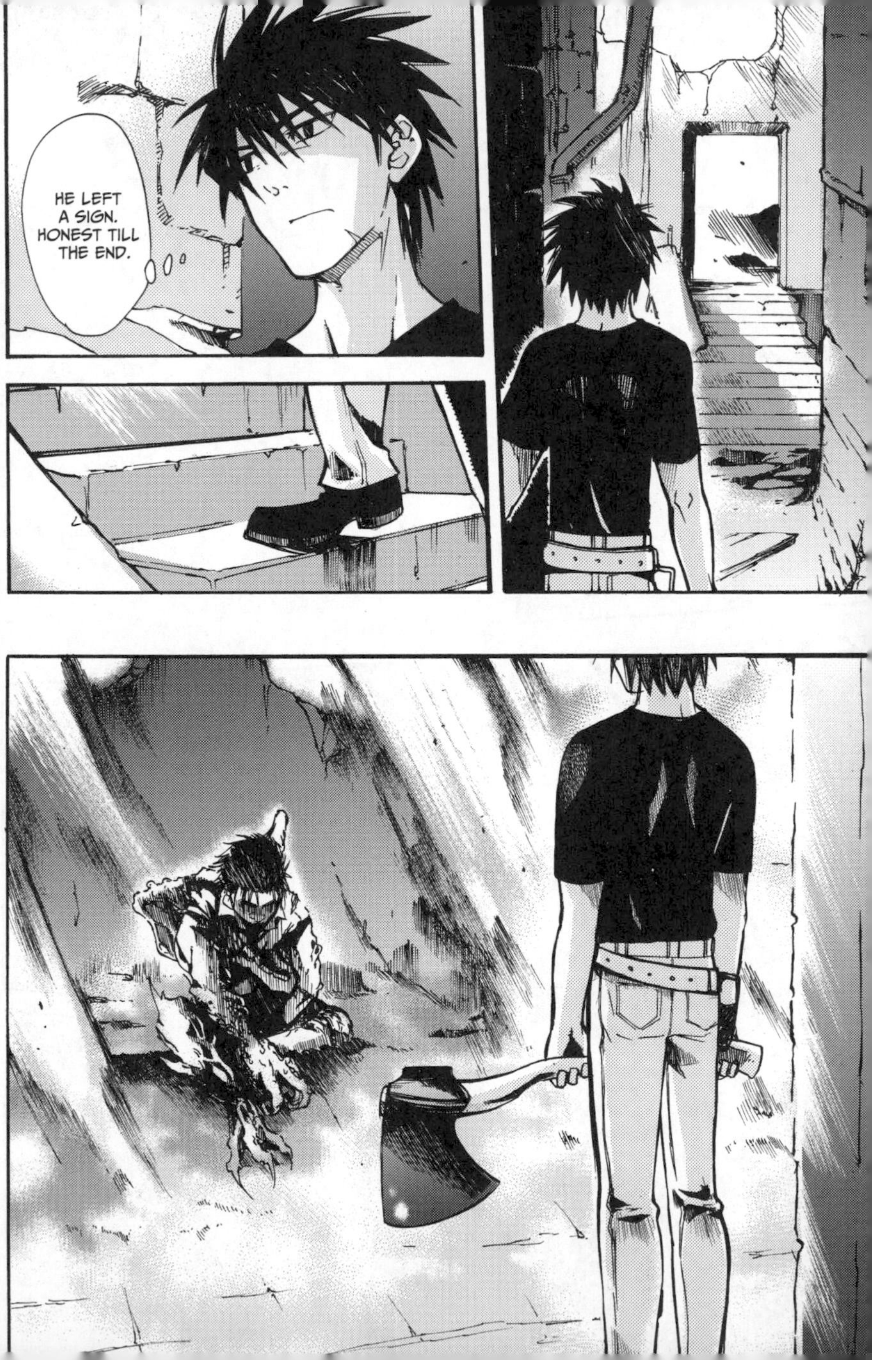
HE LEFT A SIGN. HONEST TILL THE END.

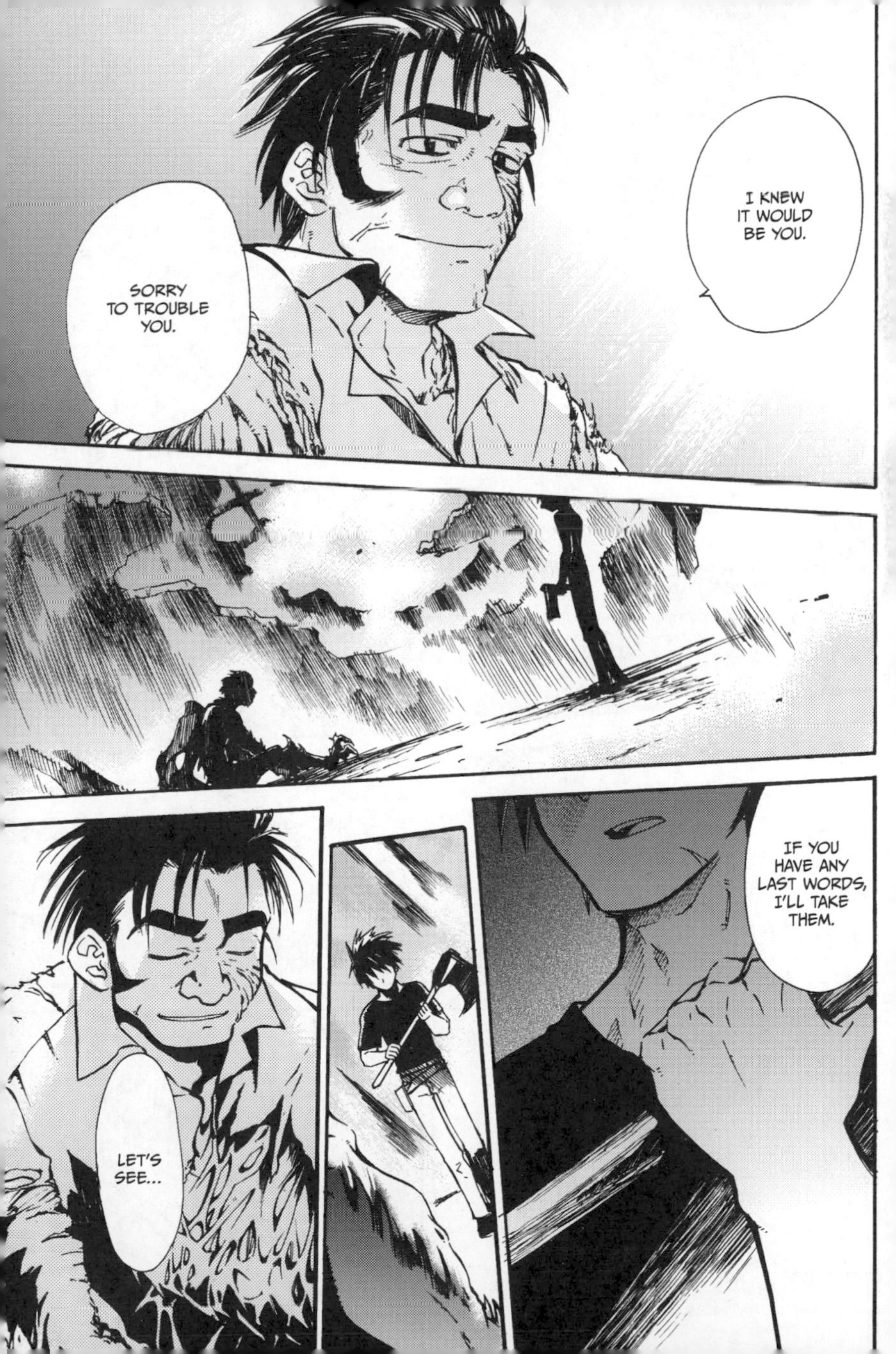
I KNEW IT WOULD BE YOU.
SORRY TO TROUBLE YOU.
IF YOU HAVE ANY LAST WORDS, I'LL TAKE THEM.
LET'S SEE...

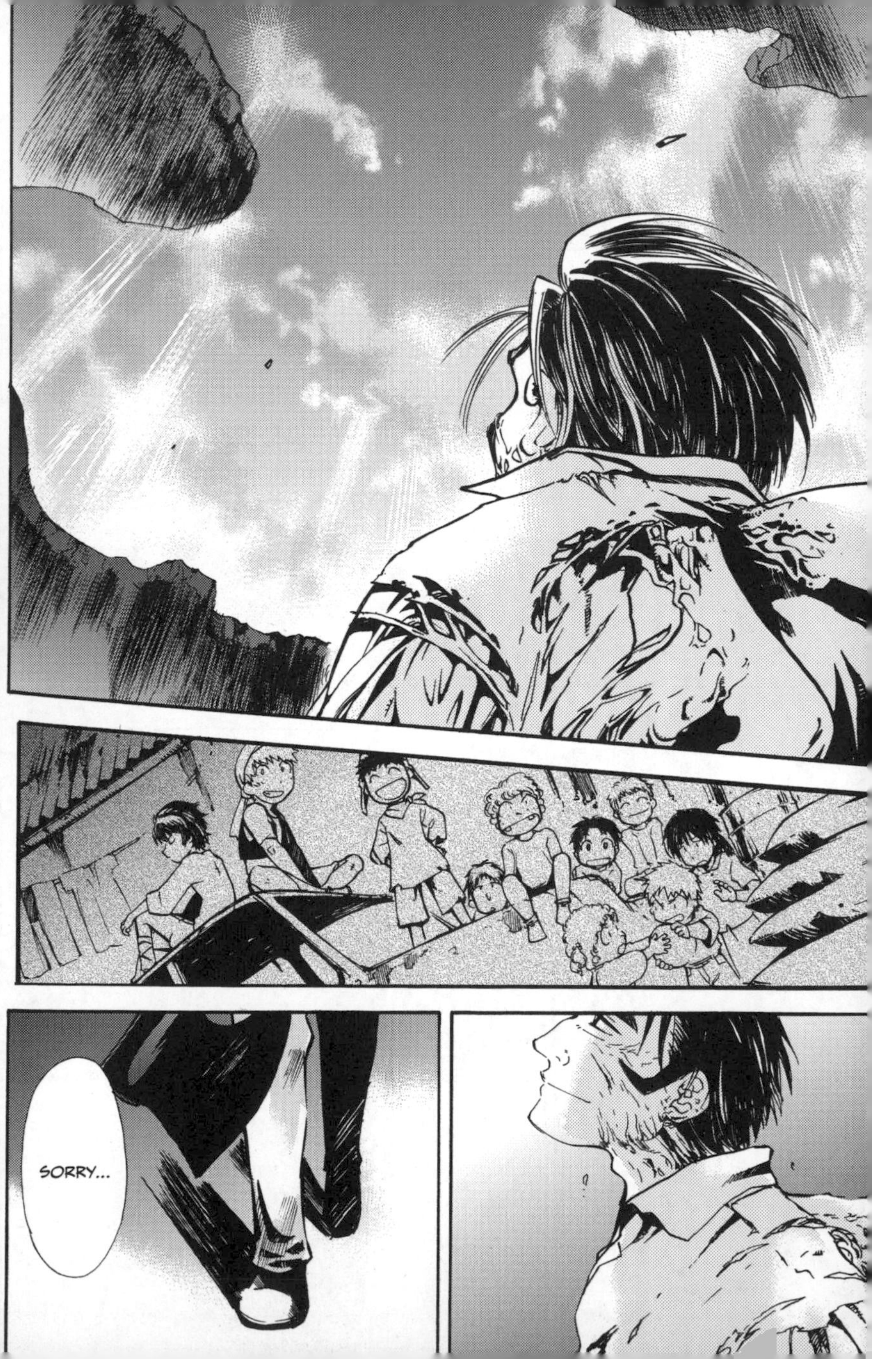
SORRY...

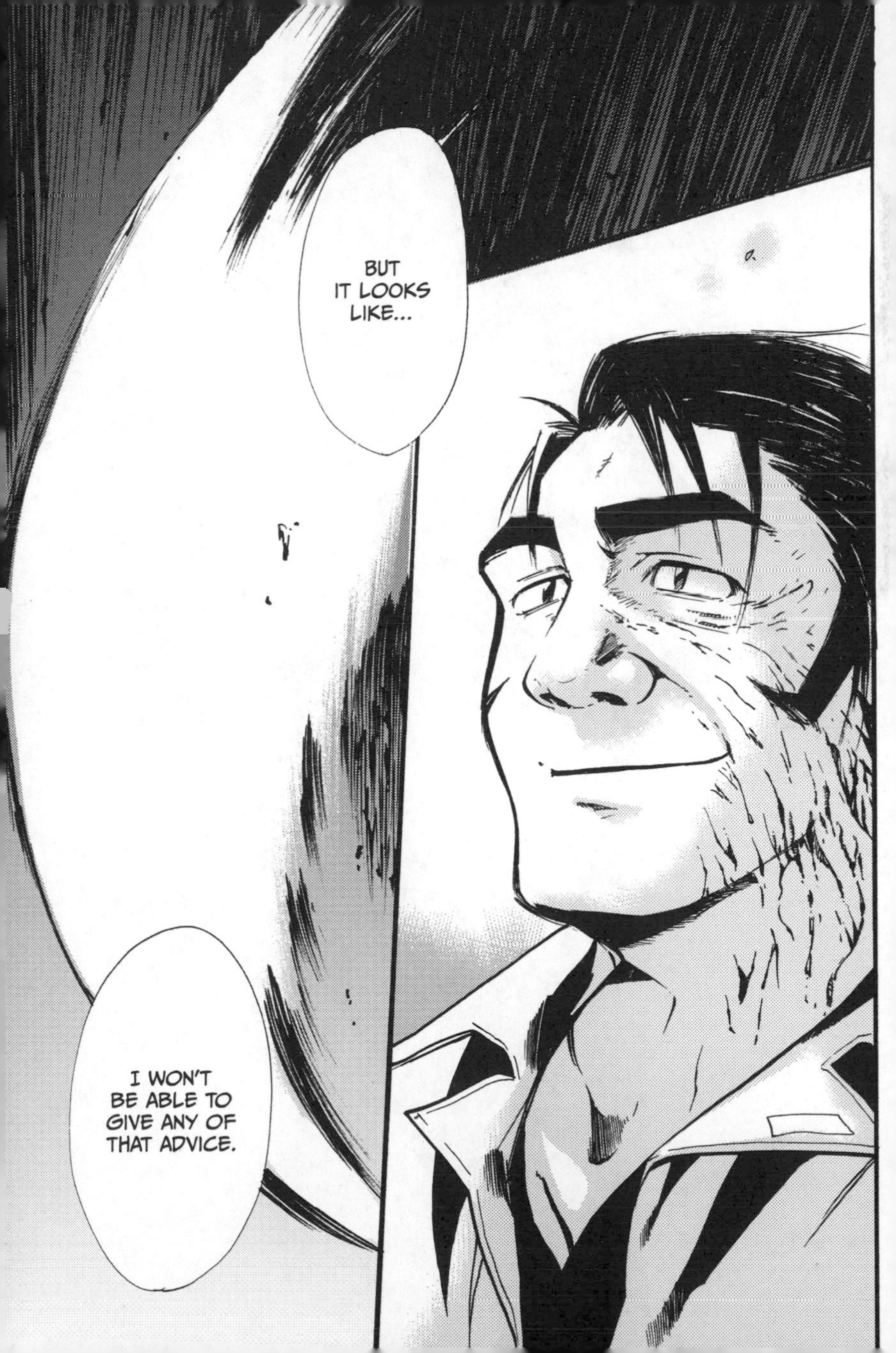
BUT IT LOOKS LIKE...
I WON'T BE ABLE TO GIVE ANY OF THAT ADVICE.

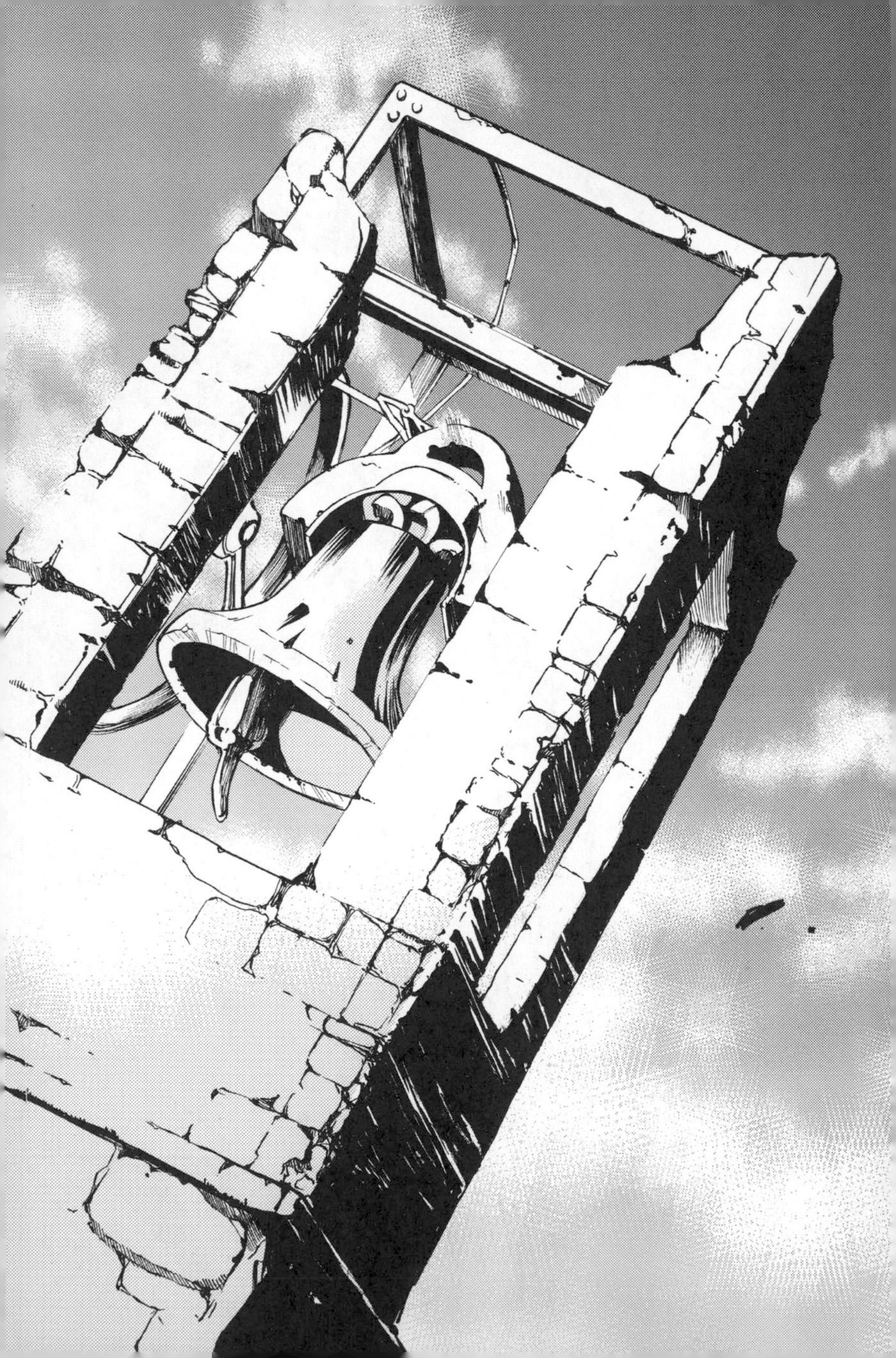

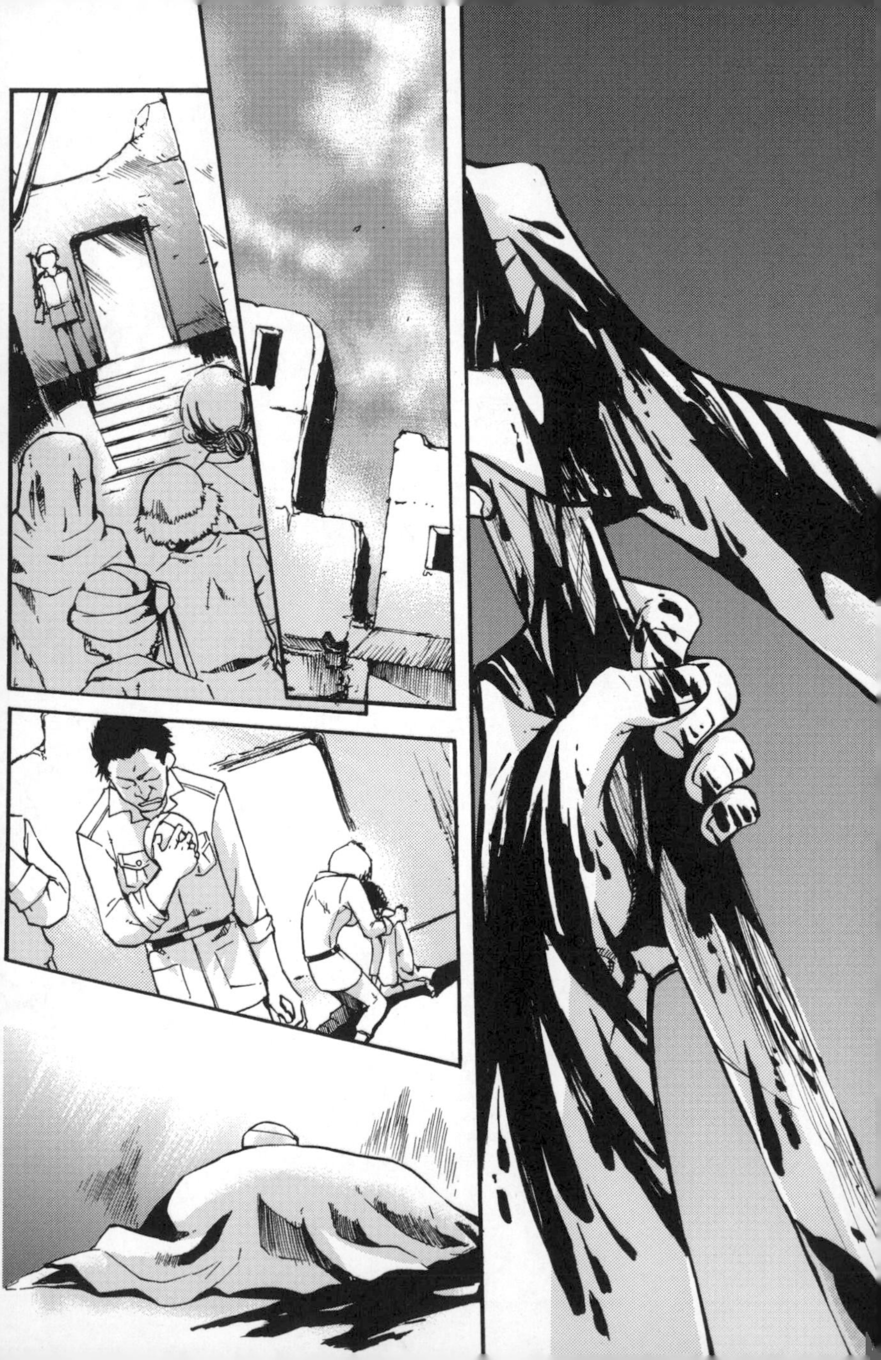

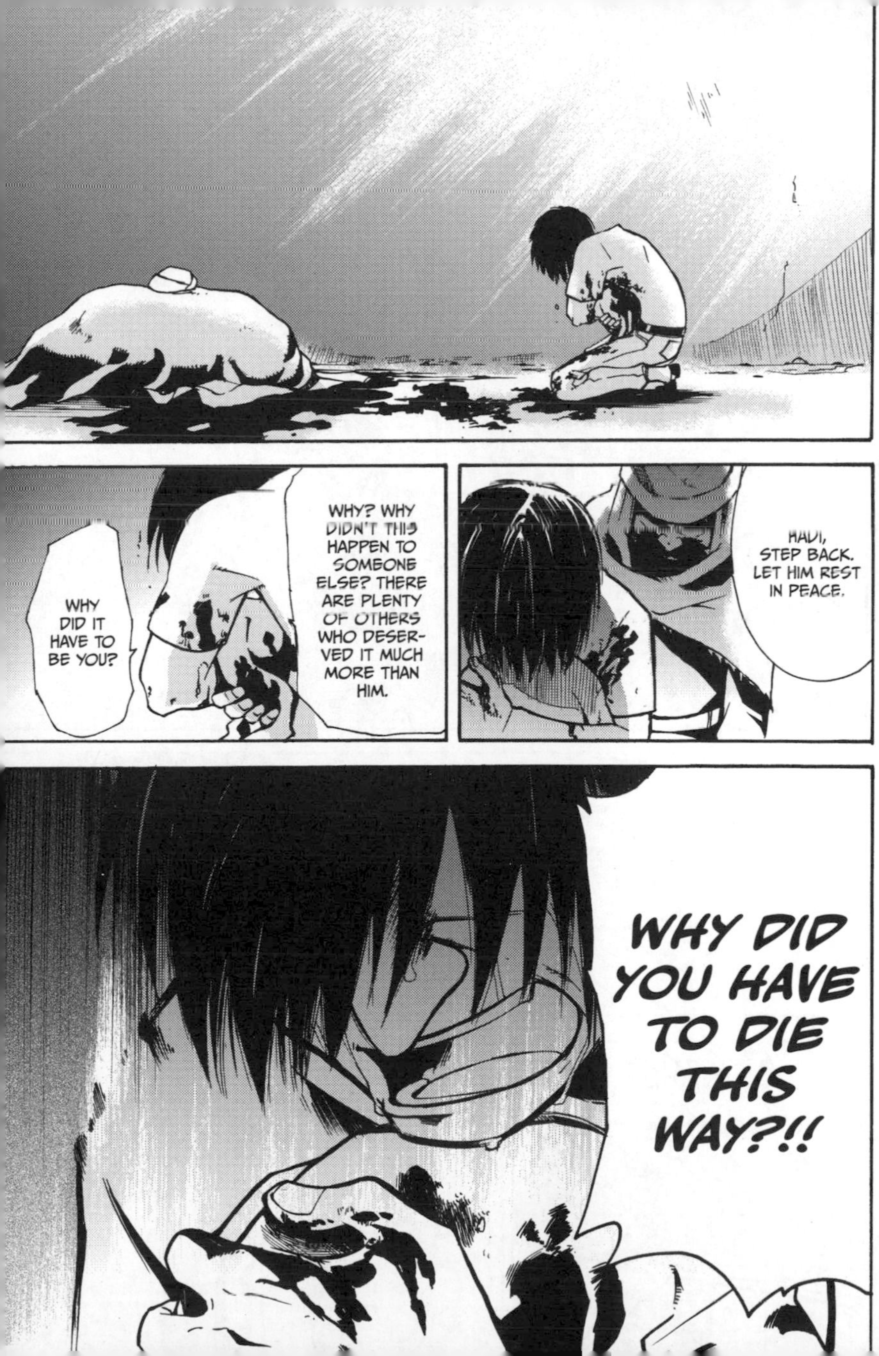
HADI, STEP BACK. LET HIM REST IN PEACE.
WHY? WHY DIDN'T THIS HAPPEN TO SOMEONE ELSE? THERE ARE PLENTY OF OTHERS WHO DESERVED IT MUCH MORE THAN HIM.
WHY DID IT HAVE TO BE YOU?
WHY DID YOU HAVE TO DIE THIS WAY?!!

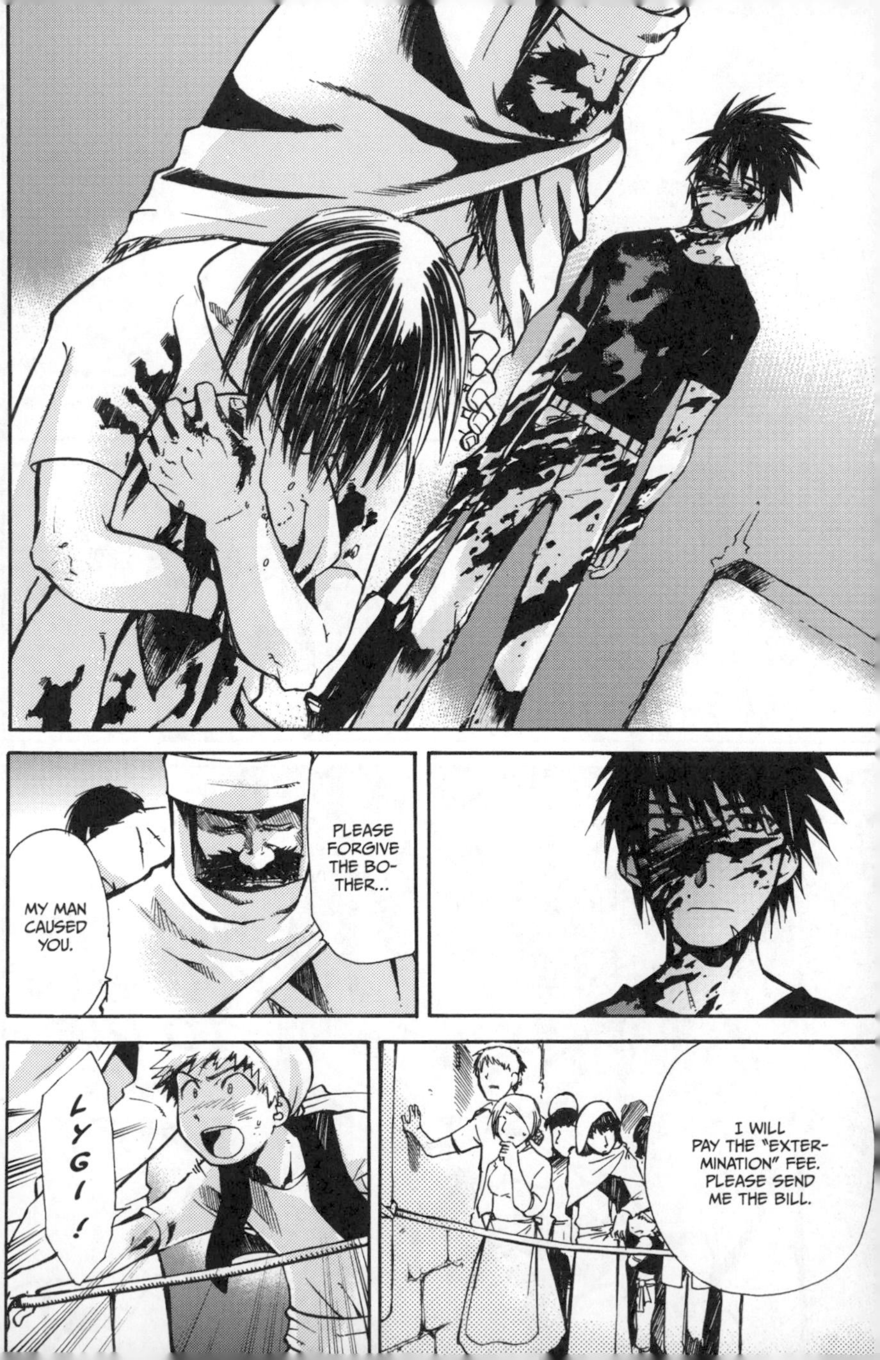
PLEASE FORGIVE THE BOTHER...
MY MAN CAUSED YOU.
I WILL PAY THE "EXTERMINATION" FEE. PLEASE SEND ME THE BILL.
LYGI!

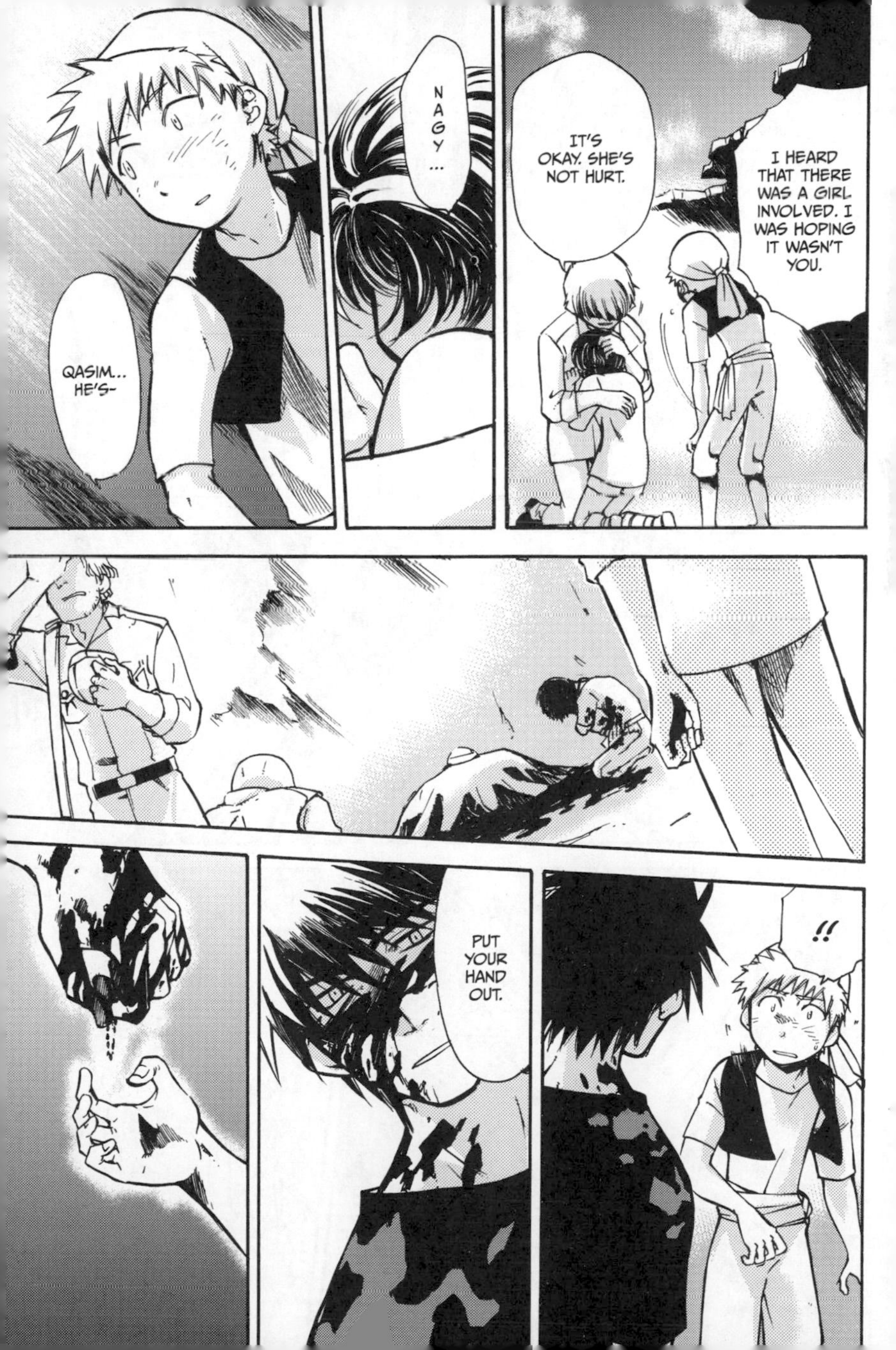
I HEARD THAT THERE WAS A GIRL INVOLVED. I WAS HOPING IT WASN'T YOU.
IT'S OKAY. SHE'S NOT HURT.
NAGY...
QASIM... HE'S-
!!
PUT YOUR HAND OUT.

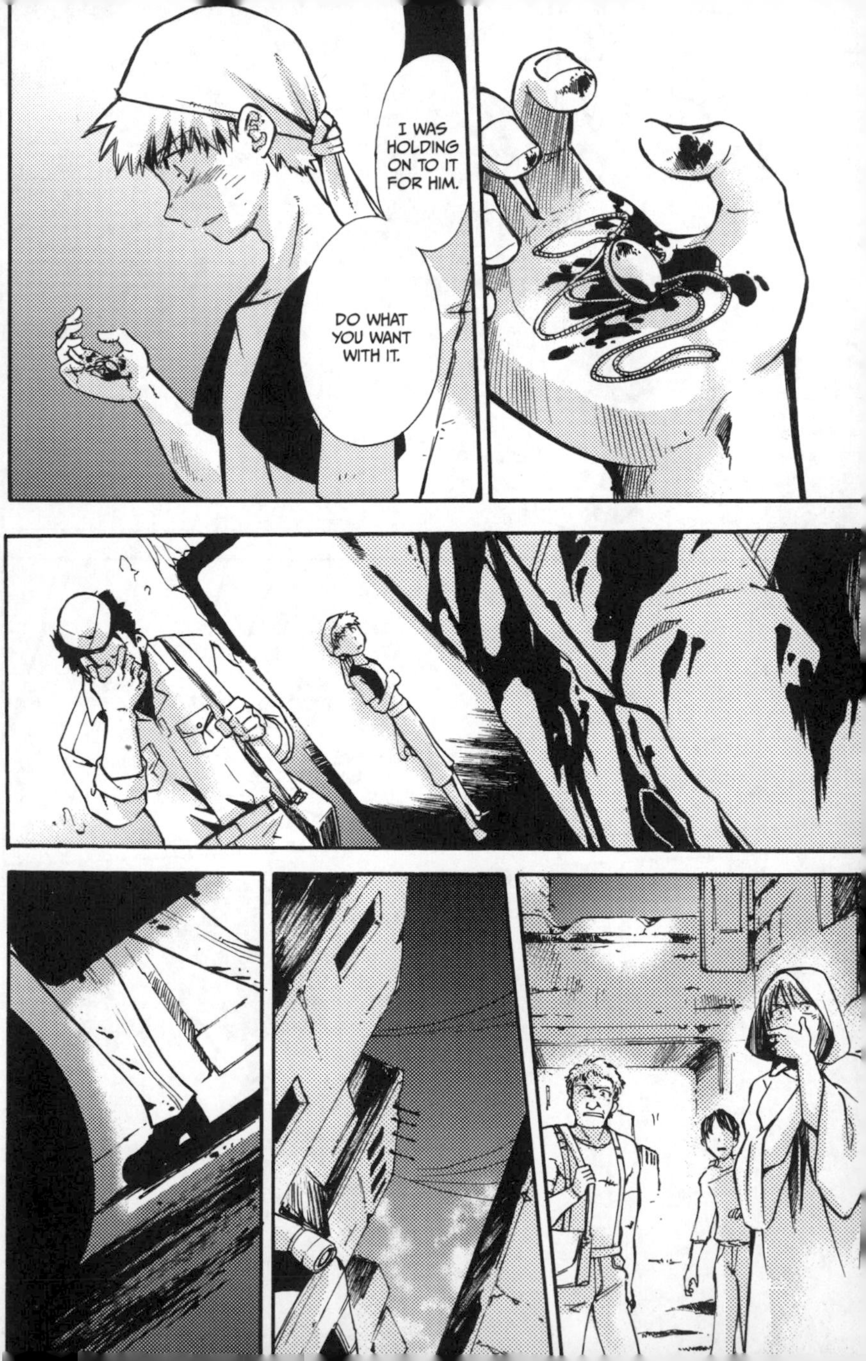
I WAS HOLDING ON TO IT FOR HIM.
DO WHAT YOU WANT WITH IT.

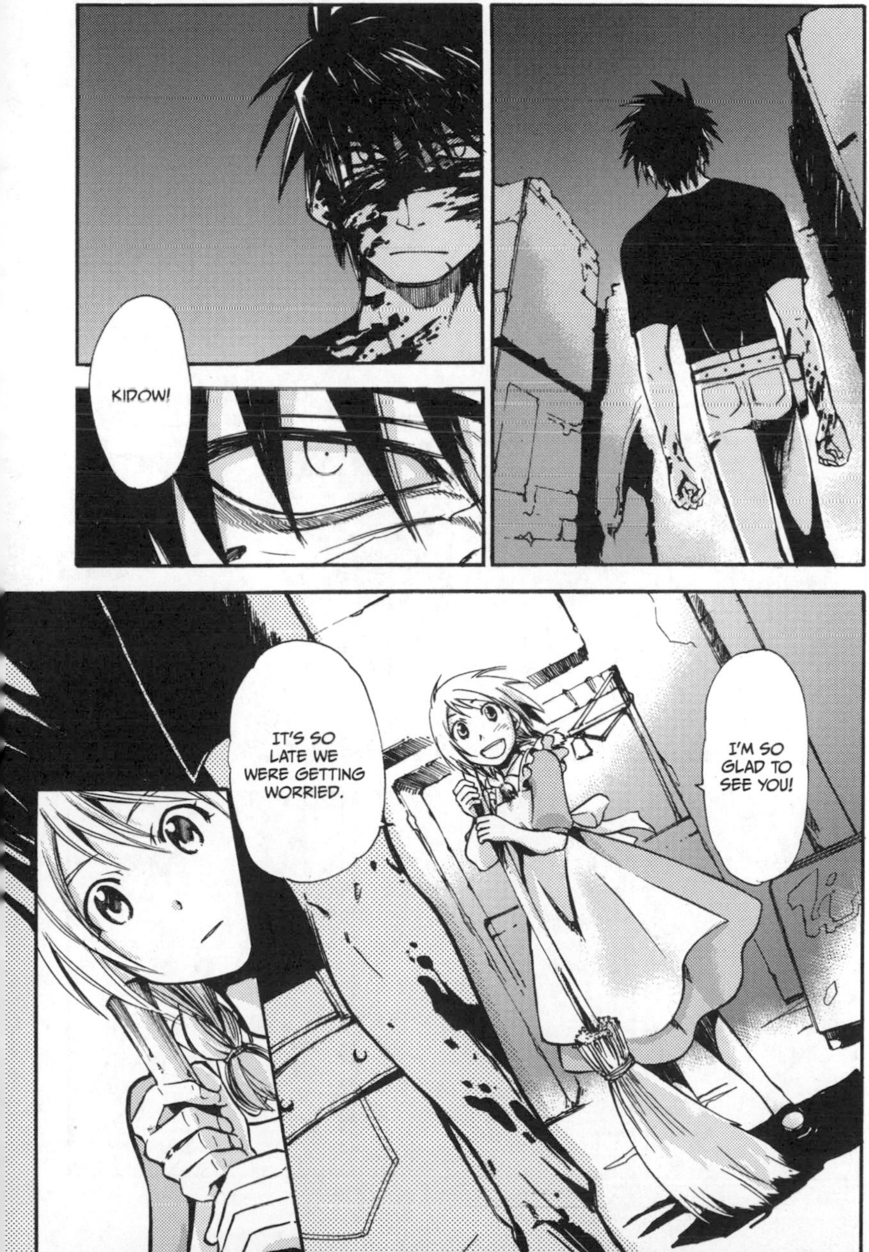
KIDOW!
I'M SO GLAD TO SEE YOU!
IT'S SO LATE WE WERE GETTING WORRIED.

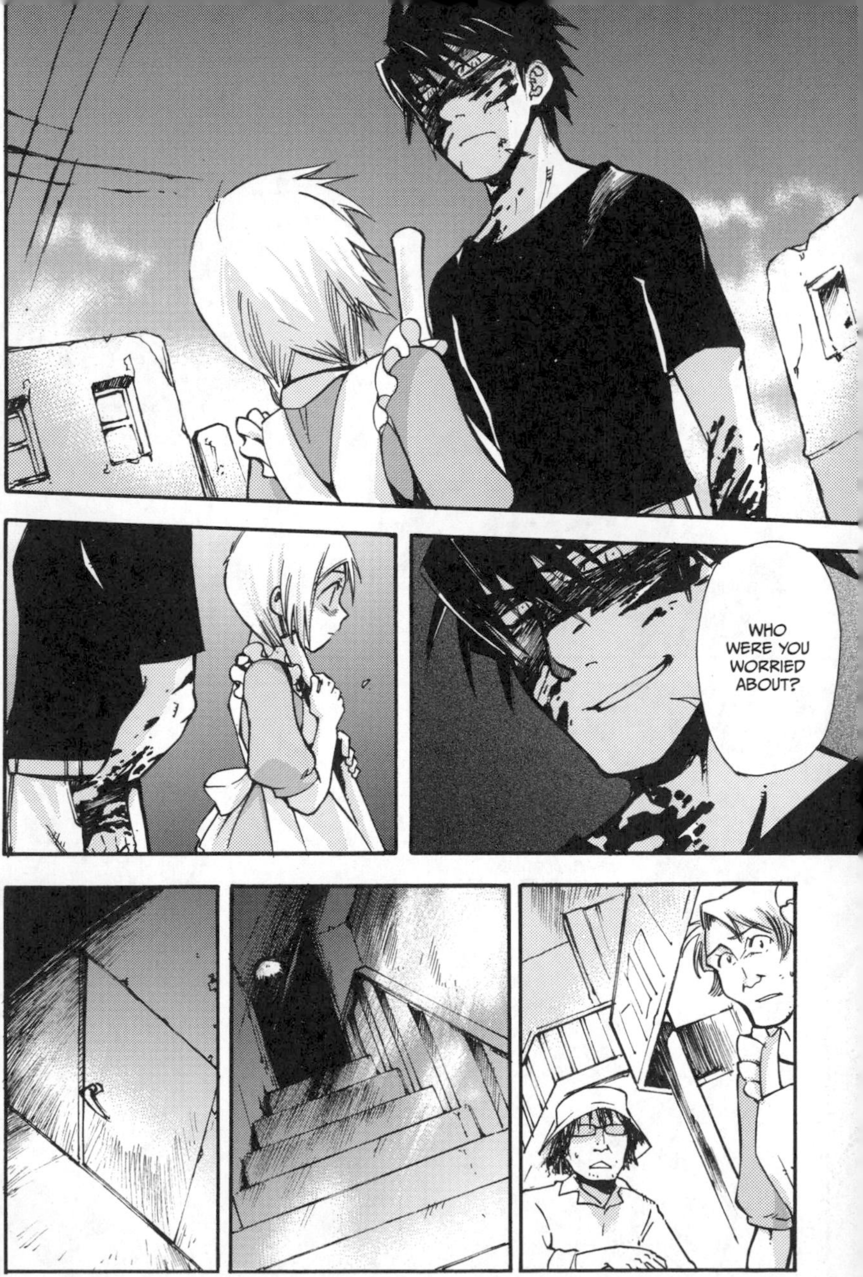
WHO WERE YOU WORRIED ABOUT?

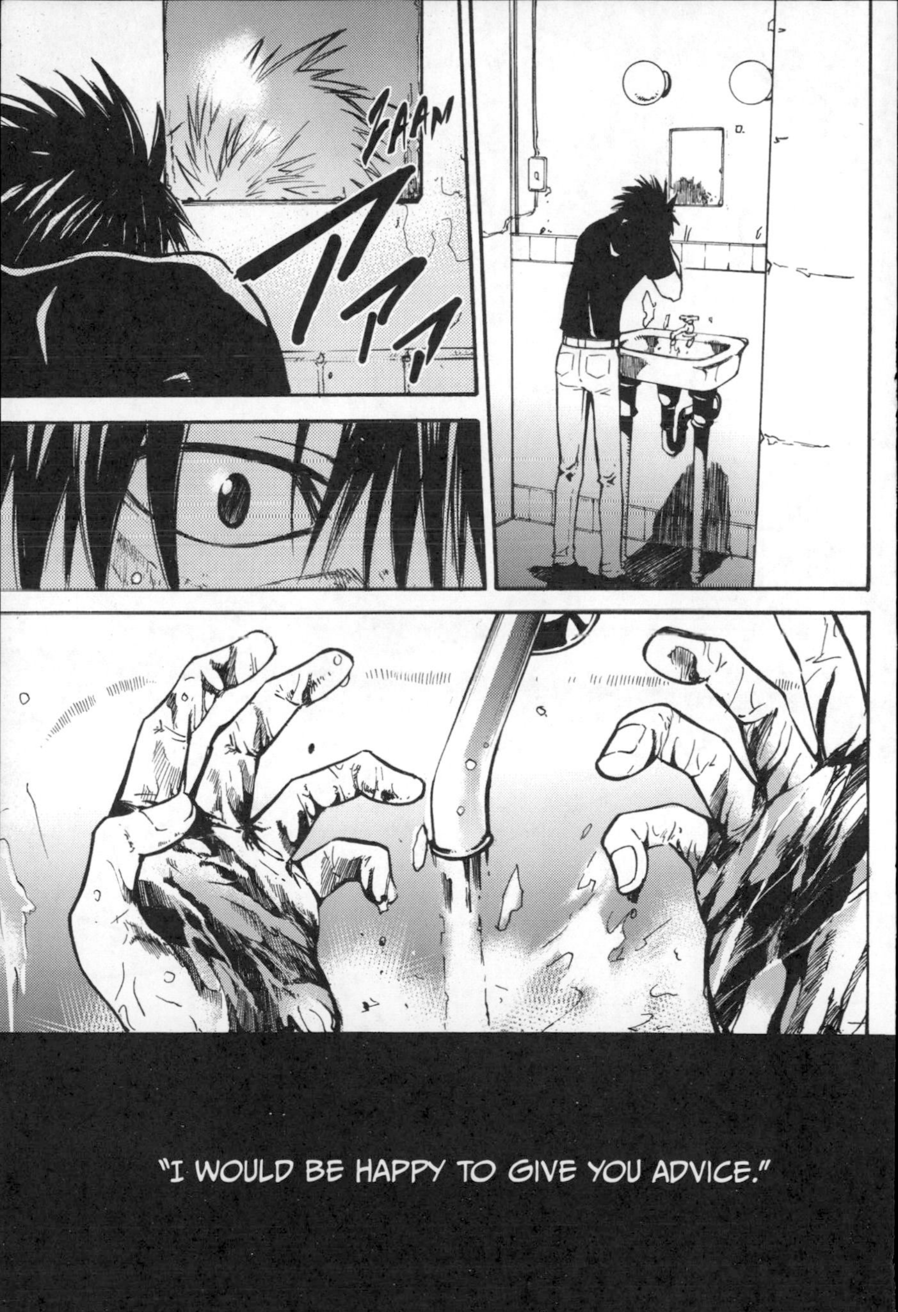
ZAAM

"I WOULD BE HAPPY TO GIVE YOU ADVICE."

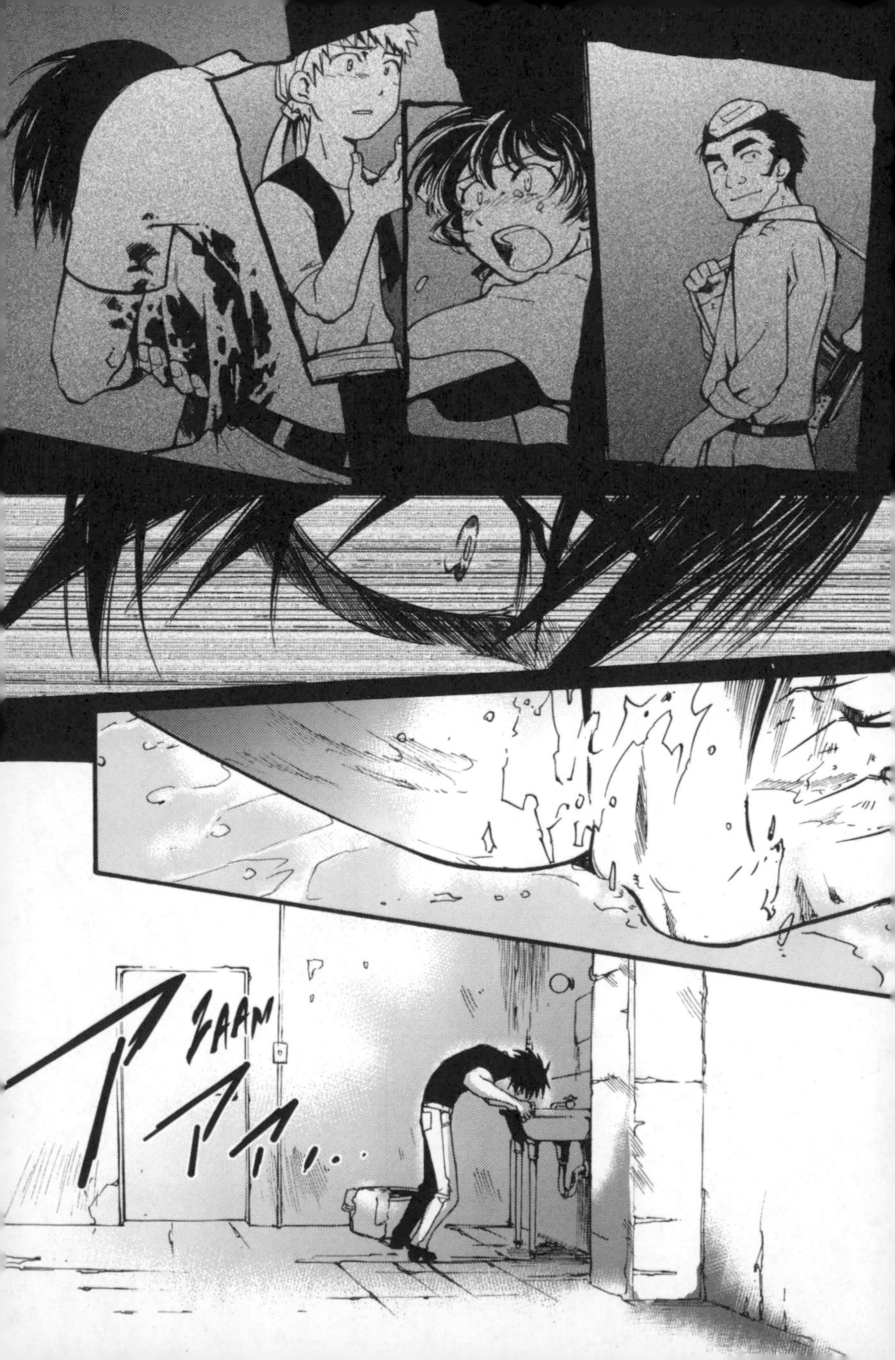
ZAAM

[CHAPTER 10]

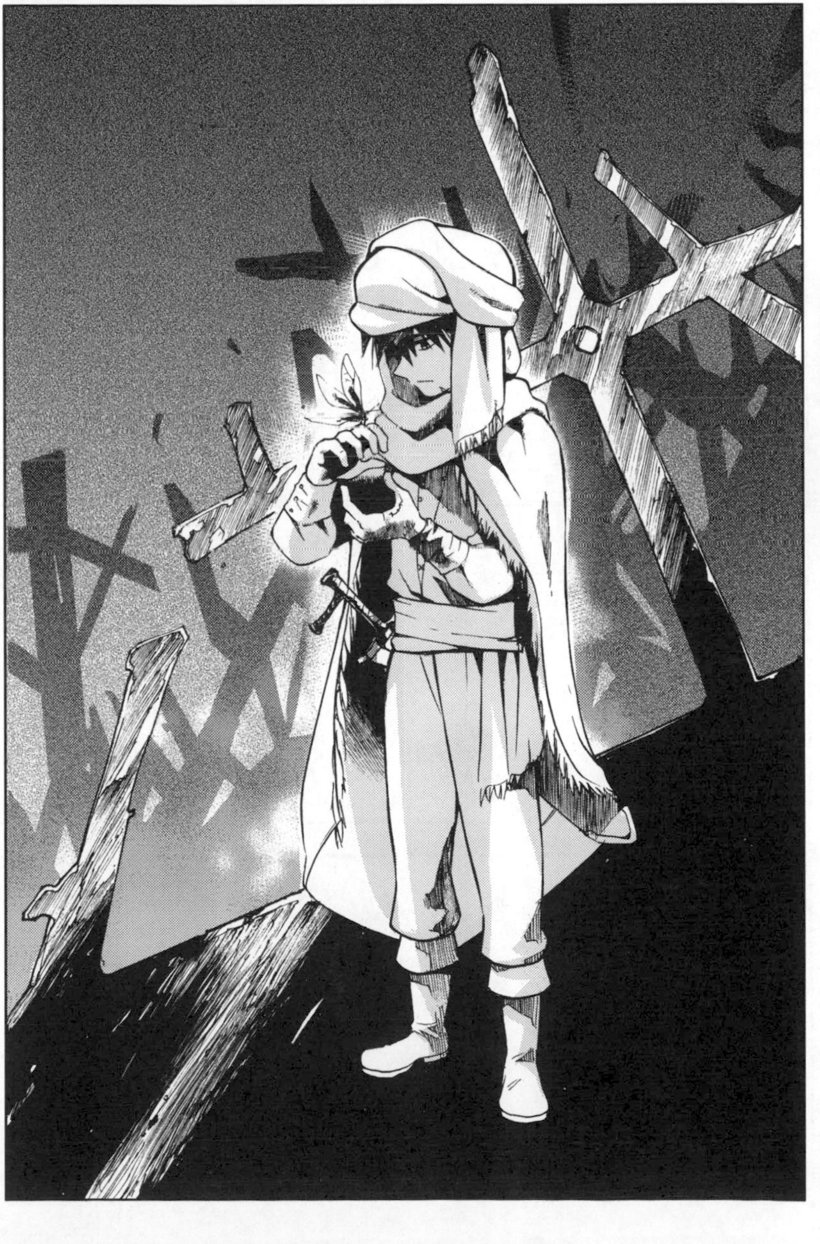

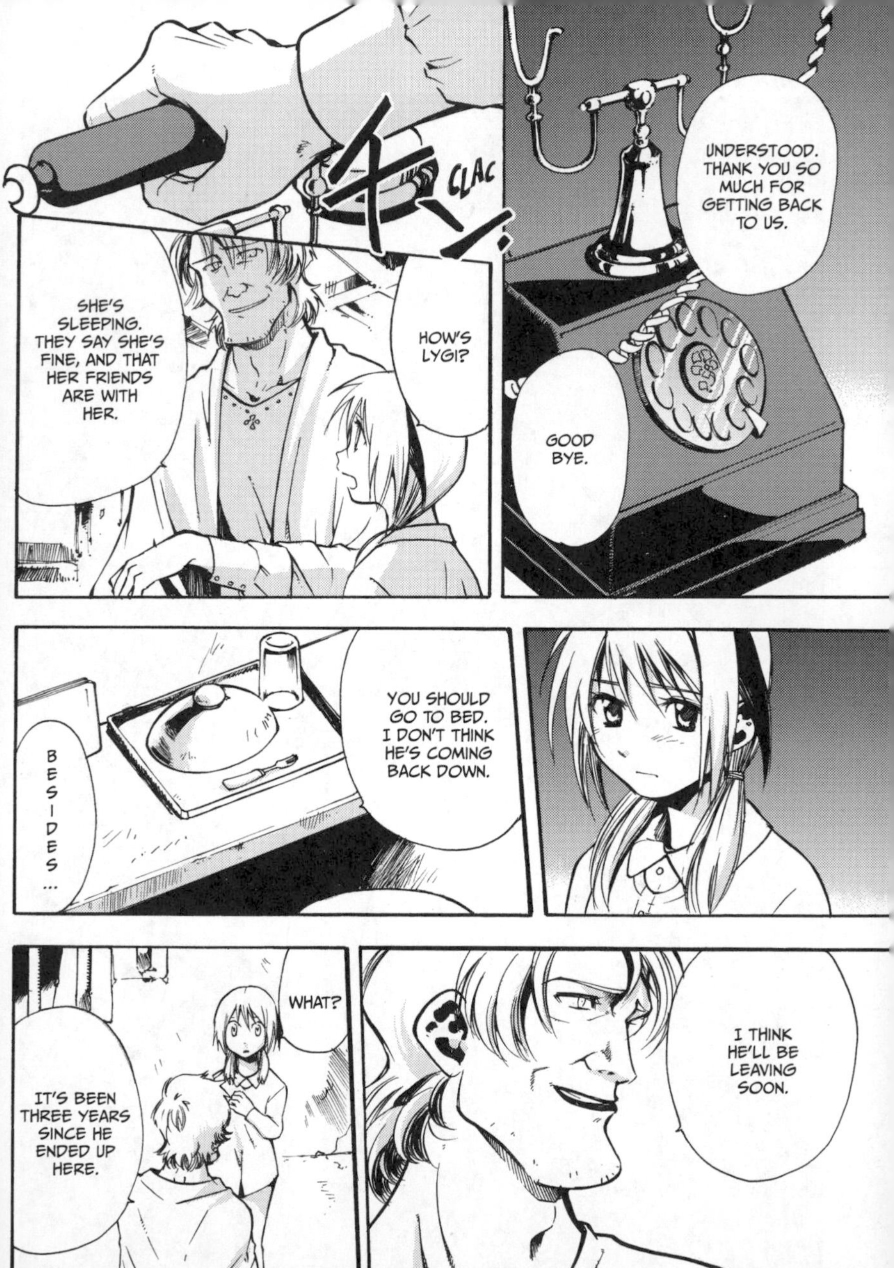
UNDERSTOOD. THANK YOU SO MUCH FOR GETTING BACK TO US.
GOOD BYE.
CLAC
HOW'S LYGI?
SHE'S SLEEPING. THEY SAY SHE'S FINE, AND THAT HER FRIENDS ARE WITH HER.
YOU SHOULD GO TO BED. I DON'T THINK HE'S COMING BACK DOWN.
BESIDES...
I THINK HE'LL BE LEAVING SOON.
WHAT?
IT'S BEEN THREE YEARS SINCE HE ENDED UP HERE.

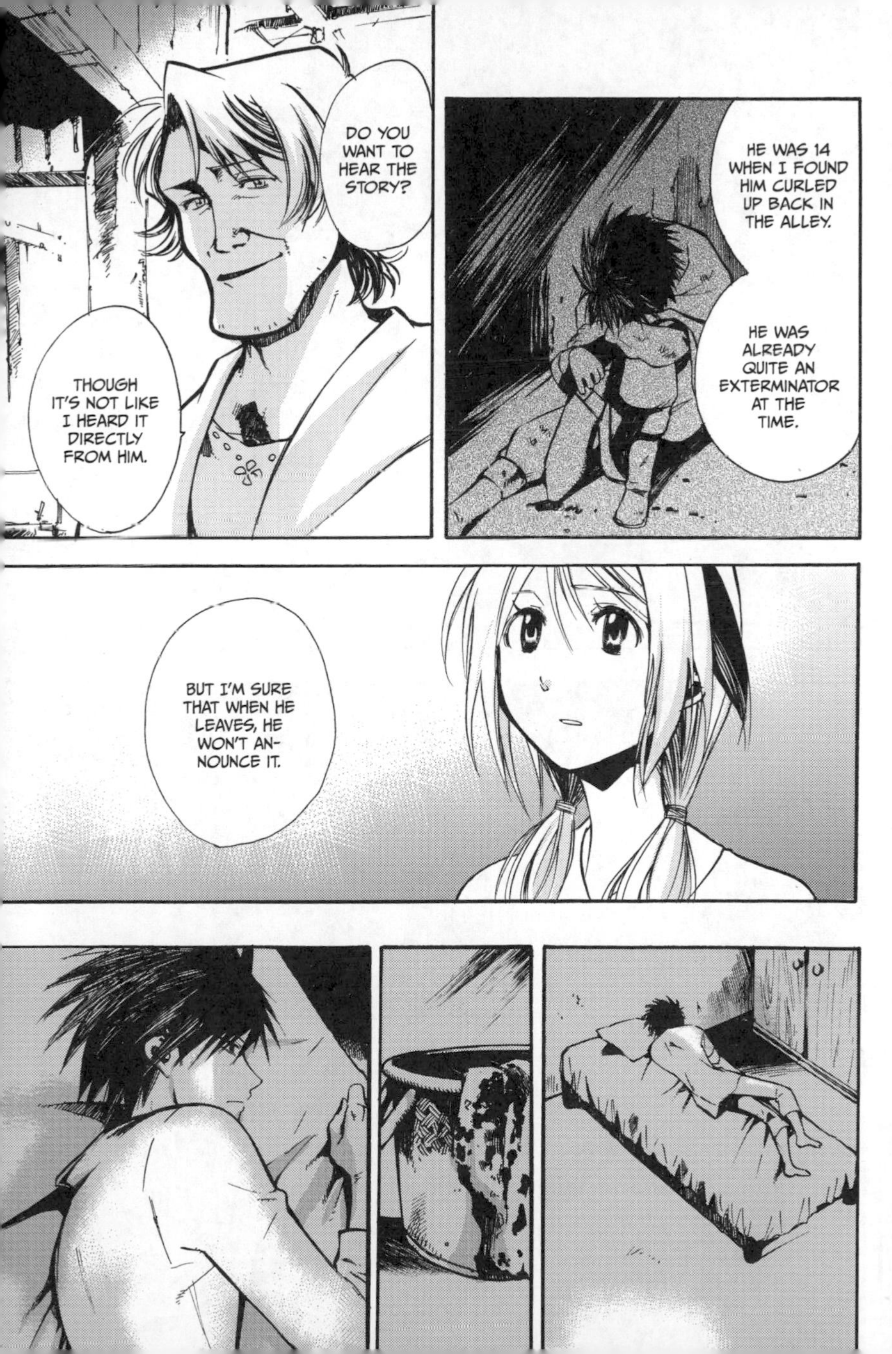
HE WAS 14 WHEN I FOUND HIM CURLED UP BACK IN THE ALLEY.
HE WAS ALREADY QUITE AN EXTERMINATOR AT THE TIME.
DO YOU WANT TO HEAR THE STORY?
THOUGH IT'S NOT LIKE I HEARD IT DIRECTLY FROM HIM.
BUT I'M SURE THAT WHEN HE LEAVES, HE WON'T AN-NOUNCE IT.

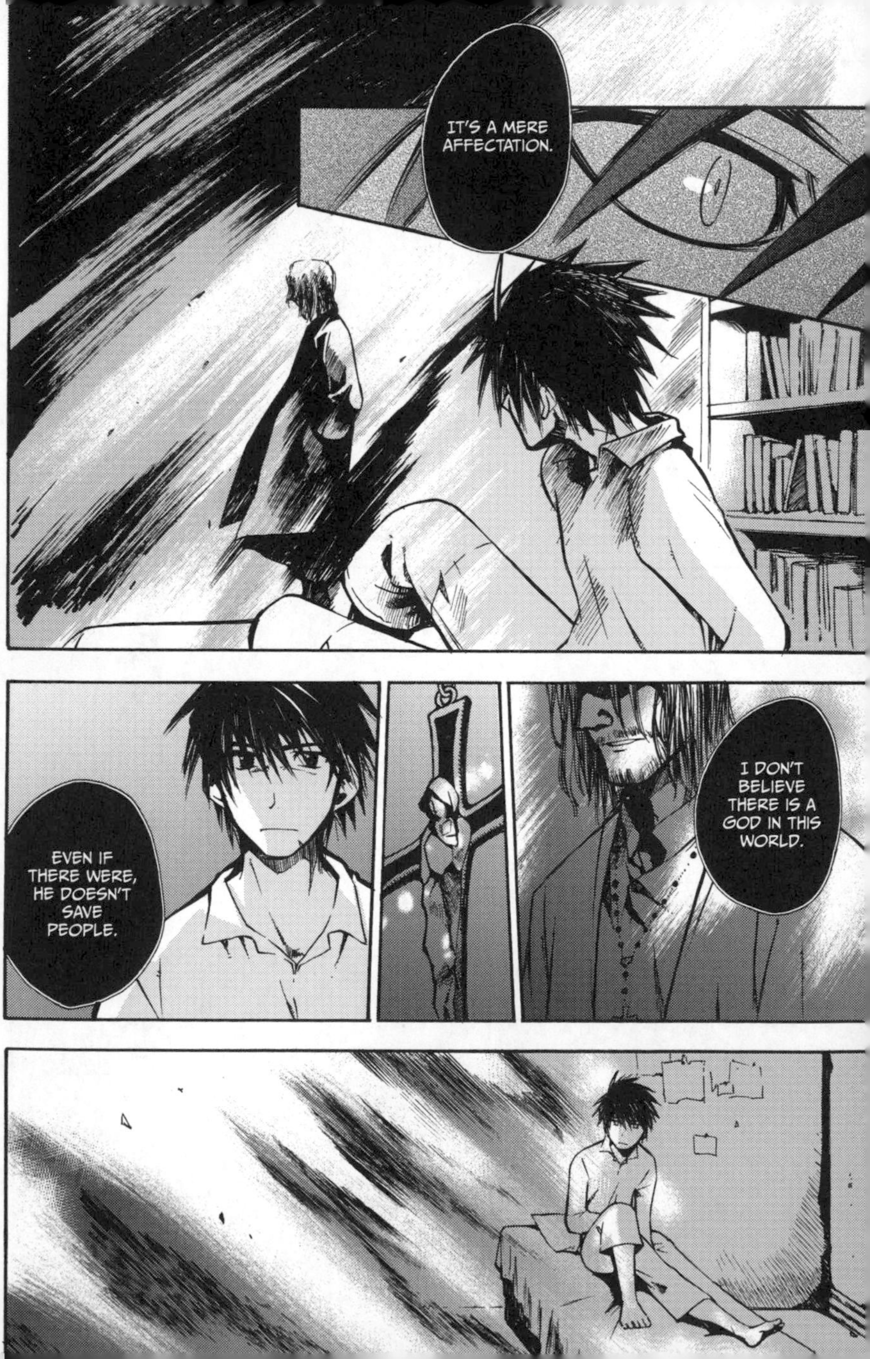
IT'S A MERE AFFECTATION.
I DON'T BELIEVE THERE IS A GOD IN THIS WORLD.
EVEN IF THERE WERE, HE DOESN'T SAVE PEOPLE.

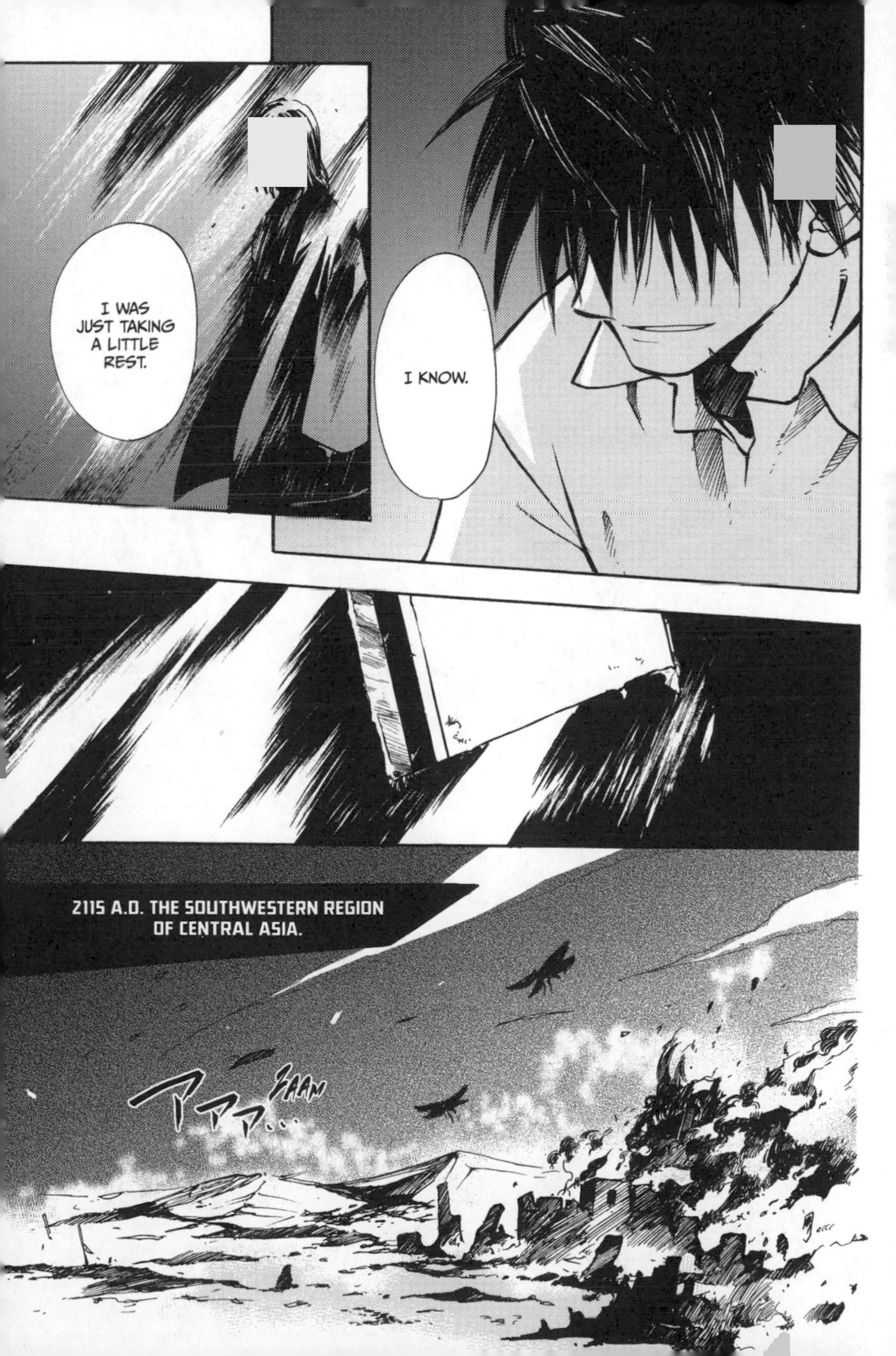
I KNOW.
I WAS JUST TAKING A LITTLE REST.
2115 A.D. THE SOUTHWESTERN REGION OF CENTRAL ASIA.
ZAAN

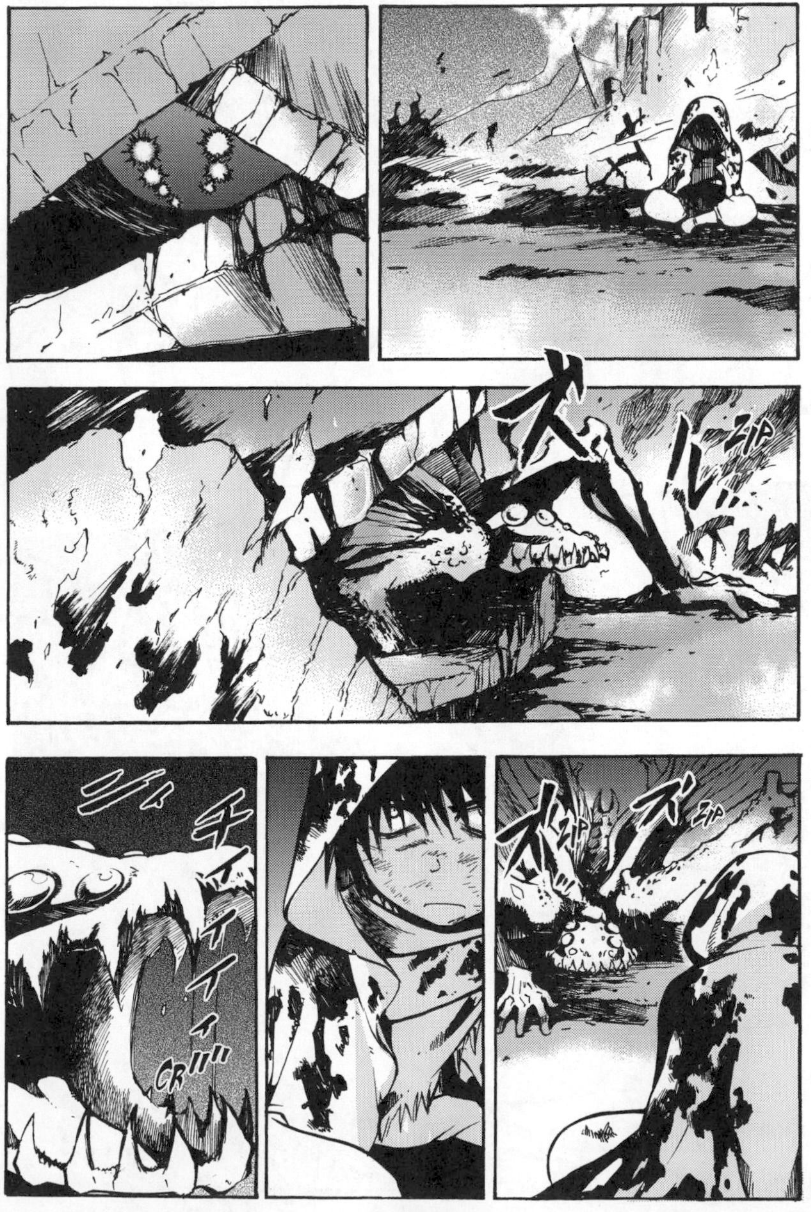
ZIP
ZIP
ZIP
CRII

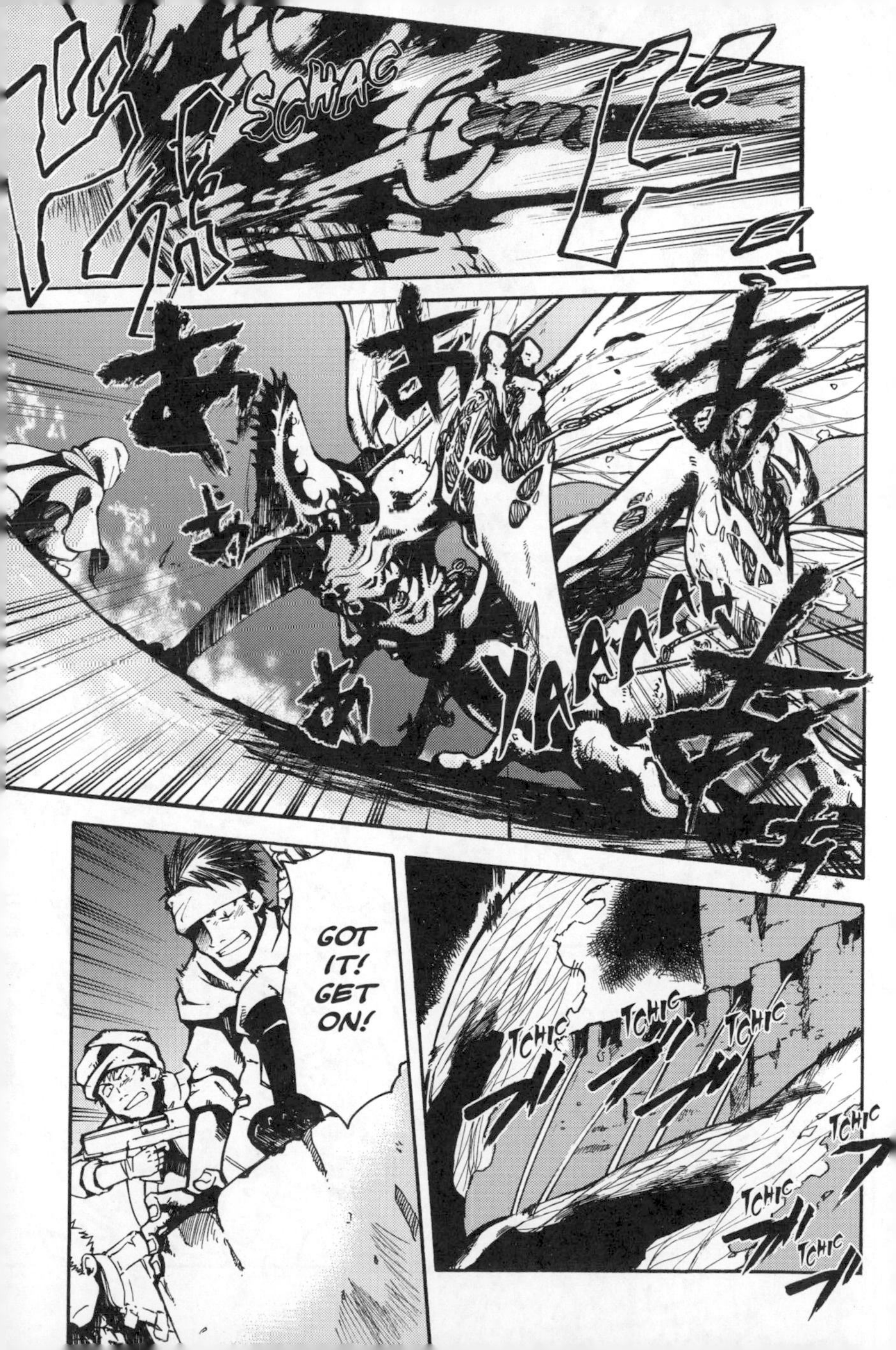
SCHAC
YAAAAH
TCHIC
TCHIC
TCHIC
TCHIC
TCHIC
TCHIC
GOT IT! GET ON!

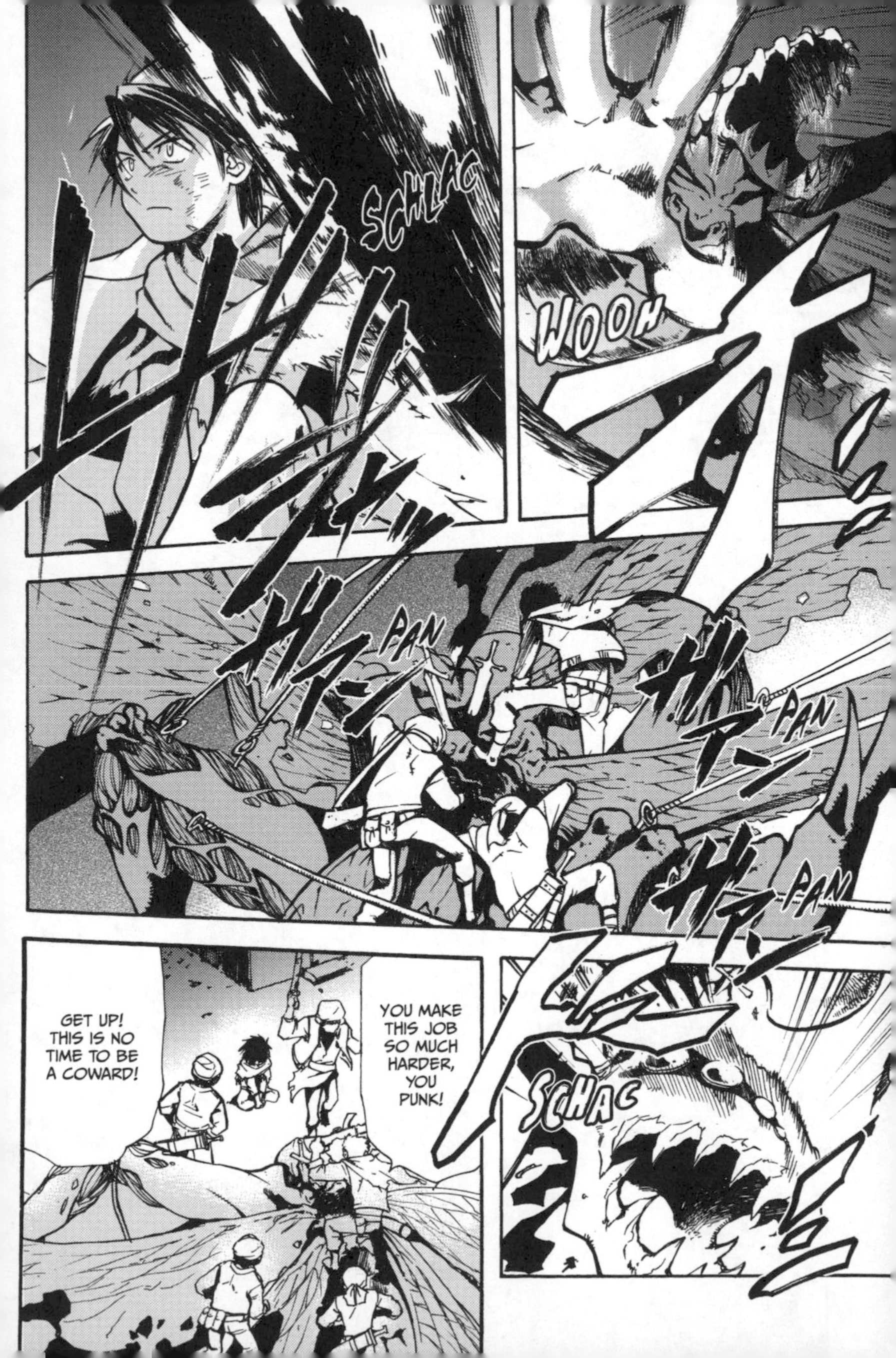
SCHLAC
WOOH
PAN
PAN
PAN
YOU MAKE THIS JOB SO MUCH HARDER, YOU PUNK!
GET UP! THIS IS NO TIME TO BE A COWARD!
SCHAC

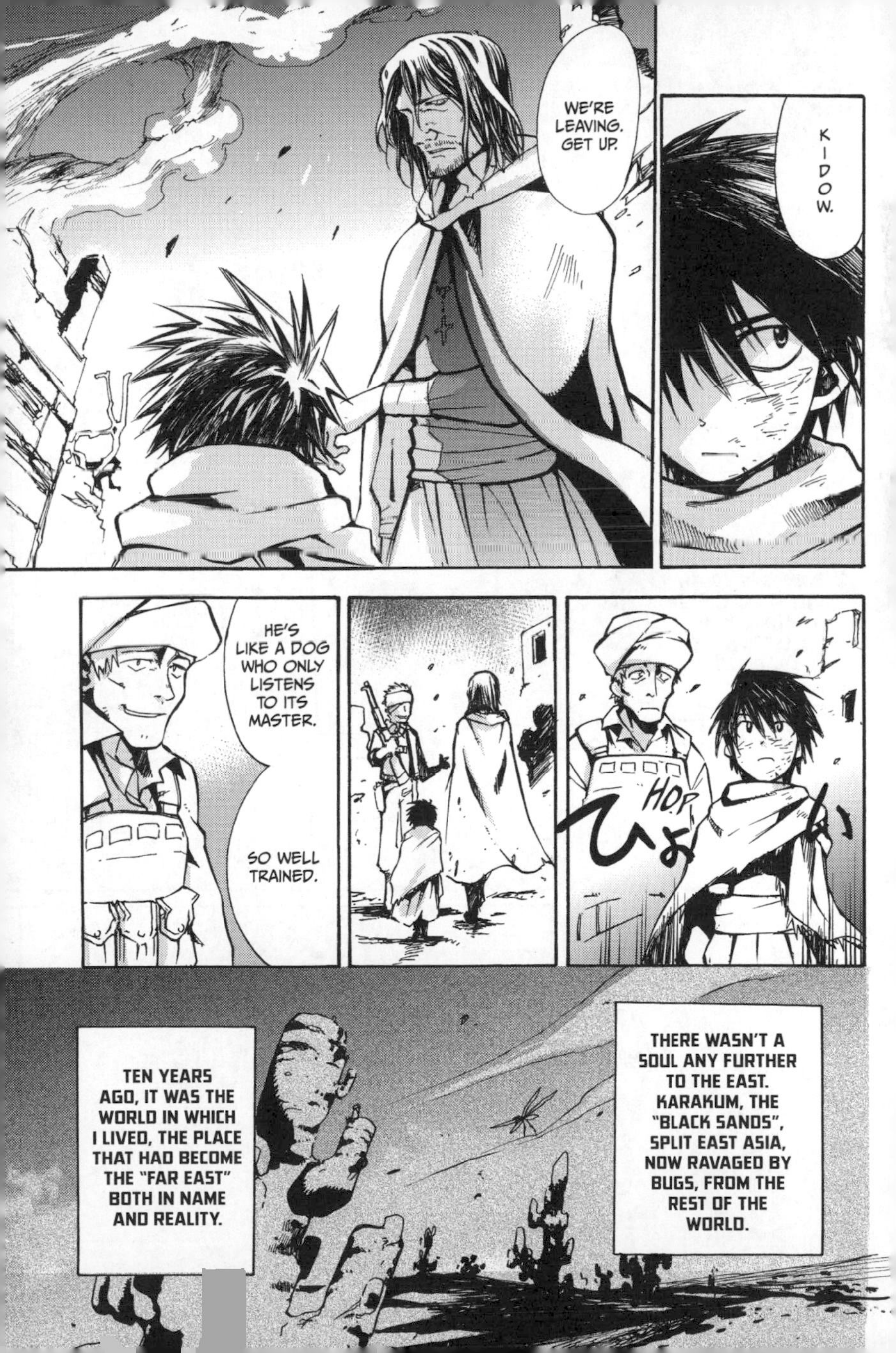
KIDOW.
WE'RE LEAVING. GET UP.
HOP
ひょい
HE'S LIKE A DOG WHO ONLY LISTENS TO ITS MASTER.
SO WELL TRAINED.
THERE WASN'T A SOUL ANY FURTHER TO THE EAST. KARAKUM, THE "BLACK SANDS", SPLIT EAST ASIA, NOW RAVAGED BY BUGS, FROM THE REST OF THE WORLD.
TEN YEARS AGO, IT WAS THE WORLD IN WHICH I LIVED, THE PLACE THAT HAD BECOME THE "FAR EAST" BOTH IN NAME AND REALITY.

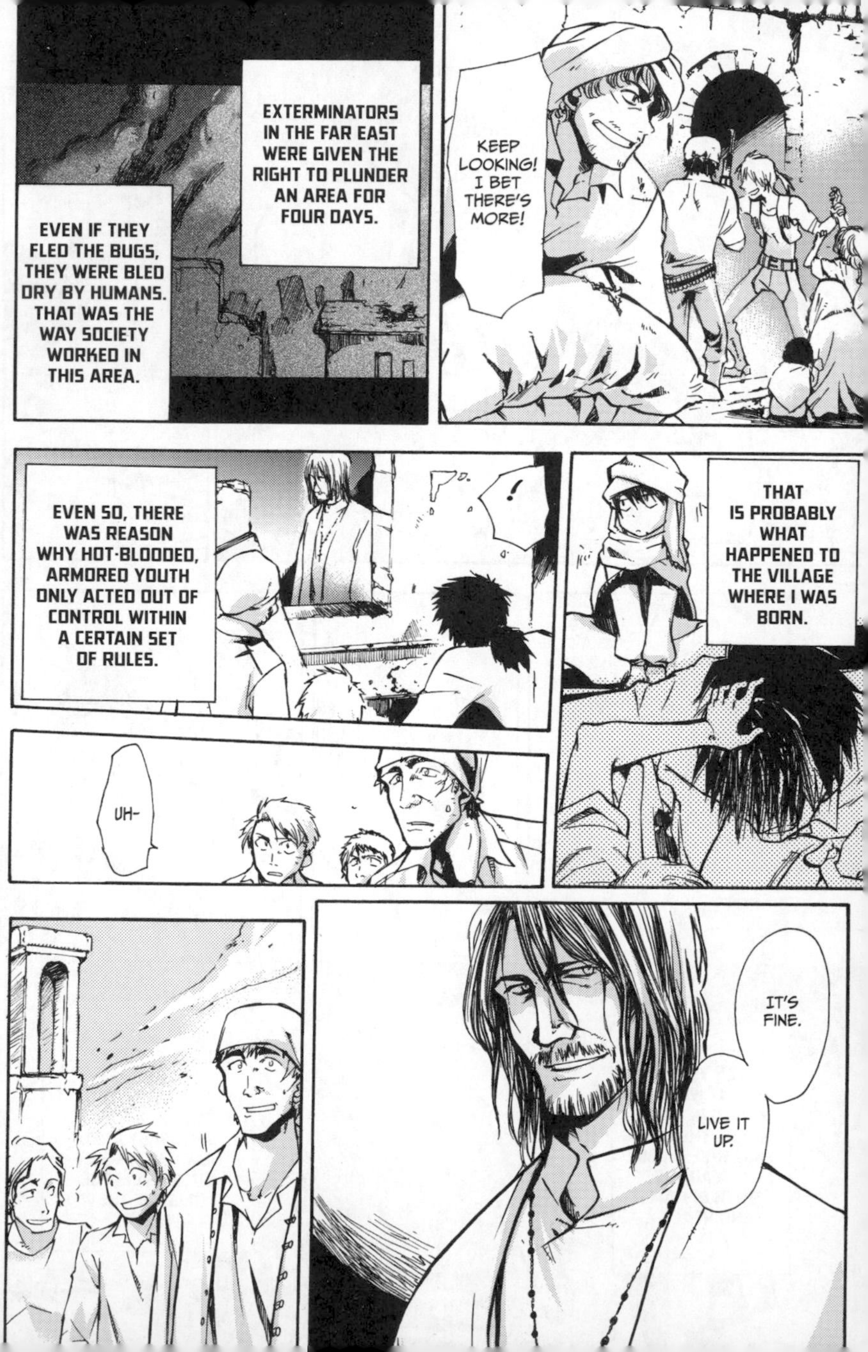
KEEP LOOKING! I BET THERE'S MORE!
EXTERMINATORS IN THE FAR EAST WERE GIVEN THE RIGHT TO PLUNDER AN AREA FOR FOUR DAYS.
EVEN IF THEY FLED THE BUGS, THEY WERE BLED DRY BY HUMANS. THAT WAS THE WAY SOCIETY WORKED IN THIS AREA.
THAT IS PROBABLY WHAT HAPPENED TO THE VILLAGE WHERE I WAS BORN.
EVEN SO, THERE WAS REASON WHY HOT-BLOODED, ARMORED YOUTH ONLY ACTED OUT OF CONTROL WITHIN A CERTAIN SET OF RULES.
UH-
IT'S FINE.
LIVE IT UP.

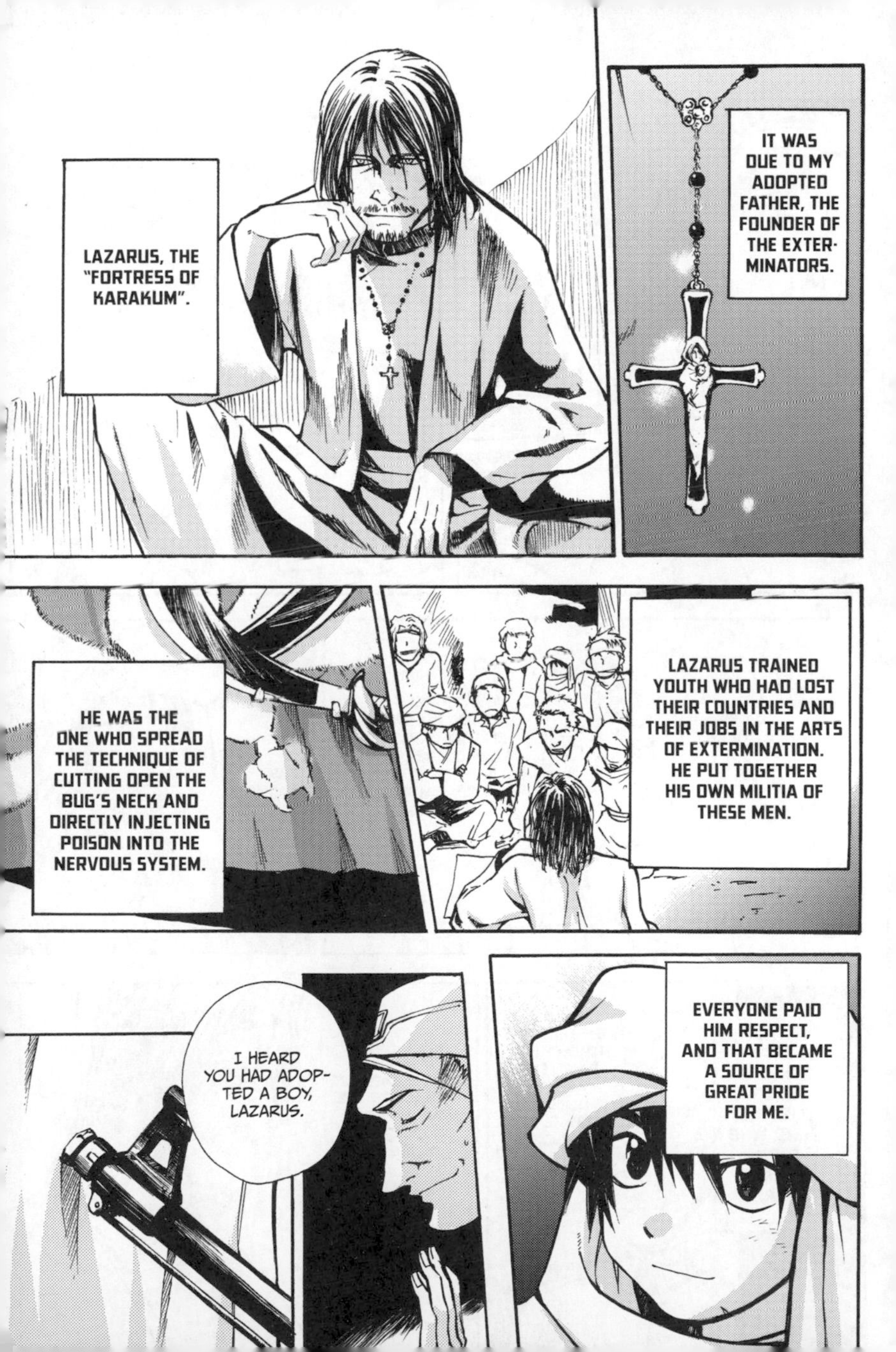
IT WAS DUE TO MY ADOPTED FATHER, THE FOUNDER OF THE EXTER-MINATORS.
LAZARUS, THE "FORTRESS OF KARAKUM".
LAZARUS TRAINED YOUTH WHO HAD LOST THEIR COUNTRIES AND THEIR JOBS IN THE ARTS OF EXTERMINATION. HE PUT TOGETHER HIS OWN MILITIA OF THESE MEN.
HE WAS THE ONE WHO SPREAD THE TECHNIQUE OF CUTTING OPEN THE BUG'S NECK AND DIRECTLY INJECTING POISON INTO THE NERVOUS SYSTEM.
EVERYONE PAID HIM RESPECT, AND THAT BECAME A SOURCE OF GREAT PRIDE FOR ME.
I HEARD YOU HAD ADOP-TED A BOY, LAZARUS.

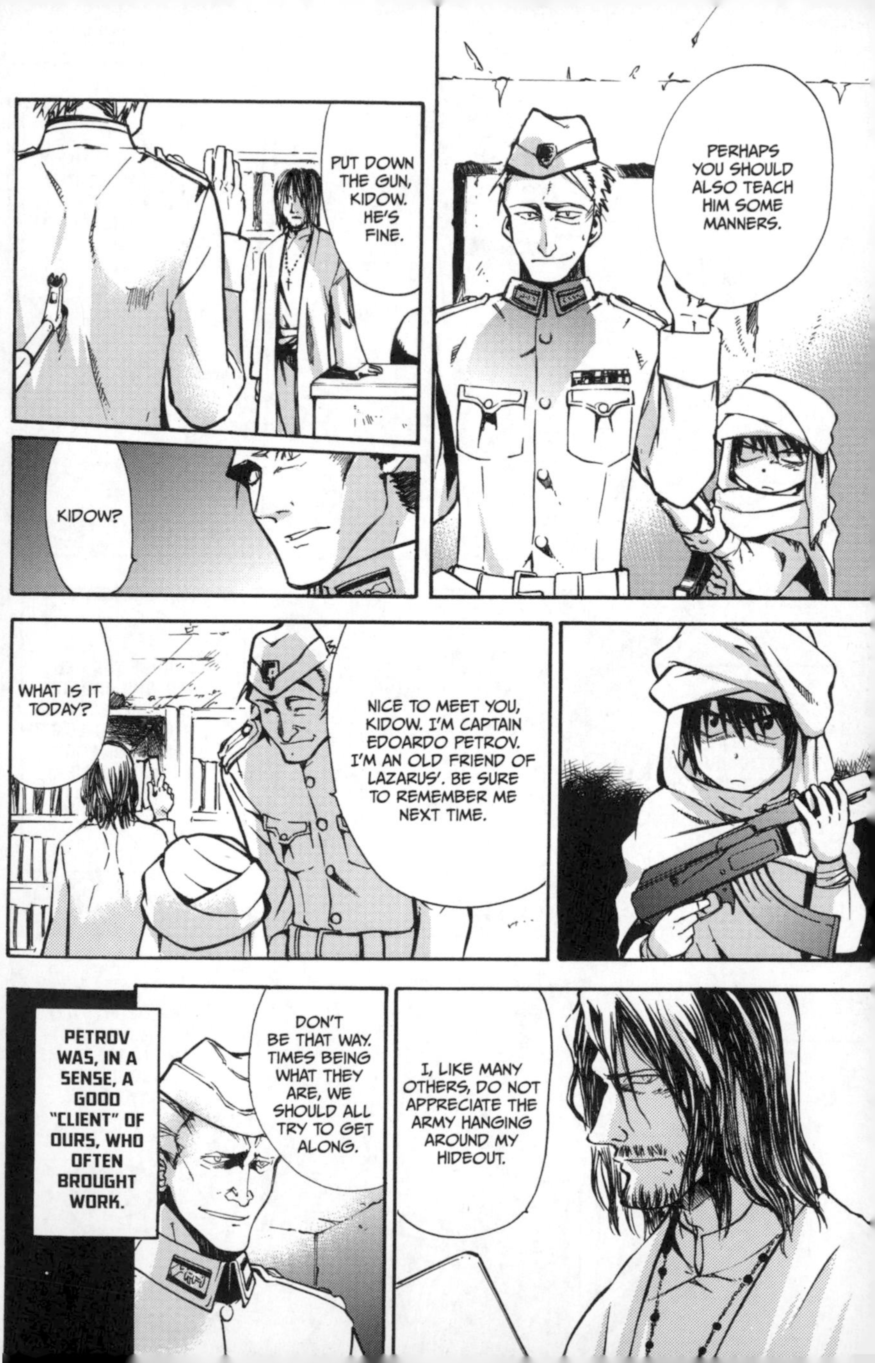
PERHAPS YOU SHOULD ALSO TEACH HIM SOME MANNERS.
PUT DOWN THE GUN, KIDOW. HE'S FINE.
KIDOW?
NICE TO MEET YOU, KIDOW. I'M CAPTAIN EDOARDO PETROV. I'M AN OLD FRIEND OF LAZARUS'. BE SURE TO REMEMBER ME NEXT TIME.
WHAT IS IT TODAY?
I, LIKE MANY OTHERS, DO NOT APPRECIATE THE ARMY HANGING AROUND MY HIDEOUT.
DON'T BE THAT WAY. TIMES BEING WHAT THEY ARE, WE SHOULD ALL TRY TO GET ALONG.
PETROV WAS, IN A SENSE, A GOOD "CLIENT" OF OURS, WHO OFTEN BROUGHT WORK.

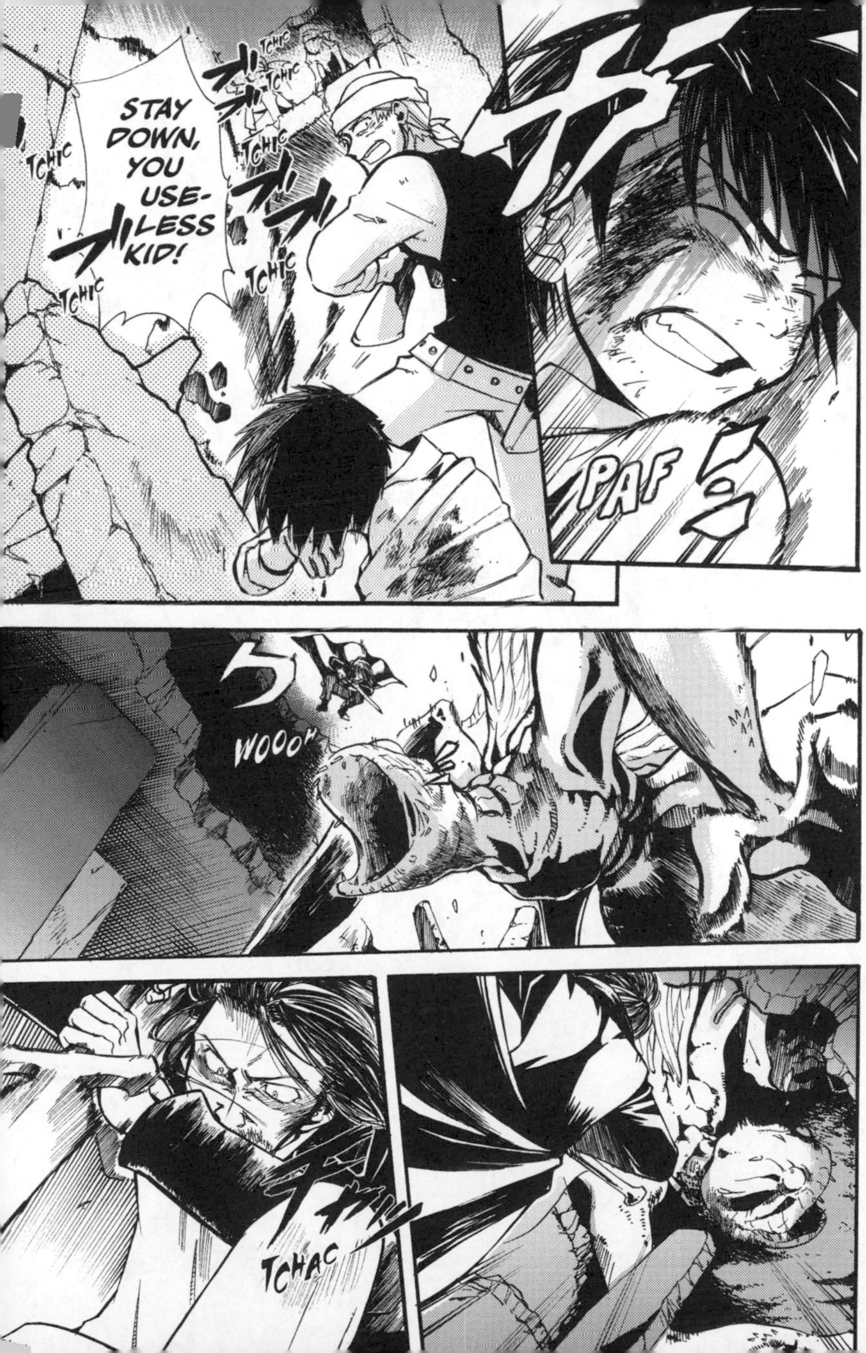
PAF
STAY DOWN, YOU USELESS KID!
TCHIC
TCHIC
TCHIC
TCHIC
TCHIC
TCHIC
WOOOH
TCHAC

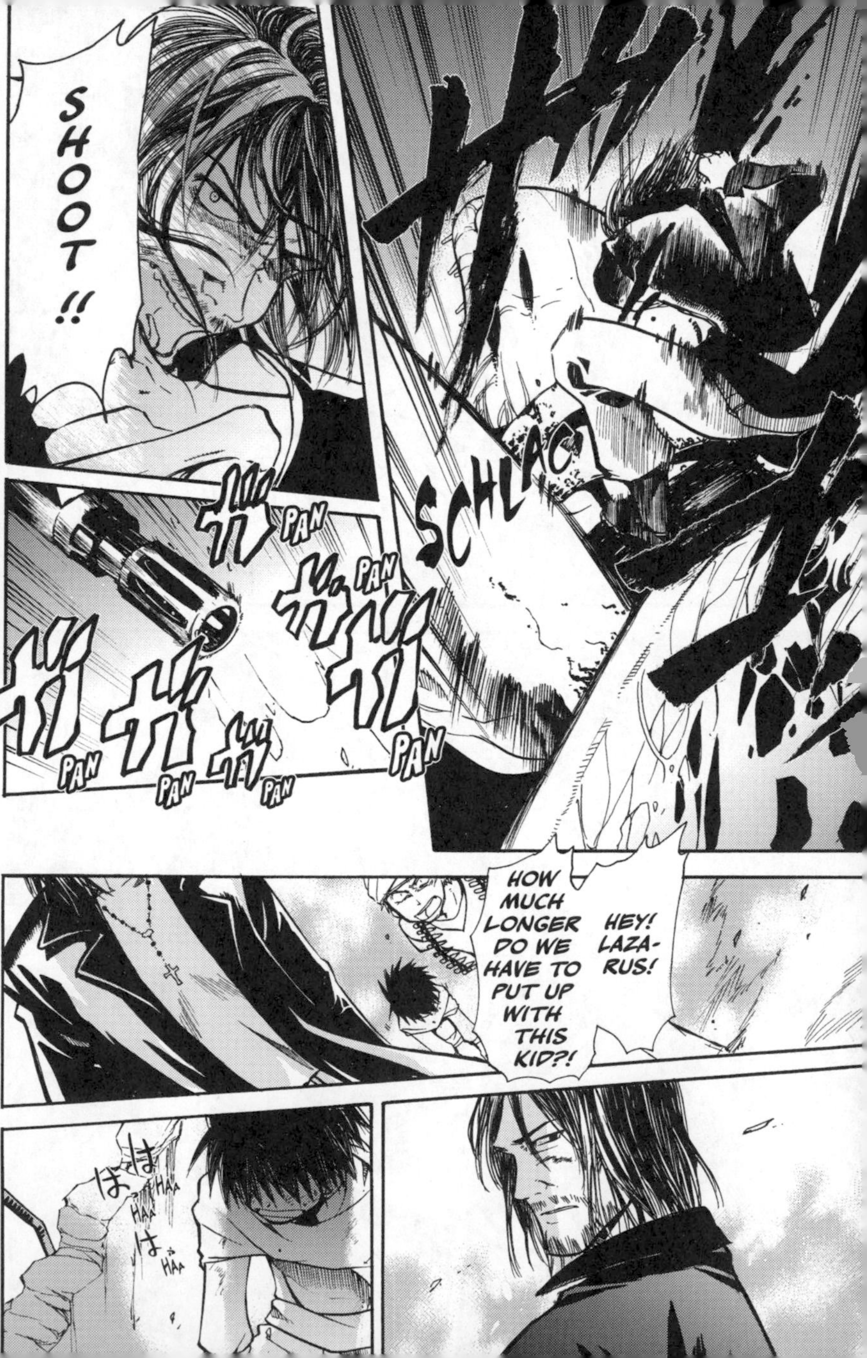
SCHLAC
SHOOT!!
PAN
PAN
PAN
PAN
PAN
PAN
HEY! LAZARUS!
HOW MUCH LONGER DO WE HAVE TO PUT UP WITH THIS KID?!
はは HAA HAA
は HAA

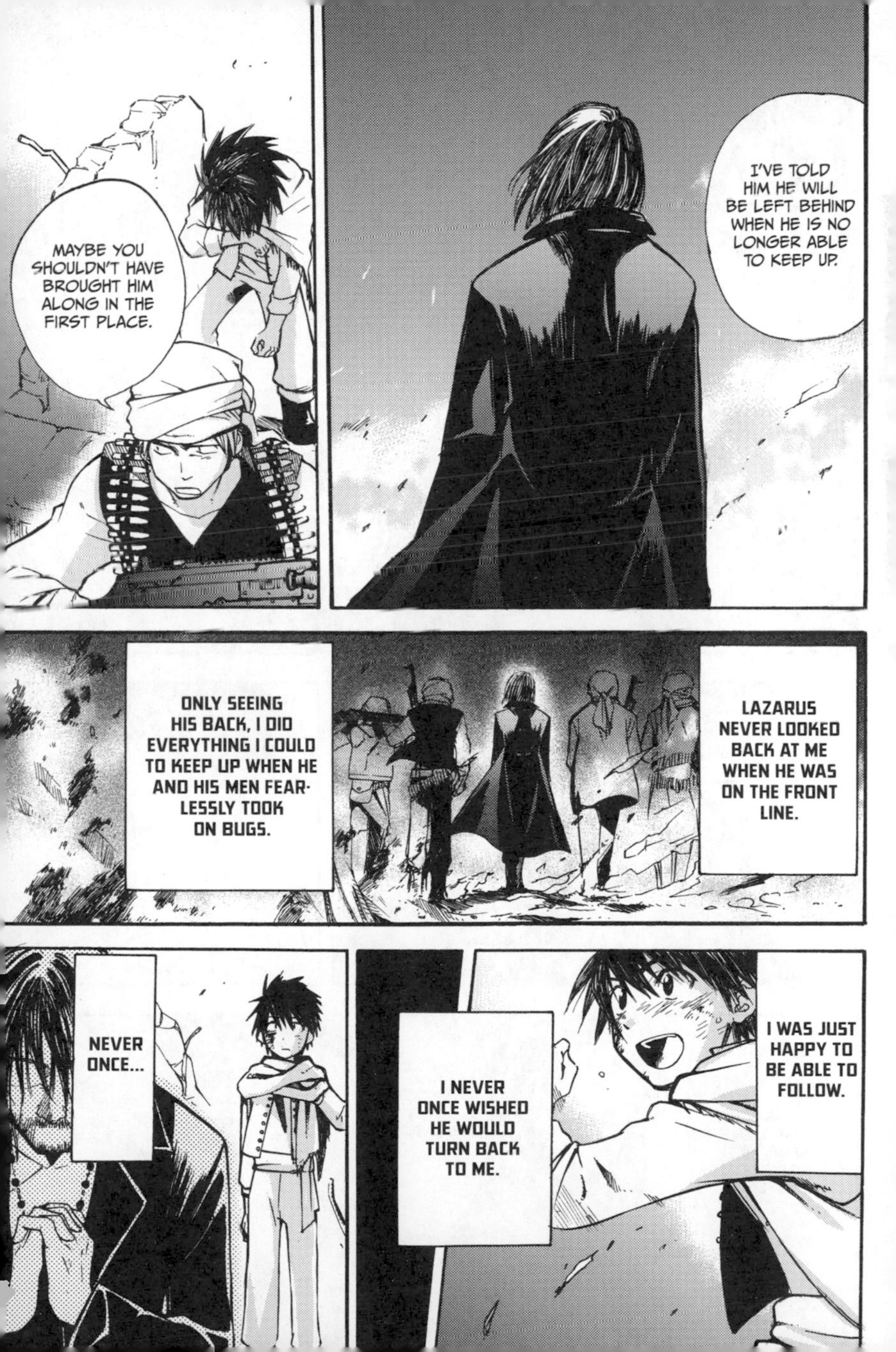
I'VE TOLD HIM HE WILL BE LEFT BEHIND WHEN HE IS NO LONGER ABLE TO KEEP UP.
MAYBE YOU SHOULDN'T HAVE BROUGHT HIM ALONG IN THE FIRST PLACE.
LAZARUS NEVER LOOKED BACK AT ME WHEN HE WAS ON THE FRONT LINE.
ONLY SEEING HIS BACK, I DID EVERYTHING I COULD TO KEEP UP WHEN HE AND HIS MEN FEAR-LESSLY TOOK ON BUGS.
I WAS JUST HAPPY TO BE ABLE TO FOLLOW.
I NEVER ONCE WISHED HE WOULD TURN BACK TO ME.
NEVER ONCE...

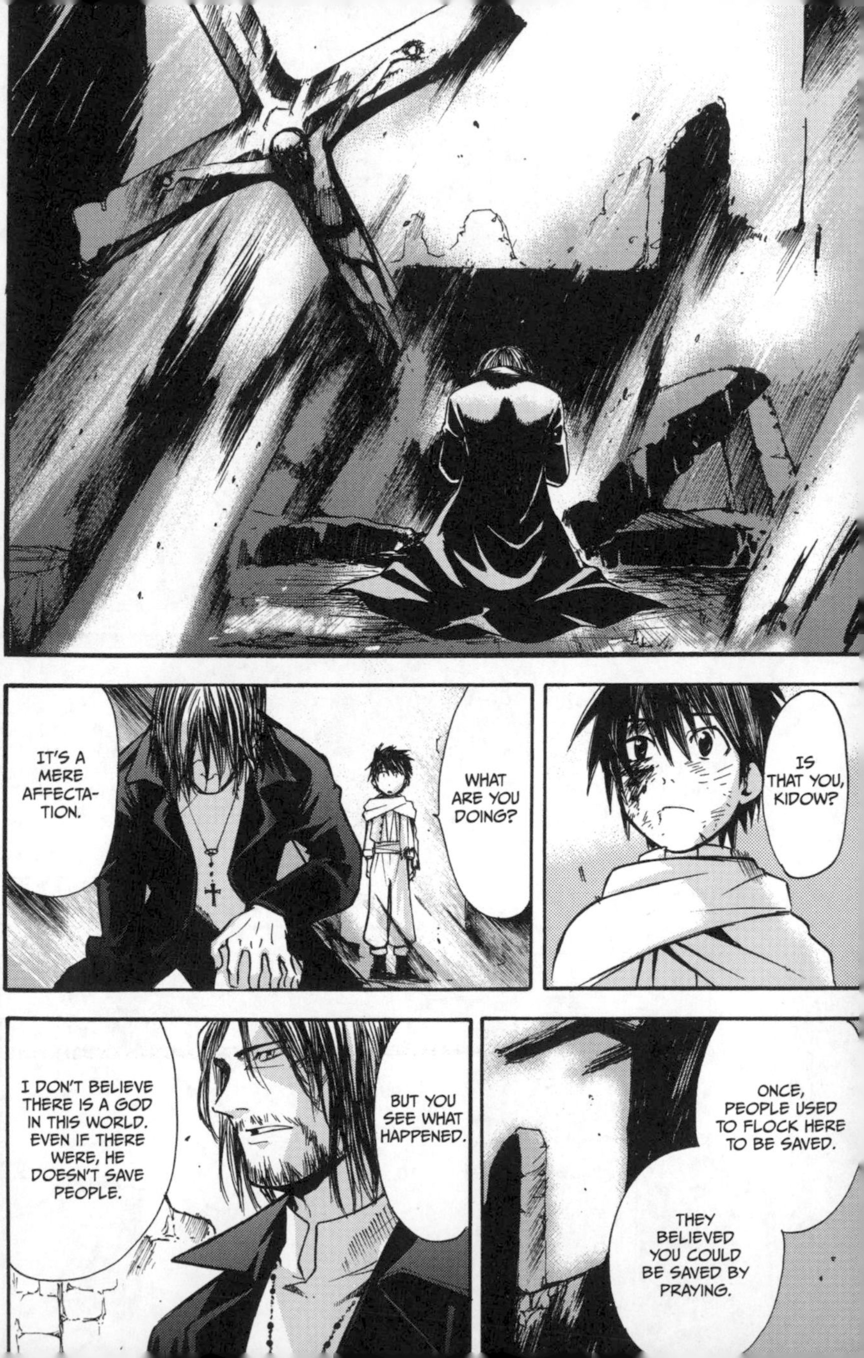
IS THAT YOU, KIDOW?
WHAT ARE YOU DOING?
IT'S A MERE AFFECTA-TION.
ONCE, PEOPLE USED TO FLOCK HERE TO BE SAVED.
THEY BELIEVED YOU COULD BE SAVED BY PRAYING.
BUT YOU SEE WHAT HAPPENED.
I DON'T BELIEVE THERE IS A GOD IN THIS WORLD. EVEN IF THERE WERE, HE DOESN'T SAVE PEOPLE.

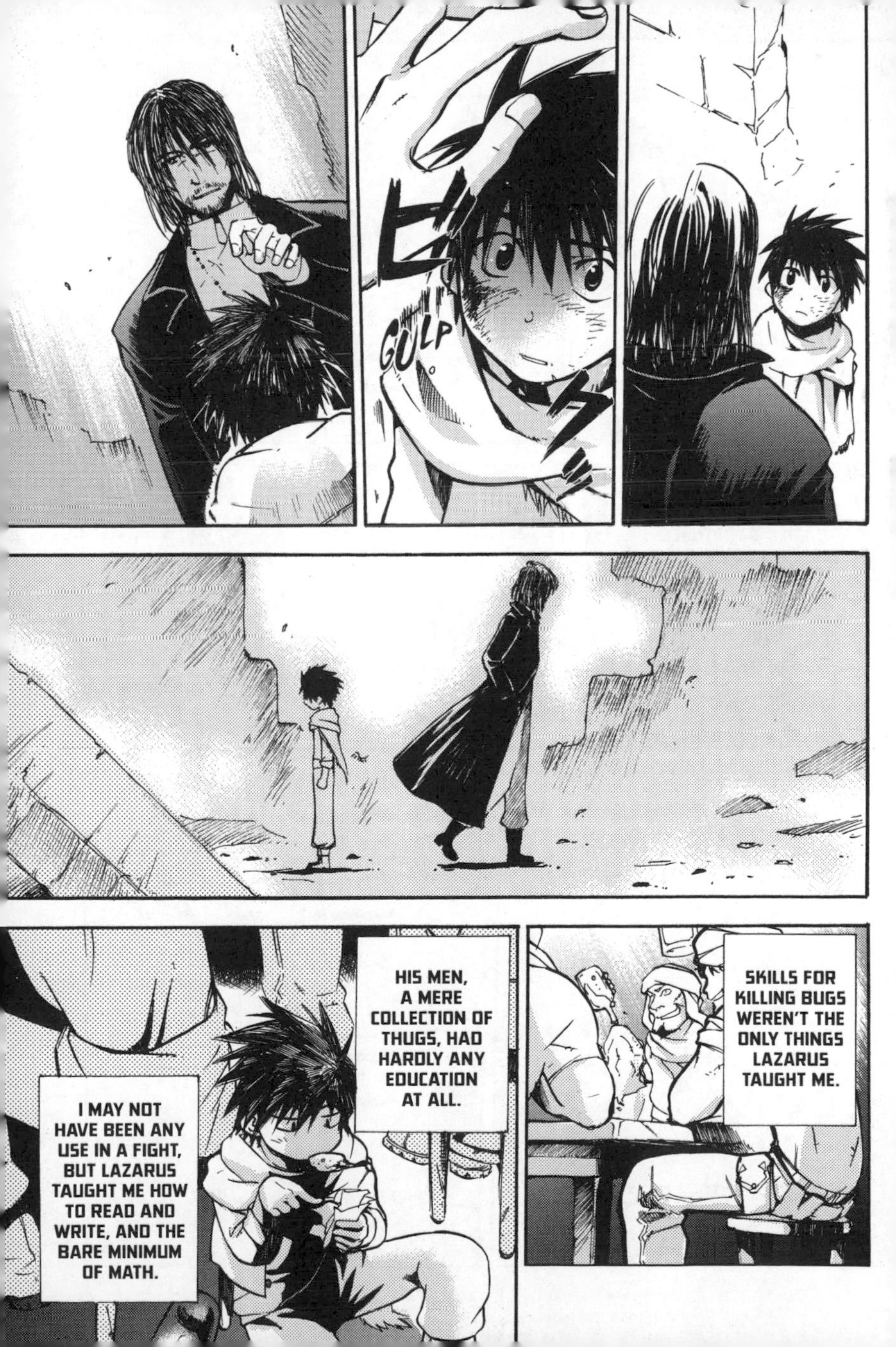
GULP
SKILLS FOR KILLING BUGS WEREN'T THE ONLY THINGS LAZARUS TAUGHT ME.
HIS MEN, A MERE COLLECTION OF THUGS, HAD HARDLY ANY EDUCATION AT ALL.
I MAY NOT HAVE BEEN ANY USE IN A FIGHT, BUT LAZARUS TAUGHT ME HOW TO READ AND WRITE, AND THE BARE MINIMUM OF MATH.

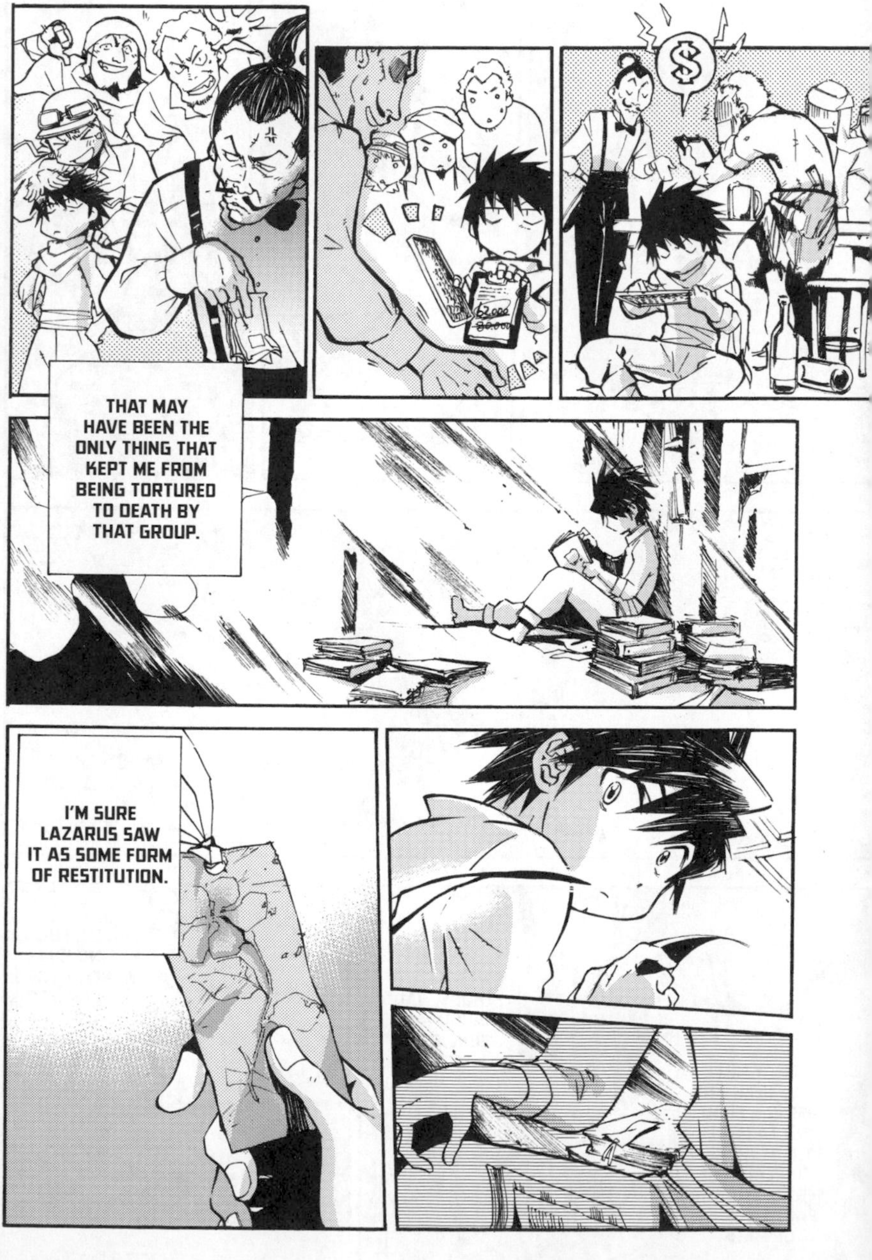
THAT MAY HAVE BEEN THE ONLY THING THAT KEPT ME FROM BEING TORTURED TO DEATH BY THAT GROUP.
I'M SURE LAZARUS SAW IT AS SOME FORM OF RESTITUTION.

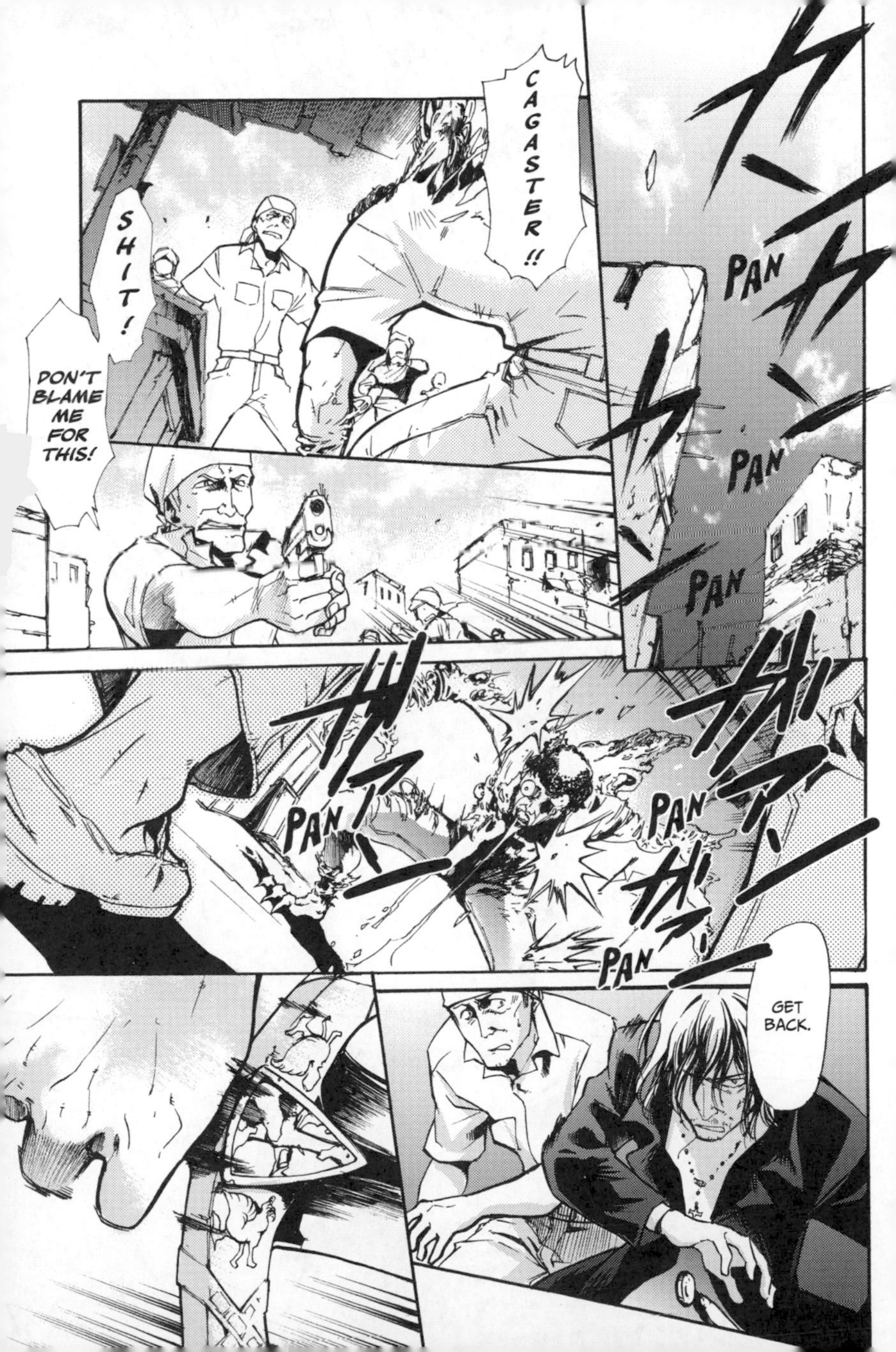

PAN
PAN
PAN
CAGASTER !!
SHIT!
DON'T BLAME ME FOR THIS!
PAN
PAN
PAN
GET BACK.

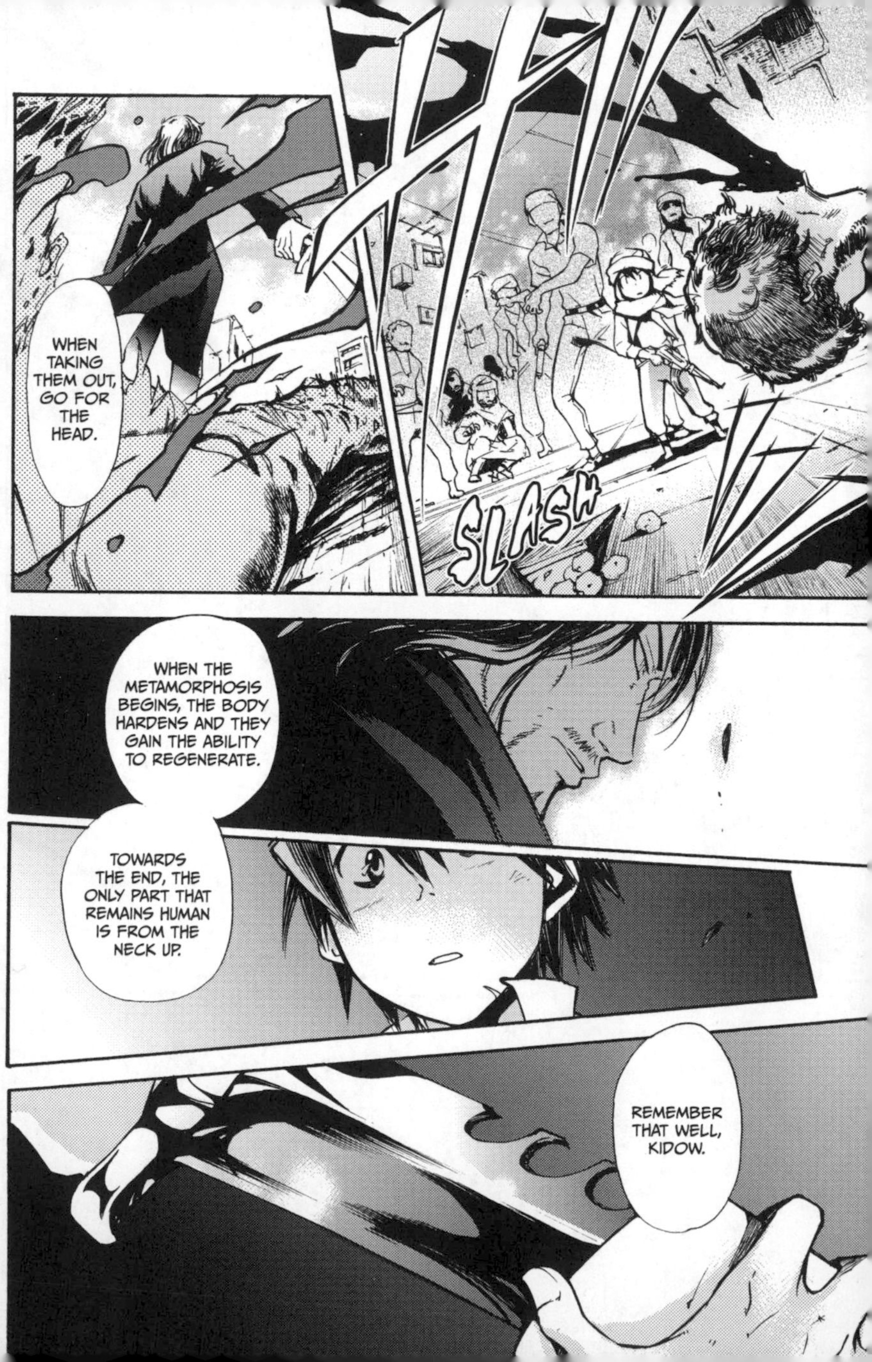
SLASH
WHEN TAKING THEM OUT, GO FOR THE HEAD.
WHEN THE METAMORPHOSIS BEGINS, THE BODY HARDENS AND THEY GAIN THE ABILITY TO REGENERATE.
TOWARDS THE END, THE ONLY PART THAT REMAINS HUMAN IS FROM THE NECK UP.
REMEMBER THAT WELL, KIDOW.

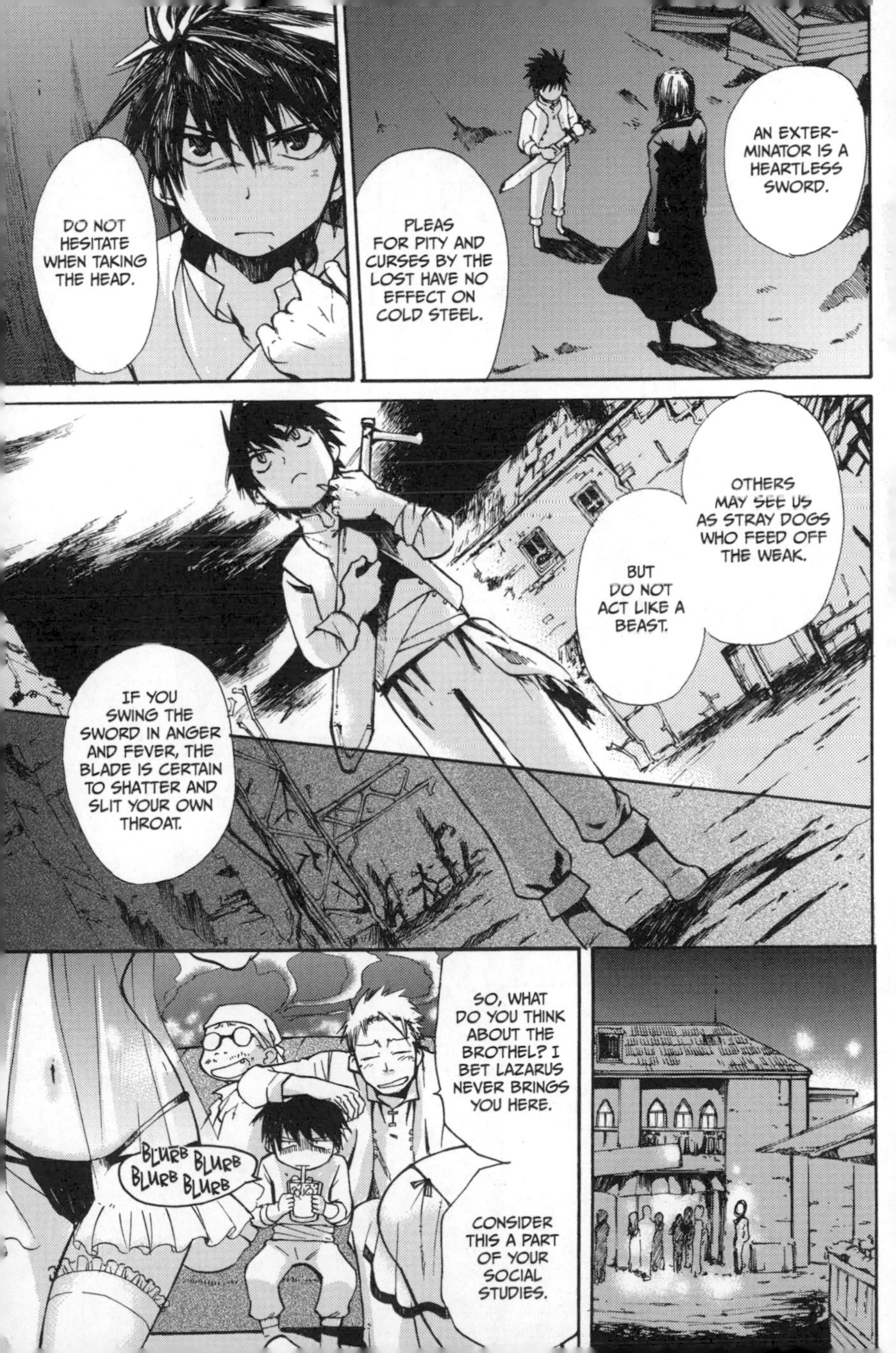
AN EXTER-MINATOR IS A HEARTLESS SWORD.
PLEAS FOR PITY AND CURSES BY THE LOST HAVE NO EFFECT ON COLD STEEL.
DO NOT HESITATE WHEN TAKING THE HEAD.
OTHERS MAY SEE US AS STRAY DOGS WHO FEED OFF THE WEAK.
BUT DO NOT ACT LIKE A BEAST.
IF YOU SWING THE SWORD IN ANGER AND FEVER, THE BLADE IS CERTAIN TO SHATTER AND SLIT YOUR OWN THROAT.
SO, WHAT DO YOU THINK ABOUT THE BROTHEL? I BET LAZARUS NEVER BRINGS YOU HERE.
CONSIDER THIS A PART OF YOUR SOCIAL STUDIES.
BLURB BLURB BLURB BLURB

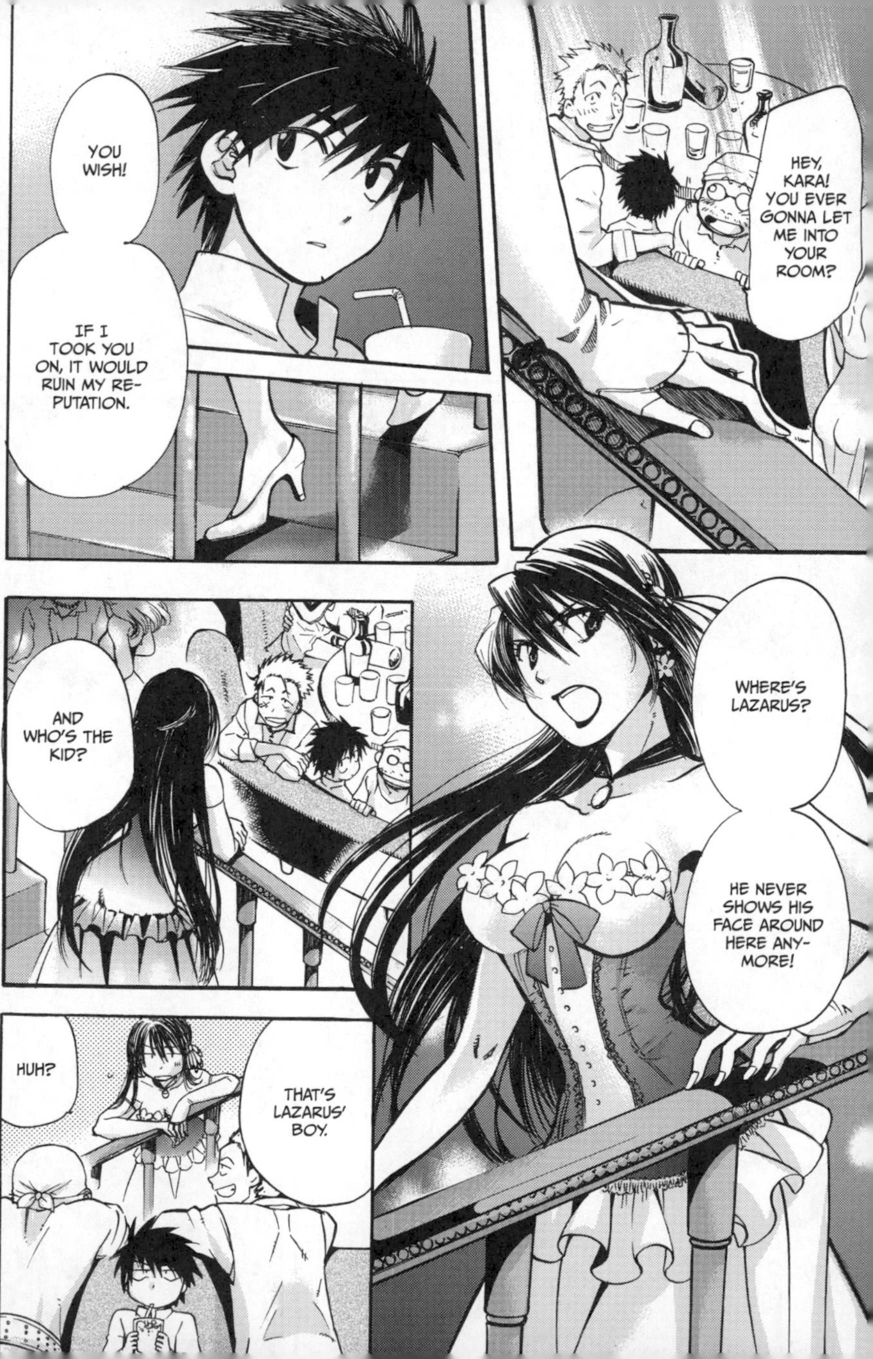
HEY, KARA! YOU EVER GONNA LET ME INTO YOUR ROOM?
YOU WISH!
IF I TOOK YOU ON, IT WOULD RUIN MY RE-PUTATION.
WHERE'S LAZARUS?
HE NEVER SHOWS HIS FACE AROUND HERE ANY-MORE!
AND WHO'S THE KID?
THAT'S LAZARUS' BOY.
HUH?

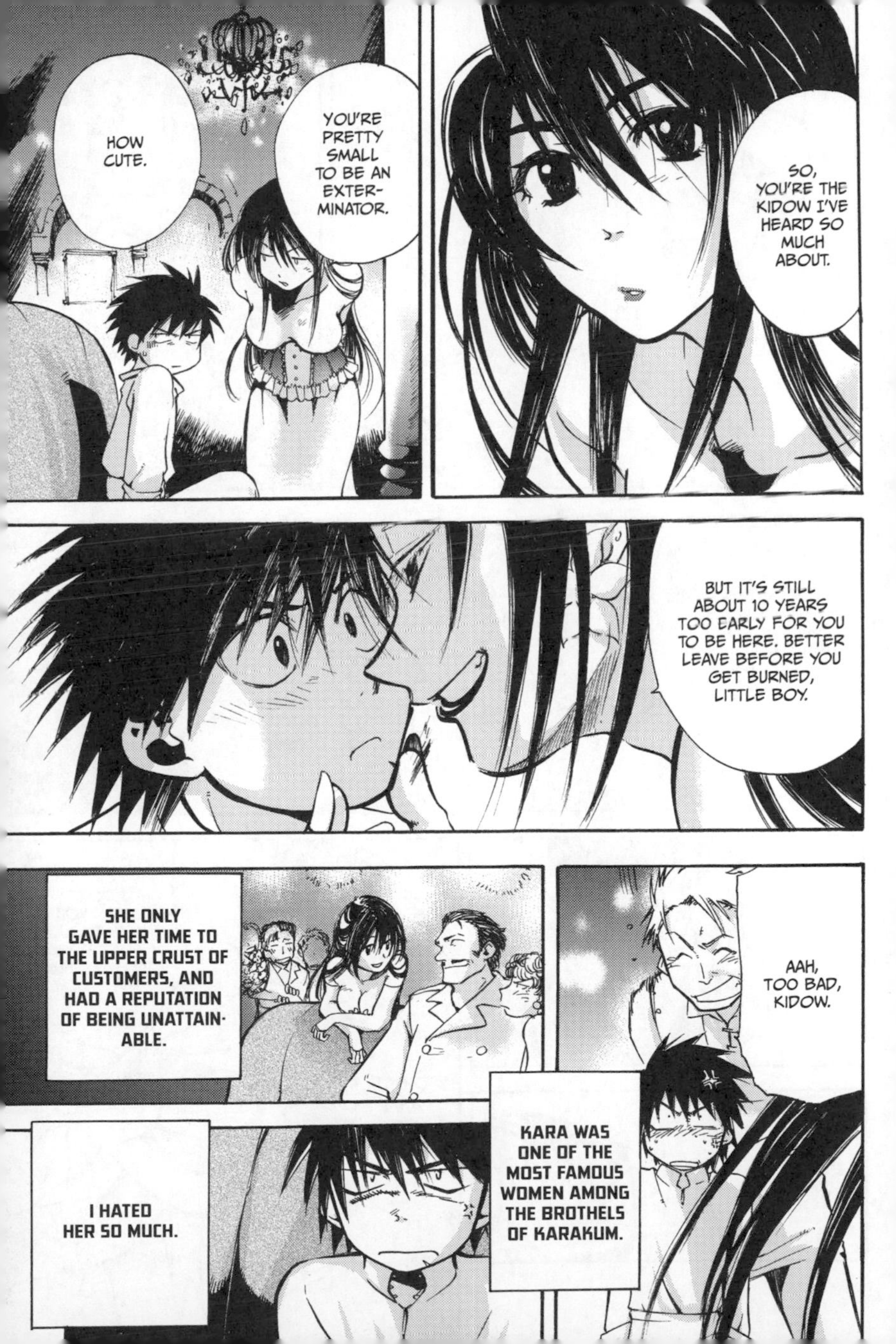
SO, YOU'RE THE KIDOW I'VE HEARD SO MUCH ABOUT.
YOU'RE PRETTY SMALL TO BE AN EXTER-MINATOR.
HOW CUTE.
BUT IT'S STILL ABOUT 10 YEARS TOO EARLY FOR YOU TO BE HERE. BETTER LEAVE BEFORE YOU GET BURNED, LITTLE BOY.
AAH, TOO BAD, KIDOW.
KARA WAS ONE OF THE MOST FAMOUS WOMEN AMONG THE BROTHELS OF KARAKUM.
SHE ONLY GAVE HER TIME TO THE UPPER CRUST OF CUSTOMERS, AND HAD A REPUTATION OF BEING UNATTAIN-ABLE.
I HATED HER SO MUCH.

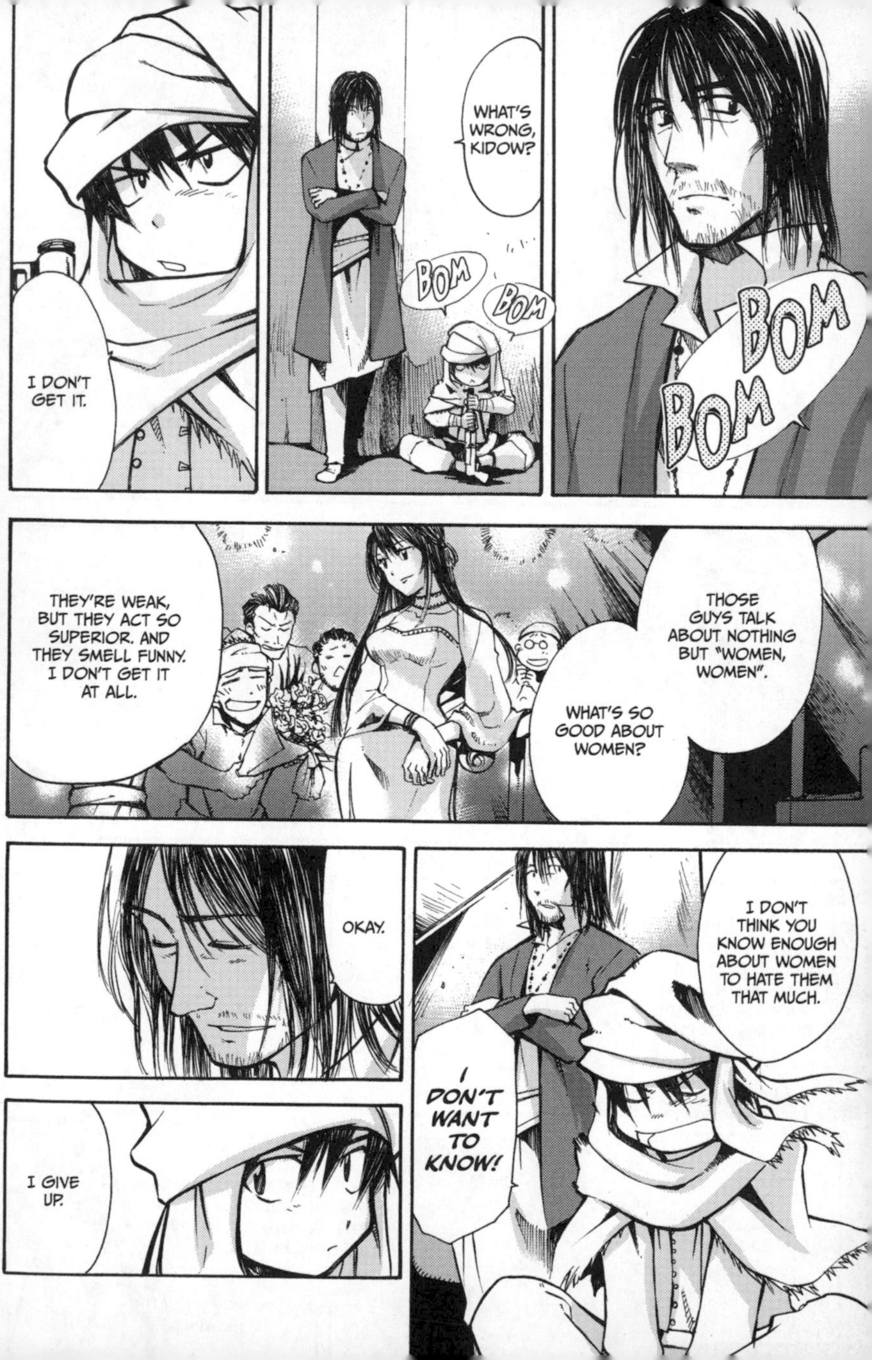
BOM BOM BOM
WHAT'S WRONG, KIDOW?
BOM
BOM
I DON'T GET IT.
THOSE GUYS TALK ABOUT NOTHING BUT "WOMEN, WOMEN".
WHAT'S SO GOOD ABOUT WOMEN?
THEY'RE WEAK, BUT THEY ACT SO SUPERIOR. AND THEY SMELL FUNNY. I DON'T GET IT AT ALL.
I DON'T THINK YOU KNOW ENOUGH ABOUT WOMEN TO HATE THEM THAT MUCH.
I DON'T WANT TO KNOW!
OKAY.
I GIVE UP.

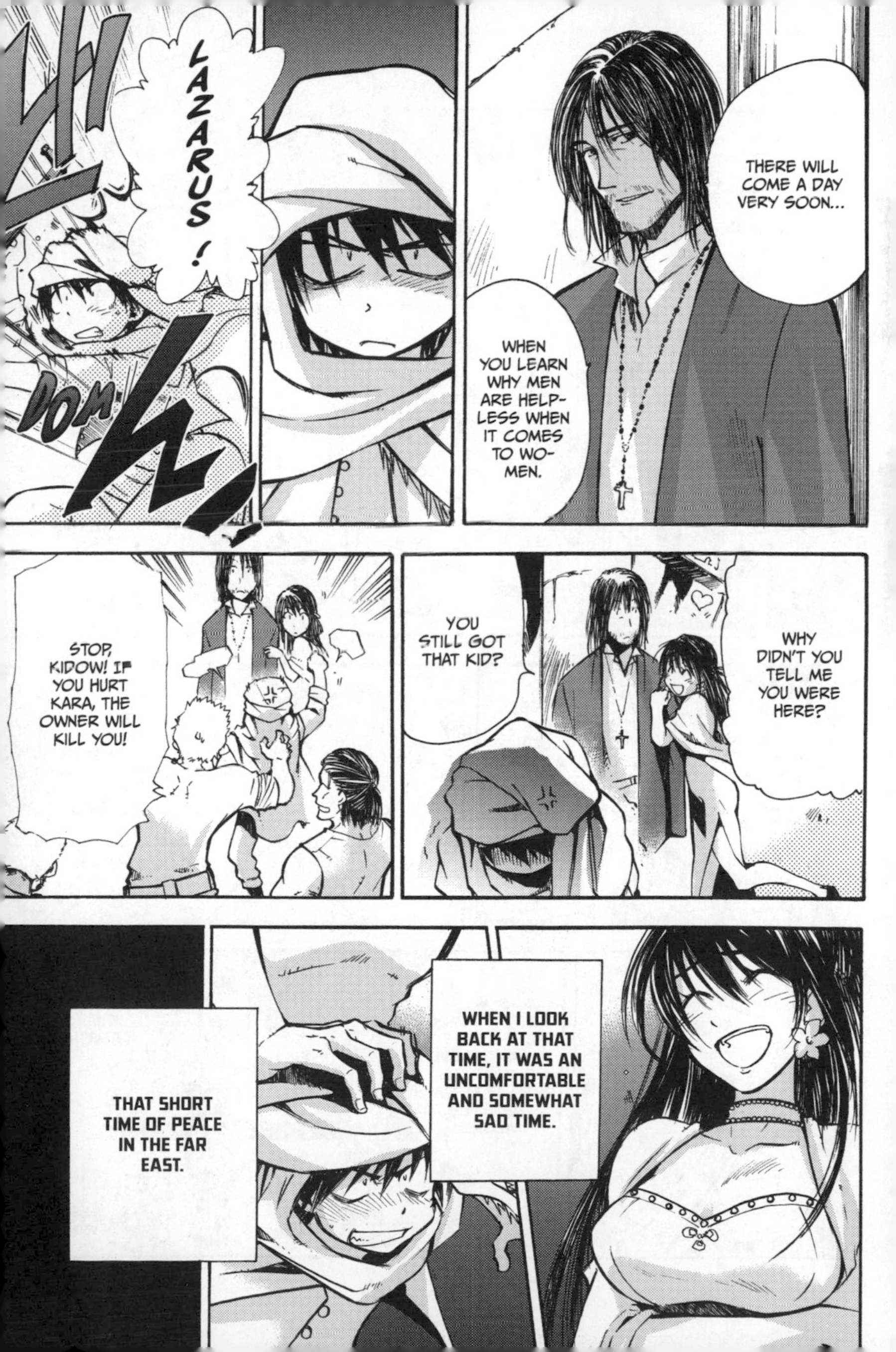
THERE WILL COME A DAY VERY SOON...
WHEN YOU LEARN WHY MEN ARE HELP-LESS WHEN IT COMES TO WO-MEN.
LAZARUS!
WHY DIDN'T YOU TELL ME YOU WERE HERE?
YOU STILL GOT THAT KID?
STOP, KIDOW! IF YOU HURT KARA, THE OWNER WILL KILL YOU!
WHEN I LOOK BACK AT THAT TIME, IT WAS AN UNCOMFORTABLE AND SOMEWHAT SAD TIME.
THAT SHORT TIME OF PEACE IN THE FAR EAST.

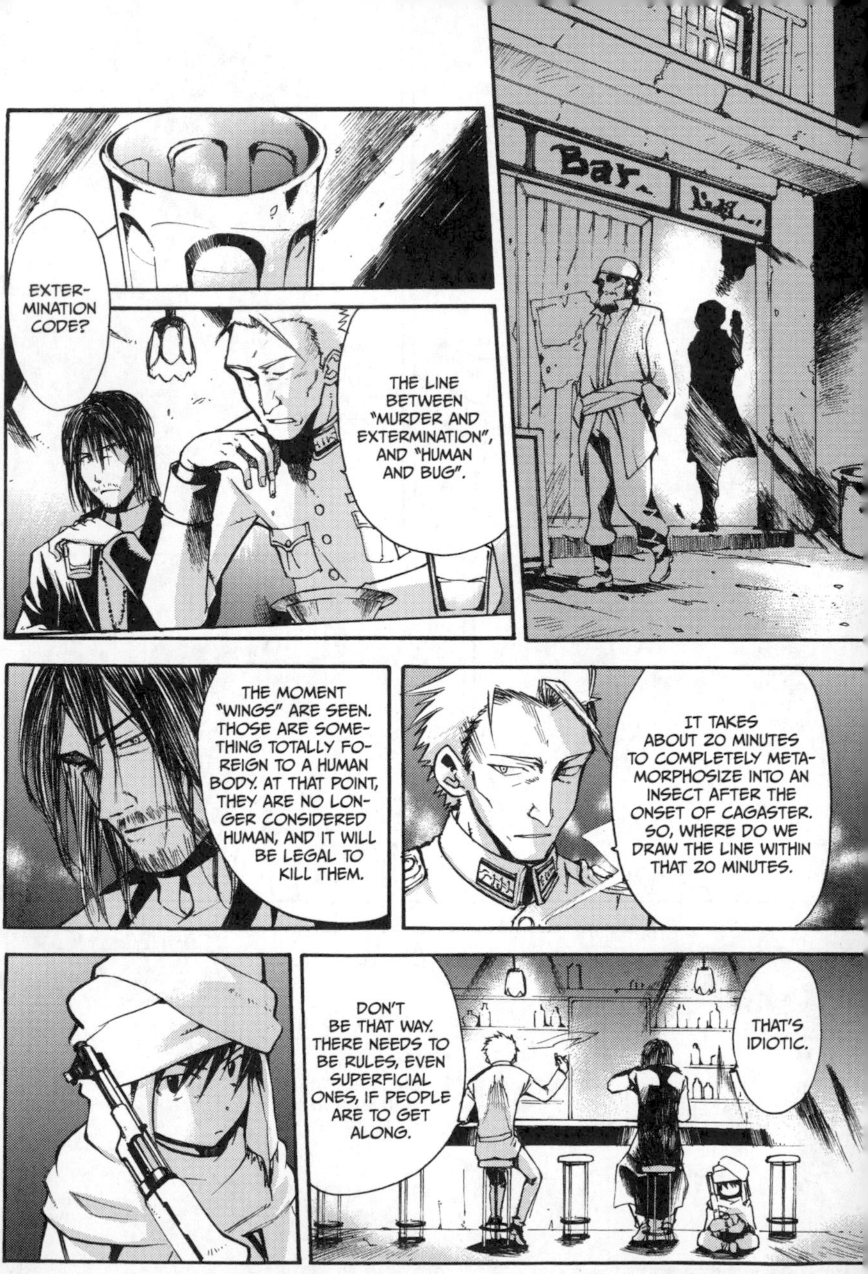
EXTERMINATION CODE?
THE LINE BETWEEN "MURDER AND EXTERMINATION", AND "HUMAN AND BUG".
IT TAKES ABOUT 20 MINUTES TO COMPLETELY METAMORPHOSIZE INTO AN INSECT AFTER THE ONSET OF CAGASTER. SO, WHERE DO WE DRAW THE LINE WITHIN THAT 20 MINUTES.
THE MOMENT "WINGS" ARE SEEN. THOSE ARE SOMETHING TOTALLY FOREIGN TO A HUMAN BODY. AT THAT POINT, THEY ARE NO LONGER CONSIDERED HUMAN, AND IT WILL BE LEGAL TO KILL THEM.
THAT'S IDIOTIC.
DON'T BE THAT WAY. THERE NEEDS TO BE RULES, EVEN SUPERFICIAL ONES, IF PEOPLE ARE TO GET ALONG.

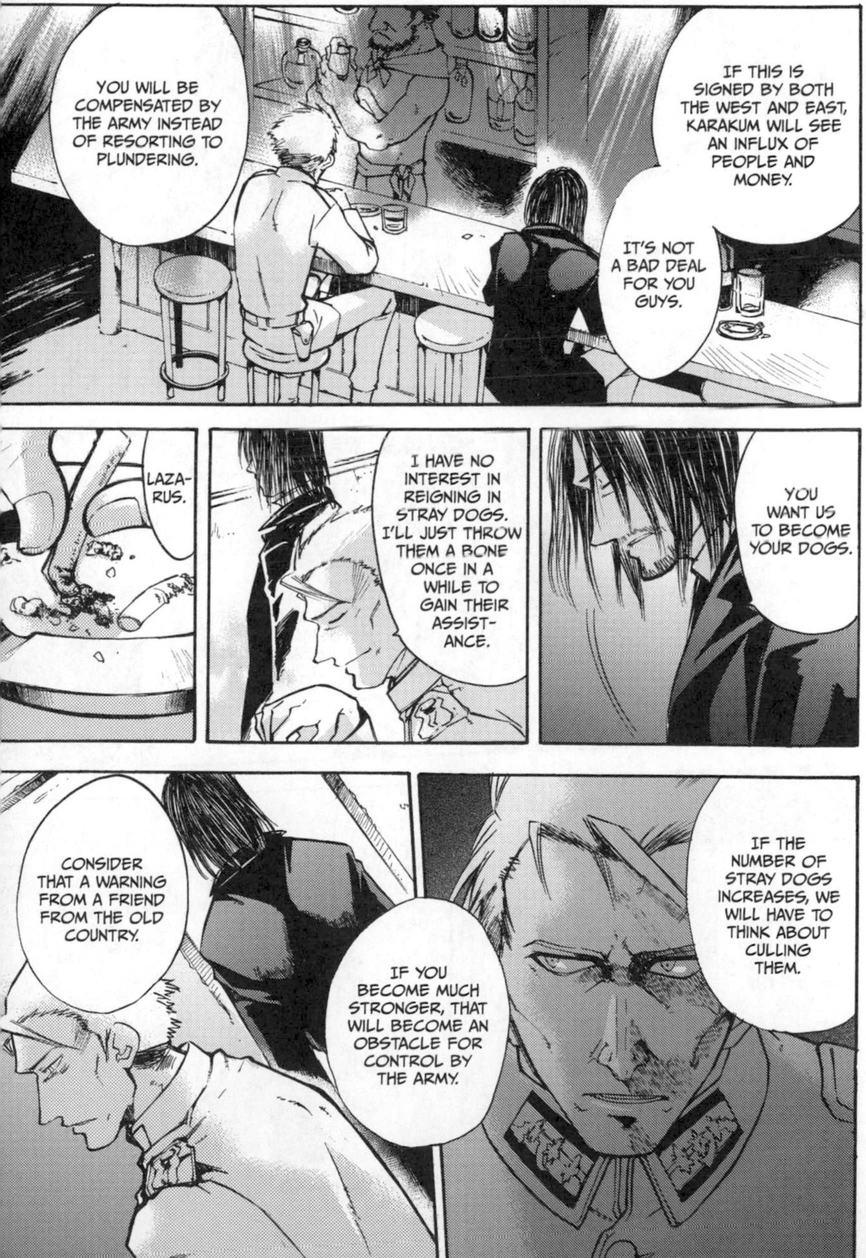
IF THIS IS SIGNED BY BOTH THE WEST AND EAST, KARAKUM WILL SEE AN INFLUX OF PEOPLE AND MONEY.
IT'S NOT A BAD DEAL FOR YOU GUYS.
YOU WILL BE COMPENSATED BY THE ARMY INSTEAD OF RESORTING TO PLUNDERING.
YOU WANT US TO BECOME YOUR DOGS.
I HAVE NO INTEREST IN REIGNING IN STRAY DOGS. I'LL JUST THROW THEM A BONE ONCE IN A WHILE TO GAIN THEIR ASSIST-ANCE.
LAZA-RUS.
IF THE NUMBER OF STRAY DOGS INCREASES, WE WILL HAVE TO THINK ABOUT CULLING THEM.
IF YOU BECOME MUCH STRONGER, THAT WILL BECOME AN OBSTACLE FOR CONTROL BY THE ARMY.
CONSIDER THAT A WARNING FROM A FRIEND FROM THE OLD COUNTRY.

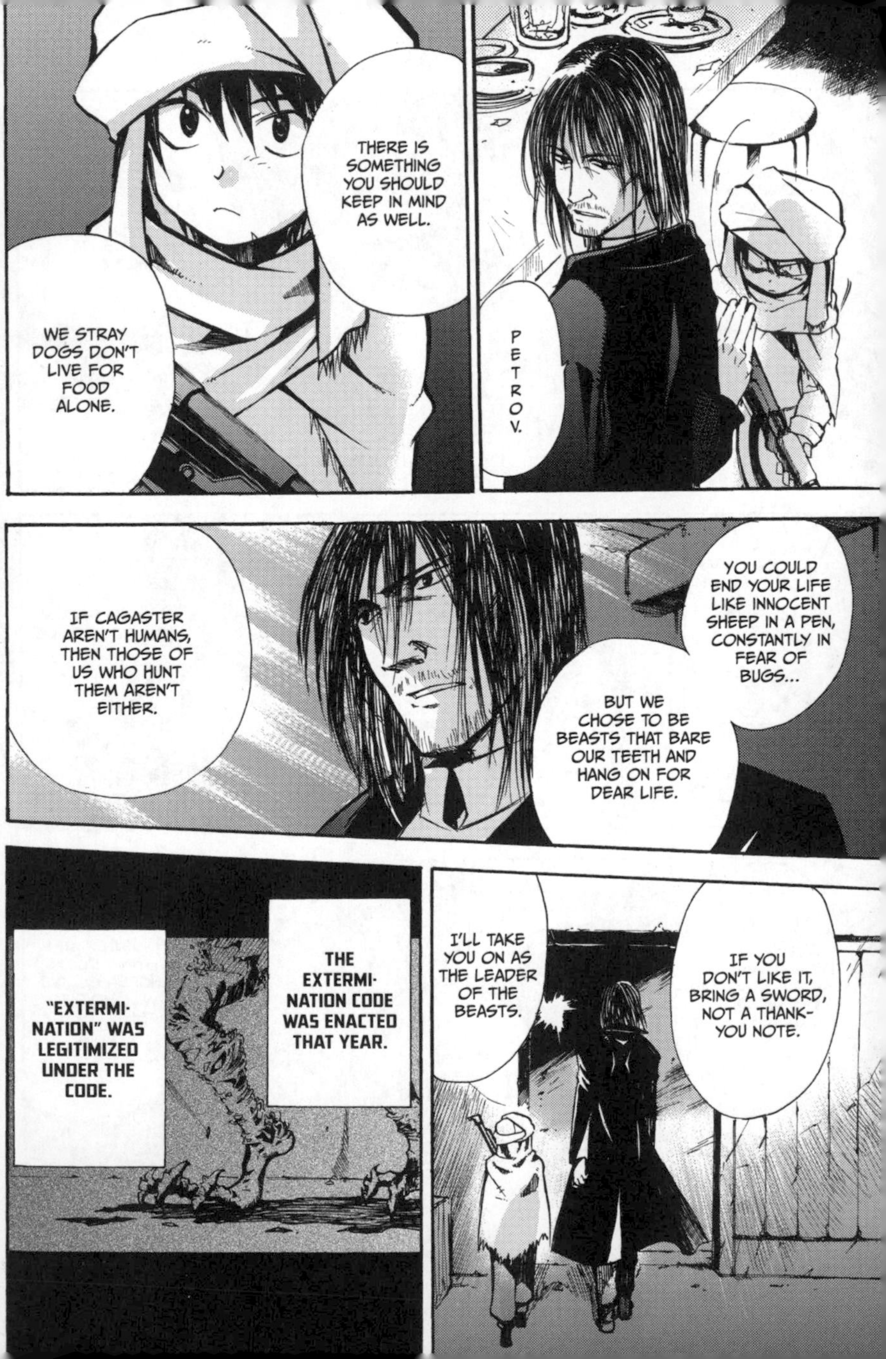
PETROV.
THERE IS SOMETHING YOU SHOULD KEEP IN MIND AS WELL.
WE STRAY DOGS DON'T LIVE FOR FOOD ALONE.
YOU COULD END YOUR LIFE LIKE INNOCENT SHEEP IN A PEN, CONSTANTLY IN FEAR OF BUGS...
BUT WE CHOSE TO BE BEASTS THAT BARE OUR TEETH AND HANG ON FOR DEAR LIFE.
IF CAGASTER AREN'T HUMANS, THEN THOSE OF US WHO HUNT THEM AREN'T EITHER.
IF YOU DON'T LIKE IT, BRING A SWORD, NOT A THANK-YOU NOTE.
I'LL TAKE YOU ON AS THE LEADER OF THE BEASTS.
THE EXTERMI-NATION CODE WAS ENACTED THAT YEAR.
"EXTERMI-NATION" WAS LEGITIMIZED UNDER THE CODE.

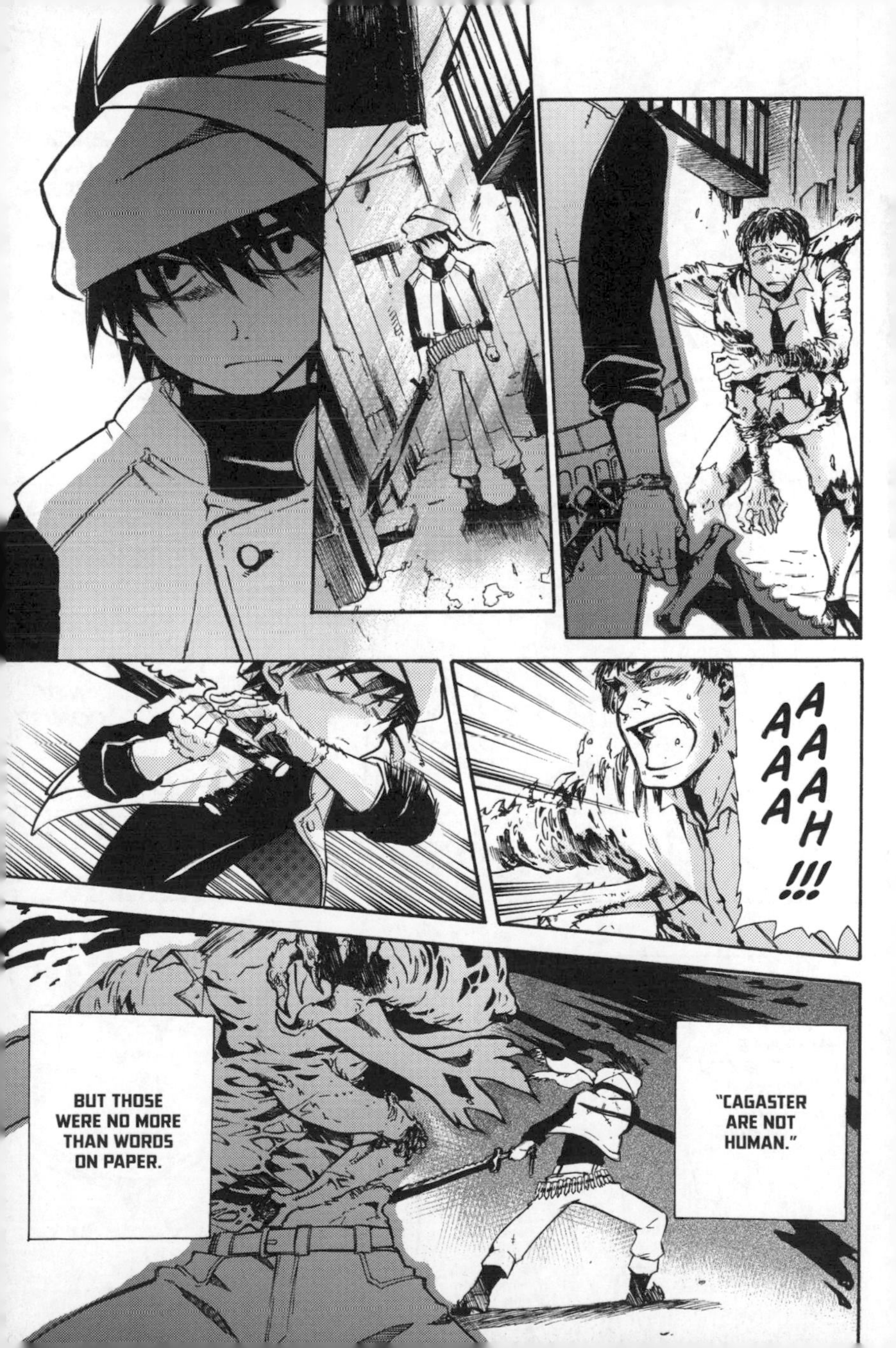
AAAAAAAH!!!
"CAGASTER ARE NOT HUMAN."
BUT THOSE WERE NO MORE THAN WORDS ON PAPER.

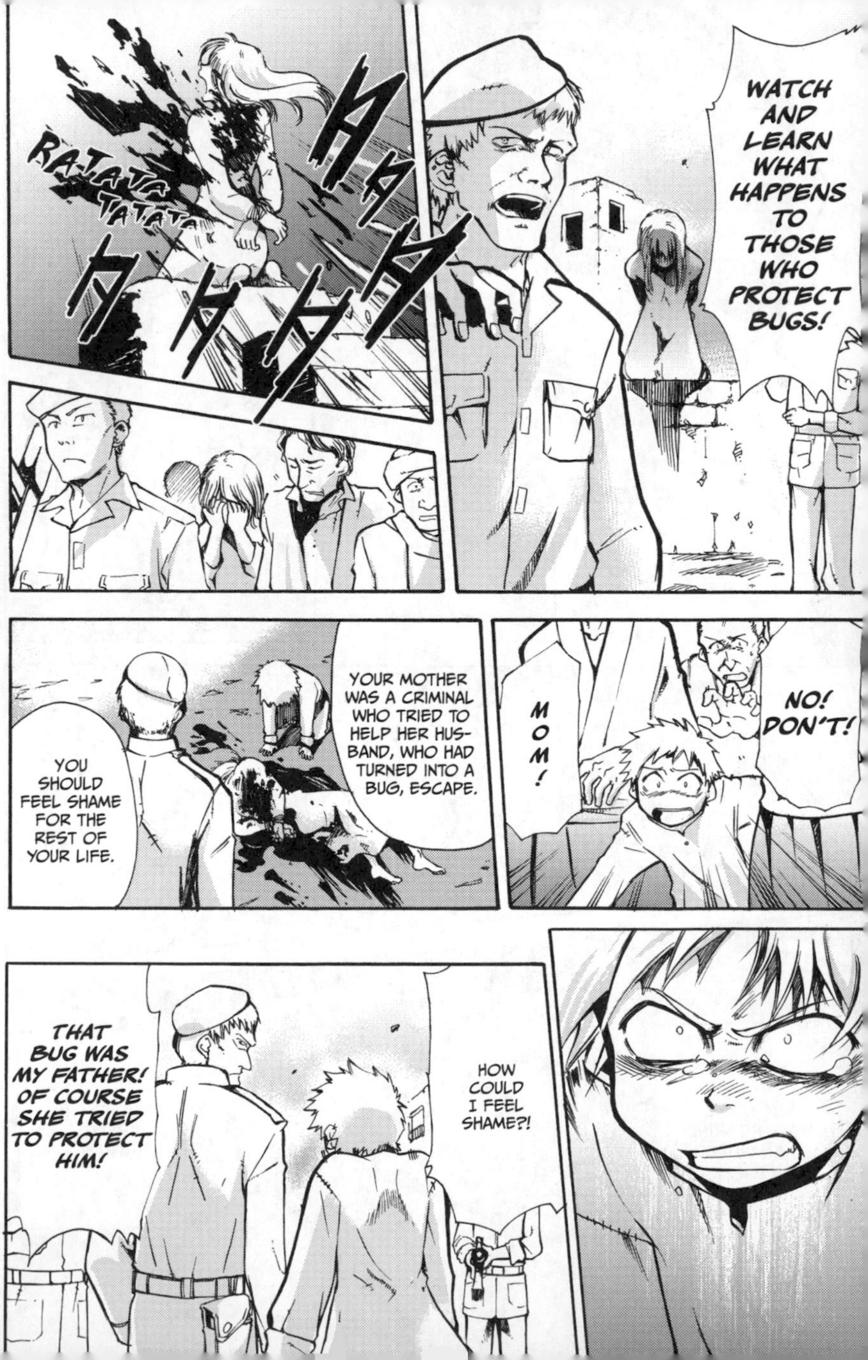
WATCH AND LEARN WHAT HAPPENS TO THOSE WHO PROTECT BUGS!
RATATATA TATATA
NO! DON'T!
MOM!
YOUR MOTHER WAS A CRIMINAL WHO TRIED TO HELP HER HUS-BAND, WHO HAD TURNED INTO A BUG, ESCAPE.
YOU SHOULD FEEL SHAME FOR THE REST OF YOUR LIFE.
HOW COULD I FEEL SHAME?!
THAT BUG WAS MY FATHER! OF COURSE SHE TRIED TO PROTECT HIM!

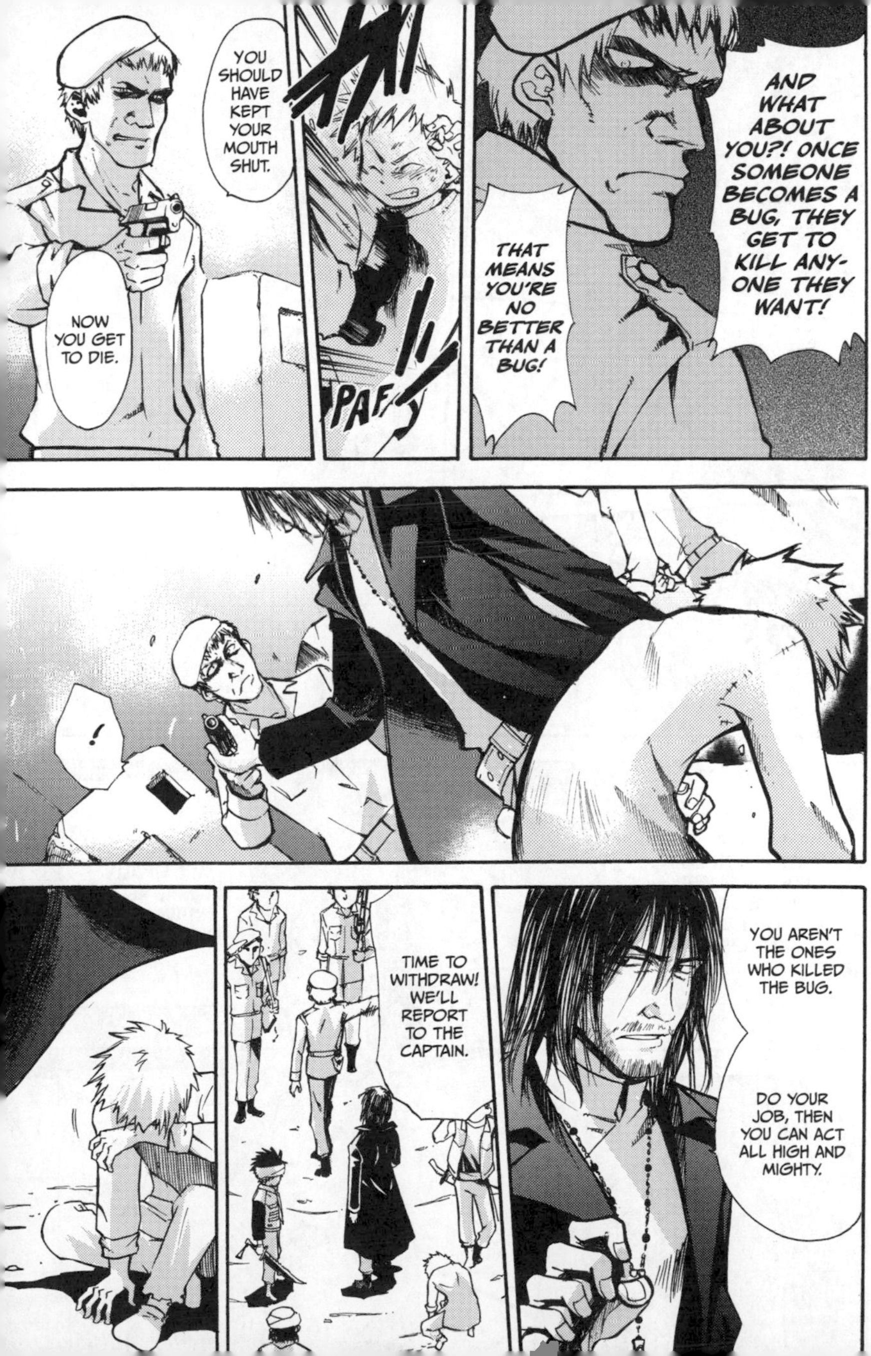
AND WHAT ABOUT YOU?! ONCE SOMEONE BECOMES A BUG, THEY GET TO KILL ANY-ONE THEY WANT!
THAT MEANS YOU'RE NO BETTER THAN A BUG!
PAF
YOU SHOULD HAVE KEPT YOUR MOUTH SHUT.
NOW YOU GET TO DIE.
!
YOU AREN'T THE ONES WHO KILLED THE BUG.
DO YOUR JOB, THEN YOU CAN ACT ALL HIGH AND MIGHTY.
TIME TO WITHDRAW! WE'LL REPORT TO THE CAPTAIN.

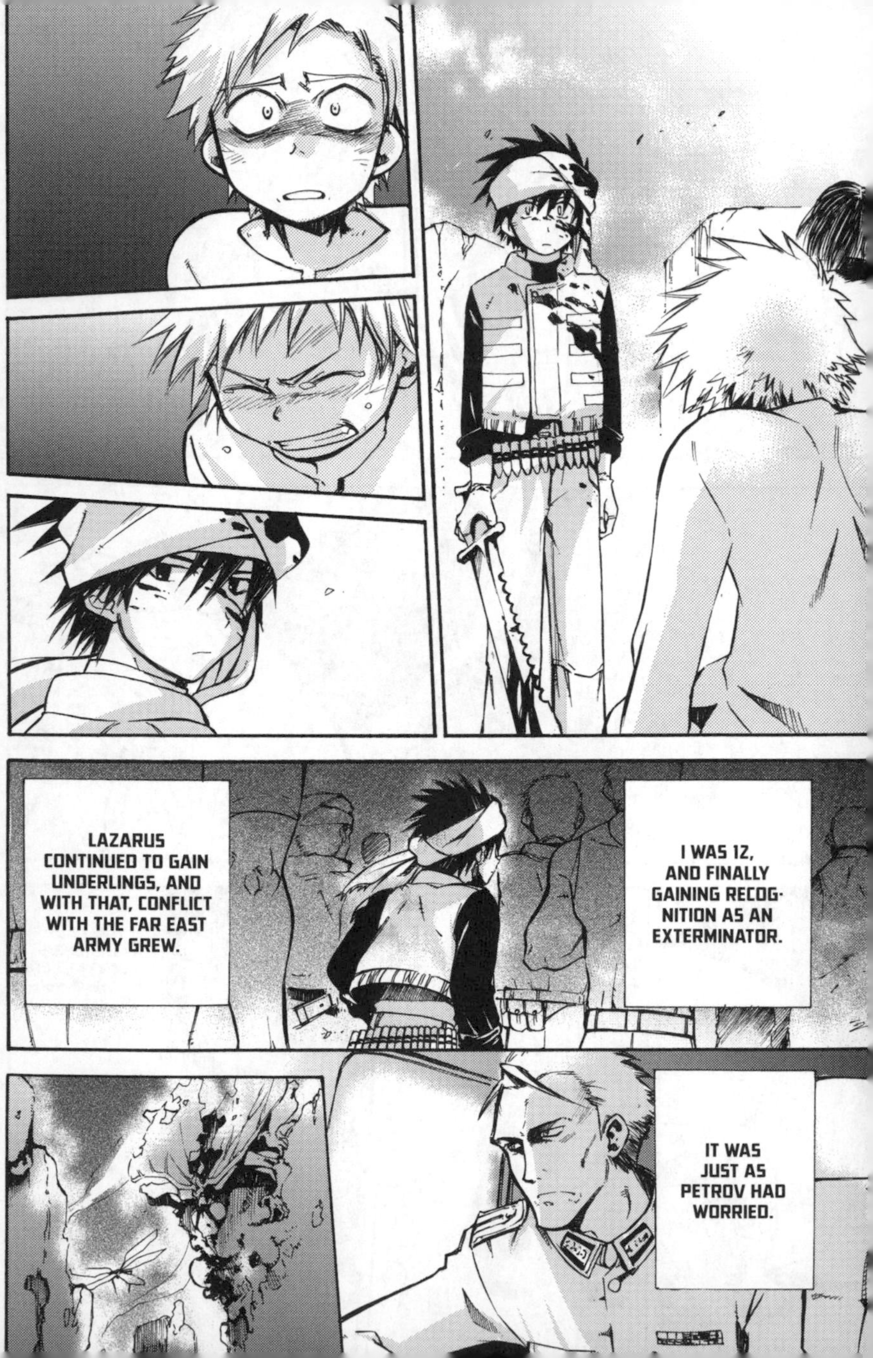
I WAS 12, AND FINALLY GAINING RECOG-NITION AS AN EXTERMINATOR.
LAZARUS CONTINUED TO GAIN UNDERLINGS, AND WITH THAT, CONFLICT WITH THE FAR EAST ARMY GREW.
IT WAS JUST AS PETROV HAD WORRIED.

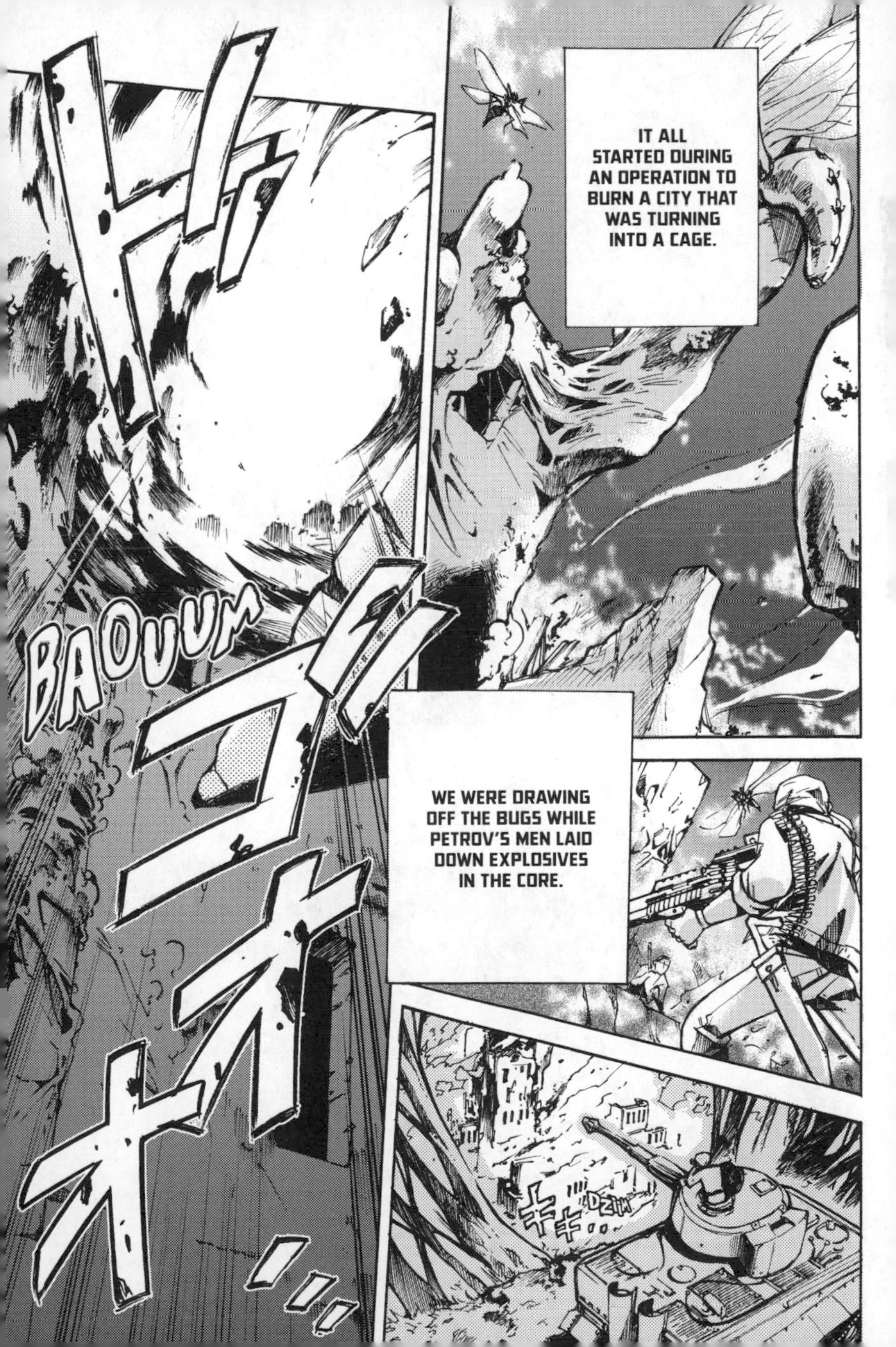
IT ALL STARTED DURING AN OPERATION TO BURN A CITY THAT WAS TURNING INTO A CAGE.
WE WERE DRAWING OFF THE BUGS WHILE PETROV'S MEN LAID DOWN EXPLOSIVES IN THE CORE.
DZIIM
BAOUUM

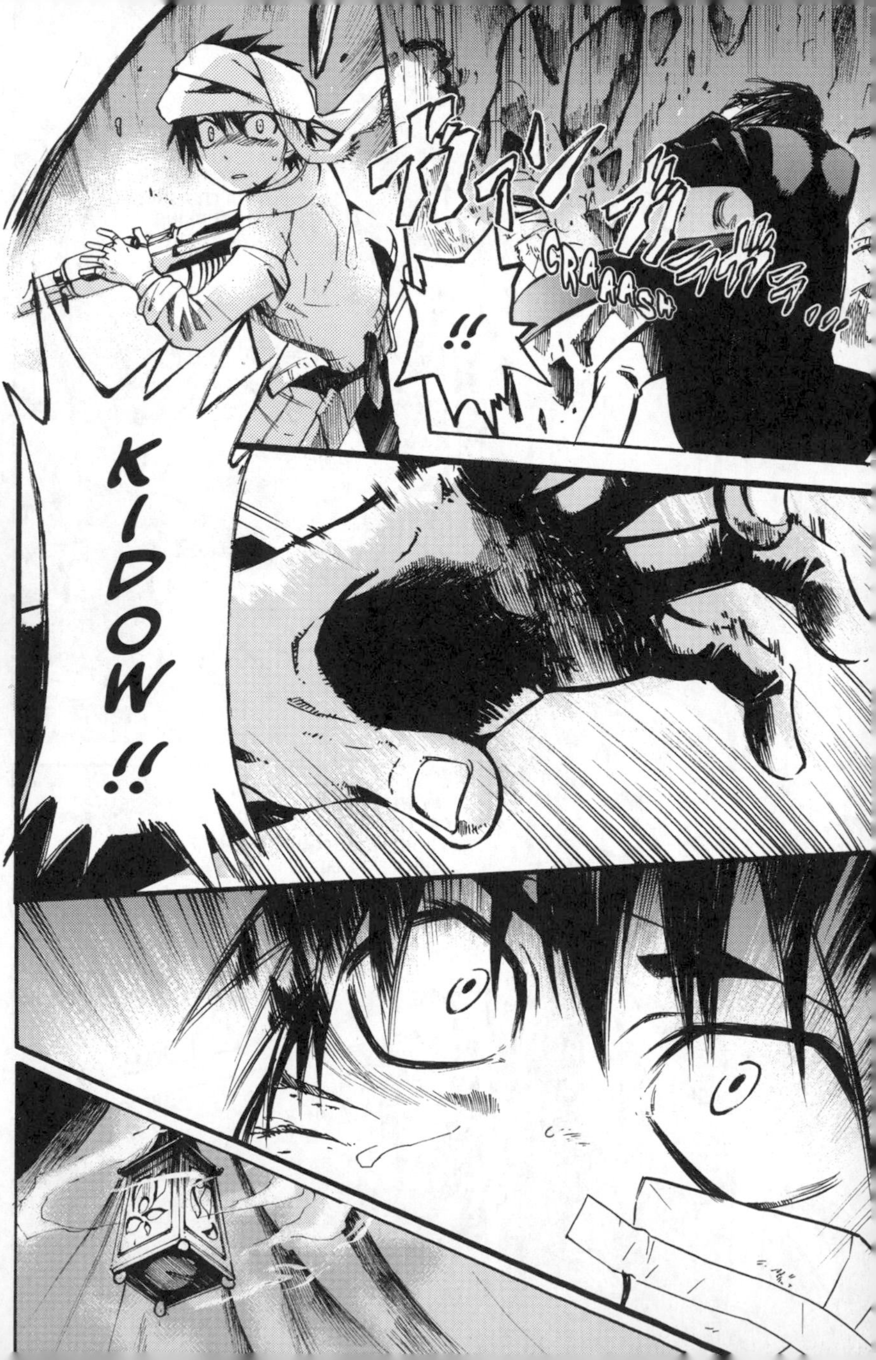
CRAAASH
!!
KIDOW !!

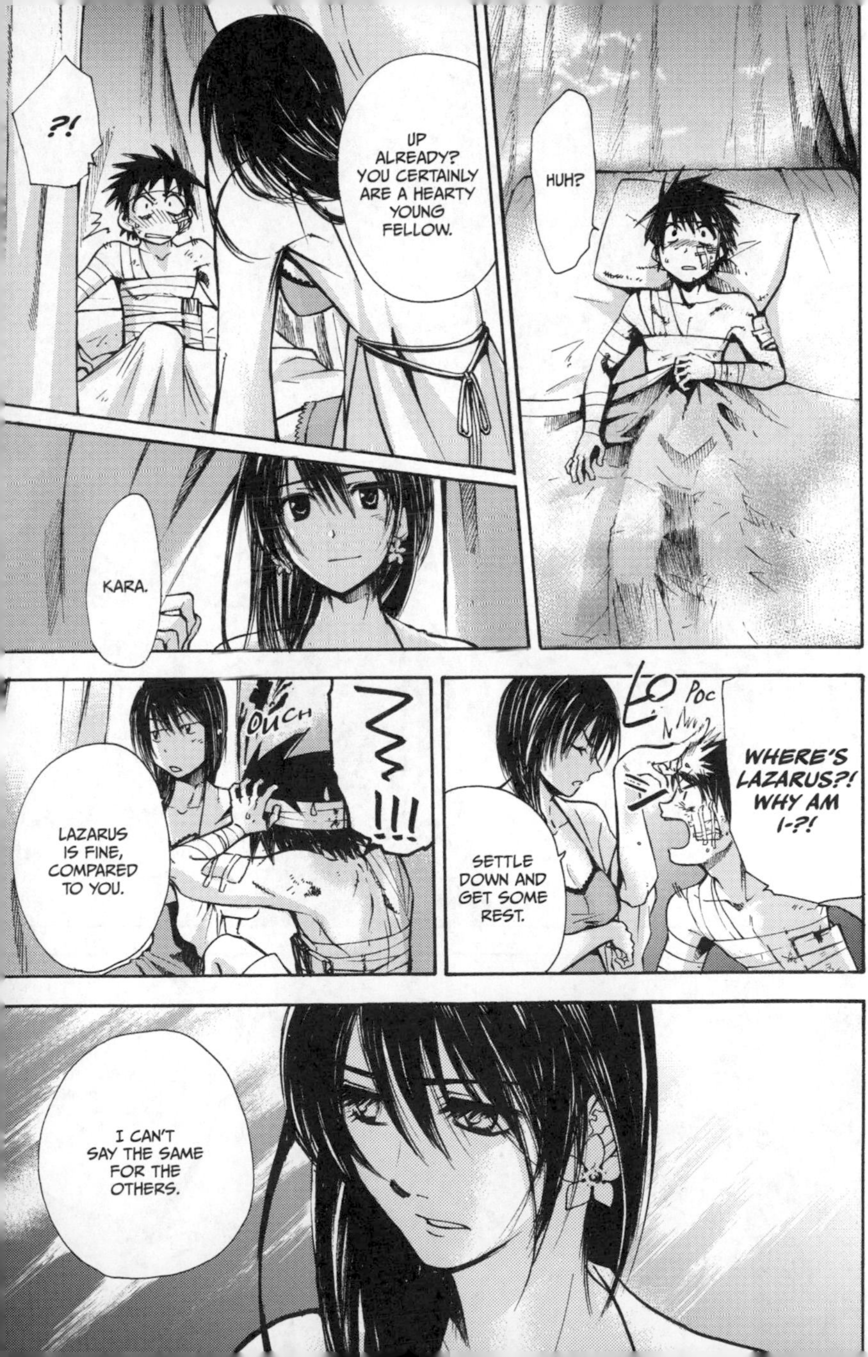
HUH?
UP ALREADY? YOU CERTAINLY ARE A HEARTY YOUNG FELLOW.
?!
KARA.
POC
WHERE'S LAZARUS?! WHY AM I-?!
SETTLE DOWN AND GET SOME REST.
OUCH
!!!
LAZARUS IS FINE, COMPARED TO YOU.
I CAN'T SAY THE SAME FOR THE OTHERS.

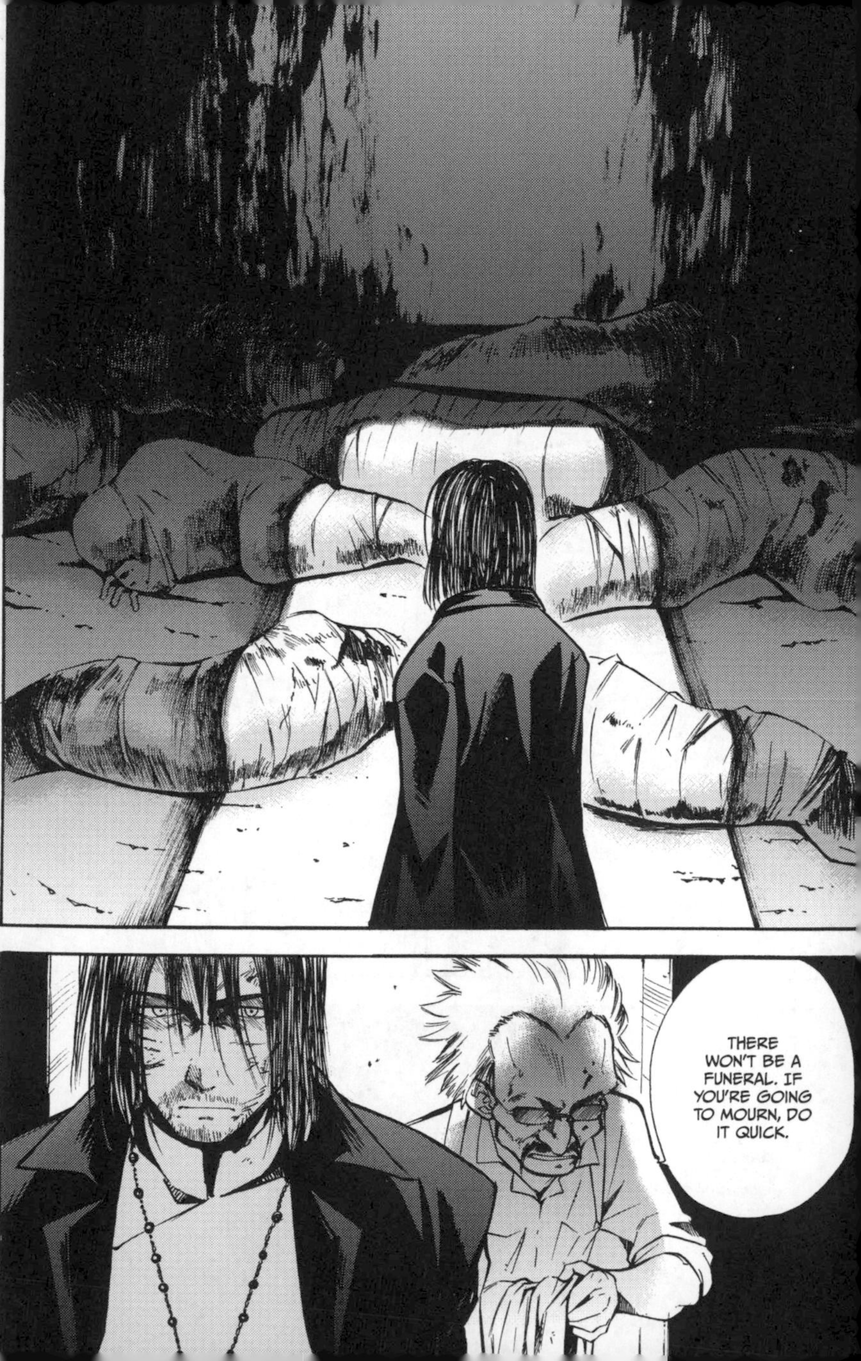
THERE WON'T BE A FUNERAL. IF YOU'RE GOING TO MOURN, DO IT QUICK.

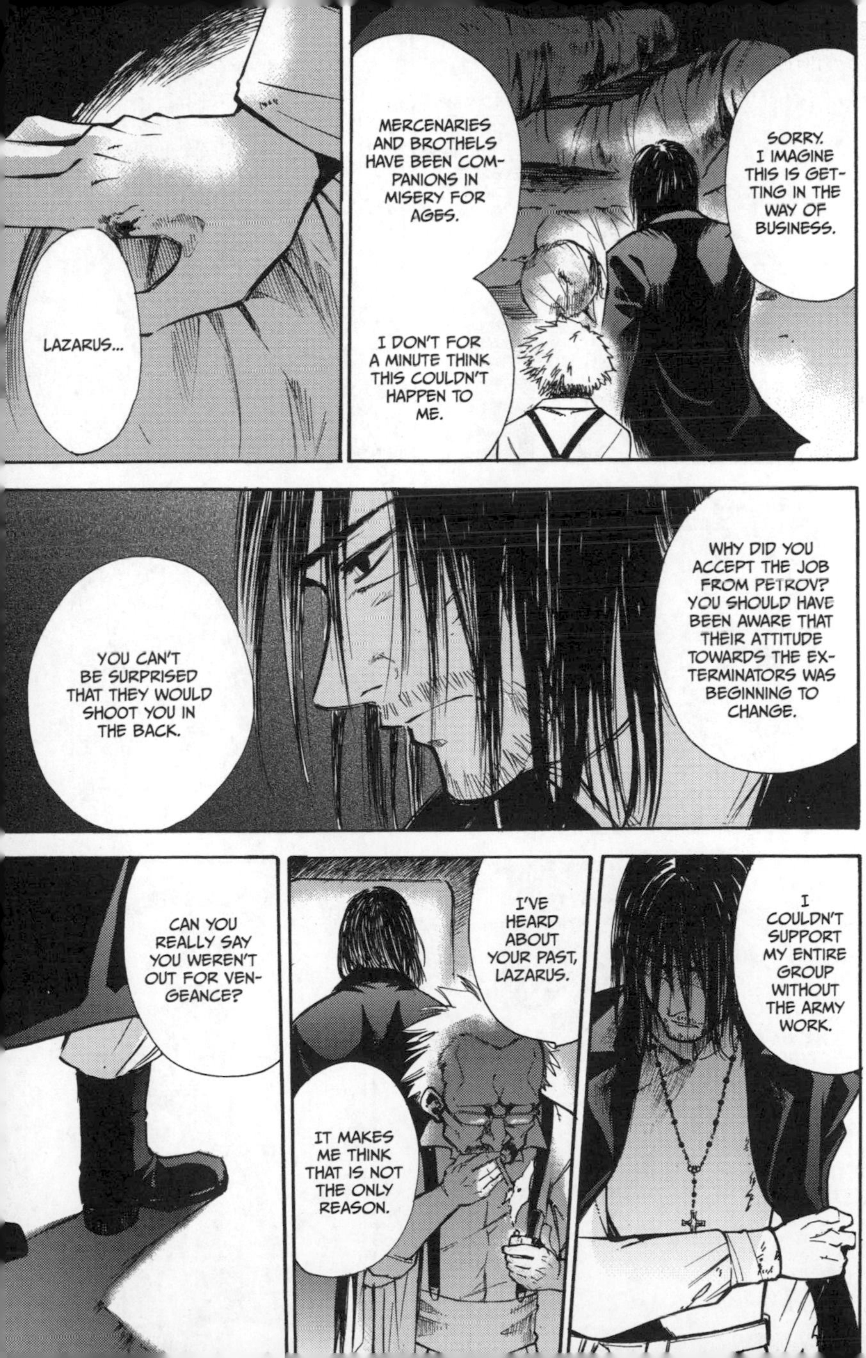
SORRY. I IMAGINE THIS IS GETTING IN THE WAY OF BUSINESS.
MERCENARIES AND BROTHELS HAVE BEEN COMPANIONS IN MISERY FOR AGES.
I DON'T FOR A MINUTE THINK THIS COULDN'T HAPPEN TO ME.
LAZARUS...
WHY DID YOU ACCEPT THE JOB FROM PETROV? YOU SHOULD HAVE BEEN AWARE THAT THEIR ATTITUDE TOWARDS THE EXTERMINATORS WAS BEGINNING TO CHANGE.
YOU CAN'T BE SURPRISED THAT THEY WOULD SHOOT YOU IN THE BACK.
I COULDN'T SUPPORT MY ENTIRE GROUP WITHOUT THE ARMY WORK.
I'VE HEARD ABOUT YOUR PAST, LAZARUS.
IT MAKES ME THINK THAT IS NOT THE ONLY REASON.
CAN YOU REALLY SAY YOU WEREN'T OUT FOR VENGEANCE?

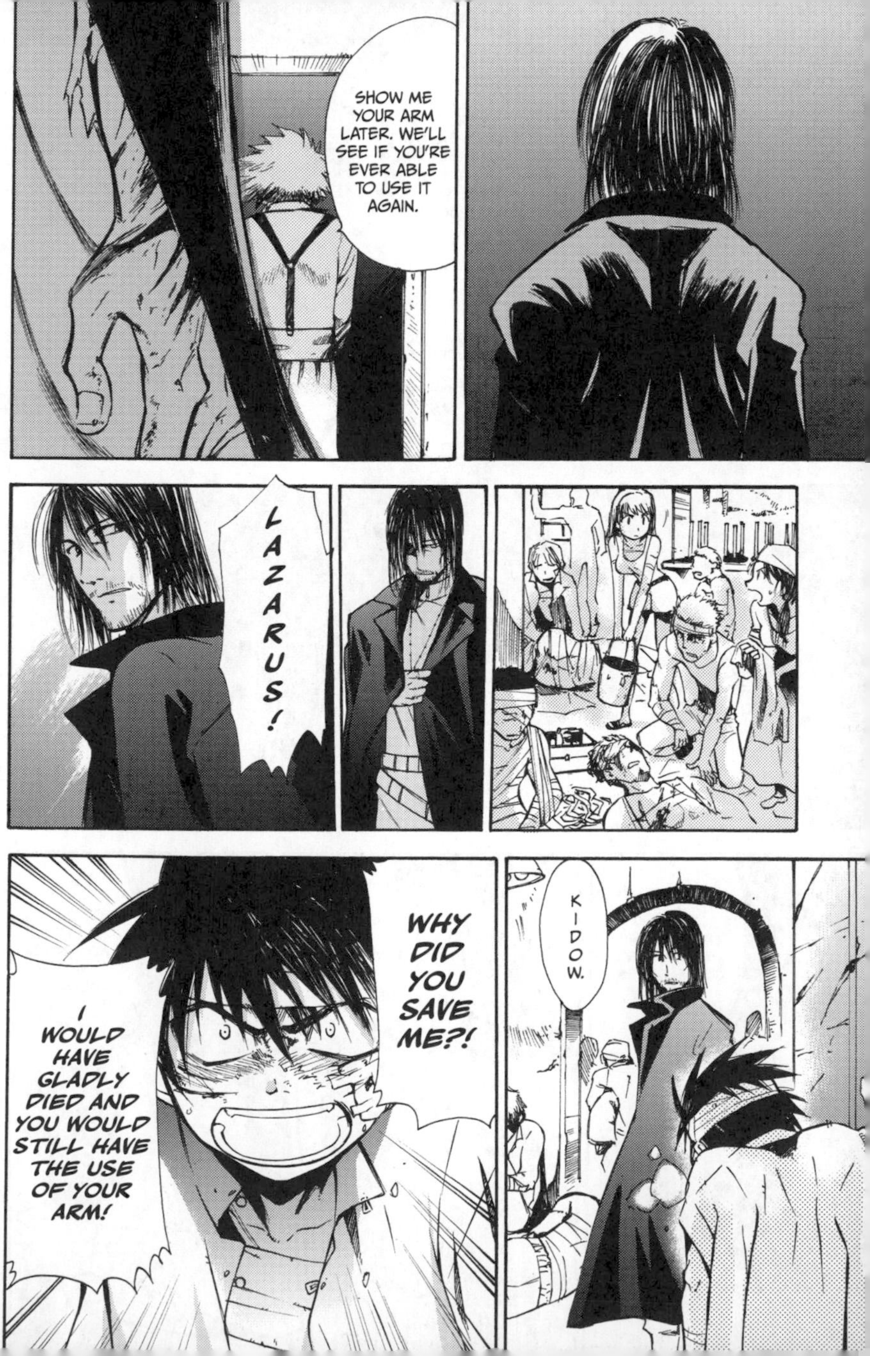
SHOW ME YOUR ARM LATER. WE'LL SEE IF YOU'RE EVER ABLE TO USE IT AGAIN.
LAZARUS!
KIDOW.
WHY DID YOU SAVE ME?!
I WOULD HAVE GLADLY DIED AND YOU WOULD STILL HAVE THE USE OF YOUR ARM!

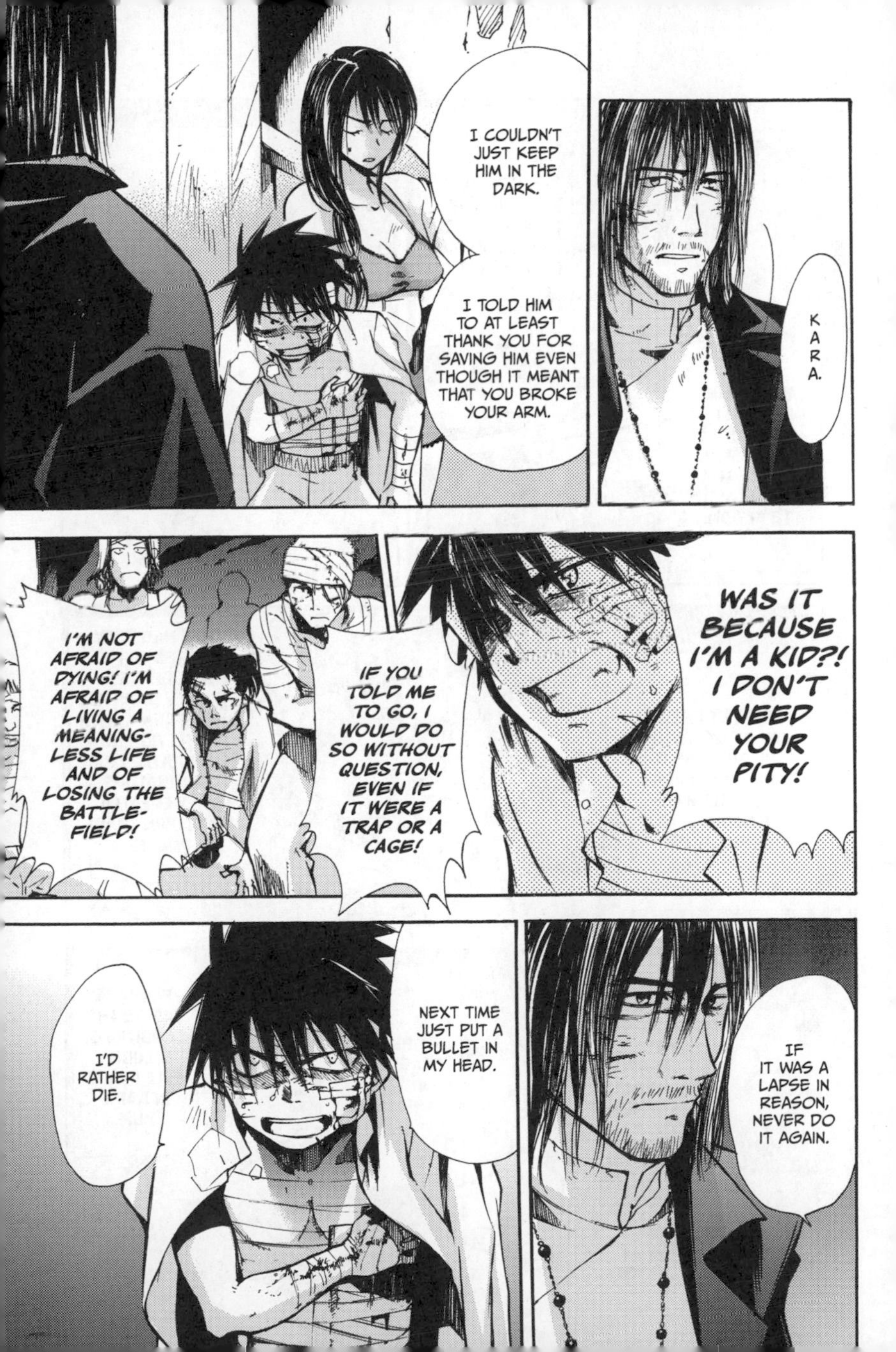
KARA.
I COULDN'T JUST KEEP HIM IN THE DARK.
I TOLD HIM TO AT LEAST THANK YOU FOR SAVING HIM EVEN THOUGH IT MEANT THAT YOU BROKE YOUR ARM.
WAS IT BECAUSE I'M A KID?! I DON'T NEED YOUR PITY!
IF YOU TOLD ME TO GO, I WOULD DO SO WITHOUT QUESTION, EVEN IF IT WERE A TRAP OR A CAGE!
I'M NOT AFRAID OF DYING! I'M AFRAID OF LIVING A MEANING-LESS LIFE AND OF LOSING THE BATTLE-FIELD!
IF IT WAS A LAPSE IN REASON, NEVER DO IT AGAIN.
NEXT TIME JUST PUT A BULLET IN MY HEAD.
I'D RATHER DIE.

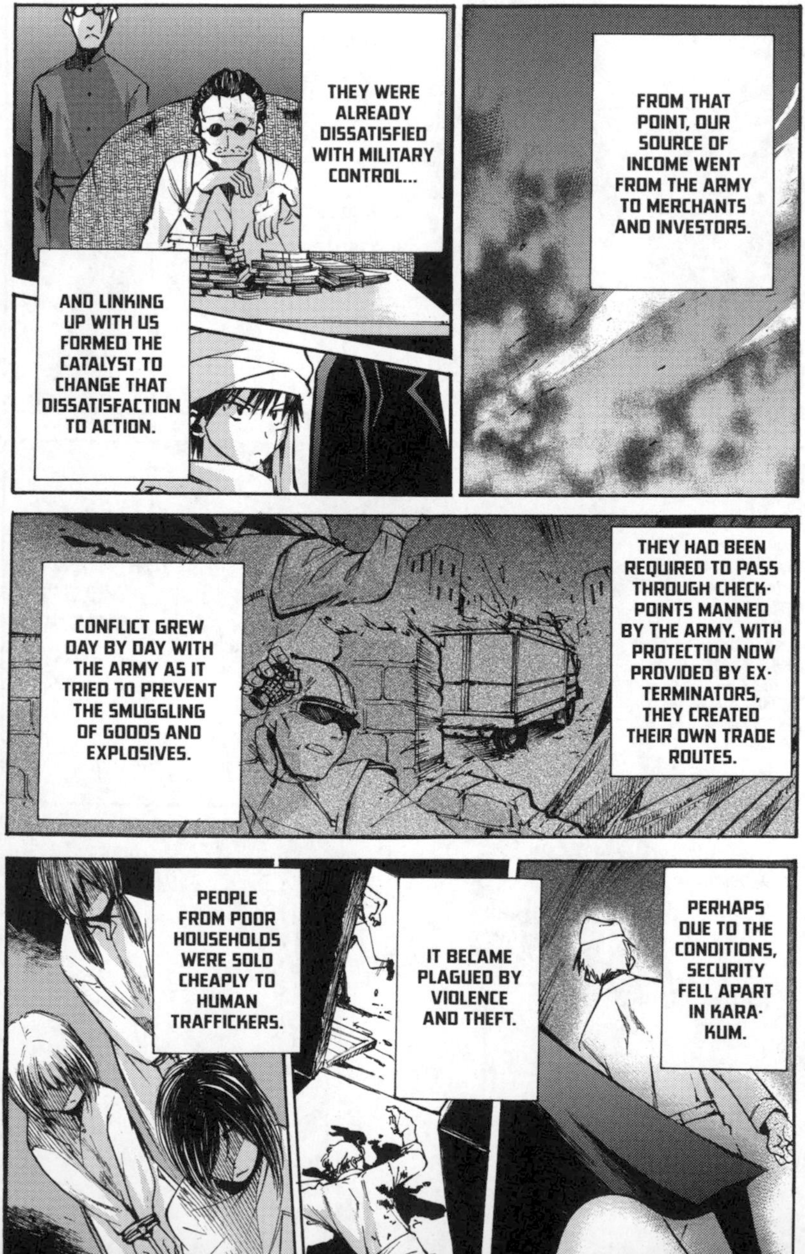
FROM THAT POINT, OUR SOURCE OF INCOME WENT FROM THE ARMY TO MERCHANTS AND INVESTORS.
THEY WERE ALREADY DISSATISFIED WITH MILITARY CONTROL...
AND LINKING UP WITH US FORMED THE CATALYST TO CHANGE THAT DISSATISFACTION TO ACTION.
THEY HAD BEEN REQUIRED TO PASS THROUGH CHECK-POINTS MANNED BY THE ARMY. WITH PROTECTION NOW PROVIDED BY EX-TERMINATORS, THEY CREATED THEIR OWN TRADE ROUTES.
CONFLICT GREW DAY BY DAY WITH THE ARMY AS IT TRIED TO PREVENT THE SMUGGLING OF GOODS AND EXPLOSIVES.
PERHAPS DUE TO THE CONDITIONS, SECURITY FELL APART IN KARA-KUM.
IT BECAME PLAGUED BY VIOLENCE AND THEFT.
PEOPLE FROM POOR HOUSEHOLDS WERE SOLD CHEAPLY TO HUMAN TRAFFICKERS.

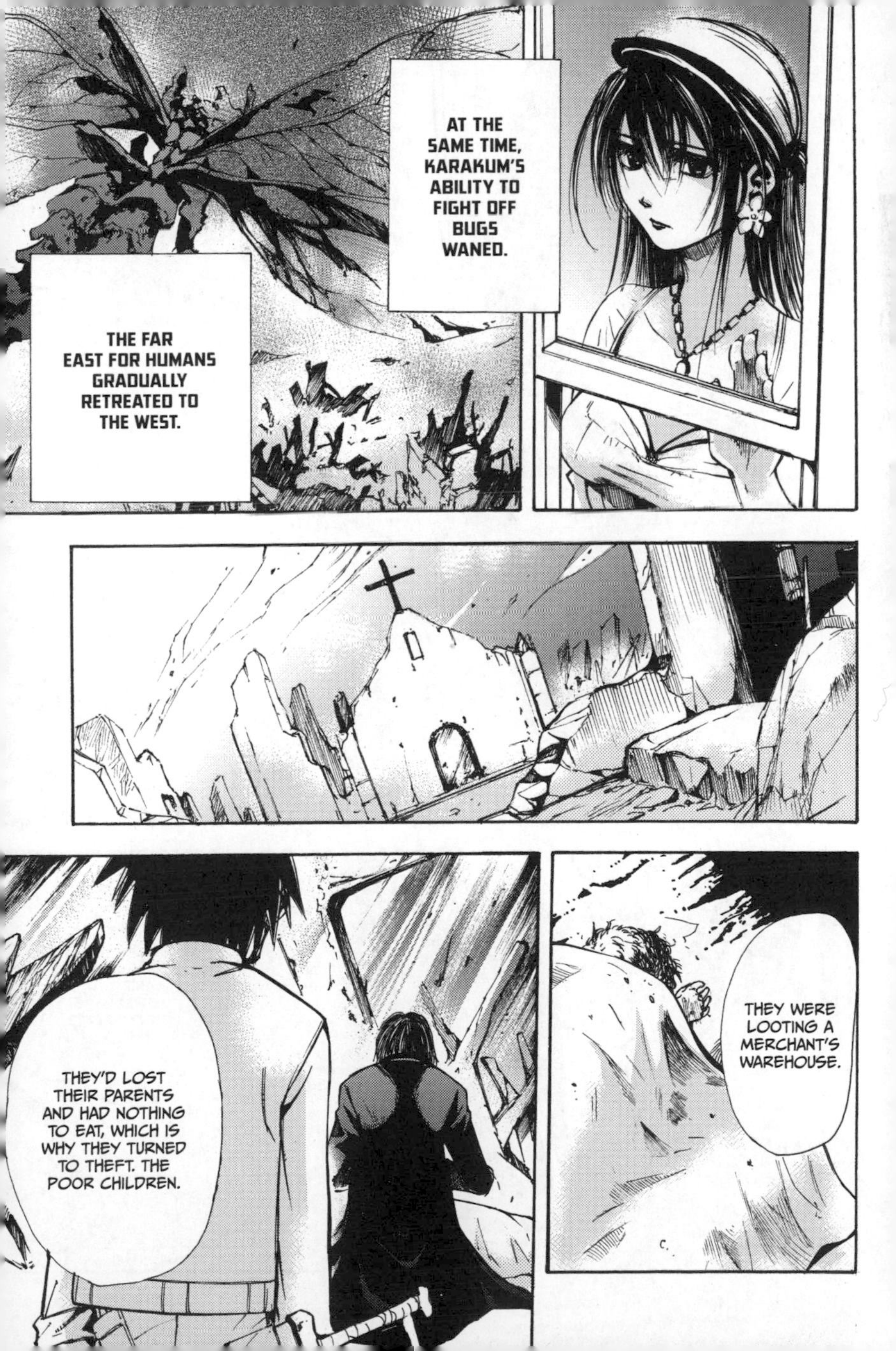
AT THE SAME TIME, KARAKUM'S ABILITY TO FIGHT OFF BUGS WANED.
THE FAR EAST FOR HUMANS GRADUALLY RETREATED TO THE WEST.
THEY WERE LOOTING A MERCHANT'S WAREHOUSE.
THEY'D LOST THEIR PARENTS AND HAD NOTHING TO EAT, WHICH IS WHY THEY TURNED TO THEFT. THE POOR CHILDREN.

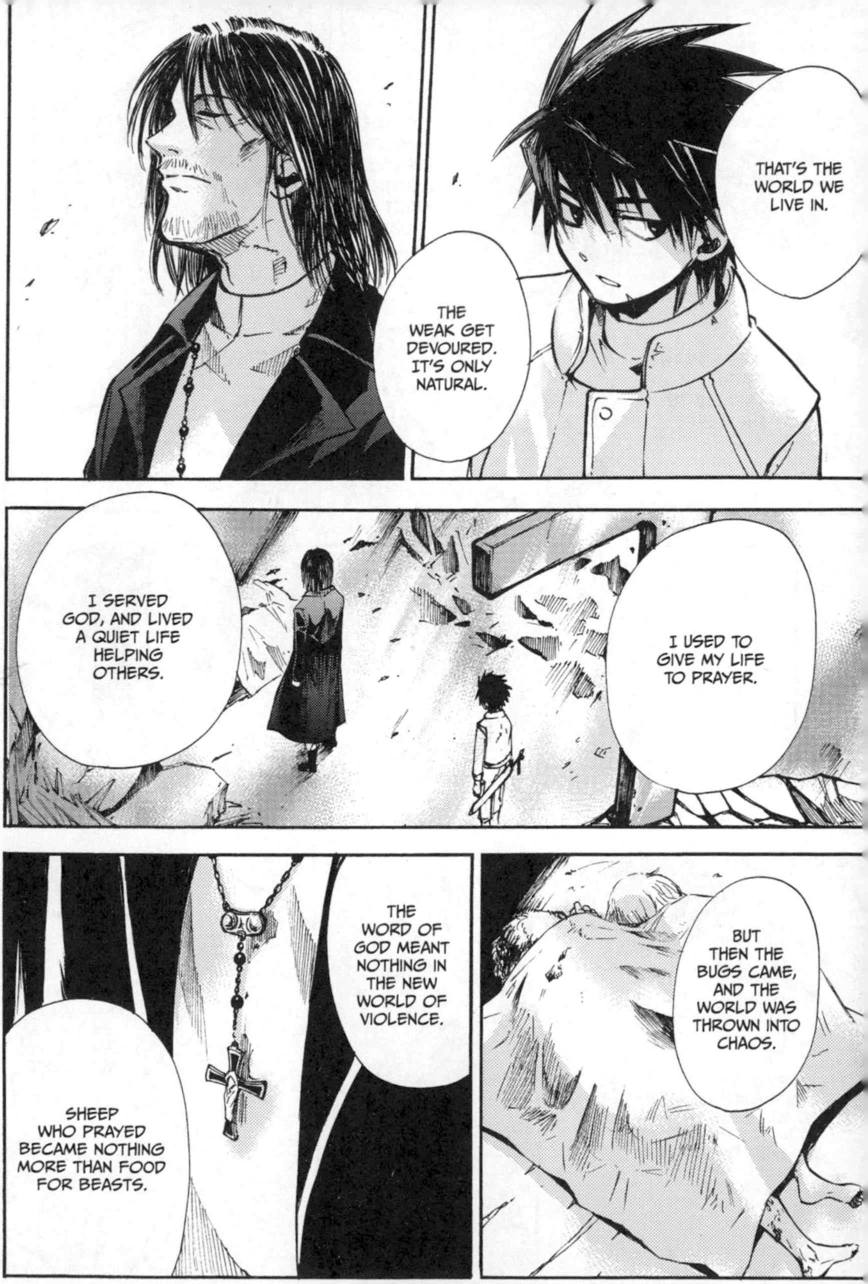
THAT'S THE WORLD WE LIVE IN.
THE WEAK GET DEVOURED. IT'S ONLY NATURAL.
I USED TO GIVE MY LIFE TO PRAYER.
I SERVED GOD, AND LIVED A QUIET LIFE HELPING OTHERS.
BUT THEN THE BUGS CAME, AND THE WORLD WAS THROWN INTO CHAOS.
THE WORD OF GOD MEANT NOTHING IN THE NEW WORLD OF VIOLENCE.
SHEEP WHO PRAYED BECAME NOTHING MORE THAN FOOD FOR BEASTS.

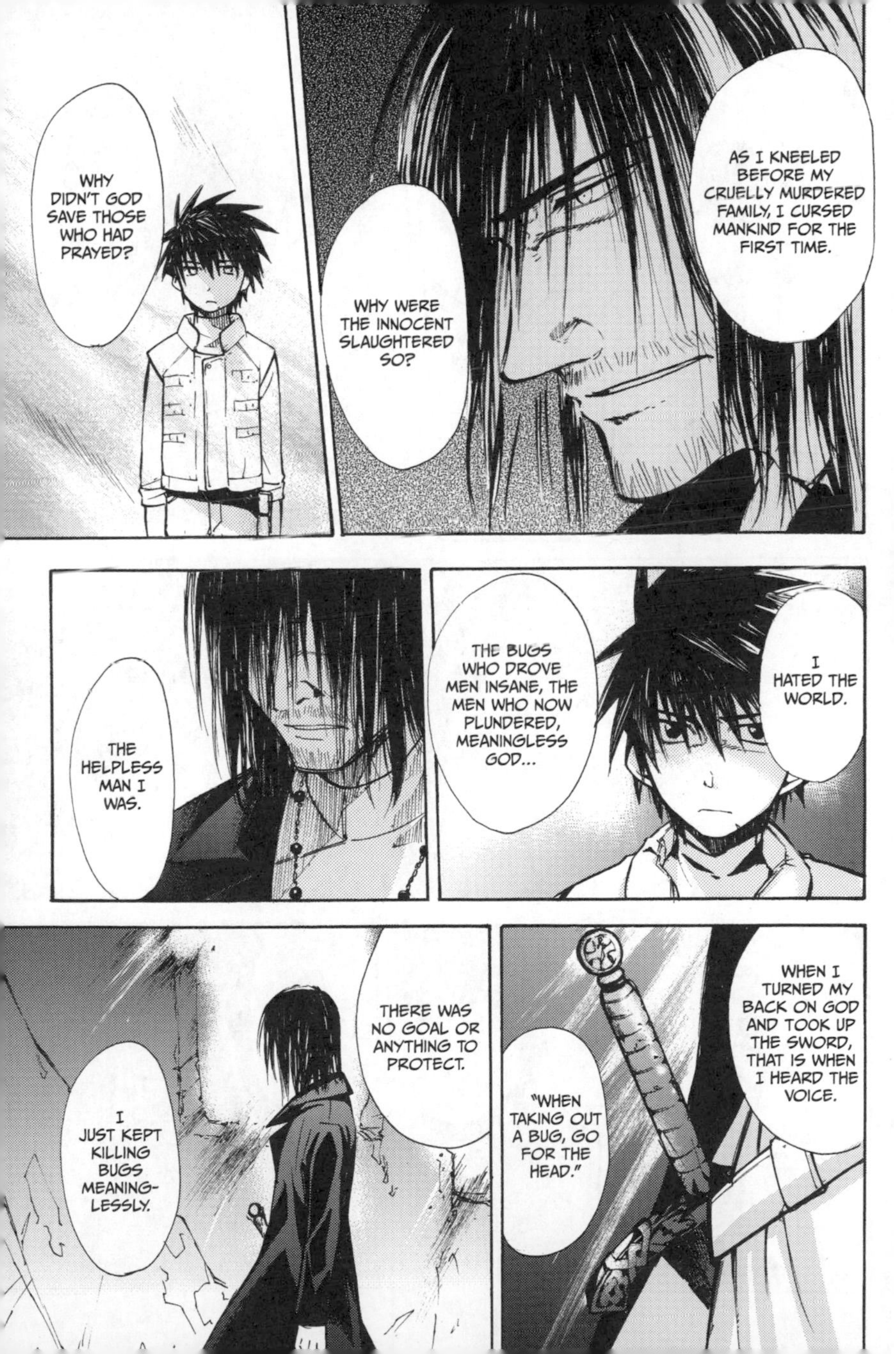
AS I KNEELED BEFORE MY CRUELLY MURDERED FAMILY, I CURSED MANKIND FOR THE FIRST TIME.
WHY WERE THE INNOCENT SLAUGHTERED SO?
WHY DIDN'T GOD SAVE THOSE WHO HAD PRAYED?
I HATED THE WORLD.
THE BUGS WHO DROVE MEN INSANE, THE MEN WHO NOW PLUNDERED, MEANINGLESS GOD...
THE HELPLESS MAN I WAS.
WHEN I TURNED MY BACK ON GOD AND TOOK UP THE SWORD, THAT IS WHEN I HEARD THE VOICE.
"WHEN TAKING OUT A BUG, GO FOR THE HEAD."
THERE WAS NO GOAL OR ANYTHING TO PROTECT.
I JUST KEPT KILLING BUGS MEANING-LESSLY.

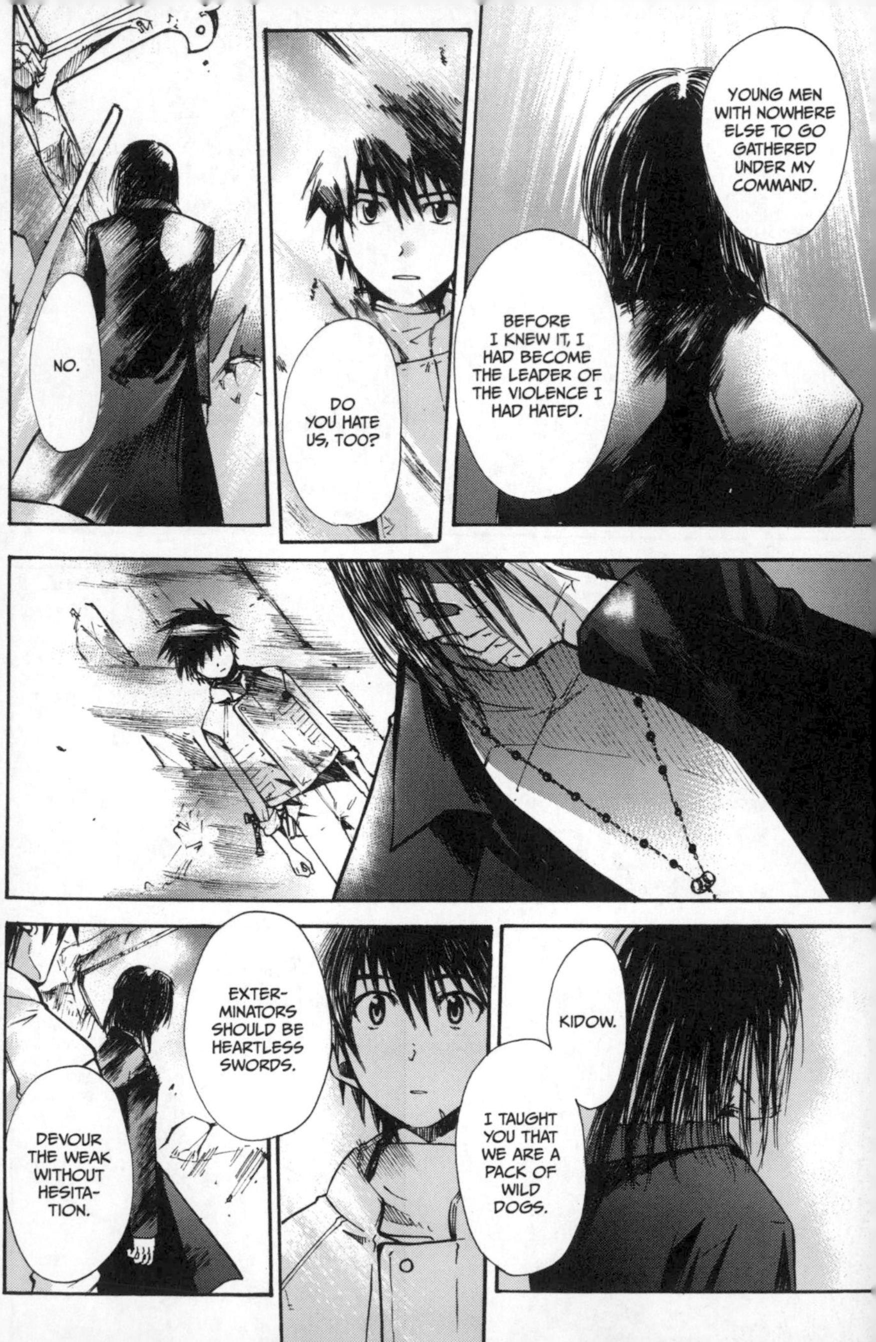
YOUNG MEN WITH NOWHERE ELSE TO GO GATHERED UNDER MY COMMAND.
BEFORE I KNEW IT, I HAD BECOME THE LEADER OF THE VIOLENCE I HAD HATED.
DO YOU HATE US, TOO?
NO.
KIDOW.
I TAUGHT YOU THAT WE ARE A PACK OF WILD DOGS.
EXTER-MINATORS SHOULD BE HEARTLESS SWORDS.
DEVOUR THE WEAK WITHOUT HESITA-TION.

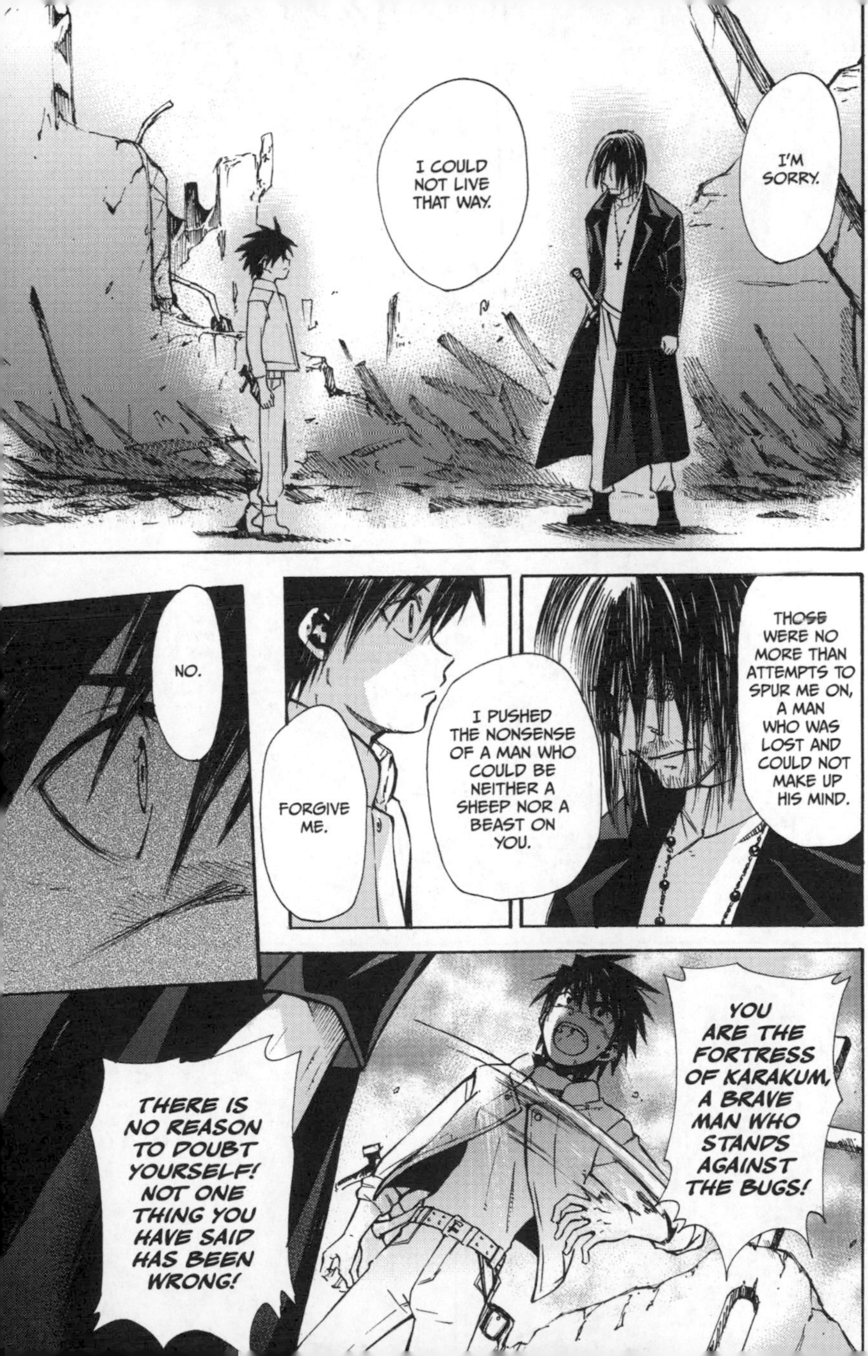

I'M SORRY.
I COULD NOT LIVE THAT WAY.
THOSE WERE NO MORE THAN ATTEMPTS TO SPUR ME ON, A MAN WHO WAS LOST AND COULD NOT MAKE UP HIS MIND.
I PUSHED THE NONSENSE OF A MAN WHO COULD BE NEITHER A SHEEP NOR A BEAST ON YOU.
FORGIVE ME.
NO.
YOU ARE THE FORTRESS OF KARAKUM, A BRAVE MAN WHO STANDS AGAINST THE BUGS!
THERE IS NO REASON TO DOUBT YOURSELF! NOT ONE THING YOU HAVE SAID HAS BEEN WRONG!

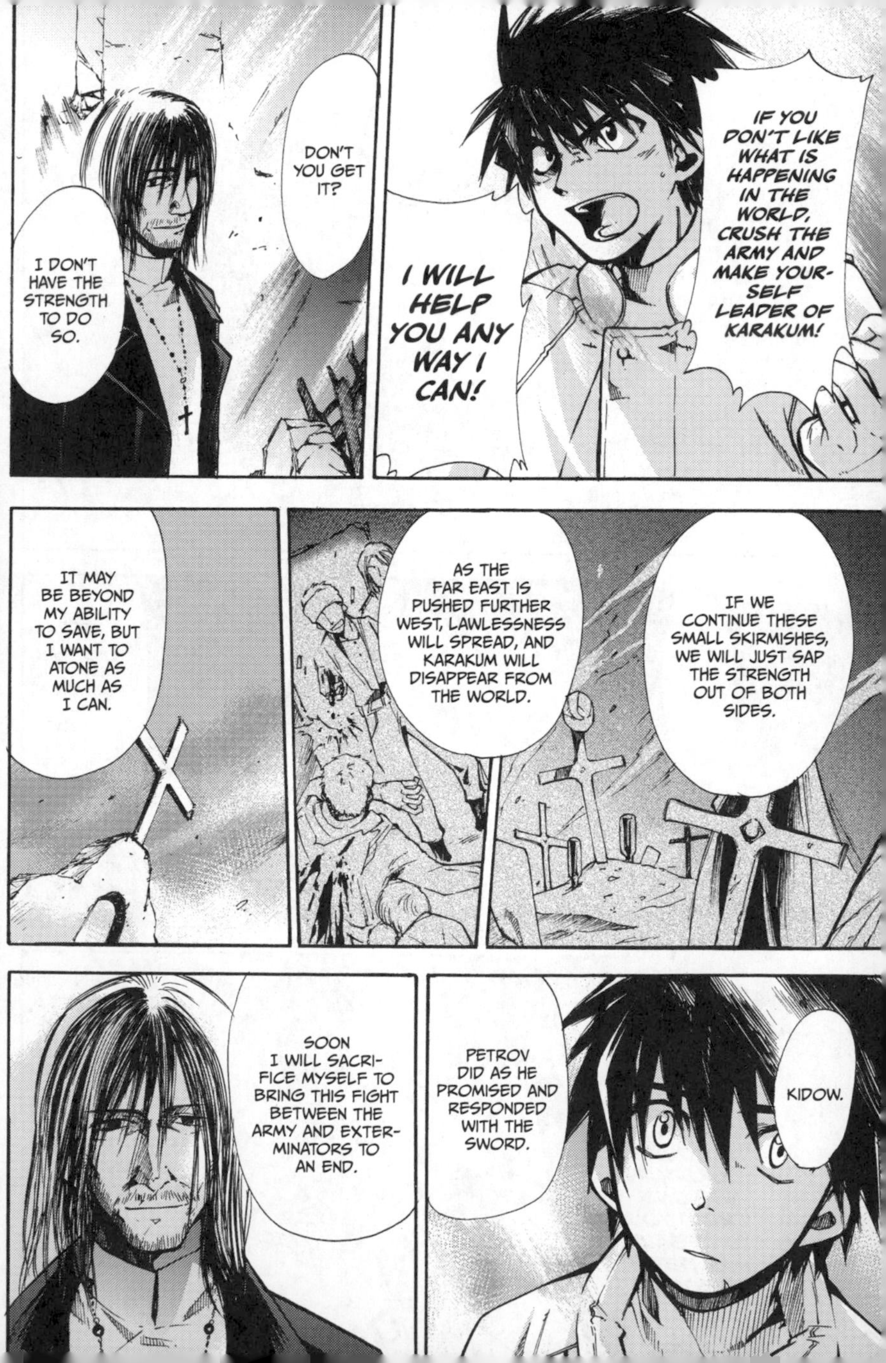
IF YOU DON'T LIKE WHAT IS HAPPENING IN THE WORLD, CRUSH THE ARMY AND MAKE YOUR-SELF LEADER OF KARAKUM!
I WILL HELP YOU ANY WAY I CAN!
DON'T YOU GET IT?
I DON'T HAVE THE STRENGTH TO DO SO.
IF WE CONTINUE THESE SMALL SKIRMISHES, WE WILL JUST SAP THE STRENGTH OUT OF BOTH SIDES.
AS THE FAR EAST IS PUSHED FURTHER WEST, LAWLESSNESS WILL SPREAD, AND KARAKUM WILL DISAPPEAR FROM THE WORLD.
IT MAY BE BEYOND MY ABILITY TO SAVE, BUT I WANT TO ATONE AS MUCH AS I CAN.
KIDOW.
PETROV DID AS HE PROMISED AND RESPONDED WITH THE SWORD.
SOON I WILL SACRI-FICE MYSELF TO BRING THIS FIGHT BETWEEN THE ARMY AND EXTER-MINATORS TO AN END.

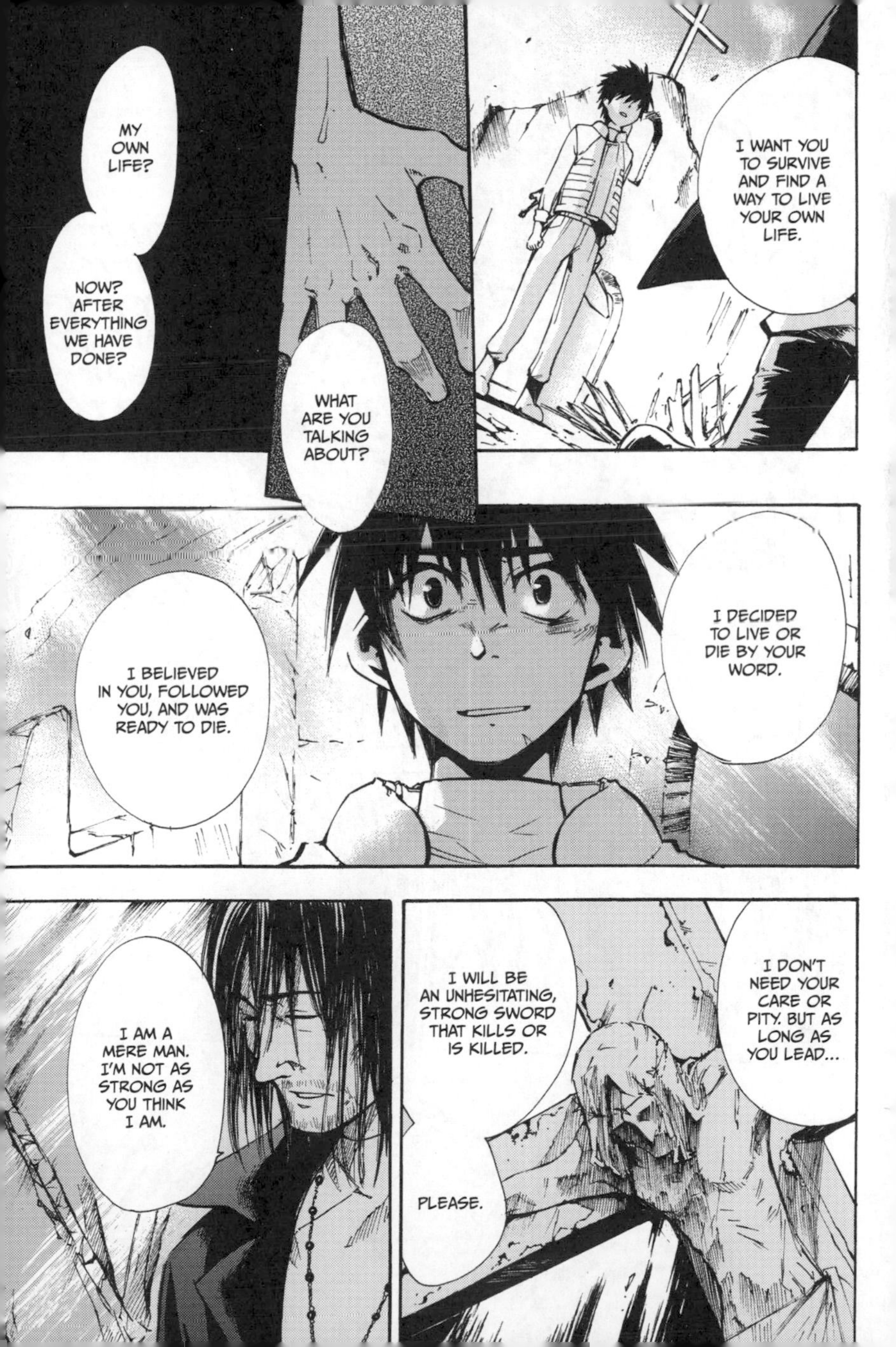
I WANT YOU TO SURVIVE AND FIND A WAY TO LIVE YOUR OWN LIFE.
WHAT ARE YOU TALKING ABOUT?
MY OWN LIFE?
NOW? AFTER EVERYTHING WE HAVE DONE?
I DECIDED TO LIVE OR DIE BY YOUR WORD.
I BELIEVED IN YOU, FOLLOWED YOU, AND WAS READY TO DIE.
I DON'T NEED YOUR CARE OR PITY. BUT AS LONG AS YOU LEAD...
I WILL BE AN UNHESITATING, STRONG SWORD THAT KILLS OR IS KILLED.
PLEASE.
I AM A MERE MAN. I'M NOT AS STRONG AS YOU THINK I AM.

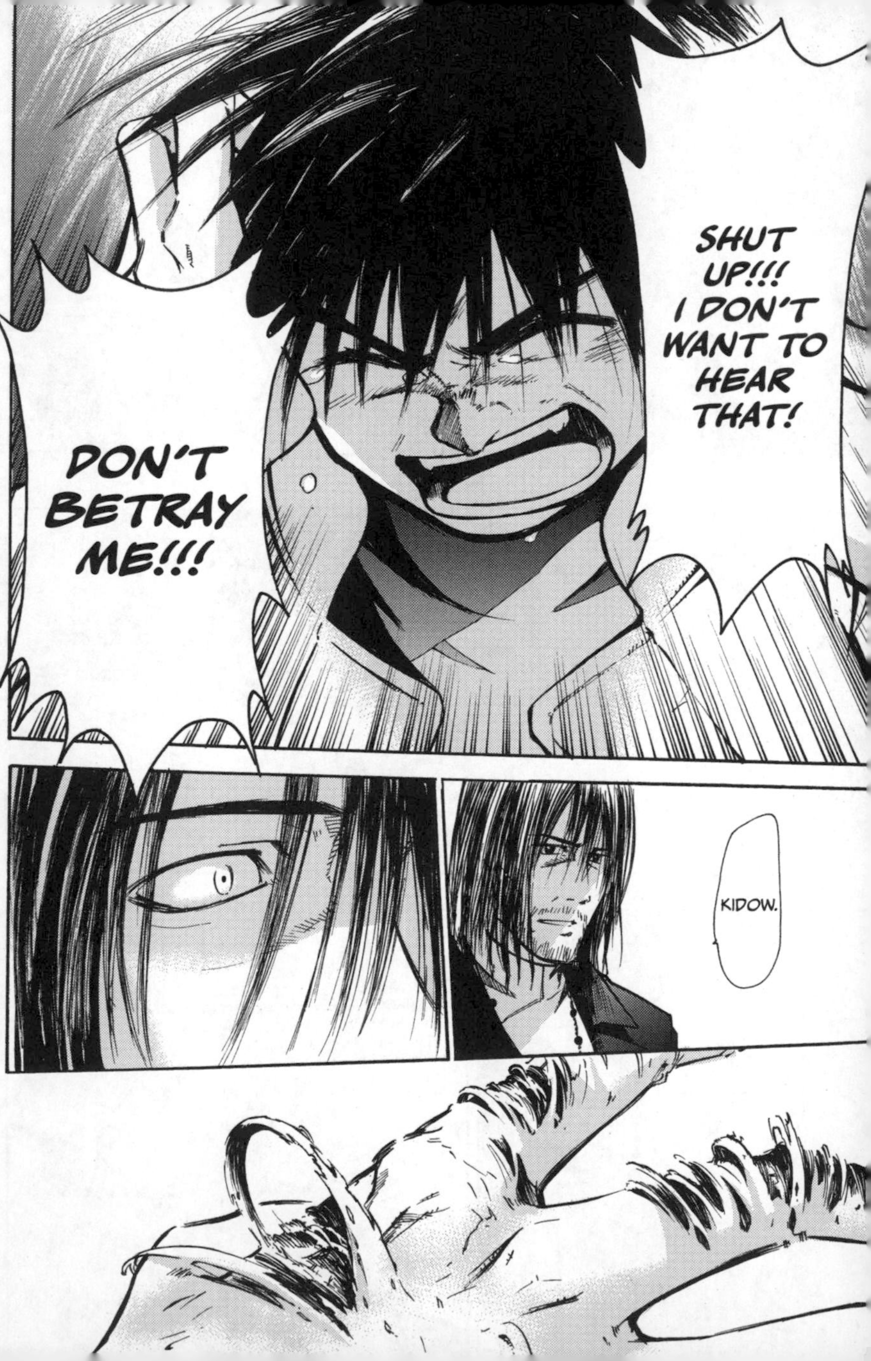
SHUT UP!!! I DON'T WANT TO HEAR THAT!
DON'T BETRAY ME!!!
KIDOW.

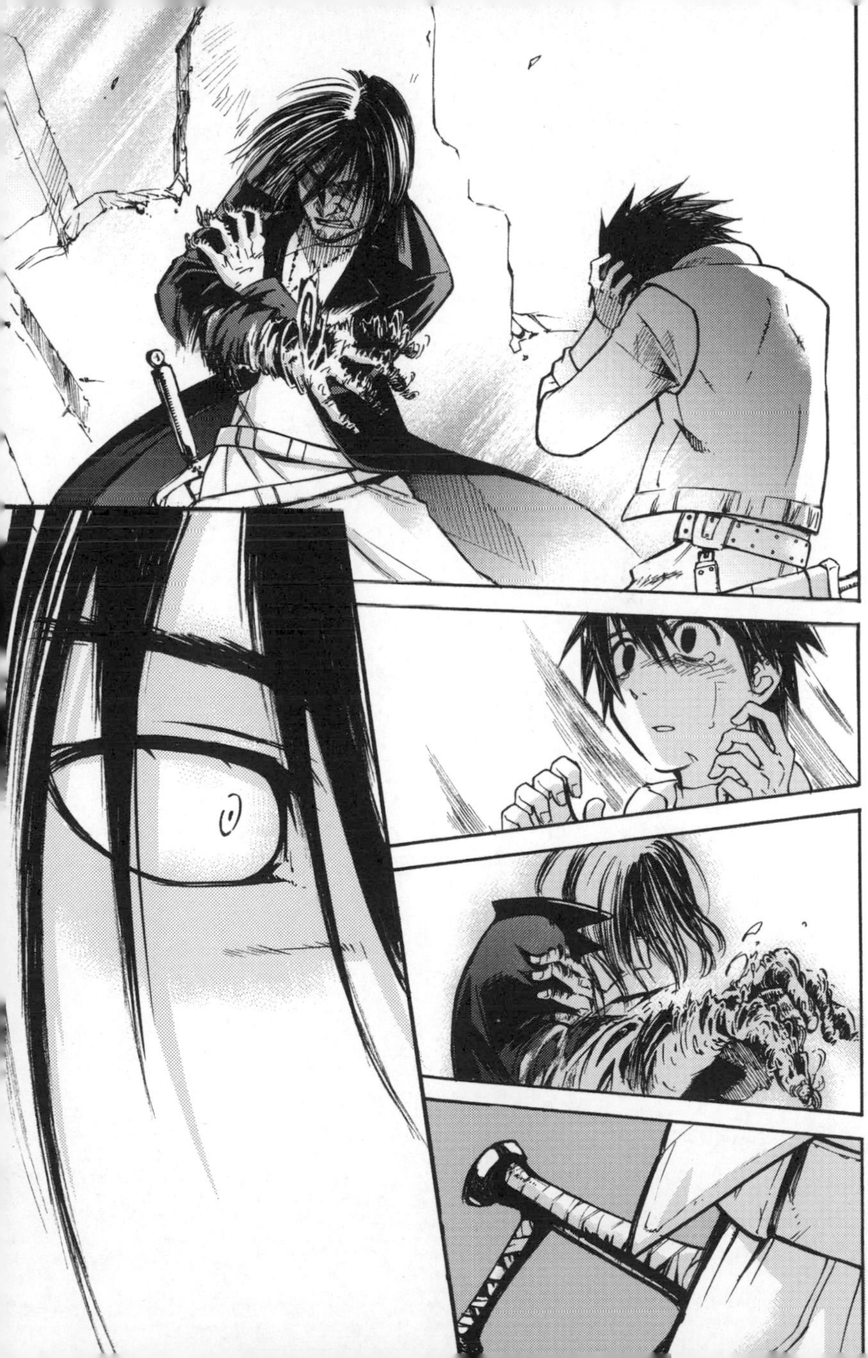

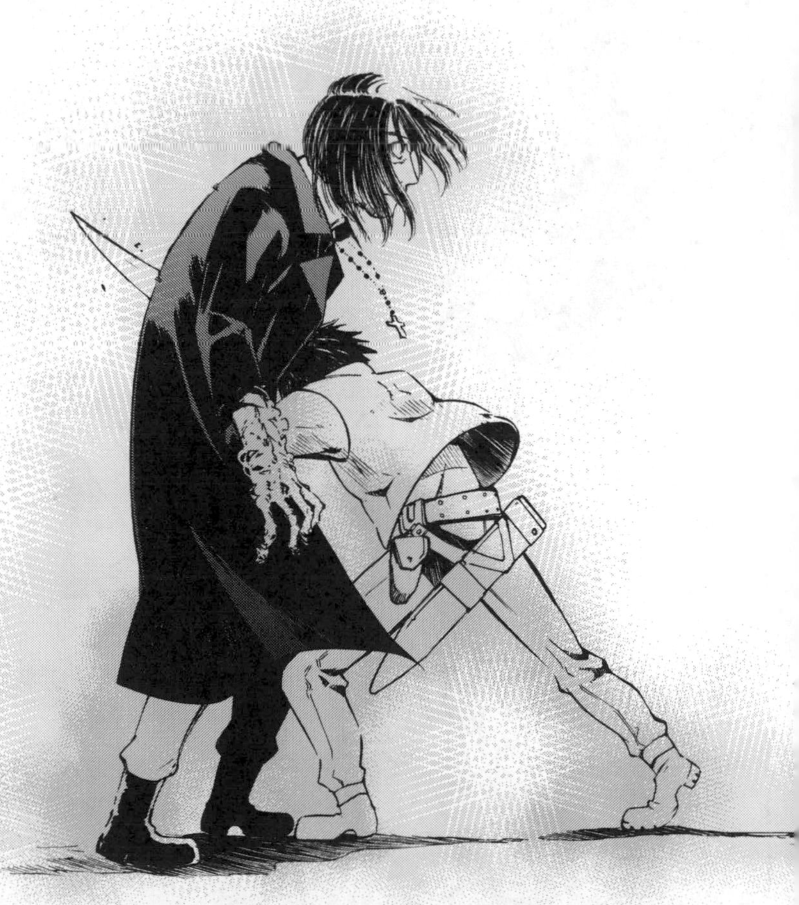

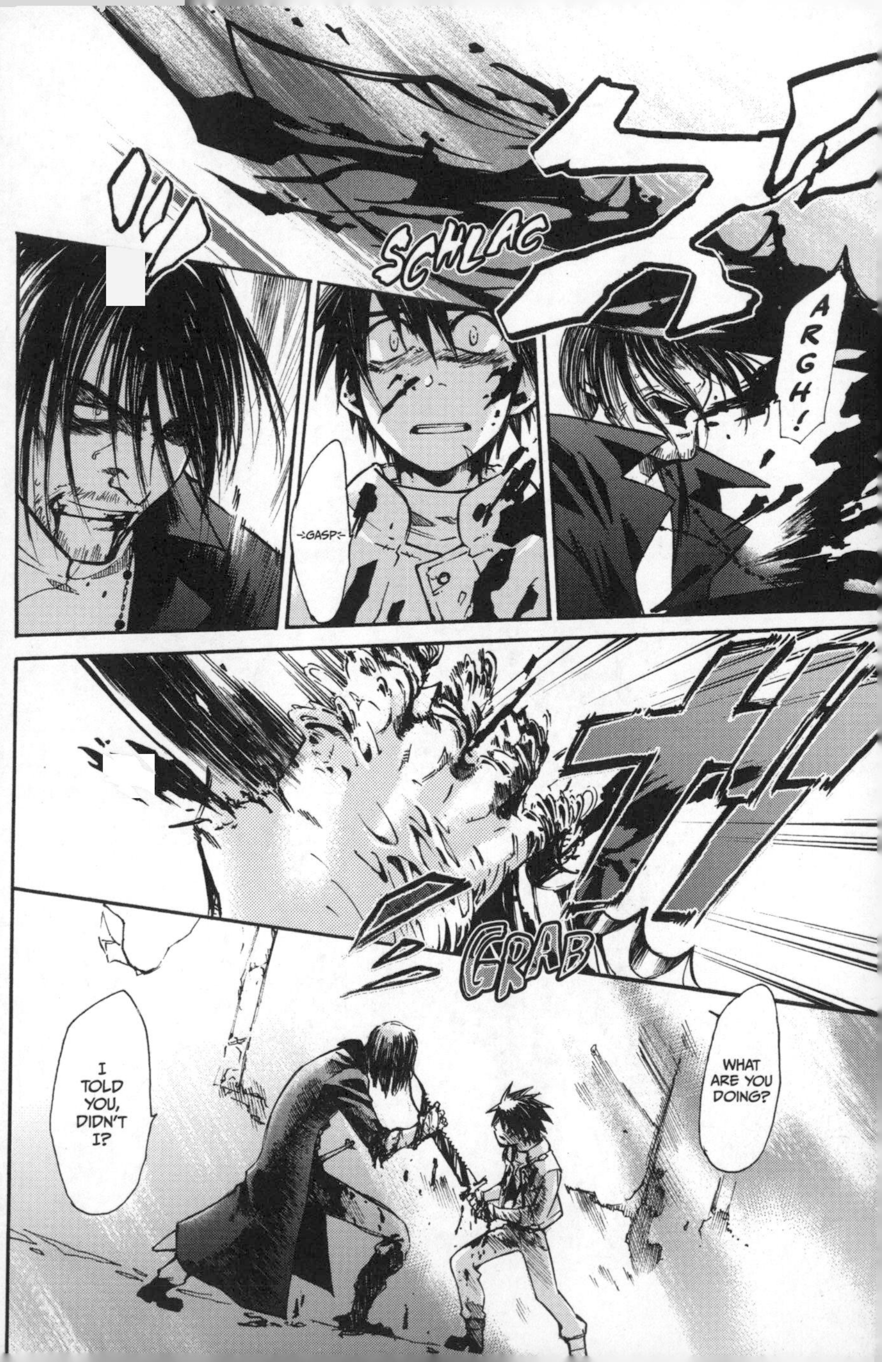
SCHLAC
ARGH!
-GASP-
GRAB
WHAT ARE YOU DOING?
I TOLD YOU, DIDN'T I?

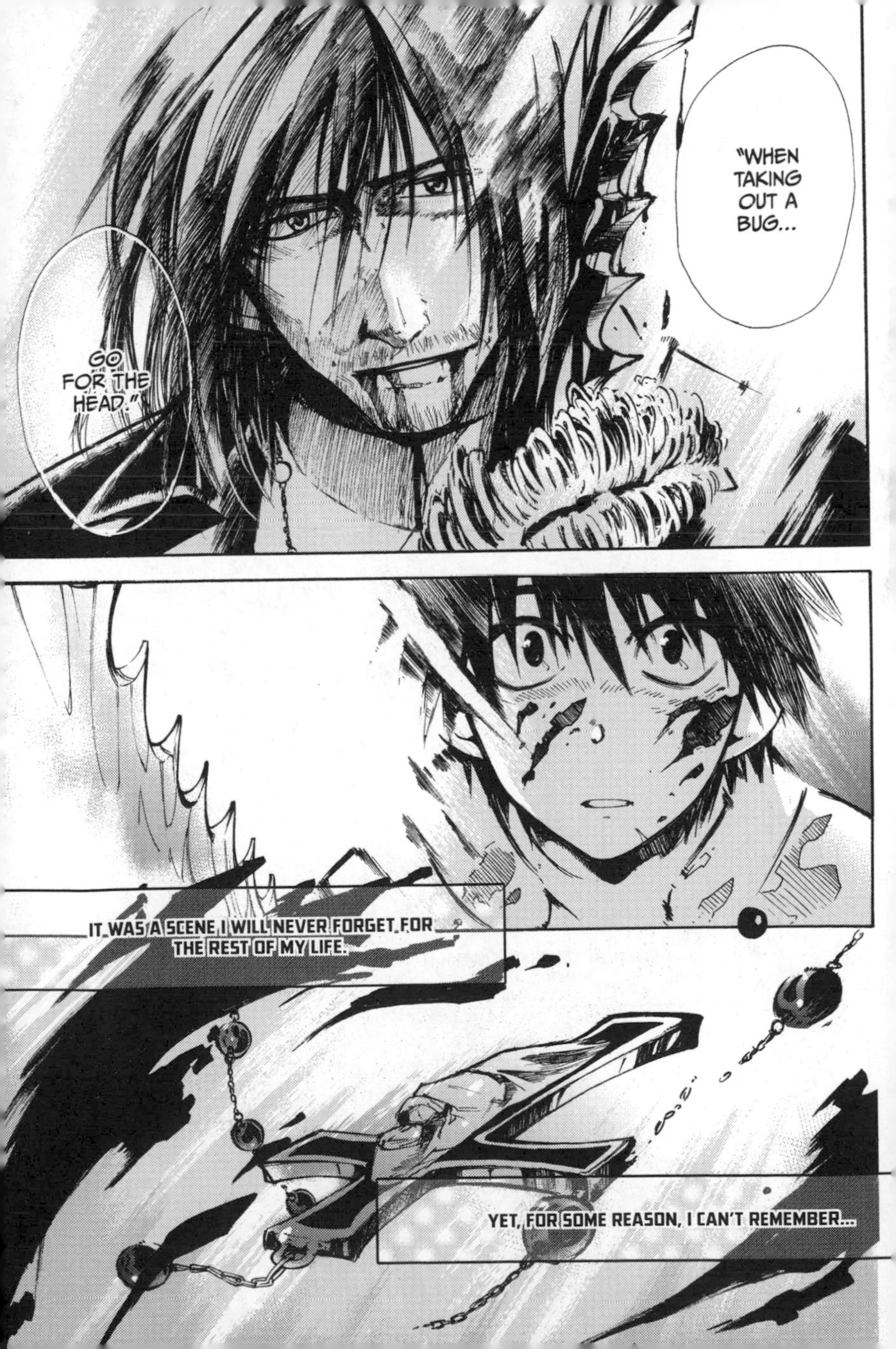
"WHEN TAKING OUT A BUG...
GO FOR THE HEAD."
IT WAS A SCENE I WILL NEVER FORGET FOR THE REST OF MY LIFE.
YET, FOR SOME REASON, I CAN'T REMEMBER...

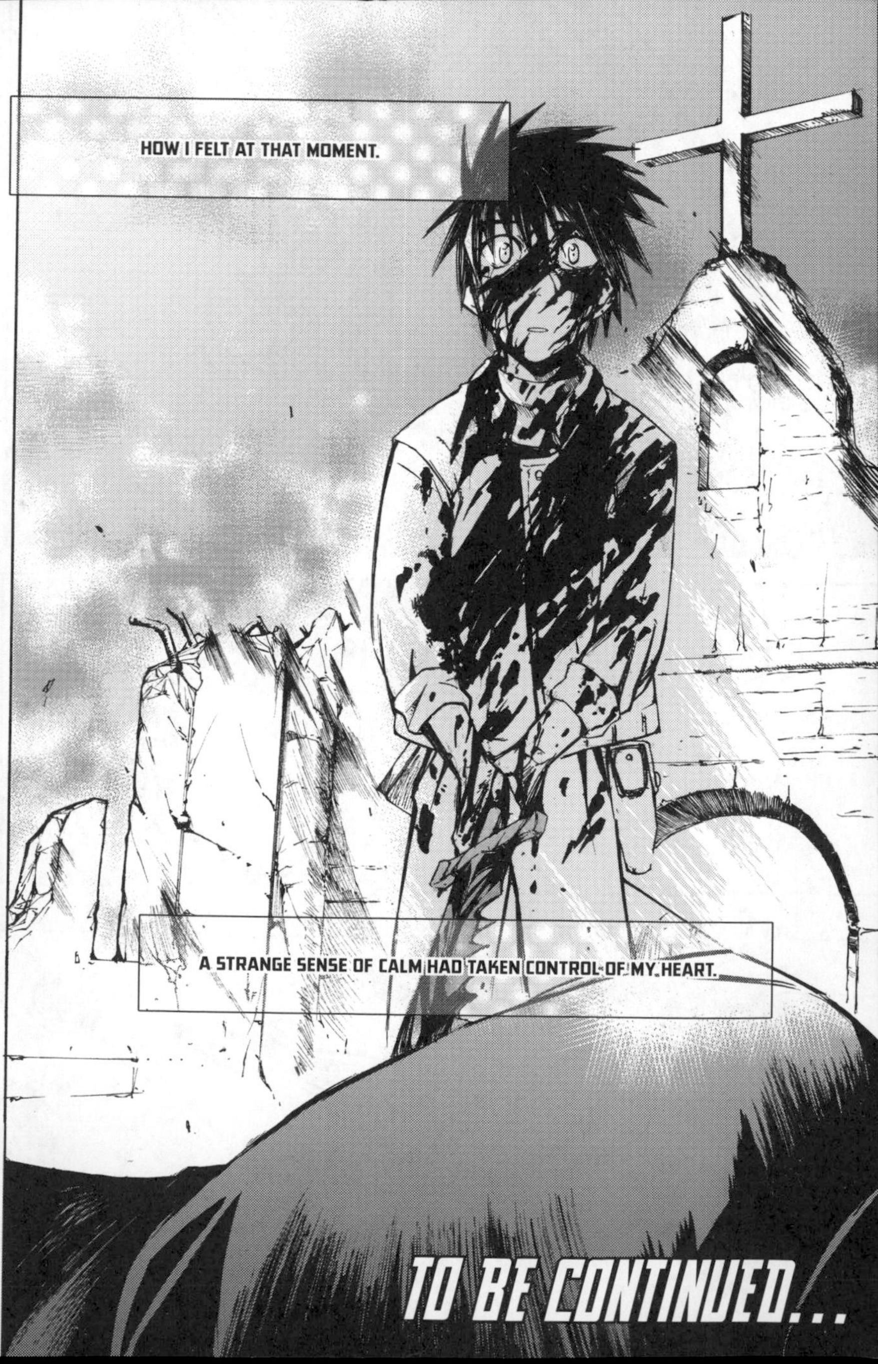
HOW I FELT AT THAT MOMENT.
A STRANGE SENSE OF CALM HAD TAKEN CONTROL OF MY HEART.
TO BE CONTINUED...